SIR WALTER RALEGH

Books by Robert Lacey

Sir Walter Ralegh   *(1974)*

The Queens of the North Atlantic   *(1973)*

Henry VIII   *(1972)*

Robert, Earl of Essex   *(1971)*

Sir Walter Ralegh

Robert Lacey

ATHENEUM

New York

1974

To Sandi

Copyright © 1973 by Robert Lacey
All rights reserved
Library of Congress catalog card number 73-80750
ISBN 0-689-10570-3 **JUN 17 '75**
Printed in the United States of America by
The Murray Printing Company, Forge Village, Massachusetts
Bound by H. Wolff, New York
First printing January 1974
Second printing April 1974

Contents

5

CONTENTS

Part 5 1597–1603 FAVOUR REGAINED

Part 6 1603–16 CAPTIVITY

Part 7 1616–18 FINAL RELEASE

List of Illustrations

Between pages 240 and 241

Walter Ralegh and Wat in 1602 (*National Portrait Gallery*)
Sherborne Castle (*Drawing by James Gibb*)
Robert Devereux, Earl of Essex (*National Portrait Gallery*)
Robert Cecil (*National Portrait Gallery*)
Sir Walter Ralegh, the hero of Cadiz (*by courtesy of the National Gallery of Ireland*)
A contemporary map of the capture of Cadiz
Henry Brooke, Lord Cobham (*by courtesy of the Earl of Ilchester; photograph by the Courtauld Institute*)

Maps

Preface

This biography springs from several recent discoveries that have thrown the career and character of Sir Walter Ralegh into an exciting new perspective, and I am happy to acknowledge the work on which my own study has been based. Professors D. B. Quinn and Agnes M. Latham have cultivated their particular fields of Raleghana with care and love for many years, and I have drawn heavily on Quinn's compilation of Ralegh's colonizing and exploratory ventures and on Miss Latham's edition of the poems. Professor Pierre Lefranc has now provided us with the definitive canon of Ralegh's prose and verse, and to his massive study of *Sir Walter Ralegh, Ecrivain* there is only to be added Peter Howe's discovery at Sherborne of the Will that sheds such a fresh perspective on several episodes in Ralegh's life. I am most grateful to Mr Howe for sparing time – with the permission of Simon Wingfield Digby, MP – to show me the Will at Sherborne.

My debt to all of them is considerable, but I owe a still greater due to Dr. A. L. Rowse, who has not only provided illumination for all Ralegh scholars with his unearthing and expounding of the Throckmorton Diary, but has helped me personally with unstinting quantities of his time and expertise. The warmth of his friendship and the excellence of his scholarship have both been an inspiration to me.

Down in the West Country Captain Walter Ralegh Gilbert provided me at Compton Castle with more than a flavour of his illustrious ancestors ten generations back, while Mrs Down kindly showed me Ralegh's birthplace at Hayes Barton. I am most grateful for the hospitality of my aunt, Mrs Ethel Winch, while I was down in Devon.

I must also thank for their particular assistance, the late Lord Salisbury, Dr Roy Strong, Hans Tasiemka and the librarians of the British Museum, Bodleian, Sealey, Cambridge University and London Libraries, together with the officials of the Public Record Office.

Jacqueline Reynolds, John Cushman, Simon Michael Bessie, Tony Godwin and Gila Curtis have all helped make the book possible. I must thank Peter Coxson for his typing and forbearance, Claus Henning for his maps, Elizabeth Webb for her picture research and Ken Carroll for his cover design.

My debt to my parents remains as ever. What I owe my employers, the *Sunday Times*, scarcely bears thinking of in terms of stolen energy and concentration. And most of all I must thank for their tolerance and love my daughter Scarlett, my son Sasha and my wife Sandi. I dedicate this book to Sandi.

ROBERT LACEY
London. May, 1973.

Ralegh's Name

Posterity has been guilty of both mis-spelling and mis-pronouncing Walter Ralegh's name. The form most usually adopted, Raleigh, was in fact never once used by Walter himself. From 9 June, 1584, when he was thirty, until his death he consistently signed himself Ralegh, and so this is the spelling I have adopted.

In his youth he was less methodical, and the variations he employed indicate clearly the way in which his name was pronounced – *Rawleyghe* for example, in 1578. This makes sense of the many puns made on his name during his lifetime – 'I have heard but rawly of thee,' said James 1 – and most of the seventy-three different contemporary spellings of his name were based on the phonetic interpretation, *raw-lee*.

Raleich was the spelling used by the French, Ralo and Ralle by the Venetians and Halley by the Dutch – while the Spaniards usually referred to him by variations of his first name: Gualtero, Guatteral, and Gualteral.

To Robert Cecil, Walter was Rawley, Raleigh, and Ralegh; to King James, he was Raulie and Raleigh; to his wife, Ralegh (except for her one use of Raleigh); to Henry Howard, Rawlegh and Rawlie; to the lord admiral, Rawlighe, and to Henry Brooke, Lord Cobham, Rawlye.

Part 1

❧

1554-82 Rise

Before he came into the public note of the world . . . he came up *through his own hard work*, not pulled up by chance, or by any gentle admittance of fortune.

Sir Robert Naunton 'Fragmenta Regalia'

❧ I ❧

West Country

You can follow today the path that first took Walter Ralegh to the sea. Up past rooting pigs and furrows of red Devon earth it runs to Hayes Wood, a skyline of branches loud with jays and woodpeckers.

Three centuries after Walter Ralegh ran along this stream-muddied track as a boy, an artist imagined him sitting down on the Devonshire beach by an upturned boat while some old sailor spun yarns of the ocean. And in the eyes of the lad is a yearning for sails and spars and distant horizons. It has become posterity's archetypal image of the boyhood of Ralegh, for we all know, just as the artist knew, that much of the adult life of this wistful, frail-looking boy was to be spent with the sea and the ships.

But there was another core element in the grand career to come – and it can be recaptured down in Devonshire. For with Walter Ralegh's love of the ocean went a love of the land – the dark earth thrown up in ramparts along the moist West Country lane that winds now, as it wound then, through Hayes Wood, the primroses and the soaring beech trees: Sir Walter was to be a very shrewd judge of how much a forest was worth. He was the son of a country gentleman who farmed the land, and from Hayes Wood one can look down across the fields his father worked to the cob-walled house of mud and straw where Walter Ralegh was born. It was among pigs and cattle that he grew up; barking farm dogs and gossiping hens. Like any West Country farmer's son he must have helped with the harvest, scrumped cider apples from the orchard, snared snub-eared rabbits, and shot birds in the woods. He saw the seagulls follow the plough-man and cows drink at the pond where the path to the sea turned into the yellow pimpled gorse. Beneath all the glittering layers of Renaissance achievement with which the years were to embellish Walter Ralegh, he remained in essence a man of the West Country, gracious on the court dance floor, daring on the deck of a ship, but feeling safest of all and most at home with his feet planted solidly on his own patch of soil. For Sir Walter Ralegh was remembered long after his death, not just as the courtier who laid down his best cloak for his queen, but as a man who 'spake broad Devonshire to his dying day'.[1]

One reason why, in later life, Sir Walter was so keen to set solid English acres to his name, was that his father had not actually owned the land that he farmed.[2] Squire Ralegh simply rented Hayes Barton, as tenant farmers live there today, and when the great Sir Walter was subsequently, at the very height of his career, cast down in disgrace, it was remarked, with a contempt only partially mitigated with admiration for the enterprise of the man, that he could scarcely be humbled to a level lower than that from which he had risen.[3] The great nobility of England, from first to last, regarded the squire's son from Hayes Barton as an upstart.

But that simply reflected their own insecurity, for Walter Ralegh's lineage was in its way more ancient and distinguished than many of theirs. Ralegh might not be a name that carried much weight up in London, but down in Devon there were at least five knightly branches of the family, and Squire Ralegh, Walter's father, sat in East Budleigh church in the very front pew with his own coat of arms carved boldly on the side. He might not own his farmhouse or the acres he worked, but he was a gentleman – *the* gentleman so far as East Budleigh was concerned. And depressed though his branch of the family might be, the neighbouring parishes of Colaton Ralegh and Combe Ralegh bore his name.

Those place-names bear their witness to this day – as does the coat of arms on the pew where young Walter, the squire's son, sat Sunday after Sunday in the Church of All Saints, East Budleigh. And right beside the pew, in the centre of the nave, lies a slab incised with a cross and strange Latin characters engraved backwards so that they need a mirror to be read in proper sequence: '*Orate pro aia Johanne Ralegh Uxrs Waltri Rale Armig Que Obiit X Die Mensi Junii Ano D. . . .*' 'Pray for the soul of Joan Ralegh, wife of Walter Ralegh, Esquire, who died the tenth day of the month of June, Anno Domini. . . .' The year of her death has been worn away, but by the time young Walter was old enough to puzzle out its hieroglyphics the date must have been at least a decade and three reigns past. For Walter was born early in the 1550s – 1554 seems the most likely date – and Joan Ralegh, the woman commemorated on that curiously carved stone, had been the first of his father's three wives. She had been a Drake – a respected Devonshire name even before the great Sir Francis made it famous. Her successor was a London merchant's daughter, one of the Darrells.[4] And then came Katherine Champernowne, sister of Sir Arthur Champernowne, vice-admiral of Devon. She was the widow of Otho Gilbert of Compton, near Torquay, and had borne him three sons – John, Humphrey and

Adrian Gilbert, sea-crazy youths whose enthusiasm was to inspire both the boys that Katherine bore in the farmhouse at Hayes Barton to Walter Ralegh Esquire – the eldest called Carew and the second named after his father.

It is a peaceful little church, All Saints at East Budleigh, but at the time when Walter Ralegh Esquire gave thanks from his front pew for his second-born son Walter it was suffering some of the worst upheavals in its history – and Squire Ralegh was one of the troublemakers. For the ways of three and a half centuries had just been overturned. Since 1189, if not earlier, the village had worshipped there, doing weekly homage to the age-established certainties of the Roman church. But then in the 1530s King Henry VIII had broken with the pope, and to East Budleigh came a new vicar, Richard Henson.[5] He brought to the village the ways of Protestantism, and presided, too, over the radical innovations of Henry's son Edward VI when religious shrines, stained glass windows and relics were destroyed and sacked by God's reformed soldiers.

To this day one can see in All Saints, East Budleigh, a strange double hagioscope or squint pierced through a staircase so that worshippers out of the direct line of vision could peer at the ornaments and statues of the magnificent high altar, and cross themselves when the host was raised in its glittering chalice. But that high altar and that chalice are no more, for they were smashed and looted by the enemies of superstition and idolatry.

Squire Walter Ralegh was one of these crusaders. His son was in later years to be accused of atheism – an imprecise term of abuse in the years of Reformation and Counter-Reformation – but of the father's piety there can be no doubt. He was a radical adherent of the new ways – a Protestant of the sort subsequent centuries were to describe as 'low church'. In the cause of purifying the House of God he had carried off from All Saints, East Budleigh, in April 1546, a fine cross of gold and silver, had the idolatrous ornament reduced to small pieces – and refused absolutely to give it back to the church.[6] A few years later he helped with the pillaging of other churches in the name of religious reform, but he was more than a profiteer, for when the testing time came he was not afraid to stand up and be counted for his Puritanism. Like his famous son, he was not frightened of being unpopular, nor of suffering in periods of adversity.

The people of Devon did not all like the new ways. In the cause of the new Protestantism it was announced that there would be no more holy water and washings, no ashes on Ash Wednesday, no palms on Palm Sunday, no crucifixes, bells or candles at the burial of the dead. Henry VIII had decreed that but two candles could be lit at the Mass. Now there were to be none at all – nor any shiftings or genuflections or signs of the cross. The comforting Latin ritual the villagers had murmured since the time they first learnt to speak was swept away for a grating metropolitan English. It was too much, too soon, and on the Monday after the Whitsun of 1549 set for the new form of service the riots started. From west Cornwall marched an army of peasants bearing crosses and candlesticks, holy bread and holy water – and a mob from mid-Devon joined in. With no standing army or police force the Government felt that only foreign mercenaries could cope with the threat. It was hardly the time for a reforming Protestant to make a public stand if he valued his popularity, property or life.

But just as the great Walter Ralegh was to show throughout his own career a cavalier indifference to the popular opinion of his fellow men, so his father chose this moment to rebuke one old woman he met mumbling over her beads while going to church. To say the rosary was old-fashioned and superstitious he told her, and it showed disrespect for the law.[7] If the gesture was kindly meant, the old woman did not take it as such. For she hurried straight to the church and interrupted the service with the news that Squire Ralegh had threatened her and all poor people. He and gentry like him, she cried, would burn down the houses of believers who refused to throw away their beads as he commanded. Incensed with fury, the congregation 'in all haste, they like a sort of wasps all flying out' swarmed after Squire Ralegh to punish him for his arrogance. They would have set upon him there and then if he had not taken refuge in another chapel, and though he managed to escape from that temporary captivity he was caught by more persistent devotees of the old order who locked him up in St Sidwell Church in Exeter and threatened to hang him. Squire Ralegh looked like paying dearly for his Protestant enthusiasm.

But in the event it was the insurgents who were hanged, for the Government's foreign army marched west and slaughtered them at Clyst St Mary. Squire Ralegh was saved, but his triumph was shortlived. At about the same time that his second-born son Walter was christened, Queen Mary came to the throne and the old faith was restored. Candlesticks, bells and rosaries, all the old comforts returned, and East Budleigh had a change of vicar to match the change of practice – John Ford, who once again held up the mass for the congregation to gaze at through the squint hole.

But Squire Ralegh and his family were of stubborn stock, and though their radical Protestantism might be out of favour, and though men and women might be going to the stake for the sake of it, the Raleghs were not afraid to bear witness to their beliefs. A cousin of Katherine Ralegh's, Sir Peter Carew, tried to get the people of Exeter to rebel against Queen Mary's plans to marry Philip of Spain and was pursued vigorously by the authorities. It was Squire Ralegh who provided him with the boat to escape to France.[8] And when Agnes Prest went to Exeter Castle as a Protestant sentenced to be burnt to death for her heresy,

> there resorted to her the wife of Walter Ralegh – a woman of noble wit and of good and godly opinions, who coming to the prison and talking with her, she said the *Creed* to the gentlewoman.[9]

Katherine Ralegh must have possessed some sort of immunity by virtue of the local importance of her husband and of her own family, but it was brave of her just the same to testify openly against Popish practices in the manner John Foxe recorded. She told Agnes Prest:

> that God dwelleth not in temples made with hands; and that the sacrament to be nothing but a remembrance of His blessed Passion. And yet (said she) as they now use it, it is but an idol, and far wide from any remembrance of Christ's body – which will not long continue, and so take it, good Mistress.

Agnes Prest did not live long enough to see that particular prophecy fulfilled. She went to the stake. But the Raleghs survived the brief years of persecution – and with the accession of Queen Elizabeth were vindicated in their faith and endurance. Squire Walter Ralegh became in 1561 churchwarden of All Saints, East Budleigh, and up in London a relative of his wife's had assumed a position of far greater importance. Through the difficult years of Mary's reign, Queen Elizabeth had been guarded and cared for by a Champernowne, Katherine Champernowne Ashley – she was probably the aunt of Katherine Champernowne Ralegh – and now Kate Ashley was the confidante not of some imprisoned and helpless princess but of the Queen of England. It was not to be long before Kate Ashley's West Country kinsmen started turning up at court – Humphrey Gilbert, Richard Grenville, Carew Ralegh, and finally young Walter himself. But that last and most brilliant advent of all lay at the beginning of Queen Elizabeth's reign, a score of years in the future.

❦ 2 ❦

France

Walter Ralegh was in later years to boast that he could count on the connections and support of 'more than a hundred gentlemen of his kindred' in his home county. There was scarcely a village or port in South Devon where he could not meet up with a kinsman, for, with five marriages between them, his thrice-wedded father and twice-wedded mother had given him a special advantage in a century and a society where blood ties counted for so much.

There was Richard Grenville of the *Revenge*. He was a cousin of Ralegh's through the Gilberts and Katherine Champernowne. Then there was Katherine's brother Sir Arthur Champernowne, young Walter's uncle. He was vice-admiral of Devon, representing the lord high admiral in local maritime affairs. The Carews, more cousins, were great seamen. Peter Carew was the man whom Squire Ralegh had helped escape from the anger of Queen Mary. George Carew was to partner Ralegh in several overseas ventures. Then there were the Gorges, Ferdinando and Butshead (or Buddockshide) and Arthur, the last of whom was to prove one of Walter Ralegh's closest friends. There were the Tremaynes and the St Legers, some links through marriage to powerful London merchants like William Sanderson, and subsequent business connections with John Hawkins and Martin Frobisher. Then, most influential of all so far as Walter Ralegh was concerned, there were the Gilberts – his half-brothers through his mother: John, Humphrey and Adrian.

Throughout his life Ralegh shared the closest friendship, interests and enthusiasms with them. Much of his boyhood must have been shaped by their influence and by their company, for though they were older than Walter – Humphrey was in his early teens when Walter was born – they lived a couple of dozen miles from Hayes Barton, at Compton on the other side of the River Exe. There their little castle stood – and still stands – finely towered and turretted in the middle of green Devonshire fields, just

out of sight of the sea. Like Hayes Barton, Compton Castle was sheltered
from coastal raiders by several miles of steep red cliffs and hillside, for it
was not long since French pirates had menaced West Country beaches, and
during the years of the Armada 'when the Spaniards were upon the
coast'[1] Compton Castle lay in the very front line of defence.

And so the remarkable children of Katherine Champernowne – four of
whom, John and Humphrey (Gilbert) and Carew and Walter (Ralegh)
were each to earn knighthoods – breathed in the atmosphere of this castle
which was to prove itself one of the cradles of Britain's overseas empire.
To this day there live at Compton, Ralegh Gilberts who, ten generations
on, keep bright the memories of their forebears who inspired the colonization of Newfoundland and Virginia and who dreamed and searched for the
route that would take them to the treasures of 'Cathay and all the other rich
parts of the world hitherto not found'.[2] Walter Ralegh was just entering
his teens when his half-brother Humphrey drew up his *Discourse* that
suggested how English ships might reach the gold, silver, spices and 'wonderful wealth of commodities of India and China by following a passage
north-west through a sea which lieth on the northside of Labrador'.

Another of his mother's adventurous family drew Walter on a course
that was to shape his life as much as the Gilberts' enthusiasm for overseas
exploration. One of his cousins, Gawain Champernowne, had married the
daughter of a French nobleman, the Comte de Montgomerie, one of the
champions of the Huguenot cause in France. Gawain had gone to live in
France and fight for his father-in-law in the vicious battles between
Protestant and Catholic that rent that country for half a century. When
the Huguenot cause fared badly his brother, Henry Champernowne
raised in Devon the black Montgomerie banner with its motto – 'let
valour end my life'. It proved a rallying call to over a hundred Devonshire
gentlemen willing to fight for the Protestant cause and the kinsmen of the
Champernownes. It was chivalry in the style of the crusades or, in our
own century, the Spanish Civil War, for the West Countrymen volunteered
to cross over the Channel and to fight at their own expense.

The romance and excitement of the adventure was one to which a lad
with Walter Ralegh's Protestant upbringing could scarcely fail to respond,
and in 1568 he packed his bags and set sail to win his spurs on the fields
of France.[3]

If Walter was born in 1554 then he was just fourteen when he first went
to fight in France. The oldest that alternative estimates of his birthdate can
make him in 1568 is sixteen. And he was to stay on the Continent for four
whole years – which by any calculations must be counted among the most
formative years of his life. Walter Ralegh was later to do battle in
many contexts – in Ireland, against Spain, in the New World, with

domestic enemies and at court – but it was these four years in France that were to shape his fighting mentality most firmly. When, imprisoned in the Tower after 1603, he wrote his *History of the World*, he was to say nothing about his battles in Ireland. But to his years in France he was to return over and over again, the men he disliked, the men he admired, the cruelties he saw, the strategy of the campaigns.

The odds against survival in France were high, for Walter, like his Devonshire comrades, went to fight at his own risk. Queen Elizabeth had made it a matter of policy that England should not get involved in this French dispute, so when the French king's ambassador protested to her that bands of Englishmen were fighting on the side of the Protestant rebels, she insisted that they had crossed the Channel without her knowledge or approval, which meant that if young Walter Ralegh were captured he could look forward to being hanged with a placard round his neck announcing execution 'for having come, contrary to the wish of the queen of England, to serve the Huguenots'.[4]

It was a rough school for a boy. Soon after Walter arrived, a superior force of Catholic mercenaries cornered 4,000 Germans fighting for the Huguenots and slaughtered every one of them, execution squads systematically slashing their way through their captives. Ralegh was lucky not to become one of their victims for he was part of the retreating Huguenot column and was only narrowly saved by the bravery of Prince Louis of Nassau.

The atrocities were not all one-sided, however. With some Huguenots Walter chased a group of Catholics into some caves in Languedoc:

which we knew not how to enter by any ladder or engine, till at last, by certain bundles of lighted straw let down by an iron chain with a weighty stone in the midst, those that defended it were so smothered that they surrendered themselves, with their plate, money and other goods therein hidden, or they must have died like bees that are smoked out of their hives.[5]

The slaughter was remorseless. When Montgomerie, Champernowne's father-in-law, captured Navarrens he put the whole garrison to the sword. So the royalists retaliated and when they took Mont-de-Maison slaughtered not only men but also women who had been throwing down stones from the walls. Treaties were made and treacherously broken, and whatever victories Walter Ralegh and his cousins helped win were set at nought by retaliatory massacres and murders that struck down Montgomerie, Coligny and many thousands of Huguenots.

Small wonder that Walter Ralegh decided:

the greatest and most grievous calamity that can come to any state is civil war . . . a misery more lamentable than can be described.

He had little time for the religious justifications that each side advanced for their

barbarous murders, devastations and other calamities . . . begun and carried on by some few great men of ambitious and turbulent spirits, deluding the people with the cloak and mask only of religion, to gain their assistance to what they did more especially aim at.[6]

Even the Huguenot leaders of his own side were not spared:

It is plain the Admiral Coligny advised the Prince of Condé to side with the Huguenots not only out of love to their persuasion but to gain a party.[7]

It was a precocious age at which to lose the simple ideals and faith of youth. When Walter Ralegh had first gone to France he was a country boy, a straightforward Devonshire lad, but by the time he returned home again, a new and lifelong facet had been engraved on his character – a worldly wisdom, a scepticism that was the fruit of disillusion. It was to run through his writing, especially his poetry, so that it is possible to scent a Ralegh verse from its atmosphere alone. It was to characterize his private life so that his less-than-reverent opinions of churchmen, their beliefs and practices were to make him notorious. It was also to dog his public persona, for few men could feel at ease with an individual who pierced so cynically through their pretensions.

❊ 3 ❊

Education

Walter Ralegh was a self-taught man and he grew up in consequence with acute interests of mind, delighting in games of words, pursuing knowledge for its own sake, and remaining all his life a voracious reader. He was to prove one of his generation's best poets and most notable writers. Not having had the energies of his boyhood blunted by pedagogues, he revelled in donnish pastimes, indulging in scientific experiments and debates on dangerous intellectual issues. This was to be the foil to his life of action, and he grew up into a true Renaissance man, moving evenly from court to battlefield to study and laboratory. The vital impulse was not artificially planted but came from some natural source – hence its energy and unpredictability.

Although Walter Ralegh went to Oxford, the surviving evidence suggests that his time there was neither lengthy nor conventional. His name appears on the register for Oriel College in 1572,[1] and one must assume that he had made himself enough money in France to pay his way through university. But he does not seem to have enjoyed the company of fellow students – junior to him in years and experience. Their undergraduate games were hardly the pastime of a hardened soldier. When two students quarrelled one came to Walter, who was obviously looked up to as the expert on such matters, to ask how he should fight a duel. He was a coward and did not fancy his chances with a sword or dagger – but he could aim an accurate bow and arrow. 'Why,' suggested Walter sardonically, 'challenge him to a match of shooting.'[2]

The only other anecdote about these years comes from John Aubrey who, in the following century, was to gather several stories about Walter Raleigh's life.

I remember that Mr Thomas Child of Worcestershire told me that Sir

Walter Ralegh borrowed a gown from him when he was at Oxford (they were both at the same College), which he never restored, nor the money for it.[3]

At least twelve months away from a degree, Walter Ralegh, comfortably enough off to retain at least two servants of his own,[4] moved down to London to England's 'third university', the Inns of Court, where would-be lawyers lived and were trained – 'always the place of esteem with the queen which, she said, fitted youth for the future'.[5] But on trial for his life in 1603 and conducting his own defence, Walter Ralegh was to claim that he had never read a word of law, for like most gentlemen he treated the Inns as casual introductions to London life, where they could taste the pleasures of men with the freedom of undergraduates. The register of the Middle Temple for 27 February 1575, reads: 'Walter Ralegh, late of Lyons Inn, Gentleman, Son of Walter Ralegh of Budleigh, County Devon, Esquire'.[6]

John Aubrey says that these years in Ralegh's life were turbulent and the records confirm this. Two of his servants were hauled up before the magistrates for riotous behaviour, and there is evidence that Walter himself was a riotous master. According to one story he sealed up with sealing wax the beard and moustache of some brawler who annoyed him in a tavern. And when, nearly forty years on, his own son, in Paris under the care of Ben Jonson, caused his tutor 'to be drunken and dead drunk, so he knew not where he was [and] thereafter laid him on a car, which he made to be drawn by pioneers through the streets, at every corner showing his governor stretched out', we are told that young Ralegh's mother 'delighted much, saying his father young was so inclined.'[7]

Yet Walter as a youth could be serious – earnest even. 1576 saw the first publication of his verse, the beginning of the collection of poems that he was to compose in his lifetime and which live to this day as sharp and vigorous as when he first penned them. For, coming up to London and gravitating naturally into the circle of his half-brother Humphrey Gilbert, Walter came into contact with the man who sparked off the earliest literary inspiration of his that has come down to our own day.

It was a case of hero worship. One of Humphrey's most notable friends was a swashbuckler called George Gascoigne, an adventurer who had, like Walter, been to the Continent as a soldier and who had also made something of a name for himself as a poet. He could turn his hand to most things – he acted as a publisher from time to time – and he clearly made a great impression on young Walter. Gascoigne's motto was, *Tam Marti quam Mercurio* – 'dedicated to Mars as to Mercury' – and Walter liked the ring of this so much that he adopted it as his own.

Gascoigne's bent was for satirical verse, which he produced as a collection under the title of the *Steel Glass*, and it was as a foreword to this book that one of Walter's poems was first published.[8]

The title of the book referred to the traditional English mirror – a plate of polished steel. But Londoners of wealth and fashion had been importing mirrors of Venetian crystal glass which, said Gascoigne, 'shows the thing much better than it is'. So it was his intention to show a more searching reflection of society. 'This Glass of Steel', explained Ralegh in his prefatory poem, might offend people, and so he was writing his dedicatory verse in order to forestall readers' outrage, and to testify to his own admiration of Gascoigne's work:

> This Glass of steel impartially doth show
> Abuses to all, to such as in it look,
> From prince to poor, from high estate to low.

Gascoigne was in the 1570s a helpful literary figure to be associated with. He achieved not a little renown in his own day and was patronized by no less a noble than Robert, Earl of Leicester, the favourite of the queen, so he did not, in fact, need Walter Ralegh to take up the cudgels on his behalf. His young protégé was, furthermore, too shy of his audience and over-reacted to the strain of coming under critical scrutiny by cocooning himself in a bombastic style, a defence mechanism that was to prove one of Walter's less than advantageous qualities. Relaxed and sensitive in private, he became stiff and arrogant under the public gaze.

Yet in the 1570s the problems of Walter Ralegh's public persona were only hints of the future. The extent of his public appearances – beyond his name featuring in slim volumes of verse – were the courtrooms of the Middlesex Petty Sessions where he went to bail out his rowdy servants. That he could employ at least two, and also stand surety up to 100 marks (£66·66) when they got into trouble indicates that he had some resources behind him. On one bail sheet he signed himself as 'Walter Rawley, Esq. of Islington' – the village to whose pond and taverns Aldersgate lads walked their girls on Sundays through the meadows – and on the other 'Walter Rawley, Esq. de Curia' – 'of the Court'. We know that three years later he was an 'Esquire of the Body Extraordinary', extraordinary meaning reserve, and an 'Esquire of the Body' being one of the young gentlemen required to wait upon the queen, particularly when she appeared in public. So we can assume that Walter Ralegh treated the Middle Temple as an antechamber not to any court of law but to the royal court at Whitehall. As Sir Robert Naunton later said, Walter's brushes with the institutions of Tudor higher education were rather incursions than sieges or settings down, for he stayed not long in a place; and being the youngest brother, and the house diminished in patrimony, he forsaw his own destiny, that he was first to rule – through want and disability to subsist otherwise – before he could come to a repose.[9]

Walter Ralegh had already set his eyes on the goal he wished to pursue – the favour of Queen Elizabeth 1.

His half-brother Humphrey was his mentor in these years. It was he who introduced Walter to George Gascoigne and the circle of young men who were eager to seek their fortune in foreign exploration. Gascoigne had fought with Gilbert in the Netherlands and now, in 1576, he returned Walter's compliments to *The Steel Glass* by writing an equally eulogistic endorsement of the *Discourse to Prove a Passage by the North West to Cathay* which Walter's half-brother had written ten years before. As well as writing the foreword, Gascoigne financed the publication of Gilbert's *Discourse* which set before the public the possibility that 'any man of our country . . . may with small danger pass in Cataie [China] . . . and all other places in the East, in much shorter time than either the Spaniards or Portingale doth.'

Accompanied by an over-simplified map, the *Discourse* was produced in 1576 as propaganda for a company that had been formed to send Martin Frobisher off to sail through the North West Passage, and though Frobisher did not, in fact, discover the riches that his shareholders hoped for, he brought back enough evidence to justify Gilbert's great hypothesis. North of the Labrador coast he found lumps of coal black stone which, when assayed back in London, were said to contain iron and possibly gold as well. He also brought back Eskimoes, one of whom, before they all died from English food and weather, put up a spectacular display of kayak handling in Bristol harbour, hitting ducks on the wing with his spear.

In the confused state of knowledge about the geography of the New World his discoveries seemed most promising. To judge from the Oriental appearance of the Eskimoes, Frobisher might have landed on the east coast of Russia – and on that assumption the Russian ambassador lodged a formal protest against the abduction of Russian subjects.[10] The vast piles of coal-black stone – well over a thousand tons of it – shipped back to England by Frobisher in the course of three voyages stimulated excitement still more and the fact that the mysterious lumps resisted all attempts to convert them into gold was set down to faults in the refining process rather than to the fact that they were no more valuable than paving stones.[11]

On 11 June 1578 Queen Elizabeth granted to her 'welbeloved servante

Sir Humphrey Gilberte of Compton' letters patent 'to discover, searche, finde out and view such remote heathen and barbarous landes, countries and territories not actually possessed of any Christian prince or people', and Walter Ralegh was to be one of the principal assistants in this enterprise. The land the brothers discovered could be disposed of 'in fee simple or otherwise according to the order of the lawes of England', and any Englishmen who chose to live in any colonies that might be set up would enjoy their full rights and privileges as subjects of Queen Elizabeth – as would their descendants 'in suche like ample manner and fourme as if they were borne and personally resideunte within our sed Realme of England'.[12]

Through the summer of 1578 the would-be colonizers of the New World scurried around London and to and from the West Country getting their expedition organized. They had a private plan that they hoped would help meet the cost of their expensive project, but it involved extra preparations. Heading for Newfoundland they would set upon the defenceless fishing fleets of Spain, Portugal and France and bring back the captured vessels and cargoes to sell in the Netherlands. In the spirit of this unashamed piracy – for England was still officially at peace with all three countries – some of Gilbert's followers seized in Dartmouth harbour a Seville merchant's boat loaded with oranges and lemons, useful supplies for the voyage. But the Privy Council, who had judiciously made no response to Humphrey Gilbert's attempt to gain his Newfoundland piracy some sort of approval, could not let so naked a larceny go unnoticed and ordered that the Spanish ship be restored to its rightful owner. They instructed the eldest of the Gilbert brothers, John, who had been knighted in 1571 and appointed to the post of vice-admiral of the county of Devon in 1572, to work with other government officials to delay Humphrey Gilbert and Walter Ralegh until they had paid compensation for the theft, since, by the time the pirated vessel had got back to its owner, all its oranges and lemons had rotted.

But it was one thing for the central government to issue such an order, and quite another to get it carried out. It was not for reasons of prestige alone that the Raleghs were so pleased to keep regional admiralty responsibilities in the family, and Sir Humphrey Gilbert and Walter Ralegh continued to prepare and equip their fleet in Dartmouth harbour in defiance of the Privy Council prohibition, sailing into the Atlantic on 26 September 1578 with 365 men in ten ships, all heavily armed and provisioned with food and drink sufficient for a whole year's sailing.

In command of the *Falcon*, a ship of the queen's which probably represented the royal stake in the venture, Walter Ralegh seemed set on a course for both fame and fortune. But almost as soon as he had unfurled his sails in the Channel he was caught by savage autumn gales that buffeted the fleet back into Plymouth harbour. Humphrey Gilbert, red-haired like Queen Elizabeth and just as quick-tempered, took out his frustration on his fellow captains. As Walter remarked, his half brother's great defect was an irascibility which tended to 'make his good service forgotten and hold hyme from the preferment he is worthy of'.[13]

The expedition lost heart. Three ships deserted, and when the remaining seven sailed out of Plymouth on 19 November 1578 and were caught by the weather yet again, they lost little time in getting back to the comfort of Dartmouth harbour – with just one exception. The young commander of the *Falcon*, sailing under the motto *Nec Mortem pto nec finem fugio* – 'I neither seek death nor flee the end' – stayed out at sea, refusing to yield to the December tempests. Walter Ralegh bravely headed the queen's vessel into the storms blowing up out of Biscay and found himself amid Spanish shipping. Determined to salvage something from the fiasco he pluckily took on some Spaniards – to be painfully worsted. There was a sharp battle in which the English fared badly and Walter Ralegh, lucky to escape death, with the royal ship badly damaged and with many of his crew killed or injured, struggled back to Devon.

But he had proved his courage and tenacity. More important, he had learnt not to rely on the command and organization of others. The next time that Walter Ralegh got involved in ventures of piracy or colonization he was to trust only in himself.

❧ 4 ❧

A Start at Court

Twenty-five years old in the spring of 1579, Walter Ralegh had been less than successful in his first command of a royal ship, but his fight with the Spaniards had incurred a repair bill for the *Falcon* which meant that – if only to discover who had caused her such expense – Elizabeth was likely to take a careful note of Kate Ashley's kinsman.

Six foot tall – a head taller than most of his contemporaries – slender, but very obviously muscular, he was a difficult man to miss, and he called attention to himself with flamboyant clothes. His boldly coloured and sharply cut costumes were to become a by-word and give added point to that famous story about the fine cloak he sacrificed to keep his queen's feet dry. He wore jewels too that sparkled on his fingers and on his doublet, stating over-explicitly the value that he set on himself. He would wear a pearl in one ear that gave him a gypsy look, and that was accentuated by his swarthy skin and dark pointed beard. His forehead was broad and high, his hair brown, flowing and curly, his nose sharp, and his mouth, under his moustache, very firm. Everything about him radiated energy and ambition. He was upright, virile and unmistakably, ostentatiously, catastrophically, proud.

His pride got him into trouble. He quarrelled with Sir Thomas Perrott, fighting a duel with him and ending up in the Fleet Prison for a week. Then he came to blows, for equally trivial reasons, with a man called Wingfield beside the Tennis Court at Whitehall.[1] This time the Privy Council sent him to the Marshalsea Prison – but his two sessions behind bars were scarcely a penance, for prisoners of quality in both the Fleet and the Marshalsea had their meals brought into them by their own servants, could receive friends at most times of day and could even go out for exercise or the occasional social engagement. In the Marshalsea Walter discovered an additional consolation, for committed to the gaol the very next day, also for feuding and quarrelsomeness, was his cousin Arthur Gorges.

In the tradition of Gasgoigne, Gorges was a soldier poet. He was to collaborate with Ralegh not only in his military and exploratory activities, but in many literary projects as well, and in the 1590s the two cousins were to compose a group of sixteen poems – *The Phoenix Nest* – the work and credit for which they shared.[2] So close were their ideas and styles that it is impossible now to apportion to one or the other author some of the poems or their component parts, and as Walter's public life became more and more multi-faceted he delegated much to Arthur Gorges, setting his name with scarcely any alteration to drafts that his cousin had prepared. The relationship which developed in these early years flowered into a fruitful and lifelong partnership.

But another friendship of this period 1579–80 proved less durable, and, in the long term, positively poisonous. Returning to London after the abortive expedition of 1578–9 Walter Ralegh fell in with the set that centred on the libertine Edward de Vere, Earl of Oxford.[3] He was an unstable young man, and although related to Lord Burghley, his touch-stone was not the prudence of the great councillor but the erratic temper of companions like Charles Arundel and Henry Howard, crypto-Catholics who vented their spleen against the Protestant establishment with anti-social antics, deliberately calculated to shock. Oxford himself had never quite recovered from a grand tour he had made to Italy, and took par-ticular delight in voicing rationalist criticisms of accepted practices and beliefs. He was no high-powered intellect – suggestions that the Virgin Mary had cuckolded Joseph represented the level of his theological debate – but he was not the sort of young man that the Privy Council, and in particular Puritan councillors like Walsingham and Leicester, liked to see allowed influence at court.

It was strange that Walter Ralegh, well aware of the realities of Elizabethan politics, should ever have associated himself with a man so obviously cut off from the mainstream of Privy Council approval. But there is a plausible explanation of his brief friendship with the Oxford circle that is suggested both by the shortness of his association and by the nature of court rivalry. Walter, open though he usually was both in friendship and in enmity, was to exhibit throughout his life a paradoxical penchant for intrigue. He could be a shocking liar and, when the oppor-tunity presented itself, he plunged into conspiracy with all the enthusiasm, if not quite the ability, of a Borgia. It was another aspect of his Renaissance tastes to plot, on occasions, the downfall, not to say the violent death, of men he embraced as friends and to tell shameless lies for the sake of political advantage.

31

This was the style in which he approached the Earl of Oxford in 1579–1580 – though he was but part of a larger framework of plottings woven around the strange passion that Queen Elizabeth conceived at the end of the 1570s for Alençon, the Protestant duke who was a claimant to the throne of France. England was split over this marriage that the queen appeared to be contemplating, factions forming for and against the French connection, and it was in the crossfire between them that Walter and the Earl of Oxford came together – and parted.

Elizabeth, menopausal and uncharacteristically erratic, had let Alençon's courtship get out of control. Though feeling at the court was inflamed against the marriage, the queen acted provocatively. She flirted indecorously with the Frenchman and allowed his envoy, Simier, to raid her bedchamber to filch her nightcap as a love token. This was a cause of general scandal, but when John Stubbs dared to protest at the royal plans to marry a foreign prince, and when the printer William Page dared publish Stubbs' protest, the queen had both men's hands struck off in a gruesome public ceremony. 'I left there a true Englishman's hand' called out Master Page as he raised the bleeding stump of his severed right wrist – and true Englishmen applauded him. Sir Christopher Hatton was in tears at the waywardness that was depressing the queen's popularity to one of the lowest ebbs of her entire reign. And the Earl of Leicester, whose secret marriage to Lettice Knollys had been revealed to Elizabeth by Alençon's creature Simier, had even more reason to resent the dominance of the French party – as well as the English nobles who supported it, most notably old Burghley and his son-in-law the Earl of Oxford.

When opposition expressed in the council chamber proved ineffective, the opponents of the French match – Leicester and Walsingham were their leaders – resorted to more devious tactics. Sir Philip Sidney was put up to writing an ostensibly unprompted letter to Elizabeth to explain the strength of Protestant feeling on the subject, and at almost the same time, Walter Ralegh, from his militantly Protestant West Country background, started making friends with the popishly inclined Oxford.

In the conspiratorial context of Counter-Reformation politics it seemed likely that if Catholic plots were afoot, the Earl of Oxford's friends like Arundel and Henry Howard would be privy to them. They were both soon to be compromised in conspiracies on behalf of Mary Queen of Scots, Howard spending some time in the Tower and Arundel dying there, and they already exhibited symptoms of being involved in the sort of intrigue which would prove to Elizabeth that the French marriage was part of a Catholic scheme to subvert her throne. It was possible that they might even compromise the great Lord Burghley himself, and Walter Ralegh, whose connections with Leicester (through the poet Gascoigne) and Walsingham (through Humphrey Gilbert) were comparatively remote, stood a good chance of winning the confidence of Oxford and his popish friends and of discovering what schemes they were plotting.

Walter played his part to perfection. Within a matter of months he became the closest friend of the Earl of Oxford. The earl's affair with Anne Vavasour, one of the queen's ladies-in-waiting, made Oxford even more *persona non grata* to many courtiers at this time – a dangerous, unreliable man to get involved with. So Walter had few rivals for the earl's companionship, associating so intimately with him that the smear of Oxford's atheism was to be remembered and held against him by those not privy to the convolutions of those times. When the Earl of Oxford and Sir Philip Sidney confronted each other as the publicly acknowledged champions of the contending factions, Oxford insulting Sidney at tennis as a 'Puppy' and Sidney disdainfully leaving the court, it was Walter Ralegh who acted as an intermediary to avoid a duel.

And then suddenly he was Oxford's friend no more, one of his bitterest enemies, in fact. And more strangely still, instead of being mistrusted by Oxford's enemies for his association with the wayward earl, whom the queen was to imprison for getting Anne Vavasour with child, it was now that he was made Esquire of the Body Extraordinary, a comparatively minor but not insignificant court position.[4]

It is difficult to escape the conclusion that this honour was a reward for some service connected with Ralegh's *volte-face* of loyalties and that Francis Walsingham, that master spy-ring operator, had played his characteristically concealed role beneath the surface of events. The fact that Ralegh was given almost immediately – despite his imprisonment for duelling and rowdiness – a command in Ireland which carried responsibility, power, and profit, strengthens the hypothesis. Furthermore it got Walter out of the country very rapidly, for Oxford was a pathological character who was said, after the tennis court confrontation, to have plotted the murder of Sir Philip Sidney. Walter Ralegh had survived his first sally across the quicksands of life at court and had won the chance in Ireland to make a real name for himself.

❧ 5 ❧

Ireland

S ir Humphrey Gilbert set the style that Walter Ralegh was to adopt in the troubled country of Ireland. Sir Humphrey had been given command of the south-west corner of the island, the province of Munster, back in 1569, and had devised a short way of dealing with all who opposed his rule: their heads were hacked off and set in a double line as a grisly guard of honour leading to the door of his tent.

Such strategy sowed dragon's teeth whose harvest is reaped to this day – but Gilbert was simply putting into practice a traditional English attitude towards the Irish that men like Walter Ralegh and Oliver Cromwell were to strengthen with even worse brutality. The English method of colonization, which gave English settlers the right to seize with the sword lands that Irishmen had held for centuries, intensified the bitterness – as Walter Ralegh saw.

> Certainly the miseries of war are never so bitter and many as when a whole nation, or a great part of it, forsaking their own seats, labour to root out the established possessions of another land, making room for themselves, their wives and children. ... The merciless terms of this controversy arm both sides with desperate resolution.[1]

But to understand was not to sympathize, for Walter Ralegh was a prime example of the English settler who caused such hardship in Ireland. He came to the country, a younger son with little wealth and no lands to inherit, with the express intention of carving out for himself from the lush and mineral-rich acres an estate whose resources he could never hope to win in England. In Ireland he could – and in due course did – secure a castle from which he could lord it over the hapless natives whose leaders, lands and faith it was his pride to have taken away. When he went to explore the jungles of South America, Walter Ralegh was to treat the

34

naked savages of the Guiana swamps with more respect and kindness than ever he showed to the Irish.

Landing in Cork in the summer of 1580, he started sharply in the way he intended to continue. Sir James Fitzgerald, a descendant of one of the many settler families who had gone native, was in the custody of Sir Warham St Leger, a relative of Ralegh's, and the two kinsmen were given the job of dealing with the rebel – which they did without compunction. The prisoner was butchered with the legalized agonies of hanging, drawing and quartering.

But within days the Fitzgeralds got their revenge, for on 25 August 1580 Walter's cousin Sir Peter Carew, out in the pleasant Irish countryside far away from the protection of the English garrison in Cork, was set upon and murdered in an ambush and George, another Carew kinsman of St Leger and Ralegh, was lucky to escape with his life. Thus Walter, within a matter of weeks, was baptized into the blood feuds of Irish colonization.

Yet before the autumn was out he got his chance to avenge his cousin's death, for a party of Italian and Spanish mercenaries landed on the far west coast of Munster at Smerwick (St Mary Wick), a town just north of Dingle Bay. They had arrived under the papal flag to strengthen the Irish revolt against the English crown, and it was the good fortune of the English that these foreigners provided precisely the sort of help that the Irish rebels did *not* need. The Irish strength in their guerrilla war was the ability of raiding parties to lay their ambushes and then to disperse into the woods and marshes. There was no single focus that their pursuers could follow, no control fortress or point of resistance they could lay siege to or destroy.

But this elaborately armed phalanx of foreign soldiers was anything but a quick-moving guerrilla band and was, if possible, still worse suited to Irish conditions than the English, for they knew even less about the terrain, and they could not even speak a language that Irish sympathizers might understand.

So, isolated out on the Smerwick peninsula, the unfortunate foreigners dug themselves in, preparing for the sort of face-to-face confrontation in which their Irish allies could be no use to them whatsoever, and for which the English had been thirsting after months of inconclusive ambushes and raids.

In command of the English forces was Lord Grey of Wilton, a pious Puritan who, when confronted with a fort from whose flagpole fluttered the papal colours and whose occupants brought to Ireland copies of the Bull excommunicating Queen Elizabeth I, had no doubt that 'the Lord of Hosts' would deliver the forces of Babylon into his hands. After four days of bombardment, on 9 November 1580, his prophecy was fulfilled and

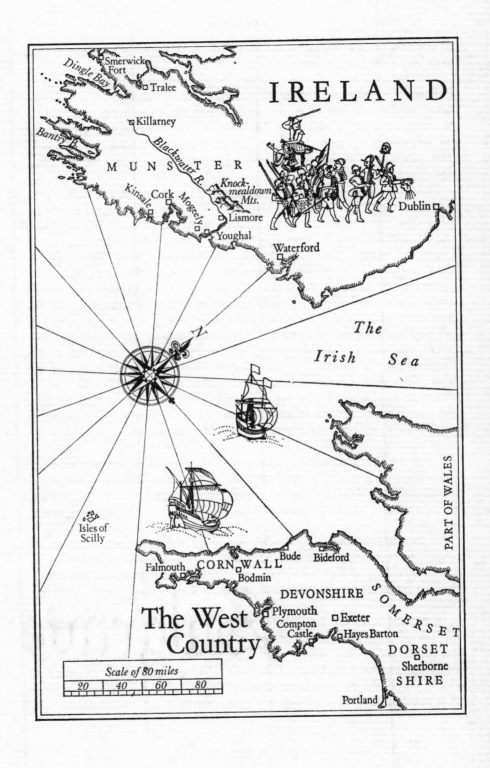

IRELAND

Smerwick Fort
Dingle Bay
Tralee
Killarney
Bantry
MUNSTER
Blackwater R.
Knock-mealdown Mts.
Kinsale Cork Mogeely
Lismore
Youghal
Waterford
Dublin

The Irish Sea

PART OF WALES

Isles of Scilly

CORNWALL
Bude Bideford
Falmouth
Bodmin
DEVONSHIRE
SOMERSET
Plymouth Exeter
Compton Castle
Hayes Barton
DORSET
Sherborne
SHIRE
Portland

The West Country

Scale of 80 miles
20   40   60   80

the garrison, hopelessly isolated, capitulated. There were some four hundred Italians and Spaniards inside, plus a couple of hundred Irish men and women. Grey had refused all their requests for a parley or permission to depart at once for Italy by sea. He insisted on nothing less than unconditional surrender and in due course the garrison hung out the white flag crying plaintively '*Misericordia, misericordia*!' At the time – and to this day – the Irish have insisted that this capitulation was based on the undertaking of Grey to spare the lives of all who laid down their arms and 'the faith of Grey' remains an Irish byword for a broken promise. But Lord Grey was quite adamant – and Englishmen in his entourage like the poet Edmund Spenser equally emphatic – that no such undertaking was ever given.

The two duty officers of the day for the English forces were Captain Mackworth and Captain Walter Ralegh, to whose lot it now fell to execute Lord Grey's orders. Two traitors, an Englishman and an Irishman who had given especial help to the papal legate had their legs and arms broken and were then hanged, as were some pregnant women who were presumed to have pandered to the invaders' lusts. And then, after their armour had been stacked in neat piles under their pikes, the defenceless Italians were systematically put to the sword. Some two hundred English soldiers had to deal with six hundred victims, so, by simple arithmetic, Walter Ralegh and his company must have slaughtered three defenceless foreigners apiece that day. Since human bones when struck with too much force could turn the soft edges of sixteenth-century blades, there were special attack drills to preserve the cutting power of the soldiers' weapons. A quick slash through the neck, almost decapitating the victim, left the sword sharp. Or, alternatively, a jab in the belly did the job just as effectively, at the same time inflicting on the victim a much slower and more agonizing end. In a matter of hours Walter Ralegh and his company could stand back and contemplate six hundred stripped corpses 'as gallant and good personages as ever were beheld', reported Grey triumphantly to the Privy Council.

It was a savage morning's work, the horror of which outraged Catholic Europe. But the Protestant Elizabeth praised Grey of Wilton, complaining only that he had spared for the sake of their ransoms certain officers whom he ought also to have massacred. English adventurers caught in Spain or Spanish colonies in similar circumstances had, after all, never been treated with any more leniency.

What Walter Ralegh thought of the slaughter in which he had played so active a role, he never directly said. But the orders he obeyed were directly in line with his own personal and family policy for dealing with the Irish. When on another occasion he asked an Irish peasant, whom he caught scavenging willow branches from a campsite, what he wanted the branches for, and was answered back impudently 'to hang English churls', Ralegh promptly had the man strung up on the spot, remarking that the branches would serve equally well to hang an insolent Irishman.

Walter Ralegh was never a merciful man. It was not in his nature to spare those who crossed him, nor had his years spent in France done anything to soften him. The sharkpool that was the Elizabethan court did not make for tenderness, nor did the West Country tradition of fierce loyalties and fierce hatreds. Forgiveness was a concept less prized than honour, consistency and the willingness to stand by first principles and friendships.

But for all his cruelty, Walter Ralegh was not a bully who would only attack when all the guns were on his side. Returning from Youghal to Cork with a small patrol on one occasion, he was surprised at a ford by an Irish ambush. Outnumbered ten to one, the half dozen Englishmen did not retreat. Walter charged boldly across the river to cut his way to the opposite bank, and when one of his patrol, a Devon man called Henry Moyle, fell off his horse to flounder at the mercy of a whole band of armed Irishmen Walter plunged back into the stream to save him, confronting the rebels single-handed. In the face of Ralegh's quarterstaff and loaded pistol they hesitated long enough for Moyle and the rest of the English to regroup and cover their leader. Rather than fight it out and risk being surprised by English reinforcements, the guerrillas melted into the trees. They were not warriors of the stand-up-and-fight variety, and realizing this Ralegh was able to pull off several notable exploits, plunging into hand-to-hand battles and routing more numerous forces though his mount was shot under him.

By the spring of 1581 Ralegh had made such a name for himself that when the president of Munster went back to London, he became one of the three deputies nominated to look after the province in his absence. In this position of responsibility he carried off his most outstanding personal achievement of all. Lord Roche of Bally, a nobleman living in a castle some twenty miles from Cork, was suspected of aiding the rebels and it was Ralegh's job to bring him in for questioning. But, as so often happened, the Irish got wind of the English plans and prepared a thousand-strong ambush to surprise the small English posse that did not number one hundred.

On this occasion, however, English counter-espionage was efficient enough to warn Ralegh of the trap. And so, under cover of darkness, Walter led his little band right through the terrain where the rebel ambush was laid. Dawn broke on the Englishmen drawn boldly up in battle order outside Lord Roche of Bally's castle, and, thrown into confusion, the Irish garrison were in no state to resist. Unlike the guerrillas who haunted the woods and bogs they were, in any case, supposed to be loyal subjects of

Queen Elizabeth. So Ralegh, with just five companions, marched up to the gates of the castle to be allowed inside.

Lord Roche invited the unexpected English guests to eat. But Walter Ralegh called a double bluff on his deceptively hospitable host, for while he graciously accepted Lord Roche's invitation, he also instructed his men to take advantage of the surface amity to infiltrate the castle casually and to secure the positions of importance. The garrison were caught off guard, so that when Ralegh requested that Lord Roche and his lady should accompany him back to Cork, and when Lord Roche refused, Ralegh simply called up his troops who were already inside the castle.

But there was still the journey back to Cork and the ambush laid by the guerrillas waiting somewhere along the way. Once again, in darkness, Walter Ralegh stalked through enemy territory, this time in the teeth of a furious storm and accompanied not only by Lord Roche and his family but by a group of Roche's own townsfolk drafted to protect their Lord, in case, in the darkness, the ambushers were not particular about whom they attacked.

Highly pleased with himself, Walter wrote over the heads of his immediate superiors to inform Walsingham and Leicester in London of his achievements and to solicit from them the reward which he considered his skill and bravery merited. Modesty was never his strong point, and not content with going behind the lord deputy's back, he also criticized his commanding officer. To Leicester he complained that he had so low an opinion of Lord Grey of Wilton that he only obeyed him because he knew it was what Leicester wanted.

I have spent some time here under the deputy, in such poor place and charge, as, were it not for that I know him to be one of yours, I would disdain it as much as to keep sheep.[2]

Walter felt that, after Smerwick, his superiors had gone soft on the Irish. Altogether tougher policies were called for, he felt, along the severe guidelines laid down by Sir Humphrey Gilbert: 'I never heard nor read of any man more feared than he is among the Irish nation.'[3]

That was a loyal thing to declare on his half-brother's behalf, but the overall sentiment of the letter, carping at men who had devoted more time, money and energy to Irish affairs than Walter would have dreamt of sacrificing, was less than likeable; and it was, in any case, based on a mistaken premise. By the autumn of 1581 much of Ireland was quieter than it had been for months, and it proved possible to discharge many of the English forces – among them Ralegh's own company. Walter could return to London and, reinforced by a useful, if self-proclaimed reputation as a pundit on Irish affairs, he could with fresh confidence seek glory on the fiercest battlefield of all – the court of Queen Elizabeth I.

❦ 6 ❦

'Fain would I climb'

Walter's way with the ladies was legendary.

> He loved a wench well [wrote John Aubrey] and one time getting up one of the maids-of-honour up against a tree in a wood ('twas his first lady), who seemed at first boarding to be something fearful of her honour and modest, she cried 'Sweet Sir Walter, what do you me ask? Will you undo me? Nay, sweet Sir Walter!' At last, as the danger and the pleasure at the same time grew higher, she cried in ecstacy 'Swisser, Swatter! Swisser, Swatter!' She proved with child. . . .[1]

Writing two generations after Walter's death, John Aubrey did not know the half of it, for Walter Ralegh, long before he had won the knighthood that impelled ladies with a proper sense of etiquette to cry out 'Sir!' to him, had had ample opportunity for sexual adventuring – though not always, perhaps, in the arboreal style that Aubrey described.

The French Wars of Religion had been hard schools of experience in every sense. When towns were put to the sword the women would be raped, and the armies of both sides travelled everywhere with camp followers who could supply the comfort of a warm embrace between cold route-marches. This was the world in which Ralegh became a man – and when he went to Ireland the opportunities for sexual experience were similar. Walter took advantage of them – as we know from a quite unexpected discovery made only a few years ago in the archives of the Sherborne estates in Dorset. These were the estates that Walter secured at the high point of his favour with Queen Elizabeth, and in a packet of deeds there was found in 1970 a will of Walter's dated July 1597 in which he left 500 marks (£331 13s. 4d.) to 'My Reputed Daughter begotten on the body of Alice Goold now in Ireland'.[2]

Where did Walter meet Alice Goold? What did she look like? Was their affair a long one? What was their daughter called? We do not know – but from the scanty evidence available we can make some plausible deductions. The dark eyes that flash out from the portraits of Sir Walter Ralegh are those of a ladies' man. The pupils are sultry and disturbing – sensuous. Those who envied his looks called him 'sour eye-lidded', for there was a brooding heaviness below his brow. His eyes could flare with temper as with passion. His turbulent emotions bubbled over to betray themselves in his features. If he was angry, eager or inflamed, he showed it, and this directness lay at the heart of the relationship he was to establish with Queen Elizabeth. In a world of sycophants he was a flatterer too, but a transparent one, a man who wore his heart on his sleeve, fierce and to-the-point. He never made any secret of what he wanted, and, as he pursued his fancy, nothing would stand in his way.

Alice Goold had a West County name. There are many Goolds, Goulds and Golds mentioned in the archives of sixteenth-century Devon, with a fair number of Alices among them[3] but it is doubtful whether any of them was Walter's Alice. For what with leaving for France so young, then going up to Oxford and the Inns of Court, Walter had little time for dalliance in Devonshire. Ireland seems a more likely field for him to have sown his wild oats, and there were, in fact, Goulds in Munster – they had been there ever since the thirteenth century[4] – especially around Cork where the English armies relaxed when they were not on patrol. This seems the most likely home for Alice, especially as Walter's will describes her as living in Ireland in 1597, and her remoteness would explain too why neither she nor her daughter attracted the attention of observers eager to report on indiscretions at court.

So on one of his visits to Ireland, and most probably in his first years there in the early 1580s, Walter met and made love to Alice Goold, fathering the baby daughter he was to remember in his will – and subsequently. For later in his career he was to serve for a period as governor of the island of Jersey, and there, according to the journal of Elie Brevint of Sark, he found time between his stints in the high round keep of Mont Orgueil Castle, to make provision for his natural daughter's future. As governor of the Channel Islands he was given charge of a young local nobleman, Daniel Dumaresq, Seigneur de Saumarez, whom he made his page and whom he married to his daughter, thus providing her with a title, albeit a foreign one. There is no evidence that she and Dumaresq had any children, and later, according to the Sark chronicle, she died in 'London or Kingston'[5] of the plague. But Walter had done his duty by her and her mother. We can infer from the gracious silence of Alice Goold that she had few complaints, and perhaps even some happy memories, from her association with Sir Walter Ralegh.

Back from Ireland he swaggered in the early 1580s and leapt from obscurity to prominence (to historical immortality indeed) with that spectacular gesture which is none the less plausible for having become a fable:

> This Captain Ralegh coming out of Ireland to the English court in good habit (his clothes being then a considerable part of his estate) found the queen walking, till, meeting with a plashy place, she seemed to scruple going thereon. Presently Ralegh cast and spread his new plush cloak on the ground; whereon the Queen trod gently over, rewarding him afterwards with many suits for his so free and seasonable tender of so fair a foot cloth.[6]

The flourish was pure Ralegh, though the story was not set down until later, and there is no reason to disbelieve it. Nor was the jaunty ploy with which he followed up his coup any more out of character. Taking a diamond ring he scratched on a latticed window of the palace: 'Fain would I climb, yet I fear to fall'.

To which Elizabeth replied, scratching her enticement immediately below with the very same diamond: 'If thy heart fail thee, climb not at all'.[7]

The two anecdotes have become fragments of that unfashionable sort of history that is handed down by word of mouth and not in learned academic tomes but that does not mean they are untrue. The episodes of the cloak and the lattice pane were obviously not the only reason why Walter Ralegh became the favourite of Elizabeth 1. He had probably caught the queen's eye soon after he returned from Humphrey Gilbert's ill-fated voyage of 1579, if not before, and another reason for his prominence at court was the fact that he could count on Walsingham and Leicester as patrons. But he was, until the early 1580s an obscure figure for all that, one of a swarm of young hopefuls, and it was not until the moment which the popular stories specify as the turning point of his fortunes – his return from Ireland – that he suddenly emerged as a favourite. And so those stories shall stand. Their romance and flamboyance certainly accord with all we know about both Walter and Elizabeth, while one representation of the coat of arms sported by Ralegh shortly after this is swathed in a heraldic cloak that would seem to be a reference to the great legend. It is the sort of visual pun the Elizabethans relished.

Another tale also has a ring of truth. Robert Naunton related that Walter Ralegh got involved in a fierce dispute with Lord Grey of Wilton over the way in which Ireland had been ruled. Ralegh had much the better in the telling of his tale; and so much that the Lords [of the Privy Council] took no small mark of the man and his parts.[8]

There was certainly a longstanding feud between Ralegh and Grey of Wilton, for Grey did not take kindly to the way in which his subordinate officer wrote behind his back to his patrons at court, and he said so in no uncertain terms.

I like neither his carriage nor his company; and, therefore, other than by direction and commandment, and what his right can require, he is not to expect [consideration] at my hands.

But Elizabeth was tickled by Ralegh's bumptiousness. She

began to be taken with his elocution and loved to hear his reasons to her demands; and the truth is, she took him for a kind of oracle, which nettled them all.[9]

'Oracle' is a word that encapsulates precisely what Walter Ralegh came to represent for Queen Elizabeth in the early 1580s, for his own style of wisdom was the quality that enhanced his physical attractiveness. It was not the prudent wisdom of a Burghley or a Walsingham – Elizabeth never considered her Walter to be Privy Council material – nor the arcane wisdom of an astrologer like John Dee, nor least of all the theological wisdom of 'her little black husband', Archbishop Whitgift. It was something else, a quality of mind of Ralegh's own. It was born of his country origins and of his cosmopolitan experience and, most of all, of his restless intellect, a dynamic wit that amused and stimulated Elizabeth for over a decade. Walter Ralegh was very good company.

It was partly his youth. Walter was in 1582 still under thirty, playful and vigorous, while Elizabeth was in her late forties. It was an intriguing gap between their ages, refreshing for both of them. Elizabeth, in her early middle age, was a well-preserved and handsome lady in her pale, fragile fashion, very different from the harridan who was in her late sixties to drive Essex to the block. That final romance of hers came to grief on an age difference that was grotesque. But Walter Ralegh, self-possessed and mature for all his boyish enthusiasms, had a firmness, an iron in the soul, that other men in her life lacked.

Leicester could be wobbly-lipped, and he was, besides, by 1582, corpulent and broken-veined, a bloated reflection of the trim Robert Dudley who had once won a young queen's heart. Christopher Hatton was too obsequious. There was in his eagerness to please something of the dancing master. William Cecil, Lord Burghley, was a counsellor not a companion, too consumed with advising his queen to spare energy to amuse her.

Robert Cecil his son, a sickly, crippled youth, was of the same stock, and, after nearly a quarter of a century, the whole Elizabethan court seemed jaded, the faces wrinkled, the paunches more blousy, the jokes old and even the quarrels predictable. Walter Ralegh was the new player the show needed to recapture its vigour.

It was thirty-five years since the young Elizabeth had flirted with Lord Thomas Seymour, the dashing lord admiral who had provided her, a shy fourteen-year-old, with her first quiverings of sexual excitement – and paid with his life for them. He had initiated her in bedroom play, snatching kisses from her and tickling her familiarly on the excuse of waking her in the morning – and she, as a consequence, had been rumoured his whore, became implicated in his treasonable ambitions and was cross-examined in the course of the proceedings that led to his death. The whole affair had been a sordid, terrifying ordeal permanently scarring the girl whose mother Anne Boleyn had suffered even more cruelly from sexual jealousies, whose first stepmother had died in childbirth, whose second stepmother was divorced, and whose third, Catherine Howard had been beheaded for adultery – all before the young Elizabeth reached her tenth birthday.

So when Walter Ralegh paid court to Queen Elizabeth, praising in his poems her eyes 'which set my fancy on a fire' and her auburn red curls 'which hold my heart in chains', words like desire and love had a very special meaning for her, and Walter had the wit to realize that. His poems to Queen Elizabeth were gracious, flattering, ardent even, but never presumptuous. Walter Ralegh knew his place, and instead of wooing with intimacies that both he and Elizabeth knew to be irrelevant to their particular relationship, he wooed with his mind, with games of words and intellectual conceits, mental exercises of the sort Elizabeth delighted in. That makes his verse particularly rich and allusive, almost too concentrated for the modern reader easily to digest. But the message is there in every poem, waiting to be unearthed from its elliptical, John Donne-like style, and when it is unveiled the flash of comprehension is the more satisfying for the unravelling that preceded it.

The vigorous composition of his poetry is the very image of the appeal its author held for Queen Elizabeth and its playful confidence a token of the intellectual harmony Walter knew that he shared with his queen.

But he knew too that such harmony had its limits, and in recognizing those limits and keeping to them Ralegh retained the favour that he had won. Having been scorched early on by intimacy, Elizabeth stayed a safe distance from its flames ever afterwards. Sir Robert Dudley, created by her favour Earl of Leicester, had, of all her paramours, got closest to her. For a time there seemed a possibility that she might perhaps marry him. But even in those months of greatest warmth and affection, Elizabeth remained emphatically a 'Virgin Queen'. Provincial gossips might swear that 'Sir Robert doth service the queen', but that only demonstrated their ignorance. For as Walter Ralegh discovered, the rivals for Elizabeth's smile went to the greatest lengths to keep each other under surveillance, and in a court where gentlemen of rival loyalties slept at the doors of royal apartments and also staffed the queen's guard, it was virtually impossible for any man to reach the bedchamber unnoticed. Elizabeth deliberately created around herself a network of jealous rivals spying on her every move and on those of their competitors, a system that guaranteed not only that she remained pure, but that she was seen to be so, and Walter Ralegh played this game to perfection. He could be many things to Queen Elizabeth – oracle, playmate, wistful suitor – but husband or master, never. That was the basis of their relationship, and it was one of its great strengths, when other friendships foundered on rocks of intimacy that Walter knew better than to approach.

It was his mind that she loved him for, with its gemlike abstractions and its earthy commonsense, its fanciful imaginings and its precise control over words. Walter was in later years to become a best-selling author writing, in addition to his poems, pamphlets whose vivid language was to capture the popular imagination, and books whose style has earned a permanent reputation. With this mastery over words he wooed her – when he was in her presence with speech, when he was away from her with the poems that conjured up his direct, restless tone of voice. Soon after he returned from Ireland he was selected, at the beginning of 1582, as a token of his new importance at court, to escort the Duke of Alençon back from London to the Netherlands where the Frenchman was 'Protector' of the Protestant cause. Walter would be travelling as one of the gentlemen in the train of the Earl of Leicester, so both suitors for Gloriana's love would have to endure for a few weeks the 'mishap, unrest, death, winter, hell, dark night' of absence from her presence. Leicester sent his queen letters. Walter could send her poems:

> What else is hell, but loss of blissful heaven?
> What darkness else, but lack of lightsome day?
> What else is death, but things of life bereaven?
> What winter else, but pleasant spring's decay?[10]

But the absence was not long, and Walter received while he was in the Netherlands a consoling indication of the new importance he had asumed. Of all the English gentlemen who had accompanied Alençon to the Low Countries, including Philip Sidney, Fulke Greville, Lord Hunsdon and the Earl of Leicester himself, it was Walter Ralegh whom William the Silent, the Prince of Orange, singled out to carry back to Queen Elizabeth a secret entreaty for help with his crusade against Spain. 'Say to the Queen for me,' said Europe's great Protestant hero to young Walter confidentially, '*Sub umbra alarum tuarum protegimur*' – 'we are defended under the shadow of thy wings.'[11]

Prince William of Orange's agents were well informed. They had picked out for their master's confidence the new man who had captured the ear of the queen of England, for Elizabeth was now, in 1582, at her happiest in Ralegh's company, giggling and laughing as she had not done for many years and – a sure sign of favour – bestowing on him a private nickname. She called him 'Warter' when she wanted to tease him over his Devonshire accent, and said that she was thirsty for 'Water' when she was in a more tender mood. It was the same game she had played with Leicester, her 'Eyes' and Hatton, her 'Sheep' or 'Mutton'.

Poor Hatton had even been proud to be dubbed his queen's 'Bell-Wether' (castrated ram), and he was most disconcerted by Ralegh's sudden pre-eminence. He took it personally when his shepherdess began to play her name game with 'Water' and he recruited in his jealousy Sir Thomas Heneage, another dancing partner of the queen's. The two men staged a protest against the new favourite – in courtly style.

One fresh October morning in 1582 as Queen Elizabeth sat on her horse ready for a day's sport 'to ride abroad in the great park to kill a doe', Heneage emerged coyly from a clump of trees bearing in his hands three incongruous gifts which he presented to the queen: a bucket, a book and a fine jewelled bodkin. The bucket, it transpired, symbolized water and thus referred to Ralegh; the book contained a letter in which Hatton reproached the queen for paying more attention to 'water' than to her own faithful 'sheep'; and the jewelled bodkin symbolized the dagger with which Hatton would stab himself if Elizabeth did not direct her love once more in his direction.

Elizabeth was delighted, and in her excitement her horse reared up so that she had to hand back the tokens to Heneage while she calmed it. Then she read her 'bell-wether's' letter 'with blushing cheeks' and murmured sweet reassurances to be passed on to the anxious Hatton. She was his shepherdess as ever, she said, and would cherish him in a meadow bounded with high banks 'so sure as no *water* nor floods should ever overthrow them. And, for better assurance that you shall not fear drowning,' she gave Heneage to take to Hatton a dove, the bird which to Noah's ark brought the good tidings that 'there should be no more destruction by *water*. . . . You should remember she was a shepherd and then you might think how dear her sheep was to her.'[12]

The convenient presence of that dove suggests that Elizabeth's part in the scenario may have been less spontaneous than it appeared, and it was certainly the sort of tableau the 'Faerie Queene' loved – flirtatious, trivial and thoroughly amusing. Walter Ralegh had jolted Hatton and Heneage out of relaxing like complacent old uncles and made them thrust for her hand like young bucks. Even old Burghley took the hint, noting down respectfully in October 1582 'the opinion of Mr Rawley upon the means of subduing the rebel in Munster'.[13] The queen bestowed on Walter an important command in Ireland and then, as she loved to do with her favourites, forbade him to take it up because she could not bear to be parted from him. She had, she told Lord Grey of Wilton, taken a 'special care' of the young man and could not spare him from her side. Lord Grey did not complain.

Walter Ralegh was the coming man. He had gambled an expensive cloak and won himself a fortune. Later he was to wager with larger stakes and find that his lucky streak was less generous, but for the moment at least he could not go wrong. In the summer of 1583 Lord Burghley paid him the sweetest homage possible when he came to Walter to implore that he would intercede with the queen on behalf of his son-in-law, the Earl of Oxford, whose catalogue of misdemeanours had been lengthened by a duel with a member of the Privy Chamber. It was indeed a sign of the times when the most powerful lord on the Privy Council had to beg on behalf of a seventeenth earl favour from a fellow who had, just a few years earlier, counted himself lucky to be numbered among the followers of that same nobleman. There was no love lost between Ralegh and Oxford, particularly after the dramatic reversal in their relative positions of power, and Walter made it clear that, in persuading Elizabeth to be merciful towards the earl, he was exerting his influence for the sake of Lord Burghley and not for his former friend.

Never a gracious loser, Walter could be an even more boorish victor. 'I am content for your sake', he wrote to Burghley, 'to lay the serpent before the fire, as much as in me lieth, that, having recovered strength, myself may be most in danger of his poison and sting.'[14] It was a gratuitously churlish comment which, though vindicated by events, gave unnecessary offence to the man who mattered – Burghley, the serpent's father-in-law. High politics was always Walter's blindspot; he had a penchant for intrigue of the type that had characterized his earlier relations with Oxford; he could lie convincingly, and he could pursue vendettas with passion. But those qualities, essential though they were to survival in Renaissance public life, did not add up to rounded political ability.

Walter had an insensitivity that was, in the end, to prove fatal. Often a poor judge of character, he was even less adept at sensing how others were reacting to his own personality. In later life marriage was to unleash his warmth, while adversity was to reveal his nobility and humanity. But in these early days of favour he rode roughshod over the sensibilities of others and built for himself the reputation of an overweening braggart.

'If any man accuseth me to my face, I will answer him with my mouth', was his response to the hostility of popular opinion, according to Fuller.[15] 'But my tail is good enough to return an answer to such who traduceth me behind my back.' He was, as John Aubrey said, 'damnable proud'.

Part 2

❊

1582-8 Favour

Sing, O Muse, of Ralegh, beloved of Majesty, plunging his lust into the body of a new world. . . .
Sing, O Muse and say, there is a spirit that is searching through America for Ralegh, in the earth, the air, the waters, up and down, for Ralegh, that lost man. . . .

William Carlos Williams, 'In the American Grain'

7

'Darling of the English Cleopatra'

The 1580s were to be Walter Ralegh's decade. He was to become one of the brightest stars in the Elizabethan firmament, a mesmeric figure, the archetype of the English Renaissance, a poet, a courtier, a soldier, a sailor, a man of arts and a man of business, forever exploring new dimensions of the spirit and of the world – and achieving everything through the spell that he cast over Elizabeth I, Queen of England.

'She is said to love this gentleman now beyond all the others,' wrote a German visitor to London in the early 1580s. 'And this must be true, because two years ago he could scarcely keep one servant, and now, with her bounty, he can keep five hundred.'[1]

As well as affection and fame, Queen Elizabeth gave Walter Ralegh wealth. Money, jewels, land, all were showered on the favourite in the years of his ascendancy. He was particularly anxious as the son of a tenant farmer to get some land to his name, and estates came among the first gifts. In April 1583 he was given the leases of two estates belonging to All Souls College Oxford and then in the following year, on 4 May 1584, he was granted one of the great foundations of the fortune he was to build up for himself – the farm of wines, the right to charge every vintner one pound a year for the right to retail wine.[2] There was enormous potential for profit in this operation, that would, in a modern bureaucratic state, be run by one of the revenue departments, and Walter Ralegh, like most of the courtiers rewarded in this way, simply sub-contracted the licence to an agent who paid for the lease with a guaranteed annual sum. If the merchant's administrative expenses proved heavy, and the revenue small, that was his bad luck: the courtier enjoyed his guaranteed income for doing next to nothing. But if the agent proved enterprising, then he also made money and everyone was better off – except the ordinary consumer who had to pay for these concealed and indirect taxes with higher prices.

In the case of Walter Ralegh's grant of wines, he sub-contracted to one Richard Browne, who guaranteed him for seven years an annual income of £700 – a sum that should be multiplied by one hundred to give some indication of its value in modern currency. The trouble was that Browne proved too industrious, enforcing his right to license vintners so zealously that he caused great offence – notably in Cambridge where the vice-chancellor jailed Browne's bailiff. On top of that Browne made for himself profits as substantial, if not greater, than the £700 he was giving Ralegh every year, and when Walter asked for some share of these profits, he was told – as he would have told Browne had the lease proved unremunerative – that a bargain was a bargain. So the courtier went back to the source of his fortune and asked the queen to call in his licence and re-grant it to him so that he could negotiate fresh terms – which Elizabeth did. Poor Browne was sacked. With the queen on his side an Elizabethan could not lose, and although one of Walter's justifications for getting his wine lease renewed had been that Browne's exactions had been harsh and unjust, Walter now set to work with the very same rigour his former agent had employed, doubling his effective income from the monopoly.

Still, the robbery was not all one way. On 26 April 1583, there appeared in the law courts of Middlesex one 'Hugh Pewe, gentleman' who was tried for stealing 'a jewel worth £80, a hatband of pearls worth £30, and five yards of silk, called damask, worth £3'[3] the property of Walter Ralegh. One problem was that Elizabeth's favourite had no proper home in which he could safely store his burgeoning possessions. But the queen came once again to the rescue, for in 1583 she bestowed upon her Walter the use of one of the great palaces of London, Durham House, whose finely turreted walls rose sheer out of the Thames where its course swung round from Westminster towards London Bridge.

> Durham House was a noble palace [wrote John Aubrey admiringly] I well remember his study, which was a little turret that looked into and over the Thames, and had the prospect which is pleasant, perhaps, as any in the world, and which not only refreshes the eye-sight but cheers the spirits, and (to my mind) I believe enlarges an ingenious man's thoughts.

Walter was not the proprietor of Durham House – it was granted him to enjoy at the royal pleasure – and he did not occupy all of it. It was a vast, rambling, fortress-like mansion, the ground floor of which was the residence of Sir Edward Darcy. But the lion's share was Ralegh's, and he made little distinction between what he borrowed and what he owned. For Londoners, Durham House rapidly became synonymous with Ralegh House, though the building had long been the London residence of the

Bishops of Durham. It was one of the row of episcopal palaces that ran along the Strand from Westminster to the City and which had in the years since the Reformation been taken by the crown from the princes of the church. With the high roof of its great hall towering above the skyline it was one of the landmarks of the capital, looking out over the fields and lanes of Lambeth marshes. The thronging water traffic going up and down the river could not see Lord Burghley's house, hidden away in the Convent Garden, but young Ralegh's residence dominated the panorama of the north bank – and the south bank, of course, was bare save for Lambeth Palace at one extremity and the playhouses and bear garden at the other.

The Bishop of Durham did not like his London residence being handed over to Queen Elizabeth's fancy man, but then he knew what had happened when the Bishop of Ely had protested at his Holborn residence being granted to Sir Christopher Hatton. 'Proud Prelate', wrote Elizabeth, 'you know what you were before I made you what you are. If you do not immediately comply with my request, I will unfrock you, by God!'[4] Ely's only compensation was permission to walk in his old garden and pick twenty bunches of roses a year – and the Bishop of Durham had not even that much for Walter Ralegh's tenancy.

'See! The knave commands the queen!' Richard Tarleton the jester called out derisively when he saw Walter one day lording his favour with Elizabeth. The queen made a face at the clown,[5] but he was so wide of the truth that he was punished with nothing harsher than a black look. He had not uncovered any guilty secret – the very contrary in fact, for Walter did *not* command the queen. The royal gifts he enjoyed were the reflection of power, not its substance – and it was because of this that Elizabeth went on giving. Men with real power did not need presents, but Walter Ralegh did. His magnificent residence, for example, meant extra expense – he had to employ some forty men and forty horses to keep the mansion operating on the level its grandeur deserved – and so in March 1584, he was treated to another of the patents that earned him so much profit and ill will – the licence to export woollen broadcloths, one of the great trading commodities of the nation. Within a year Ralegh was netting £3,500 annually from the turnover of this commerce – a profits tax today of, say, well over a third of a million pounds, or the best part of a million dollars, and straight into Walter Ralegh's pocket. It was no wonder that after a year or so of such revenues Burghley protested that Ralegh's energetic enforcement was creating bad feeling in the trade and making the patents harder to administer in the future. Thus in the case of the wool patent, the Merchant Adventurers of Exeter took particular exception to Ralegh's representatives.

But that local squabble does not appear to have harmed Ralegh's candidacy for the parliament of 1584, in which he represented the county of Devon along with his kinsman Sir William Courtenay. Aged thirty, pre-eminent in the queen's favour, and now a member of parliament for his own home county, Walter Ralegh was a very different figure from the captain who had returned from the Irish wars just three years previously, and the House of Commons seem gently to have reminded their fashionable new recruit of just how recent his eminence was, for as a sly Westminster joke, the bejewelled Walter was given a position of responsibility as soon as he arrived – a seat on a committee charged with surveying and restraining excessively ostentatious dress.

At the beginning of 1584 Queen Elizabeth rounded off the first stage of her new favourite's pre-eminence by bestowing on him a knighthood to go with all his other honours, a signal honour, for she was not generous with her knighthoods. He was entitled to a little flourish of triumph, and so he commissioned a West Country antiquary, John Hooker, to unearth the details of his family's former greatness. John Hooker discovered that the new Sir Walter Ralegh did indeed spring from noble stock. There had been a Sir John de Ralegh who had married the daughter of D'Amerie Clare, a descendant of Henry I. So Walter Ralegh had royal blood in his veins! He could vaunt himself as a long-lost Plantaganet.

A Jesuit charting the spiralling ascent of this Devonshire Puritan's son, sourly noted that the 'darling of the English Cleopatra' wore pearls on his shoes alone that were worth £6,000.[6] But the priest's religious loyalties got the better of his regard for the truth, for Elizabeth was no Cleopatra and Ralegh no Antony – at least when he was wooing the queen, and the insinuation that Walter squandered his wealth on sartorial ostentation was also unfair. Though he did indeed lavish a fortune on his clothes and personal appearance (peacock is too waddling an epithet for him, he was more of a dragonfly) Walter Ralegh also put much of his income to solid effect. He invested soundly in some profitable business ventures, and devoted vast sums to the enterprise that has contributed as much to his immortality as the tale of his bemired cloak – the planting of the New World with English-speaking peoples.

❧ 8 ❧

New Worlds

I
n the spring of 1584 the junior member of parliament for the county of Devon, just entering his thirties, presented to the House of Commons a decisive document in the history of two nations. He asked his fellow members formally to confirm a grant of Letters Patent offered by the queen to:

> ... our trusty and well-beloved servant Walter Ralegh Esquire ... to discover, search, find out and view such remote, heathen and barbarous lands, countries and territories, not actually possessed of any Christian prince, nor inhabited by Christian people.[1]

And that right they duly granted him.

It was no accident that this charter to found an English empire in America, signed and sealed by Queen Elizabeth on 25 March 1584, should sound so similar to that granted to Sir Humphrey Gilbert six years earlier, for Walter Ralegh, inspired by his half-brother to build an empire that spanned the Atlantic had taken over Gilbert's mantle as prime mover in the English exploration of the New World.

After the abortive voyage of 1578 from which only Walter had emerged with anything approaching credit, Sir Humphrey Gilbert had continued his efforts to discover the North West Passage to the riches of the East, and had made good use of the favour his brother had won with the queen. Walter had been able to raise £2,000 to help finance another Gilbert expedition to the New World in 1583 – a substantial sum, say £200,000, or half a million dollars in modern terms – and had also provided a ship, the *Bark Ralegh* of 200 tons, sizeable, fast and heavily armed, a real buccaneer's vessel, commanded by Michael Butler, who had been a lieutenant of Ralegh's in Ireland.

Queen Elizabeth herself, having lost money on Humphrey Gilbert's previous venture, risked nothing of substance on this second enterprise –

contributing principally and typically the last-minute decision that Gilbert should not, after all, be allowed to sail with his ships. It was felt – quite correctly – that he was 'a man of no good happe by sea'. But Walter Ralegh could not let such a slur on his family's naval reputation go unanswered. He pleaded with Elizabeth and was able on 17 March 1583 triumphantly to write to Humphrey sending him not only the queen's good wishes for a successful voyage but a little gift symbolizing the royal hope that his luck at sea would now change for the better.

But the good luck charm failed Humphrey Gilbert cruelly. Not two days out of Plymouth, in June 1583, his fleet of five ships struck a storm and the prime vessel, the *Bark Ralegh*, whose tonnage was almost as large as the other four ships put together, turned back to harbour. Captain Butler claimed that contagious sickness had made it impossible to go on, but Humphrey Gilbert put his desertion down to less excusable reasons: 'I pray you, solicit my brother Ralegh to make them an example to all knaves', he demanded. Since the *Bark Ralegh* was a buccaneering ship there were all sorts of reasons why the vessel might have turned back: supplies might have been embezzled, or the crew resentful of Gilbert. Privateers were, in any case, usually fair weather sailors.

Then, on the other side of the Atlantic, disaster struck again. In a dense fog the *Delight*, a 120-ton vessel second in size to the *Bark Ralegh*, ran onto a sandbank and some eighty-five men of her crew perished miserably. The tragedy confirmed all that the sceptics had said about Sir Humphrey Gilbert, for now he was left with only three vessels, the *Golden Hind* of Weymouth, 40 tons, the *Swallow*, 40 tons, and a frail little pinnace, the *Squirrel* of just 10 tons. To encourage his surviving men, Gilbert picked on the minuscule *Squirrel* as his flagship – in defiance of their protests that the mountainous waves on the journey home would swamp him. 'I will not forsake my little company going homeward', he said, 'with whom I have passed so many storm and perils.' But he would have been safer on a larger ship. North of the Azores in early September 1583, the three vessels were tossed by 'terrible seas, breaking short and high Pyramid-wise' and the watches on the *Golden Hind* and the *Swallow* lost sight of the little *Squirrel* in the troughs of the waves. Once the *Golden Hind* managed to get close, to see Gilbert sitting calmly in the stern of his craft reading a book. 'We are as near to heaven by sea as by land', he called in somewhat mournful encouragement to his men, before the wind swept his ship out ahead of the *Hind* whose watches followed his dipping lights through the evening and into the night. And then about midnight, with the sea and winds as turbulent as ever, the *Squirrel*'s lights vanished into a trough and did not emerge again.

So passed away Walter Ralegh's Pathfinder, and it was with a deliberate sense of picking up a dead brother's sword that Walter, in the spring of 1584, applied for the Letters Patent that would continue Humphrey Gilbert's work in the New World – though he was far from being the sole mover in colonial enterprise. Humphrey had built up both in the West Country and particularly in London a wide circle of New World enthusiasts who swapped abilities and resources and into whose company Ralegh had naturally moved when he came to the capital. Now Walter, the rising man at court, became the figurehead of this group of like-minded friends lobbying for the establishment of an English empire overseas.

Their propagandist was Richard Hakluyt, a clergyman whose writings and researchers were to provide both the inspiration and the chronicle of Elizabethan exploits on the sea. He was chaplain to the English embassy in Paris in 1583, but came back to write 'at the request and direction of the righte worshipfull Mr Walter Raghley, nowe Knight' *A Discourse Concerning Westerne Planting*. This was to be the glamorous brochure, the prospectus to arouse interest and support for Walter Ralegh's New World venture.

Hakluyt had a namesake, an elder cousin, who had first fired him with the excitement of exploration and who was a member of the Middle Temple at the same time Walter Ralegh was there. The younger Richard Hakluyt described vividly what it was like to visit his cousin's chambers, floating away from the Inns of Court on dreams of faraway lands:

I do remember that being a youth, and one of her Majesty's scholars at Westminster (that fruitful nursery) it was my hap to visit the chamber of Mr Richard Hakluyt my cousin, a gentleman of the Middle Temple, well known unto you, at a time when I found lying open upon his board certain books of Cosmography, with a universal Map: he seeing me somewhat curious ... pointed with his wand to all the known Seas, Gulfs, Bays, Straights, Capes, Rivers, Empires, Kingdoms, Dukedoms and Territories of each part. ... From the Map he brought me to the Bible and turning to the 107th Psalm, directed me to the 23rd and 24th verses, where I read that 'they which go down to the sea in ships and occupy great waters, these see the works of the lord, and his wonders in the deep'.[2]

Fired with the same enthusiasm, both Richard Hakluyts became advocates of Walter Ralegh's great project – and the younger one had, before he began working with Walter, done much to educate informed opinion in matters of colonization. He had published in 1582 the first of his anthologies, *Divers Voyages touching the Discoveries of America*, describing the explorations of pioneers like the Cabots and Robert Thorne of Bristol, and then, two years later, came the propaganda work on Ralegh's behalf.

England could not but gain by planting a colony on the west of the

Atlantic, argued Hakluyt. The Reformed Religion would be spread, 'numbers of idle men' could be sent over and be set to work, and the produce of the settlers would help England to become self-supporting. Wine, olive oil and silk at present imported from Europe could be produced there – not to mention gold, silver, copper and pearls. There was always the chance of piercing the North West Passage to China and India, and, most interestingly of all, the strategic position intended for Ralegh's colonists, plum in the centre of the North American coastline, would provide an ideal base for attacking England's enemies in two directions. English ships could strike north to raid the foreign fishing fleets off Newfoundland, and south towards the West Indies and the Spanish Main, returning with their loot to their base without risking the long Atlantic crossing. This was the crux of the argument, for Walter Ralegh had already experienced personally and through his half-brother's death, the cruelty of the Atlantic. Gone were the days when English pirates could hover off the coast of Spain picking off the treasure ships as they returned one by one. Armed escorts now guarded the convoys all the way from Cuba to Cadiz and Seville. To capture isolated galleons a pirate had to cross the Atlantic and take his chances cruising the Caribbean, hoping to catch his prey somewhere between the Spanish Main ports and Havana, where all the treasure ships met up to cross the Atlantic under escort. How convenient if English privateers could just sneak down from a base north of Florida, their ships, supplies, crew and guns fresh, not weakened by an ocean crossing.

It was a daring plan:

> If you touch Philip [in the Caribbean], you touch the apple of his eye; for take away his treasure, which is *nervus belli* and which he hath almost [entirely] out of his West Indies, his old bands of soldiers will soon be dissolved, his purpose defeated, his powers and strength diminished, his pride abated, and his tyranny utterly suppressed.[3]

English seamen like Ralegh would, furthermore, make themselves rich men in the process.

This was where another of Ralegh's friends, William Sanderson, became interested in western planting. As Philip Sidney wrote, if Richard Hakluyt was 'a very good trumpet' for Ralegh, William Sanderson, one of the great London merchants, was in a financial sense his 'great friend to all such noble and worthy actions'. He was married to Walter's niece and acted as Ralegh's chief link to the merchants of the City of London – men like Sir Lionel Ducket and Sir Thomas Smythe – and to risk the capital that they were prepared to invest in maritime adventure which might bring them profit. As a token of the fact that he was no ordinary fur-trimmed merchant, William Sanderson called his sons after the great sea-scavengers of the age, Ralegh, Drake and Cavendish – Thomas Cavendish being the Suffolk man who was shortly to circumnavigate the globe,[4] and it was largely with Sanderson money that John Davis, the Gilberts' kindly, scientific neighbour from Sandridge on the river Dart, was able, after the death of Sir Humphrey, to take over the search for the North West Passage, and navigate right up the strait named after him to 73° – a record distance along the Greenland coast which he christened 'Sanderson his Hope'.[5]

William Sanderson seems to have been Walter Ralegh's business manager and in 1584 he became one of the chief assistants in Ralegh's imperial ambitions, his financial expertise and resources representing a major factor in the speed with which the expedition to the New World was organized.

Another background influence was equally significant. Dr John Dee, the mysterious Welsh wizard whose astrological magic had been consulted back in 1558 to set Elizabeth's coronation date as the well-omened 15 January, had been one of the mentors of Humphrey Gilbert at Court and he had taken Walter Ralegh under his wing as well. He had travelled on the Continent meeting in person astronomers and geographers like the great Mercator, studied charts showing European ideas of where the North West Passage lay and brought back to England the cross-staff, or *balestila*, an improved instrument for measuring the height of heavenly bodies. He was the guru of Elizabethan exploration, and all the world came to his house by the Thames at Mortlake to examine his wonderful instruments: Drake, Frobisher, Davis, the Gilberts and Ralegh, the merchants of the Muscovy Company and even the queen's dwarf, Mrs Thomasin, and Queen Elizabeth herself – though Her Majesty was, in fact, more interested in the doctor's reputed dabblings in the black arts than in his solid scientific achievement: with his long white beard and black skullcap Dr Dee looked the very image of a black magician.

In the private diary for 18 April, 1583, the old man noted:

The queen went from Richmond towards Greenwich, and at her going on horseback being new up, she called for me by Mr Ralegh, his putting her in mind, and she said: '*Quod defertur non sufertur*' and gave me her right hand to kiss.

'What is deferred is not put off for ever.' Walter had obviously been trying to obtain some sort of court position for the old scientist as a token of gratitude for all that Dee's researches had done to help transatlantic venture, for it was the huge chart of the North American coastline which Dr John Dee had prepared in 1580 that provided the basis for Walter Ralegh's North American strategy.

You can see the chart still in the British Museum,[6] a long vellum roll about three foot by four, and looking at the fretwork of bays and inlets that Dr Dee traced so painstakingly from Canada down around the Cape of Florida to Mexico, it is easy to see why Walter Ralegh chose for his colony the position that he did. His overall strategy called for some sheltered and defensible bay between the West Indies and the Newfoundland Grand Banks. There, right in the middle of Dee's somewhat lopsided coastline opens a circular little bay – Bahia de Santa Maria – which, with its double row of islands inside it, looks like a natural harbour that could be fortified. This bay, lying towards the north of the modern Carolinas in the Mediterranean belt of climate seemed the obvious spot for Ralegh's settlement.

Dr Dee had got the information for his seminal map from a Portuguese pilot, Simon Fernandez, and this Fernandez was himself no stranger to the Ralegh family, for he had made for Humphrey Gilbert a voyage of reconnaissance to the New World in 1580, and was to play a leading role in the navigation of Walter Ralegh's own expedition, sailing as flagship master and pilot in all of them. He, like Ralegh, was obsessed with buccaneering at the expense of Spanish shipping, for the Portuguese had never had any love for the Spanish – particularly after Philip of Spain annexed their kingdom in 1580.

A renegade Portuguese and a Welsh magician, these were strange assistants for Walter Ralegh's greatest claim to historical fame, and one other inspiration was more unexpected still. In 1580 Dr Dee had advised that when it came to tackling navigation there was nothing like a good mathematician[7] to master the problems of geography and chronology and in 1583, with his colonization project looming up, Walter Ralegh set about searching for such a man. He found him in the mathematician Thomas Hariot, who became immediately one of his most trusted and loyal assistants.

Hariot had studied at St Mary's Hall, Oxford and won his degree in 1580, the year Ralegh went to Ireland. He was taken on by Walter as a teacher of 'the mathematical sciences' and installed with all his instruments in Durham House. There, for nearly a dozen years, from 1583 or 1584 until 1595, he held a running series of seminars and lectures on practical mathematics with special reference to the problems of navigation and astronomy. These were not public lectures but were restricted to Ralegh's men alone, the pilots and captains who sailed his ships – informal training courses. Hariot was the cartographical master, preparing the maps and charts that the mariners of the Ralegh fleet would use, comparing different versions with experienced navigators like Fernandez who knew the routes in question – and gaining personal experience himself. For that was the other half of his job. Having gathered together all the instruments and charts and instructed the ships' crews in their use, Thomas Hariot was to sail across the Atlantic with them and there examine and map out Walter Ralegh's new domain.

What Thomas Hariot achieved in this direction was, in the context of world-wide exploration, worth a dozen previous voyages of discovery put together. The expedition that Walter Ralegh was preparing in England in 1583 and 1584, represented, from an international point of view, little that was truly original. There were, after all, scores of Spaniards who commuted across the Atlantic twice a year. Fishermen had been going to and from the Grand Banks for centuries, and there had for nearly half a century existed in the New World full-scale Spanish cities with stone-built cathedrals and palaces that would put most English provincial towns to shame. The significant thing about Walter Ralegh's project, and the achievement that was to make his expedition the foundation of colonial enterprise for a whole century to come was Thomas Hariot's scientific work in cataloguing everything he saw and in describing it minutely.

Weather, coastline, vegetation, flora, fauna, human inhabitants, all went into the great volume Thomas Hariot was to publish on his return and which, translated into Latin, French and German became a standard point of reference for all New World activities thereafter. Teaching himself some Algonquin Indian dialect, Thomas Hariot was able, along with the expedition's brilliant artist John White, to make one of the most eminent contributions to the tradition of the scientific explorer, being imitated almost immediately by Thomas Cavendish, who took Hariot's friend Hues on his circumnavigation, and by the Earl of Cumberland who hired the mathematician Edward Wright in 1589. For initiating in England this great tradition, which was later to continue with the work of Captain James Cook and culminate eventually, of course, in the mind-bending work of Charles Darwin in the *Beagle*, Sir Walter Ralegh must take the credit.

The man he chose for the job was remarkable – far more than an industrious servant and zealous notemaker, a truly original mind. Up onto the leads of Durham House in 1590 Hariot took his optical instruments and worked out new techniques for charting the stars. He was a friend of the playwright Christopher Marlowe, the psychic ambitions of whose *Dr Faustus* were so akin to Thomas Hariot's own intellectual appetite. He corresponded with the great Kepler, not as some research student anxious for help, but as the authority on optics to whom the eminent German went for advice; in the preparation of Ralegh's *History of the World* he was to be a principal assistant, and, above all, he remained a loyal and honest friend to Walter Ralegh not only in the days of his patron's glory, but also in the years when it was less profitable, pleasant or even safe to acknowledge him.

To complete the preparations just one more ingredient was necessary – a reconnaissance to be made of the area proposed for settlement, and so on 27 April 1584, just a few weeks after the sealing of Walter Ralegh's Letters Patent to the new empire, two ships sailed out of Plymouth harbour to map out the route and prepare the way for the main party. It is an indication of the efficiency of Walter Ralegh's team not only that this preliminary survey was made, but that it was despatched so promptly. No Spanish agents saw it go.

The captains of the ships were two more of Ralegh's clients, members of his now sizeable retinue, Philip Amadas, a twenty-year-old gentleman from Plymouth, and Arthur Barlow. Their pilot was Simon Fernandez, who led them straight down the pirate route to the Canaries, across to the West Indies and then, catching the Gulf Stream off Cuba, up the coast of Florida and what is now the Carolinas towards the inlet, St Mary's Bay, that had looked so promising on old John Dee's map. It was not exactly as the doctor had drawn it, but Fernandez knew the coast and the shelter they were looking for, and in the middle of July 1584, Walter Ralegh's man landed on Hatarask Island formally taking possession for 'the queen's most excellent majesty' of a land which Barlow described as:

> very sandy and low towards the water's side, but so full of grapes, as the very beating and surge of the sea overflowed them, of which we found such plenty, as well there as in all places else, both on the sand and on the green soil of the hills, as in the plains, as well as on every little shrub, as also climbing towards the tops of high cedars.[8]

It was Barlow's job to make this new territory sound like a land of milk and honey, but it is obvious that he, Amadas and Fernandez were all genuinely exhilarated by the Mediterranean warmth and pastoral attraction of their empire-to-be. Indians who appeared on the third day were curious and friendly, very anxious to trade – 'most gentle, loving and faithful, void of all guile and treason, and such as lived after the manner of the golden age', enthused Barlow. 'The earth bringeth forth all things in abundance, as in the first creation, without toil or labour.'

It seemed a veritable Garden of Eden. Peas were planted and shot up 14 inches in ten days, and the local chief entertained the English visitors most graciously to a feast of corn porridge, pumpkin, fish, venison, fruit and sassafras-flavoured water. He replied to his guests' questions about the name they should give to the area with the words 'Wind gand con' – 'What gay clothes you are wearing!' and so his sartorial compliment temporarily became the colony's name, which Barlow, Amadas and Fernandez bore proudly home along with two Indians, Manteo and Wanchese, who agreed to travel to England to work out a system of translation with Thomas Hariot in Durham House.

By the middle of September 1585 the scouts were back in London and in October Walter Ralegh presented to the queen Richard Hakluyt's *Discourse* together with Manteo and Wanchese, dressed respectably in brown taffeta rather than the 'wild animal skin over the shoulders and fur over the privies!'[9] which, Queen Elizabeth was interested to learn, was their normal garb. Barlow's report, containing not only descriptions of fertility and friendliness, but hints of precious stones and metals for the digging, set the seal on the first stage of the project. All that was needed now was a name for the colony that Walter Ralegh was to found – for Windgandcon, apart from its true meaning which was only discovered later, did not roll off the tongue with much panache.

It was left to Queen Elizabeth to provide the title that could bring glory to her own reputation and inspiration to the men who adventured in her name, and in February 1585 it was formally confirmed that Sir Walter Ralegh's new settlement, colony, empire, would be known as Virginia.

The Colonization of 1585

Sir Walter Ralegh did not travel to Virginia. The queen who gave him the wealth to launch the enterprise that has made his name famous on both sides of the Atlantic, decreed that he must stay in England by her side. But she compensated him with a profitable and prestigious court office as Master of Horse, a fine title – *Walteri Ralegh Militis Domini et Gubernatoria Virginiae*, (Walter Ralegh, Knight, Lord and Governor of Virginia) – and financial assistance. The purpose of Richard Hakluyt's *Discourse Concerning Westerne Planting* had been to argue that the Virginian enterprise was not a project for private sponsorship and that Government backing was essential, and Elizabeth yielded to its suggestions to a surprising extent. She lent her *Tyger*, a prime ship of the Royal Navy, donated £400 worth of gunpowder from the royal magazine and, in addition to her grants of wine and cloth licences that enabled Walter to raise both ready cash and credit, gave Ralegh's lieutenants the right to 'take up' men and ships with press gangs, as in time of war.

The *Tyger* was a fine flagship and to sail in her as his admiral Walter recruited a fine man of action, his cousin Sir Richard Grenville from Buckland Abbey. Older than Ralegh, Grenville was related to him by marriage through the St Legers of Bideford, had passed through the Inns of Court, been abroad as a soldier of fortune to fight both the Turks and the Irish, and served as an MP for many years. He had begged the queen in vain to let him follow Magellan's route to the Pacific – the mission that Francis Drake carried off with such glory – so now, invited to ferry the Virginia colonists across the Atlantic, he declared himself 'willing to hazard himself in this voyage' out of the 'love he bore unto Sir Walter Ralegh, together with a disposition he had to attempt honourable actions worthy of honour.'[1]

That repetition of the word 'honour' was significant, for Richard Grenville was a touchy individual, whose whole life proved a preamble to his proud and fruitless end in the *Revenge*. His task was to get the colonists established in Virginia and then, once they had settled down, to return home. But the human side of this job required a flexibility that he lacked, and Walter's choice as governor of the colony, the man who would have day-to-day responsibility for the settlement after Grenville had taken his fleet home, was similarly out of key. Ralph Lane, a young and wealthy gentleman with a taste for adventure – he had shares in privateers and had appropriated rebel lands in Ireland with zest – had no obvious qualifications for the position. It was just that Elizabeth, whose equerry he was, favoured him.

In both these two figureheads there was something lacking. They never succeeded in meshing into a team as Barlow and Amadas had in their reconnaissance the previous year, for they had little in common.

The less eminent members of the party, however, were fully to vindicate the trust placed in them – Thomas Hariot, in particular, along with his artist John White. Trained as a surveyor, White had already seen the New World as a member of Frobisher's expedition of 1577, and it was probably the sensitive sketches of Eskimoes he had brought back then which recommended him to Ralegh. Also in the party, as high marshal, which meant that he would arbitrate in all disputes and enforce discipline, was Thomas Cavendish, the future circumnavigator, who was taking to Virginia the *Elizabeth*, his small bark of 50 tons. Amadas, the scout of the previous year, came too in Ralegh's *Roebuck*, with the title of Admiral of Virginia, and his fellow pathfinder, Barlow was probably in command of the *Dorothie*, another of Ralegh's own vessels. The master and pilot of Grenville's flagship was Simon Fernandez, and there were, in all, some five hundred men in the party, just 108 of whom were classed as colonists. Their names, unfortunately, though all recorded on Richard Hakluyt's roll of honour, tell us little. Three were from the household of Sir Francis Walsingham, who had invested money of his own in the enterprise, and we can guess from the West Country names – there was a Rowse and a Prideaux of Pastowe – that many were clients of Grenville, the Gilberts and Ralegh. There was a Gorges – Sir Edward – and also two German miners and a Jewish mineral expert from Prague, Joachim Ganz, whose name was anglicized on the manifest to Doughan Gannes. In the treasure-seeking skills of these three foreign experts lay a broad hint of one of the colonists' principal ambitions.

On 9 April 1585 the expedition sailed, a formidable company of men and ships which Spanish spies anxiously estimated at 'no fewer than sixteen vessels in which Ralegh intends to convey four hundred men',[2] which underestimated the manpower by about one hundred and doubled the actual number of boats. But Spain was quite right to be anxious, for open war between Spain and England was now close and Richard Grenville had every intention of attacking Spanish shipping on his way both to and from Virginia. To take Spanish prizes was the most rapid way Walter Ralegh's heavy investment in the Virginia enterprise could be recouped, and so, like the scouting ships of the previous year, the *Tyger*, *Roebuck* and other ships headed along the privateering route south to the Canaries and then across by Columbus's route to the West Indies. There, on the island of St John, Grenville immediately erected a fort. This spot, unashamedly selected on Spanish territory, must have been fixed as a rendezvous point by Ralegh before the expedition sailed, for the *Elizabeth*, having been separated from the main fleet by a storm off Portugal, rejoined the party here on 19 May 1585.

The local Spanish garrison was helpless and Grenville was in such strength that the Spaniards wondered whether he intended to stay permanently. But the English concern was simply to build a new pinnace to replace one that had been lost crossing the Atlantic. The *Tyger* had on board all the iron, sails and cordage it needed, and with the new pinnace built, Grenville moved on, carving deep in a tree trunk an inscription which the Spaniards anxiously copied down: it stated that the *Tyger* and *Elizabeth* were about to sail 'in good health, glory be to God. 1585'.

The next few days demonstrated what success an English fleet stationed on the American side of the Atlantic could expect in the Caribbean. With the greatest of ease four Spanish ships were captured, their cargoes of 'good and rich fraight' seized and their wealthier passengers ransomed. One of these tried to find out the ultimate objective of the English, but Grenville – already well known to the Spaniards as 'Greenfield' or '*Verde Campo*' – simply gave him the impression, duly passed on to the king of Spain, that he was heading for an uncolonized part of the Caribbean like Dominica.

The next port of call of Ralegh's little fleet was Isabela, the colonial capital Columbus had first founded on the island of Hispaniola, and there, despite, or perhaps because of their previous plunderings, the Englishmen were treated with hospitality by the garrison. There was a feast at which the English fleet's orchestra – brought along as a means of communicating between ships after dark and also to amuse the Virginian Indians – gave a concert 'with which the Spaniards were more than delighted', and then three white bulls were brought down from the mountains to provide quarry for a hunt, which the English greatly enjoyed. Gifts were exchanged, and next day, instead of plundering his hosts, Grenville paid for as many cattle as he could crowd on his ships' decks, as well as ginger, pears and tobacco to be sold in England.

The fleet moved on through the Bahamas up the coast of Florida to

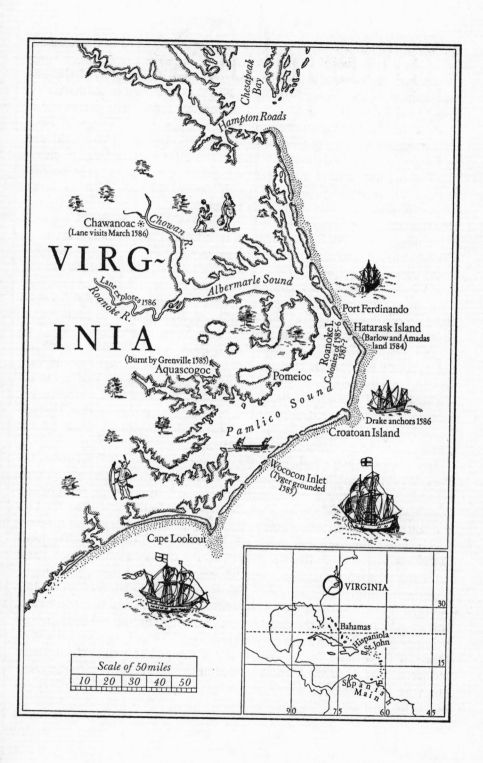

Chesapeak Bay

Hampton Roads

Chawanoac ☼
(Lane visits March 1586)

Chowan R.

VIRG~

Lane explores 1586
Roanoke R.

Albermarle Sound

Port Ferdinando

Hatarask Island
(Barlow and Amadas land 1584)

Roanoke I.
Colonies of 1585-6
1587-?

INIA

(Burnt by Grenville 1585)
Aquascogoc

Pomeioc

Pamlico Sound

Drake anchors 1586

Croatoan Island

Wococon Inlet
(Tyger grounded 1585)

Cape Lookout

Scale of 50 miles

| 10 | 20 | 30 | 40 | 50 |

VIRGINIA

30

Bahamas

Hispaniola
St. John

Spanish Main

15

90   75   60   45

arrive, at the end of June 1585, at the long sausage-shaped offshore islands which protected the bay John Dee had identified as the Bahia de Santa Maria – today known as Pamlico Sound – and here occurred the first major upset of the voyage, for Simon Fernandez, instead of sailing up the coast to the inlet he had navigated the previous year with Amadas and Barlow, tried to take a short cut into the Sound through Wococon Inlet. The passage over the sand bar was not deep enough, and though the rest of the fleet just scraped through – literally – the *Tyger* grounded. The shock strained her timbers and water rushed into her hold. She was floated again and her leaks resealed, but her supply of provisions, the expedition's largest single cargo, was completely ruined.

After the expedition returned there were to be insinuations that Fernandez was a double-agent, paid to sabotage the whole venture by Philip of Spain. But if he really had been in King Philip's pay, there were many more effective methods by which he could have betrayed the expedition whose success he had worked so hard to secure, and if he had been an Englishman and not a Portuguese, the explanation of his mistake would have been complacency and over-confidence, an eagerness to show off his local knowledge to those who had not been on the coast before.

The accident did at least prove that Spanish vessels would have a hard job breaking into Pamlico Sound, and the huge lake-like harbour – so vast that in 1524 Verrazzano had thought he had discovered the Pacific Ocean – seemed well sheltered from the Atlantic by its off-shore sandbanks. Grenville was able to embark on his ship's barge, an ordinary little Thames river boat, and set off with a longboat and the pinnace built in the Caribbean to search for a site for a settlement.

It was a remarkable little party that went off to prospect England's first New World colony in three open boats little larger than dinghies. There was Sir Richard, the West Country knight, Thomas Hariot, the Oxford mathematician turned geographer, Manteo, the Indian who had been to the court of the great white queen, Amadas, the Plymouth gentleman who had brought him back, Cavendish who was later to cross the Pacific, John White whose drawings have immortalized the reconnaissance, Ralph Lane who was to govern the colony and 'divers other Gentlemen', all brought together to this foreign lagoon by the work and inspiration of Sir Walter Ralegh. A score of miles they rowed and sailed, then beached and struck inland over fertile soil that is today rich farming land, to reach an Indian village – Pomeiooc. It was a circular little encampment surrounded with a fence of stakes and in the centre was a fire round which the Indians gathered. They seemed friendly, welcoming the strange white men and allowing John White to sketch their mat-covered houses and their sleeping platforms inside.

The countryside seemed promising, but it was not the sort of site the English were seeking. The flat fields provided no obvious defence. So back to their boats the explorers went and rowed south round creeks and bays to another Indian settlement, Aquascogoc, whose inhabitants proved friendly too. But here a trivial incident became the occasion for a misunderstanding with grave implications, for a small silver cup mysteriously disappeared from the Englishmen's baggage. Sir Richard Grenville immediately assumed the worst and set the local chief the task of discovering the cup and its thief before he next returned. But Hariot and his Indian interpreters did not succeed in impressing on the chief the great significance that the white commander set by this trinket, for when Grenville returned to Aquascogoc a few days later, having inspected the village of Secoton, the cup was still missing. The Englishman immediately ordered the Aquascogoc settlement to be burnt and the crops in the fields around to be devastated.

It was easy work to accomplish, and within hours the mat huts lay gutted and the meadows all trampled. The thieving savages had been taught a lesson. But it was not, of course, the lesson that Sir Richard intended, and learning it well, the Indians were to make the English pay dearly for it in the future. Returning to the anchored ships of the main party at the end of July 1585, the scouts had stored up trouble for the future, and had still not found a suitable site for their settlement.

So the whole fleet moved up the coast, travelling some sixty miles along the low dunes and sand bars that separated the ocean from Pamlico Sound, to arrive early in August at the spot where Amadas and Barlow had landed the previous year. There to greet the party was Granganimeo, the chief who had provided Ralegh's advance party with the name of Windgandcon for the area. He could not by then have heard of Grenville's reprisals down the coast and was delighted not only to welcome the Englishmen but to offer them an island, Roanoke, nicely situated inside the sand bars, as a site for their colony. Barlow had already seen the spot, fertile, watered, wooded and defensible, and the Indian's offer was gratefully accepted. Without more ado the colonists started unloading their supplies, while one of the Spanish ships captured in the Caribbean was sent back to England under the command of John Arundel, to obtain from Sir Walter Ralegh provisions to replace the cargo that had been lost when the *Tyger* ran aground.

All was set fair for Sir Walter Ralegh's colony. Through the early weeks of August 1585 his 108 settlers worked at building themselves houses and defences on Roanoke Island where they could spend the winter, and at the end of the month Richard Grenville set sail for England in the *Tyger*, his task completed. He had landed his Virginians with food, stores and cattle on a promising site and could now hand over the settlement as a going concern to Governor Ralph Lane. He had, furthermore, by taking those four Spanish prizes in the Caribbean done much to set the finances of the whole project on a credit footing, and one more prize he took on the way home produced a solid dividend for all Ralegh's investors. Returning to England by the route she had come, the *Tyger* overhauled off Bermuda a Spanish freighter of 33 tons, the *Santa Maria de San Vincente* loaded with sugar and ginger worth £50,000, and Sir Richard was able personally to take his booty into Plymouth harbour on 18 October 1595, the *Tyger* having gone ahead with the news of his imminent arrival.

Sir Walter Ralegh and other 'worshipfull friends' came down to the port to congratulate their captain whose piracy had netted some £10,000 worth of profit they could share. It had been a most successful year. Earlier that summer, just as the colonists were arriving at Virginia, two ships due to carry their relief supplies had been ordered by the queen to join instead a raiding expedition to Newfoundland, a diversion which had seemed a disaster until the ships returned having snatched £60,000 worth of loot from Spanish and Portuguese ships in the Atlantic. This profit meant that a really well stocked relief expedition could be sent to Virginia the following spring, and that the handsome dividends from the year's activities would make it easy to attract investors for future ventures. More colonies could be set up and the Virginia seaboard lined in due course with havens for English privateers. No longer would the New World be a monopoly of the Spanish.

Antonio de Espejo had two years earlier explored New Mexico and reported silver mines at a longitude we now know to be incorrect, but which in the 1580s sounded like the back door of Virginia. So prospects of treasure seemed opening as well. With over one hundred men settled and industriously establishing an American empire in his name, Sir Walter Ralegh could, in 1585, congratulate himself not only on his personal achievements but on swinging English history into a bold new course.

✥ 10 ✥

The Call of the West

Walter Ralegh wanted to get back to the West. In London he was the talk of the town. Yet his fame was double-edged – magnificent but malicious. 'Sir Walter Ralegh', wrote a follower of Essex, 'he is the best-hated man of the world, in court, city and country.'[1]

Life at the pinnacle of Elizabethan society was a lonely experience, very different from the certainties of Walter's farmhouse upbringing in Devonshire. From France to Oxford, London, Ireland and the court Walter Ralegh had progressed, a succession of situations in which he had never been able once to relax. To escape to the fields of Devonshire, to return to his roots, was a relief he needed very badly, and so it was in July 1584 that he had written to Richard Duke, the landlord of Hayes Barton where he was born and grew up, to ask if he could purchase the property that his father had rented. 'I will most willingly give whatsoever in your conscience you shall deem it worth', he wrote, and, in addition to this blank cheque he offered that 'if at any time you shall have occasion to use me, you shall find me a thankful friend to you and yours.'

But the prospect of influence in high places meant little to Richard Duke, for though Walter Ralegh stressed that 'for the natural disposition I have to that place [Hayes Barton], being born in that house, I had rather seat myself there than anywhere else',[2] the landlord would not sell. Walter was denied the triumph of returning in grandeur to his birthplace and providing for his family a focus they had lost after the death of his father in February 1581.

Old Walter had died too early to witness the success of his son, but in 1584 his wife, Katherine Champernowne was still alive, having suffered the grief of her son Humphrey's death in the *Squirrel* the previous year. Walter's eminence must have been a consolation to her, but once he had left home he was never again very close to his mother. Katherine lived on

71

quietly in the West for another ten years until her death in 1594, and the inventory of possessions in her will suggests, even, that Walter was a less than dutiful son. For there is no mention of exotic filial gifts brought back from the New World or looted from Spanish ships, and no evidence that Walter was passing on to her even a small portion of his vast income as favourite. Old Katherine left debts – she had run heavily into the red at the butcher's, and had not settled her accounts with the apothecary or with the grocer[3] – and this was not a result of extravagant living. Her bequests showed a humble enough lifestyle: to Mistress Katherine Hooker 'the bed wherein I lie, my saddle and saddle-cloth, the little salt [cellar] and two spoons, one pair of holland sheets, the little board with the green carpet. To Emlyn Baker, the great salt cellar in part payment for 40 shillings' – another debt, and to her waiting woman, Mary Wheare, '20s, all the apparel that I wear, besides a writing she hath to show'. This probably set out the wages due to her.

It was a modest end for a lady whose sons had cut such a dash in the world. But Katherine was looked after by at least one servant and, to judge from the fact that she had a saddle and saddle-cloth to bequeath, she enjoyed a healthy and reasonably strenuous old age. It is quite possible that she was too proud to accept her son's charity and conceivable even that she disapproved of the way in which he had created his fortune, making eyes at a middle-aged woman.

Yet whatever Walter's relationship with his mother, his protectiveness on behalf of the rest of his family was exemplary and he was particularly close to his elder brother Carew, a genial, somewhat lumbering fellow whom Walter cut in on both his business deals and the benefits of his eminence. Two minor posts that flowed from the royal favour were the governorship of the fort at Portland Bill, an important strategic position at the southernmost tip of Dorset, and the rangership of Gillingham forest, extensive acres of woodland reserved for the royal hunt just north of Shaftesbury. So while holding both these positions in name Walter passed over their effective administration and their profits to his brother. Carew, too much of a yokel to make a good courtier, was thus able to carve out a niche for himself in the county of Dorset, enjoying the local prestige of two royal positions, hunting the rich game of Gillingham and parading his little garrison at Portland and, doubtless, providing hospitality for his famous younger brother whenever he rode to and from the West, for Dorset made a good overnight break in Walter's long journey from Plymouth to London.

It was a journey that Walter came to make more and more frequently in the 1580s, for, in 1585, in the same summer that his colonists in Virginia were seeking a site for their settlement, Elizabeth bestowed upon him one of the premier West Country honours. From July 1585 Walter Ralegh could go back to Devon and Cornwall not as some jumped-up metropolitan magnate but as Lord Warden of the Stannaries, the head of the tin miners of Devon and Cornwall, whose strong local commonwealth had age-old laws and customs of its own.

Tin was, with wool and lead, one of England's principal exports, and the mines of Cornwall and south-west Devon were in the sixteenth century, as they remained until recent time, the principal source of tin for the western world. The metal made the south-western tip of England one of Renaissance Europe's great industrial areas, with German and Dutch engineers coming over to supervise the excavations, and London merchants channelling investment into ventures like the St Just copper workings from which ore was transported across the Bristol Channel to South Wales. It was smelted at Neath and the freighters returned to Cornwall with timber to shore up underground workings that went to a depth of 40 or 50 fathoms – one small part of a complicated, curiously modern undertaking complete with capitalist entrepreneurs and an industrial proletariat – 'ten thousand or twelve thousand of the roughest and most mutinous men in England'.[4] Supervising it all on behalf of the crown after July 1585 was Sir Walter Ralegh.

It was his financial responsibility as lord warden of the stannaries to ensure that the crown received its fair share of the West Country's mineral profits, there were opportunities for him to take a personal commission on the sale of tin, and his legal and social duty was to administer the local laws and regulations that were a reminder of how Cornwall had, like Brittany and Wales, once been an independent Celtic state. So up on Crockern Tor, in the very heart of Dartmoor, cut off by mists and wild country from the world – where once stood a granite table and seats hewed from the solid rock – Sir Walter Ralegh could sit in judgement over the stannary courts. Under his jurisdiction too were the stannary parliaments, thriving institutions which were expanding so ambitiously that, in 1588, they were to petition the crown that the local centres of industry should be empowered to send more representatives to their meetings.

Commercial disputes formed the bulk of the stannary business over which Walter Ralegh and his representatives had to adjudicate – with the ultimate appeal for his petitioners lying in the right to take their case to London. But there were social disputes as well. Richard Grenville had used the stannary courts to prosecute one Thomas Hilling for slander of his father-in-law, Sir John St Leger, and just as, in modern times, miners have been ruled exempt from forcible conscription into the nation's armed forces, so in the sixteenth century Walter Ralegh's tinners could not be called up for the county musters. They had their own separate military arrangements, and were also, on account of the revenue the crown derived from their tin, exempt from ordinary taxation. Being placed at the head of this independently inclined society provided Walter Ralegh with a healthy antidote to court life and politics, and strengthened his prestige in the area of the country which always meant most to him. Soon after he was given the job a client of Lord Burghley's protested that 'no man is more hated than him [Ralegh] – none more cursed daily of the poor through the gift of the cloths to him [the licence to export broadcloths] – his pride is intolerable, without regard for any, as the world knows.'[5] But that was a complaint based essentially on court politics. Whatever resentment Walter Ralegh's cloth and wine licences aroused in London, down in the West Country his administration of the stannaries won him respect throughout a region notoriously jealous with its affections.

In September 1585 Walter's local power base was fortified still further when he was made Lord Lieutenant of Cornwall, a political appointment arising from the need, especially acute under the threat of a Spanish invasion, to ensure that the independence of the stannaries did not conflict with the greater national interest. There was in the fiscal and military privileges of the stannaries, a certain potential for friction whenever the Privy Council, through the Lord Lieutenant, called for ship money to finance the fleet or men to march with the musters for the miners had the right to ignore the national interest in favour of the local. So the problem was avoided by placing the same man at the head of both jurisdictions.

But the appointment was more than a political convenience. It was also an endorsement of Walter Ralegh's personal qualities – official recognition of his energy and ability to organize, for with the prospect of Spanish soldiers landing upon the south coast, Cornwall and Devon became the front line of national defence. It was not a job for an effete courtier, and the compliment paid to Walter was emphasized by the fact that he was then the only mere knight to hold the lord lieutenancy of any county. His job was to assemble, train and arm the militia, survey the coast, identify the areas most likely to be attacked by invading troops, strengthen the defences throughout the county, make sure the alarm beacons were in readiness, keep all strongholds stocked with arms and ammunition and, apart from all these military duties, to assess and collect the taxes levied on the country. It needed a man and a half and Cornwall was lucky that, as Aubrey said of Ralegh, 'he was no slug'. Queen Elizabeth was well aware that though her Walter might not be the politic individual she needed on her Privy Council, he had the vigour needed for such a job in the firing line.

He also had the right connections. Even in the direct national emergency there was little prospect of galvanizing the counties of Devon and

Cornwall into action without the cooperation of the 'hundred gentry'[6] Walter Ralegh was so proud to count as his kinsmen, and this was the importance of the third local appointment he received at this time, Admiral of the West. His responsibility as Vice-Admiral was to be the representative in the West of the Lord High Admiral, and generally to see that the queen's ships in Devon and Cornwall were in top fighting shape. But the job also gave him the sort of perquisite that had been illustrated back in 1578 when Sir John Gilbert had mysteriously failed to prevent his brother Humphrey's expedition from leaving Dartmouth harbour in defiance of the Privy Council. The vice-admiral could help his friends, which meant that, at the cost of a few privateers avoiding customs duties or punishment for their piracy, the Government could count on the self-interested support of the local community for the Privy Council nominee. It was a system that was obviously open to abuse. A vice-admiral who let every buccaneer escape scot free could be counter-productive. But in these years punishing pirates was incidental to the Privy Council's main purpose – and they very much needed a representative like Ralegh who could cherish the friendship of the pirates against the day when the Spaniards arrived off the coast.

It helped, of course, to have a pirate in the job. Even if Walter Ralegh had never won the favour of the queen of England he would have made himself wealthy, and probably famous, as a buccaneer in his own right, and a most businesslike buccaneer at that. For through the 1580s it is possible to trace his investments and dividends in piracy multiplying in a steady fashion that was independent of those revenues that were the consequence of favour.

Walter Ralegh had ships out raiding on his behalf as early as 1582, probably financed by the profits of his time in France. From a family with strong sea-going connections and a fiercely Protestant tradition, it was natural for him to be drawn into the maritime equivalent of his activities as a Protestant freebooter in France and Ireland. Catholic shipping was the particular object of the West Country buccaneers in the 1570s and 1580s and by 1582 Walter had enough capital to his name to finance the construction of a purpose-built private warship, the *Bark Ralegh*, a sleek sea-raider which made no pretence at being a merchant vessel.

Nor was this Walter Ralegh's only privateering vessel. He had other ships that he owned, the *Roebuck*, for example, named after the heraldic beast of the Ralegh coat of arms, and Walter would charter captains and their crews to sail on his behalf or on behalf of a syndicate in which costs – and profits – were shared. Thus the records of English piracy in the latter part of Queen Elizabeth's reign – which are, of course, by their nature sketchy – are dotted with references to Walter Ralegh, his partners and their ships:

the *Bark Randall* owned by John Randall of Southampton, was financed by Walter and Sir George Carey and brought home some fabulous cargoes – pepper, cloves, mace, sugar, ivory, brazil-wood and precious stones worth well over £23,000; the *Bark Burton*, a Plymouth raider financed, apparently, by Walter Ralegh alone, brought home from just one voyage cochineal, hides and other goods valued at £10,000; and the *Pilgrim*, a ship whose captain, Jacob Whiddon, was the 'admiral' of the Ralegh pirate fleet, captured valuable sumach, raisins and almonds valued at £500.

Less glamorous cargoes also proved worth the taking. The *Bark Ralegh* brought home at least one valuable cargo of fish and an unnamed Bristol ship which Walter financed with a little syndicate of Bristol merchants also raided foreign fishing vessels. Salt, corn, barley, figs, brass pans, tallow, cider or stagskins, none were too lowly to scavenge, for, shipping costs apart, they cost nothing, and Walter's friends and relatives soon saw the profit in the game. William Sanderson shared in nearly £7,000 worth of prizes from one voyage alone, and Adrian Gilbert, the youngest of Walter's half-brothers, invested in a ship that sailed with Thomas Cavendish, a great navigator, but also a great pirate as well.

Not that Cavendish, Ralegh or any of the other adventurers would have answered to the name of pirate. We should, technically, refer to their activities as privateering – the forcible seizure and confiscation of ships and cargoes trading with an enemy power. But 'privateer' as a word was not, in fact, used in this sense until the seventeenth century – the Elizabethans used the term 'voluntary' to distinguish a licensed adventurer from a pirate – and the facts of life of Renaissance international relations made the distinction academic.

From the beginning to the end of Queen Elizabeth's reign there was scarcely a year when there were not two European powers engaged in hostilities that involved each licensing armed ships, including English ships, to disrupt the trade of the other. Thus the French Protestants licensed *corsaires* to prey on merchantmen suspected of trading with the Catholics, and vice versa, while the revolt of the Netherlands against their Spanish occupiers provided an even more fruitful source of privateering employment. William of Orange issued many letters of marque entitling Englishmen, particularly West Countrymen, to attack Spanish shipping, while the Prince of Condé acted in the same capacity for the French Protestants. Privateering was the most substantial link between the Huguenots and the Protestants of the Devon and Cornish coast towns – one reason why back in 1568 Gawain Champernowne had been able to recruit so many to fight for him in France – and it was an activity which Elizabeth's Government both tolerated and profited from since the English customs taxed everything that came into the country whether it represented the products of conventional trade or the reward of privateering.

What went on when a 'voluntary' crossed the horizon no one knew, provided, of course, that he had the sense and the decency not to attack English vessels, and this is why piracy is the most accurate description of the main activity of England's south coast ports at this period.

Then in May 1585 Queen Elizabeth herself started licensing 'voluntaries'. The Spaniards had suddenly confiscated the cargoes of English ships in Spanish harbours – only one vessel, the *Primrose*, escaped to bring home the news of the arrests. There was an immediate public outcry, but as Walter Ralegh complained, Queen Elizabeth was averse to any direct armed response to King Philip's provocations. So to license private reprisal seemed the best reaction, suiting the purposes both of Elizabeth's seamen and of the queen's sly style of international relations. In these reprisals Walter Ralegh became involved both as a privateer and, after September of that year, as vice-admiral of the West.

Vessels of Sir Walter Ralegh's privateering fleet attacked during the war with Spain some Italian traders freighting to Florence a collection of magnificent cargoes: pepper, cloves, musk, mace, sugar, ivory, brazilwood, cinnamon, rubies, ambergris, civet, diamonds, oriental pearls and wheat.[6] The English pirates carried off booty worth £25,000, a rich haul split between Ralegh and his partners, with his captains and crews taking their share as well.

But their coup turned out to be troublesome, for through an Italian merchant living in London, Filippo Corsini, Walter Ralegh's victims complained bitterly to the English court of admiralty which, when openly appealed to in this fashion could, with decency, do little else but uphold their petition. Ralegh's ships, it was ruled, had no right to attack the Italians.

The injured Italians, however, had not reckoned on the fact that Ralegh's men had sold all their loot within a fortnight of getting back to Weymouth. So though Corsini had a warrant to re-possess all his colleagues' stolen cargoes it was simply impractical for him to recover them.

The Italian's task was made still more difficult by the fact that the admiralty officers through whom he had to work were, like Walter Ralegh, involved in piracy themselves, and that the English navy as a whole relied very much on the reinforcement of the privateering fleets. This was the age of hiatus when sea power assumed a significance it had never previously possessed in European affairs, but when the official navies of the nations could not match up to the demands that were made on them. Not until the days of Cromwell and Admiral Blake was it realistic to talk of a navy in the modern sense. The sea powers of northern Europe – the Dutch and the

French as much as the English – relied on their pirates when it came to waging a maritime war. So the Lord Admiral Charles Howard had little reason to make fussy enquiries as to the rights and wrongs of privateering activities on distant waters. He personally had developed a profitable business, in any case, selling open letters patent that were a *carte blanche* for piracy, and then investing his money in the privateering expeditions he considered to have the best chance of success.

Down in Plymouth, the vice-admiral of the West had little need to feel scruples about the private use to which he put his government office, with his immediate superior competing vigorously, and on occasions collaborating with him in providing financial support for piracy. Poor Corsini never retrieved the cargoes of his Italian friends from Sir Walter Ralegh.

Through the winter of 1585 to 1586 the attack on Spain intensified, despite the fact that war still was not declared. Not content with licensing privateers, Elizabeth had despatched the Newfoundland raiding expedition into which Ralegh's Virginia relief ships had been diverted with such profit, and now in the same September that he became vice-admiral, Walter invested[7] in a large fleet organized by Sir Francis Drake to raid the Spanish ports in America: twenty-nine vessels, 2,300 soldiers and sailors and £60,000 financial backing, including £20,000 from the queen herself. Frobisher was the second in command, and the expedition wrought havoc in the Caribbean. Santo Domingo and Cartagena were captured and ransomed, shattering body blows at the Spanish empire which also guaranteed substantial profits for the backers of the voyage.

But the expedition did more for Walter Ralegh than secure a return on his investment, for Francis Drake performed for Walter two special favours. Having cruised for several months in the Caribbean he led his ships, in May 1586, north towards Florida, the Spanish colony nearest to the Virginia settlement. The English attacked the Spanish post at St Augustine, razing its fortifications and driving its garrison into the interior, and then, having removed that threat to the English colony further up the coast Drake continued north to carry relief supplies to Governor Ralph Lane and his hundred settlers who had been struggling with the problems of winter on Roanoke and were now coming up to complete their first year in America.

At precisely the same time as Drake was heading north to Virginia, Sir Richard Grenville and a little fleet of relief ships were setting off westwards across the Atlantic on the same mission, leaving Devon on 2 May 1586 – and they were following another supply ship sent off by Ralegh a few weeks earlier. So Walter Ralegh could feel confident that by the high summer of 1586 the Colony of Virginia would be strengthened and refreshed by two well-provisioned relief expeditions.

But would Governor Lane and his men still be alive to welcome the reinforcements when they arrived, and would they be at all anxious to stay in the New World after their lonely months beleaguered on little Roanoke Island through the winter of 1585-6? What had been happening to Sir Walter Ralegh's settlers?

❦ II ❦

Ralph Lane's Colony

Governor Lane had not been sad to be left in sole command of his colonists on Roanoke Island by Sir Richard Grenville in August 1585, for he had had fierce arguments with his commander. Grenville was certainly, as Lane complained, a man of 'intolerable pride'. But the record of his life glowed with determination – sheer uncomprising guts – and the story of the Roanoke settlement from 1585–6 indicates that this was a quality lacking in the more politic Ralph Lane.

Still, as a fortification organizer, Lane showed himself expert. He had worked in Ireland planning the defences of the south-west coast against the possibility of a Spanish invasion, and now he had the same enemy to frustrate on similar terrain. Building a strong fort was not difficult on Roanoke Island, which was heavily wooded. The main problem was to conceal it from Spanish reconnaissance parties who might sail up the coast from Florida, and modern excavations indicate that Lane managed this with some skill. Between 1947 and 1953 archaeologists uncovered the site of his Roanoke fort which turned out to be small – some seventy feet square – but with strong defences which were invisible from the sea. Around the outside was a ditch and rampart and inside a double-storey building in which stores and ammunition could be guarded.

Immediately neighbouring the little citadel were the huts in which the settlers lived, and adjoining them an Indian village. But there is no evidence that much land was enclosed for cultivation; indeed we know that the Englishmen relied heavily on their Indian neighbours for food, and this must be counted one of the great weaknesses of Walter Ralegh's first colony. Ambitious though Governor Lane was for his settlement, he was primarily a military commander, and his colonists were essentially soldiers. They were not given any land to make their own and they served from beginning to end of the venture simply for wages and military perquisites

– plunder from ships captured on the voyage out or from any treasure discovered in the New World. The fact that there were among them no women and children indicates how far they were from the concept. of planting a permanent and self-sustaining society with a life and identity of its own in the New World, and their system of provisioning was essentially that of a garrison in occupied territory, the ordinary soldiers looking to their superiors to supply rations, and the officers foraging with the cooperation – or at the expense – of the indigenous population. Planting and harvesting their own crops was not a soldierly priority, and this inevitably placed a strain on their relations with the local Indians.

Thomas Hariot was in charge of the colony's scientific activities and was liaison officer with the native population, and these two jobs he combined by playing tricks with his optical instruments to amuse the Indians. He used a lens to kindle a fire as if by magic, then magnified or inverted the image of his amazed onlookers. His games with a magnet also won him a ready audience – which he needed as the winter of 1585 grew deeper, for the colonists were almost totally dependent on the Indians for supplies. The Caribbean plants and fruit that survived the grounding of the *Tyger* did not survive transplantation, and such livestock as remained was soon consumed. In the autumn of 1585 the Englishmen were hunting in the woods of Roanoke in earnest – and Hariot noted the deficiencies in their stores in that respect. The settlers did not possess enough fowling pieces or traps.

Necessity now injected a disruptive and eventually fatal ingredient into the relationship between Walter Ralegh's colony and the Roanoke Indians. Naivety on both sides made for tragedy. The Indians welcomed the white men with generosity, not suspecting that the motive inspiring the god-like apparitions might be cupidity for treasure and land. The Englishmen, for their part, took the simple kindness of their hosts as a native characteristic, not understanding that it derived from the special circumstances of their own appearance from beyond the horizon and that once they had settled and showed themselves to be ordinary human neighbours then they would no longer be in a privileged position.

Nor did they realize the special complications that Indian husbandry, or the lack of it, would create. For the local population did not farm on a European basis, producing a surplus with which they could trade and on which they could survive until the next harvest came along. They stockpiled little and in the months before the new crops ripened they were often reduced to eating shellfish, roots and berries. So, with the best will in the world, it was difficult for them to support over a hundred hungry Europeans throughout the winter of 1585 to 1586. Eager though they were to barter for knives, bells and beads, by the time Christmas 1585 arrived they had little to offer in exchange and the novelty of such trinkets had worn off. Their chief Wingina had, furthermore, worked out by then what the balance of trade should be between his own people and the foreigners, and he made very sure that the Englishmen gave full value for all the food they received.

One typical problem was fish – which, with the scarcity of meat, became one of the staples of the colonists' diet. The Englishmen lacked nets or rods and so relied upon traps of reeds built by the Indians – baskets in the water which needed frequent repairs and maintenance work. The Europeans were either unable or unwilling to maintain these fish weirs themselves, and so, even in this apparently simple business, were totally dependent on their hosts. A further aggravation was the infection the foreigners brought with them. The colonists carried all the measles and chicken pox germs to which Europeans had built up immunity but to which the Indians had no defence, and it was soon noticed how people mysteriously died after the white men had visited their villages. This confirmed the visitors' magic powers and made for respect, but it was a fearful, grudging homage.

By the beginning of 1586 Chief Wingina was disenchanted with the Virginia settlement – and so was Governor Ralph Lane. Though he realized that, given time and a great deal of hard work, Walter Ralegh's project could just about survive, neither he nor the majority of the colonists had put their lives at risk for the sake of an agricultural existence no more prosperous than their less hazardous lives at home. They had crossed the Atlantic for treasure or a route to the Indies – and without one or other of those things, or preferably both, there was little more future in Virginia than in Ireland.

'The discovery of a good mine . . . or a passage to the South Sea, or some way to do it, and nothing else can bring this country in request to be inhabited by our nation', wrote Lane. His analysis was pessimistic, but realistic too, for the Virginia colony needed a spectacular commodity of small bulk and high price if it were to prosper, and Lane had discovered that Roanoke Island could not fulfil its intended function as a privateering base. It lacked a safe deep water harbour, and useful though the off-shore sandbars might be in handicapping hostile shipping, they presented just as much of a hazard to English vessels.

So as the weather improved and the Virginia colony emerged from the winter of 1586, Ralph Lane set about discovering a more suitable location for a settlement. He had already sent a scouting party up the coast, and the charts drawn by John White indicate they reached the mouth of the Chesapeake Strait – a fine deep water harbour lying in the southern corner of modern Virginia (Roanoke Island lies in modern North Carolina). Even more significant than the harbour's potential as a privateering base was the fact that it lay at the mouth of a wide channel flowing strongly from the west – which to Lane was significant as the direction in which lay China, India and the Pacific, for neither he nor his contemporaries could visualize the vast expanse of the North American landmass. The Pacific could be reached across the narrow Isthmus of Panama, so why not further up the coast and through a channel of the type whose mouth John White had charted?

So late in February or early March 1586 Ralph Lane set off to investigate, striking out along the Albermarle Sound, itself a broad channel flowing from the right direction. After over one hundred miles the Englishmen found themselves travelling up a narrowing river, the Chowan, to arrive at a large Indian settlement of the same name, Chawanoac, whose chief, Menatonon, gave Lane as much help as he could in his efforts to map out the territory west of Virginia. One story he told reinforced what the English already knew about Chesapeake. If Lane continued up the Chowan for three days, then struck north overland for four days he would come to a deep bay where another Indian tribe had established a settlement on a most defensible island. That sounded like Chesapeake, the sort of base the English were looking for, and if Lane followed the Chowan back south to where it met the Roanoke River, said Menatonon, and then followed the Roanoke towards its head waters he would find another tribe who possessed copper in abundance and who lived close to a great sea. That sea sounded to Lane like the Pacific, and the copper he excitedly transmogrified into gold.

Thanking Menatonon, Ralph Lane retraced his steps to Roanoke with two alternative courses to choose from. He could head north for Chesapeake, taking advantage of his own scout's experience, to re-found his colony by the deep water bay that Menatonon had described. Or he could gamble on the possibility of discovering gold and the Pacific Ocean at the end of the Roanoke River. There was little doubt which course he would adopt, for even if the colony could be safely re-established at Chesapeake, he would still need his crock of gold, his own personal discovery to take back in triumph to Sir Walter Ralegh. So a few weeks before Easter 1586 Lane set off again with forty men in small boats heading for the Roanoke River in search of treasure and the route to Cathay.

But Chief Wingina, whose people were now enduring the discomfort of surviving until the spring maize was ready to pick and who had had enough of working to support the white man, decided to take advantage of Lane's absence.

While providing the English with guides and every assistance for their journey up the Roanoke River he secretly sent messengers to the Indians living along the Albermarle Sound to tell them that it was Lane's intention to attack them. They should desert their villages taking their food supplies with them. So when Lane and his party set out they found every settlement they came across mysteriously deserted. Not putting this down at first to any sinister reason they forged ahead until they were 160 miles from base with only two days' supplies in hand. Excited by the prospect of the copper they were sure would be gold, the English pushed still further inland until eventually their provisions were exhausted completely. They were in a perilous position and now, completely cut off from any reinforcements, with no supplies to withstand a siege, they heard the sound of an Indian war chant through the trees. There was a volley of arrows, and only a stiff riposte of musket fire drove off an attacking party of braves. It looked as if Wingina's plot had succeeded. Meanwhile, back on Roanoke Island, the chief was engaged in psychological warfare with the few score colonists left to guard the fort. He told them that Lane had died in the interior, and he tried, furthermore, to persuade his own tribe to desert Roanoke leaving the Englishmen to die of starvation.

But the chief underestimated Ralph Lane and his followers. The Englishmen might be inept at cultivating maize or maintaining fish weirs, but isolated without food in hostile country they exhibited both endurance and resolution. Having killed, cooked and eaten the mastiffs they had brought with them as watch dogs, the English got back into their boats and, making rapid time on the downstream current, reached Albermarle Sound by Easter Sunday 1586. Back on Roanoke Island Lane got rapidly to the bottom of Wingina's plots against him, and, when he discovered that the chief was planning a physical assault on the colony with the help of Indians from the mainland, acted promptly to forstall the coup.

Wingina had withdrawn from Roanoke Island to the mainland, ordering his people not to trade with the English and to sabotage the fish weirs they were using, so that Lane had had to send twenty men down the coast to Croatoan Island to forage for food and to keep a lookout for English ships. With the English dispersed, Wingina's plan was to gather several hundred braves on the mainland on the pretext of attending a funeral ceremony, to steal over to Roanoke Island in the dead of night, fire the houses of Lane, Hariot and the other leaders and then knock out their brains as they came running out of their huts sleepy and defenceless. With the leaders dead the rest of the colonists would be easy prey.

But Ralph Lane heard of the plot through an Indian captured on one of his patrols. Wanchese, one of the Indians taken by Walter Ralegh to the court of Queen Elizabeth, had reverted to his native allegiance, and Manteo was suspected by his tribe of having sold out to the English. So it was through his prisoner that Lane discovered Wingina's strategy, and he went on 1 June 1586, with a bodyguard to confront the chief in person.

The pre-arranged watchword was a pious one, 'Christ, our Victory', and when Lane uttered it his little band of followers opened fire. The Indian leaders fell dead – except for Wingina himself who dropped to the ground merely feigning death. But when he scrambled up to escape into the woods he was 'shot through the buttocks' by one of Lane's Irish soldiers and then pursued by another one, who emerged from the trees in triumph with the bleeding head of the Indian chief in his hand.

One week later the lookouts down on Croatoan sighted no less than twenty-three sail coming up the coast – it was the fleet of Sir Francis Drake, sailing north from its triumph in the Caribbean to investigate Sir Walter Ralegh's colony. Apart from being anxious to help the settlers, Sir Francis was keen to see what possibility Virginia offered for future raids on the Spanish Main.

He was disappointed, for Roanoke could not provide the harbour all had hoped for. Only Drake's smaller ships could negotiate the sand bars into Pamlico Sound, and the rest of the fleet had to anchor some two miles off the beach in the open sea. But Sir Francis was generous to the colonists. He gave the lookouts a letter to Roanoke Island offering Lane fresh supplies and also boats and sailors who could help with further explorations or a bodily transfer of the colony to a more sheltered harbour. Drake knew that Ralegh was planning at least one major relief expedition that summer, so the sailors he left could come home with that relief fleet.

On 11 June 1586, Lane came down the coast to thank Drake for his offer, asking him to take home the sick and wounded among the colonists and to replace them by oarsmen and craftsmen. He was pleased to accept the offer of shipping, particularly the 70-ton *Francis* which could just negotiate its way into Pamlico Sound and was thus suited to help move the colony up the coast to Chesapeake Bay. Having that ship also meant that the colonists could later, if they wished, sail home to England. But at this stage there seems to have been no question of deserting Virginia, simply of transplanting the site of settlement. A group of colonists went on board the *Francis* to help transfer the food and equipment which was sufficient to last them for four months, and they were busying themselves about this task out beyond the sand bars when, on 13 June 1586, a tremendous thunderstorm blew up. For several days and nights the weather raged fiercely, whipping up water spouts and waves that drove Drake's ships out into the open sea.

But when the weather cleared on 16 June 1586, and the fleet started regrouping, it was seen that the *Francis*, which had some of the most responsible colonists and many stores on board, was continuing its course towards the horizon. The great tempest seems finally to have cracked the resolve of the settlers, while the crew of the *Francis* must have been glad of a pretext to head for home with their Caribbean loot rather than stay marooned on the hazardous shores of Virginia ferrying settlers and stores to and fro along the coast. They had had a chance to talk to the colonists and hear about the hazards of living among the Indians, while they had been able to feed the Virginians' anxieties with tales of the looming confrontation in Europe. Since the conflict with Spain had led to the diversion of the relief expedition planned to sail the previous summer, it was possible that war priorities would keep Grenville away this year as well.

Ralph Lane was now in a difficult position. He was intending to return to England later that summer with the relief fleet, but he had no means of knowing that the fleet was definitely on its way – was only a few weeks over the horizon, in fact. Drake knew little more than he did, having left England the previous autumn, the best part of nine months past. It was quite possible that national priorities had detained all Ralegh's ships in the English Channel, and Drake's explanation of how the previous September's relief expedition had been diverted to raid the Spanish fishing fleets off Newfoundland did not inspire confidence in the imminent arrival of Sir Richard Grenville. Lane did not personally look forward to seeing Grenville, in any case, and the storm, together with the desertion of the colonists on board the *Francis*, was a demoralizing and significant sign: 'the very hand of God, as it seemed, stretched out to take us from thence'. Drake generously offered more sailors and stores and another ship, the *Bark Bonner*. But this was too large to bring into Pamlico Sound – she was of 170 tons – and the staying power of the remaining colonists had been fatally eroded.

At a meeting of all the Virginians it was decided to write off their losses and to ask Drake to take them all home – including Manteo the Indian who could hope for little welcome from his people once the news of Wingina's murder had spread. The request was put into writing so that Ralegh should know that the suggestion to leave had not come from Drake, and on 18 June 1586, the entire fleet, after a hasty transfer of belongings from Roanoke, set sail for England.

Two days later another English sail appeared over the horizon. It was the supply ship sent out by Walter Ralegh ahead of the main relief expedition, but just a few hours too late to save the first Virginia colony. Finding no one but savages on Roanoke they turned round and took their stores back to England.

A couple of weeks later Sir Richard Grenville's main fleet also turned up, to discover the mysteriously empty fort and the huts deserted in such haste. Grenville travelled for miles around Roanoke trying to discover what had become of Lane and his men, but extracting no information from the Indians. Perhaps, without Hariot, the English could not be bothered to communicate with the savages. Perhaps, mindful of the fate of Wingina, the Indians kept out of the new visitors' way or maintained a conspiracy of silence.

Grenville decided to leave on Roanoke a holding party of just over a dozen men to guard the settlement until a new body of colonists could be recruited, and he made sure they were 'furnished plentifully with all manner of provisions for two years'. But he disregarded the fact that if over a hundred men could not survive on Roanoke for less than one year, a score would hardly last double the time. None of the possible reasons for the island being deserted – the elimination of Lane and his men by Spaniards, Indians or disease, or their departure in search of another position for their colony – recommended Roanoke itself as a propitious settlement site, but though Grenville certainly had in his fleet far more than fifteen or twenty men to spare, that was all he left to keep Walter Ralegh's settlement in America alive before he headed back east to indulge in his favourite maritime pastime, privateering. He proved as successful at it as ever, arriving in Bideford in December 1586 with six prizes, among them a galleon from Puerto Rico rich in sugar, ginger and hides.

Once again Walter Ralegh and his co-investors had got their capital back and dividends besides. But with Ralph Lane and his men, who had arrived in Portsmouth at the end of July, busily justifying their over-hasty desertion of Roanoke with tales of the perils of life in Virginia, it was impossible not to wonder whether simple privateering would not be more profitable. The settlement itself had proved a financial liability and it was difficult to see how it could become the exuberant source of wealth that had once been hoped for. Even before Lane and his men returned, merchants in Exeter had in January 1586 refused a subscription to the colony.[1]

But Sir Walter Ralegh himself was determined not to lose face in the great venture that he had made his own. Though the merchants of Exeter might be unwilling to risk their money, William Sanderson was as keen as ever, while Richard Hakluyt continued a trusty 'trumpet'. From Paris he put out stories that ran round Europe of the English empire that Walter Ralegh was creating in the New World, and, studying the data that the colonists had brought back, he urged the launching of a fresh settlement on Chesapeake Bay with the whole basis of the colony re-thought. The old system of paying the settlers wages should be discontinued and, instead, every man should be given a stake of his own and made to feel a partner in the new society he was creating.

Through the autumn and winter of 1586, Walter Ralegh worked on this new joint stock basis, offering 500 acres to every man prepared to settle seriously in Virginia and to build up a permanent community there with wives, children and its own rights of self-government. The governor of the new colony-company would be the enthusiastic 'American' whose drawings were already doing so much to propagandize the New World – John White.

The two great chroniclers of Virginia, White and Hariot, had brought back a mass of documentation with them from Roanoke and while one busied himself with the preparations for Ralegh's new venture of which he would be governor, the other set himself to collate all they had recorded into a work that could both stand as a monument to the first Roanoke settlement and encourage support for its successor. For over a year Thomas Hariot worked to produce the volume he modestly entitled *A Briefe and True Report of the New Found Land of Virginia*. Englishmen had heard about America; now they discovered it was not fairy land, but a real country with soil and animals and native inhabitants. John White's photograph-like drawings emphasized its authenticity and reality still more, and Richard Hakluyt, an expert contriver of 'best-sellers', got White's drawings turned into engravings by the Dutchman Theodor de Bry so that multi-lingual illustrated editions were being sold all over Europe by the 1590s.

Hariot's evocative prose recreates precisely the texture of life for those first Virginia colonists:

> The bears of this country are good meat, the inhabitants in time of winter do use to take and eat many, so also some times did we. . . . As soon as they have spiall [perception] of a man they presently run away, and then, being chased, they climb and get up the next tree they can, from whence with arrows they are shot down stark dead, or with those wounds that they may after easily be killed; we sometimes shot them down with our callivers.

The settlers looked at the Indians' farming methods and observed how 'they never fatten with muck, dung or any other thing, neither plough nor dig it [the land] as we in England'. Instead, just a few days before planting, the men and women:

> only break the upper part of the ground to raise up the weeds, grass and old stubs of corn stalks with their roots. The which after a day or two's drying in the sun, being scraped up into many small heaps, to save them labour for carrying away, they burn into ashes. And whereas some may think that they use the ashes for to better the ground, I say that then they would either disperse the ashes abroad, which we observed they do not, except the heaps be great: or else would take special care to set their corn where the ashes lie, which also we find they are careless of. And this is all the husbanding of their ground that they use.

Hariot explained how each village appeared to be self-sufficient, often speaking its own language, and that there were very few chiefs with more than a handful of villages to their name.

Some religion they have already [records the *Report* hopefully]. They believe that there are many Gods, which they call *Montoac*, but of different sorts and degrees, one only chief and great God, which hath been from all eternity. Who, as they affirm, when he purposed to make the world, made first other gods . . . and after the Sun, Moon and stars as petty gods. . . . First, they say, were made waters, out of which by the gods was made all diversity of creatures that are visible or invisible. For mankind they say a woman was made first, which by the working of one of the gods conceived and brought forth children. . . .
They think that all the gods are of human shape and therefore they represent them by images in the form of men. . . .
They believe also [in] the immortality of the soul, that after this life as soon as the soul is departed from the body, according to the works it hath done, it is either carried to heaven, the habitation of the gods, there to enjoy perpetual bliss and happiness, or else to a great pit or hole, which they think to be the furthest parts of their part of the world towards the sunset, there to burn continually: the place they call *Popogusso*.

It was only when Hariot described the relations between the native inhabitants and the English that his account became less thorough. To read of Chief Wingina joining in the white man's psalm singing one would imagine that gentle coexistence between Englishman and Indian was easy to achieve. There is no mention of how Wingina came to make war on the colony nor how he died, simply the remark that 'some of our companie towards the end of the year, showed themselves too fierce in slaying some of the people'.

Hariot's economic predictions for Virginia, too, were more optimistic than the facts could justify. He realized, as Ralph Lane had realized, that the solid but unexciting agricultural products of the area were poor substitutes for the precious metals Elizabethans assumed to be the main object of New World planting. So his *Briefe and True Report* made much of the copper mines Lane had been told of and set great store by a hoard of 5,000 beautiful pearls that had been obtained by barter with the Indians. These had been intended as a present to Queen Elizabeth – but had been lost overboard in the indecent flurry that had attended the colonists' departure with Francis Drake. Hariot predicted great wealth for the colony, and his *Report* lists products that have remained staple products of the Carolinas to this day; cedar wood for furniture and wainscoting, pitch, tar, turpentine and other pine derivatives, all valuable as naval stores and – most lucrative of all in the sixteenth century – sassafras, a bark essence thought to cure venereal disease. Sassafras, in fact, became so sought after in London in the following years, prices being inflamed to the ridiculous level of 20 shillings a pound by demand from venereal disease sufferers,[2] that in the first decade of the next century at least two expeditions were made to New England in search of it.[3]

But the premier product of all (and this too was prized as a cure for venereal disease) was tobacco. In his *Report* Hariot, who was to become England's earliest recorded tobacco cancer victim, dwelt lovingly on its comforts. It was, he wrote, 'of so precious estimation amongst the Indians that they think their gods are marvellously delighted therewith'. For in addition to the pleasure of 'drinking' [i.e. smoking] the drug, it was also a medicine which 'purgeth superfluous phlegm and other gross humours, and openeth all the pores and passages of the body'.

Hariot brought back with him the Virginia clay pipe which the Indians used for smoking the weed, and Sir Walter Ralegh promptly adopted it and made it fashionable at court, his championing of tobacco inspiring two more anecdotes to live on like the tale of the cloak and puddle. Talking to the queen one day Ralegh boasted that he knew so much about tobacco that he could weigh the smoke it produced. Always keen for a wager, Elizabeth bet him he could not make good his claim, whereupon Walter called for scales. Pinching some tobacco shreddings from the gilded leather pouch he always carried with him, he carefully weighed the amount he needed to fill his long stemmed pipe, smoked it and then weighed the ashes. Subtracting this second weight from the first he produced the answer that would win his wager, Elizabeth remarking as she paid up that she had heard of men 'who turned gold into smoke, but Ralegh was the first who turned smoke into gold'.[4] Then there is the story of how Walter's manservant, seeing smoke coming from his master's nose and mouth, promptly doused the royal favourite with a bucket of cold water. The very chair in which Walter sat as he puffed and was soaked is solemnly pointed out in more than one of the houses which the modern tourist can visit in pursuit of Ralegh.

Hentzner, the German traveller, noted 'at bull-baiting, bear-whipping and everywhere else, the English are constantly smoking the Nikotian weed which is called tobacco'. So popular was the weed that it became necessary to put up 'no smoking' notices in churches, and at the trial of the Earl of Essex the French ambassador observed how the peers made themselves 'silly' with smoking.

Plain tobacco had been introduced to the country by Sir John Hawkins in 1565, if not earlier through Spain, but at the beginning of the seventeenth century it was Walter Ralegh whom critics of smoking singled out for attack. 'It seems a miracle to me', said King James I, 'how a custom springing from so vile a ground, and brought in by a father so generally hated, should be welcomed.' Was the drug that the king and the Puritans denounced so vehemently more potent than the tobacco that fills modern cigarettes? It must have had a special kick to make a whole jury of peers silly, but then the Elizabethans were stimulated by the strangest substances. When Falstaff was attempting to have his wicked way with the merry wives of Windsor and felt that his passion had need of arousing, he called on the sky to 'rain potatoes'. This unlikely aphrodisiac was, of course, also a fresh discovery brought over from the New World and associated then and ever since with the name of Sir Walter Ralegh. So Hariot's *Briefe and True Report*, Walter's own flamboyant propagandizing and the general excitement at the opening up of the New World meant that the first lord and governor of Virginia had, without ever setting foot in North America, earned a permanent place in the folklore and history not only of that continent but also of the small European off-shore island that gave it life.

✤ 12 ✤

The Queen's Lover

One Christmas time before Sir Walter Ralegh had made his name as a colonizer of the New World, a Pomeranian traveller, Leopold von Wedel,[1] had watched Queen Elizabeth at dinner in the presence chamber at Greenwich, one of her favourite palaces. Elizabeth liked to move around her residences, to Whitehall, Hampton Court and Nonesuch down in Surrey, and Greenwich pleased her particularly in the winter. She liked to go hunting in Greenwich Park, relaxing in the saddle without being too far away from the centre of affairs. It was but a short boat ride with the tide back up the river past the Tower of London, St Paul's and Durham House to Westminster and Whitehall. And Christmas usually put her in an especially good humour, for this was the time when all the grasping caterpillars around her had to offer presents as some repayment for the favours bestowed on them during the year, and when too, in honour of the season, they dressed themselves in their most brilliant plumage. Christmas was a good time to see the Elizabethan court at its finest, and von Wedel, like the earnest German tourist that he was, took advantage of the spectator facilities to observe the ceremonies at close range, turning up at Greenwich on 27 December 1584, to watch the queen of England eat her dinner.

To the right of Elizabeth stood her famous courtiers: Leicester, Burghley, Hatton, Lord Charles Howard and Ralegh. The German noticed how much Queen Elizabeth chattered. She ate scarcely anything for 'as a rule, she talks with scarcely a break', but when she did ask one of her menfolk to speak to her then she expected him to kneel humbly before her until she gave him permission to rise. Her grandees appeared to revel in this obsequiousness.

Food seemed an incidental part of the proceedings. 'When the first dishes had been removed and others put on the table, the queen did not stay much longer.' Two bishops stepped forward and said grace – that was not an unusual number of prelates to have hanging around the court – and then followed a ritual of physical cleansing to match the spiritual purification. Three noblemen knelt down in front of the queen bearing 'a large covered bowl of silver gilt'. Two more carried her towel, and the lord chamberlain also stood by to look after the royal ring while the royal hands were washed. With the help of these six eminent peers of the realm Elizabeth I performed her ablutions.

Specially favoured guests were then granted the privilege of a private word in the queen's ear. A young earl's son was taken aside into a bay window and, kneeling before his sovereign, was allowed several minutes of conversation.

Feeling more at ease now, the fifty-year-old queen pulled up a cushion and squatted down on the floor casually to talk to another young gentleman, and then a countess was beckoned over for a gossip – though this lady too had to kneel like all the men while the queen lolled back on her cushion.

Then the dancing began, and while the music played, a succession of courtiers went over for talks long and short with the queen. The first dance had, by etiquette, to be executed by the senior courtiers, but after that the younger bloods took off their swords and cloaks and took over the dance floor.

Walter Ralegh seemed particularly close to the queen this winter evening as she laughed and joked. He was obviously a very special friend, and Elizabeth giggled to see a little speck of dirt on his face. She got out her handkerchief to wipe it away, but before she could touch his cheek Ralegh had thrust up his own hand to wipe the smut away himself. There was playfulness and gaiety bubbling between the pair of them, for this was still the early summer of their relationship. They were entranced with each other, Elizabeth showering her Walter with gifts, and Walter presenting to the queen his flattering, fanciful poems:

> ... when I found my self to you was true,
> I lov'd myself, because my self lov'd you.[2]

But it was not only to Queen Elizabeth that Walter Ralegh addressed his verse. He was one of the most handsome men at court and one of the most forceful too, and two poems of his suggest that his charms did not go unnoticed by members of the fair sex apart from the queen. There was a married lady, Lady Leighton, the wife of Sir Thomas Leighton, an eminent personality who was constable of the Tower of London, a privy councillor and governor of the Channel Islands – an important defence post that Walter was to hold later in his career. Sir Thomas was a busy man, and his duties in Jersey tended to keep him away from London when his wife, as one of the ladies in waiting to the queen, inevitably saw a lot of Sir Walter Ralegh. Her christian name was Elizabeth and she was a daughter of Sir Francis Knollys, the privy councillor whose eldest daughter Lettice had secretly married the Earl of Leicester after the mysterious death of Amy Robsart. Elizabeth certainly aroused the most ardent desire in Sir Walter Ralegh. He wrote her a poem which, we are told, he dropped into her pocket one day when he brushed past her at court:

> Would God thou knewst the depth of my desire!
> Then might I hope, though nought I can deserve,
> Some drop of grace would quench my scorching fire.[3]

Billets doux like that needed to be passed to their intended surreptitiously, particularly if the writer were a favourite of Queen Elizabeth's and the lady were one of her maids of honour, for Elizabeth adopted a most possessive attitude so far as the virtue of her own lady attendants was concerned. Ralegh was better advised to direct his attentions in another direction, particularly in view of the power that Lady Elizabeth's husband Sir Thomas possessed. Ralegh dropped just one poem into the pocket of Lady Leighton then concentrated on easier game.

Ann Vavasour was a different proposition. She was famous for her beauty and charm – and also for the generosity with which she distributed her favours. She was no tart but, on the other hand, she did not tease. In later life she was to give herself freely to Sir Henry Lee, living so openly as his mistress that she was eventually buried with him. She had also been a lover of Ralegh's great enemy, the Earl of Oxford, and had borne a child by him, for which indiscretion they had both been sent to the Tower for a spell. Walter Ralegh's poem to Ann Vavasour, sententiously entitled 'The Advice', was couched in the high moral tone that a Dutch Uncle might adopt, but knowing how zestful were Walter's own animal passions it seems more likely that he was advising her to repulse the advances of other suitors the more fully to surrender to his own:

> Many desire, but few or none deserve
> To win the fort of thy most constant will.
> Therefore take heed, let fancy never swerve
> But unto him that will defend thee still.[4]

Did Walter Ralegh get his way? Or was his sermon to Ann Vavasour sincerely intended – disinterested counsel from a friend to a friend? If the latter were the case it would not be entirely out of character, for Walter, feckless though he often was, always had measured advice aplenty to offer to the rest of the world. He had the knack of putting high moral sentiments into words which sounded neither banal nor pretentious. In love, in despair or in mourning, Walter could summon up the right sentence to cheer or console – a well considered sentiment. It went with the actor in him, that lack of selfconsciousness that can enable the less sensitive to utter words of wisdom when more feeling souls are silenced. His dealings with Lady Leighton, Ann Vavasour – or Alice Gould – did not inhibit him from composing a tirade against faithless and flirtatious love:

> Farewell false love, the oracle of lies,
> A mortal foe and enemy to rest,
> An envious boy from whom all cares arise,
> A bastard vile, a beast with rage possess'd,
> A way of error, a temple full of treason,
> In all effects contrary unto reason.[5]

These words are taken from the contra tenor part of the ballad that William Byrd made out of Ralegh's 'Farewell to False Love', a ballad that achieved great success in the 1580s – for popular opinion endorsed Queen Elizabeth's own opinion of Walter's versifying talents. The vividness of his imagery and the polished glitter of his style earned him glory – and Elizabeth could bask in its reflection. No wonder she loved him! How could she not be taken with a man whose beard turned up *naturally* ?[6] No curling tongs for Walter Ralegh. He was a natural, an original, parading before her his Indians 'like white Moors' and puffing his foul-smelling silver pipe, dashing off poems one moment and fighting duels the next. She had tired in time of all her favourites, and she was to tire in due course of Walter Ralegh as well, but with Walter the process took longer to work itself out. There were so many sides to him. He was overflowing with adventures and schemes, some that he really wished seriously to pursue, others that he dreamed up just to amuse her. He was an expensive favourite – but he was worth it. The quicksilver in him was part Celtic, part Mediterranean. There was a lushness to his tastes. He seemed to be for ever gambling, staking all on the next throw for the sake of the risk as much as for the sake of winning. He was exhilarating, unpredictable company, for in the depths of his spirit he was, as the next century was to discern, a true revolutionary, an intelligence not afraid to affront the established principles and prejudices of his day. Posterity was rightly to see him as one of the great pillars of the England of Elizabeth, of its very soul and essence.

When the German von Wedel repeated the gossip he had heard that Sir Walter Ralegh was the lover of Queen Elizabeth he was closer to the truth than he realized – though not in the salacious fashion that he intended. For in the originality and vigour of his mind Sir Walter Ralegh shared with Queen Elizabeth for a period of her life a rare part of her spirit that she shared with no one else – not with Hatton, Burghley, Essex, or even with the great Earl of Leicester himself.

Ralegh enjoyed a special intimacy that the others could only envy. But, like Walter himself, Queen Elizabeth was multi-faceted. She existed in several dimensions at once, and in these other spheres – affairs of state, for example – Walter Ralegh was allotted a less than prominent role to play.

❧ 13 ❧

Political Ambitions

Sir Walter Ralegh always wanted to be more than just a creature of the court. It was one thing to be known as the man who had introduced smoking to English social life, who founded England's first colony in the New World, who wrote poems or who had the ear of Queen Elizabeth, but Walter knew, as those who envied him knew, that his glittering network of achievements was, in essence, little stronger than a spider's web all spun from the gossamer of one woman's affection.

He had always realized that the royal favour was a mortal thing that could die, and now in 1585 came a forceful reminder of that. Christopher Hatton had already shown how jealous he was of 'Water', and now the Earl of Leicester showed his feelings – and in sharper style.

Portly, slow and visibly ageing, Leicester appreciated that he could not compete with Walter Ralegh's beauty and youth. But Walter himself, now thirty years old, was no boy either, and so in 1585 the Earl of Leicester pushed into the royal circle his stepson, Robert Devereux, Earl of Essex, a red-haired, bright-eyed youth of seventeen burning with all the enthusiasms that pleased the ageing queen. He seemed a Galahad resurrected from a by-gone age, overflowing with chivalry and eagerness for battle-field honour, blessed with all the polished accomplishments a Renaissance courtier needed, but also retaining, as Walter Ralegh retained, unlicked traces of his upbringing in one of England's wilder corners – in Essex's case, Wales. This hint of roughness scarce mastered seemed to excite Elizabeth as she grew older. After a quarter of a century of courtly smoothness she warmed to the inner fire of a Ralegh or an Essex.

But it was inevitable, as Leicester had intended, that these two Mercuries would find it difficult to coexist in the royal favour. Elizabeth was delighted by the prospect of two handsome stallions competing for her, but it was not a contest that Walter Ralegh relished. He had age against him – and pedigree as well. Robert Devereux might only be a second earl, but he was a peer just the same, and had behind him all the power and connections of his step-father, Leicester. If Walter wanted to survive at court he would have to embed his future in a more substantial base than Elizabeth's emotions. He was not in danger of losing his head – that was not Elizabeth's style. But he would lose with the royal favour his fortune and, even more rapidly, his credit. All he had to his name were trading privileges on which a term had been set, and a knighthood that meant little without substantial estates he could call his own. In terms of freehold land he possessed little more than his father had.

As a court favourite and nothing more Walter was particularly vulnerable to Elizabeth's whims. Lord Burghley earned her trust as a diligent bureaucrat, Francis Walsingham as the master of a first-rate spy-system and Leicester had transformed himself from being a paramour to taking over military responsibilities that made him effectively the commander-in-chief of England's land forces. The trick was for Walter Ralegh to transfer his reputation in the same fashion, to persuade Elizabeth that he was not interested in competing in the style of an Essex for her smiles, but that he was made of sterner stuff. With a seat on the Privy Council Walter could contemplate the progress of an Essex with equanimity, and so it was, in the summer of 1586, at the same time as Ralph Lane and his colonists were returning to England, that the royal favourite tried to prove he was more than just a courtier.

It was through his privateering that Walter won the opportunity to show that his political skills could rival those of Walsingham. For, a few days after he had despatched Grenville on his fruitless relief mission to Virginia, he sent down to the Azores two minute privateers, the *Mary Spark* and the *Serpent*, pinnaces of only 50 and 35 tons respectively, who, after a spectacularly profitable series of raids, returned to England with a high-ranking Spaniard among their prisoners, Don Pedro Sarmiento de Gamboa, the governor of the Spanish possessions around the Straits of Magellan and Patagonia. Ralegh went down to Plymouth to reward his sailors and to greet Sarmiento in person. The man was the Spanish equivalent of a Hawkins, a Grenville or, indeed, of a Ralegh, a distinguished catch who could be counted on to command a high ransom – or who might, in a more subtle fashion, assist with an oblique plot Walter was hatching.

The scheme was essentially a Trojan Horse ruse – the basic ploy which seems, on more than one occasion, to have represented the limit of Walter's melodramatic political imagination – and it imitated the stratagem of John Hawkins who had for many years, with the consent of the queen and Privy Council, maintained 'secret' contacts with Spain. Hawkins had told King Philip that he was tired of serving Queen Elizabeth and would be happy to advance Spanish projects against her – and he had been paid in Spanish gold for his apparent treachery. In fact, he informed the Privy Council of whatever Spanish information he received – which seems, from what we know, to have been comparatively scanty. Now Walter Ralegh attempted to use his Spanish captive, Sarmiento, to set up a similar connection with Madrid. By offering his services through Sarmiento to Philip he should be able to enrich himself with a Spanish pension and, if he could coax enough hard information from the enemy, also set himself up as an exclusive intelligence source which the Privy Council would have to consult regularly and, with luck, co-opt on a permanent basis.

So Walter Ralegh waived the large ransom he could have received for the release of Sarmiento, and instead suggested that his captive should simply return to Spain a free man to make two propositions to King Philip. The first was that Ralegh should sell one, or possibly two, warships from his private fleet to Philip for 5,000 crowns. The second was that Walter would do all in his power to frustrate the activities at the English court of Don Antonio, the pretender to the throne of Portugal which Philip had annexed in 1580. The two suggestions were plausible. To trade with your enemy, even in the instruments of war, was not considered unusual in the sixteenth century – had the deal come to anything, it would not have been his newest ships that Ralegh sold to Philip – and so far as Walter's second suggestion was concerned, there were many at the English court, Queen Elizabeth among them, who considered the Portuguese pretender, Don Antonio, an unreliable and troublesome imposition on English hospitality. Walsingham, Leicester and Lord Admiral Howard believed that assisting the Portuguese claimant was a useful way of troubling Philip of Spain, but Burghley had still to be convinced that Don Antonio was worth the heavy investments and risks he wished the English to venture in regaining his throne.

Ralegh's explanation to Philip, furthermore, of why he was renouncing over a decade of warfare against the forces of Spanish Catholicism was also fairly convincing. He needed the money Spain could pay for his help, and, he could claim with perfect truthfulness, that he was anxious about the stability of his position at the English court. He could see that Elizabeth's favour would not last for ever, and that Spanish support could provide security against less happy times. 'If he [Ralegh] would really look after Your Majesty's interests in that country [England]', explained Sarmiento to Philip, 'apart from the direct reward he would receive, Your Majesty's support, when occasion arose, might prevent him from falling.'

It was not an unconvincing ploy and Sarmiento, anxious to get safely back to Spain, had no reason to probe its weaknesses too firmly. Ralegh introduced him, furthermore, to the queen and Lord Burghley who gave him messages of their own for King Philip. They were reluctant to get involved in a full scale war with Spain and so put forward the tentative suggestion that English privateering might be curbed if Spain were to adopt a less aggressive attitude towards ordinary English trading ships.

Ralegh seemed well set to start up an honest brokerage in international affairs, and an accident that befell Sarmiento on his way back to Madrid served to raise Walter's stock even higher. Passing through a Protestant area of France, the Spaniard was arrested by Huguenot troops. Mendoza, the Spanish ambassador exiled from London to Paris, was quite unable to secure his release and it was Walter Ralegh who used his Protestant contacts to persuade Henri of Navarre to let the Spaniard go. Walter was empowered, furthermore, to negotiate on this occasion in the name of Queen Elizabeth – a small but hopeful token of royal trust in matters of state. Ralegh sent two agents over to France and Sarmiento was allowed to proceed on his way to Madrid.

Greatly impressed, Mendoza wrote excitedly to Madrid, 'I am assured that he [Ralegh] is very cold about [England's] naval preparations and is trying secretly to dissuade the queen from them. He is much more desirous of sending to Spain his own two ships for sale than to use them for robbery.'[1]

But King Philip proved less gullible than his foreign representatives. He had learnt to see through John Hawkins's claims of friendship – he had taken to scrawling horrified expletives in the margins of documents that mentioned the name of 'Achines' (Hawkins) – and now he saw no more reason to trust 'Guatteral' (Walter Ralegh). 'As for [Ralegh] sending for sale the two ships he mentions', wrote Philip to Mendoza scornfully, 'that is out of the question, in the first place to avoid his being looked upon with suspicion in his own country . . . and secondly, to guard ourselves against the coming of the ships under this pretext being a feint or trick upon us (which is far from being improbable). But you need only mention the first reason to him.'[2]

So ended Walter Ralegh's attempt to play the double-agent abroad. But the episode had several sequels. By coincidence, the Spanish ambassador who, some three decades later, helped secure the death of Walter Ralegh at the hands of James I was a nephew of Sarmiento and, of more causal significance, Sarmiento himself, who had geographical enthusiasms very similar to Ralegh's own, told his English captor of a mysterious wedge of South America that few Europeans had explored and which, lying between the basins of the Orinoco and Amazon rivers, was to play an even greater role in Ralegh's life than Virginia – 'that mighty, rich and beautiful empire of Guiana and . . . that great and golden city, which the Spaniards call

El Dorado.' Walter Ralegh did not gain from his Spanish go-between the influence in foreign affairs that he hoped for, but he did gain a dream, a soaring, hopeless, impossible vision that came more and more to dominate his life – and eventually brought about his death.

But in the mid 1580s no one in England had time for lost cities of gold. The immediate pressure of events was boiling up into the confrontation that Queen Elizabeth had spent a score of years trying to avoid, between Protestant and Catholic and between England and Spain. In December 1585 the Earl of Leicester had gone to the Netherlands, taking English troops to confront the armies of Spain for the first time in a capacity officially acknowledged by Elizabeth – and taking with him as one of his lieutenants the young Earl of Essex. It left Sir Walter Ralegh much freer at court, but the Earl of Leicester was well aware of the dangers of being out of the royal presence for long and kept up from the Netherlands a barrage of complaints against Walter, whom he feared was taking advantage of his absence. Walsingham had to write to the earl reassuring him 'by Her Majesty's command' and 'upon her honour' that 'the gentleman hath done good offices for you' and Walter himself wrote to explain to Leicester that, though Elizabeth had been annoyed by the behaviour of the English in the Netherlands, she was now better satisfied: 'the queen is on very good terms with you and, thanks be to God, well pacified; and you are again her "Sweet Robin".'[3]

In August 1586 bells rang in London for the capture of Anthony Babington and other young Catholic gentlemen who had planned to murder Queen Elizabeth, to release Mary Queen of Scots from her imprisonment and to place her on the throne of England with the help of Spanish troops ferried over from the Netherlands. The cunning devices Walsingham had employed to expose the conspiracy – and to incriminate Mary irredeemably – showed up Ralegh's own espionage attempts as inexperienced fumblings, though that was not for lack of trying on Walter's part. He had attempted, in fact, through his secretary William Langherne to gain access to the Queen of Scots' secrets by approaching her agent Thomas Morgan[4] and had had dealings with Anthony Babington as well. Before the traitor was due to be executed, Babington offered Ralegh £1,000 if he could obtain him a pardon from the queen, and in Paris Mendoza told Philip that Ralegh had known all about the conspiracy before it was discovered.

Some historians have cited this as evidence that Walter Ralegh was playing a disloyal role in these intrigues, but there is no evidence to suggest this, for Walsingham's agents investigated every aspect of the conspiracy thoroughly and would have pursued any such suspicion with rigour. The facts indicate, indeed, that Walter may have been trying in some way to play the same sort of double role he attempted to set up through Sarmiento, and certainly Elizabeth singled Ralegh out as the man to benefit most from Babington's crimes, bestowing upon him in March 1587 almost all the traitor's estates.

It was an enormous reward for Walter. At the stroke of a pen he became a substantial landowner with manors scattered as far afield as Lincolnshire, Derbyshire and Nottinghamshire, for almost the only thing that Elizabeth's grant of 1587 kept back from all the Babington possessions was 'a certain curious clock, reserved to Her Majesty's personal use'.

In this same year came further confirmation of the royal favour. When Sir Christopher Hatton was raised to the position of lord chancellor, to his vacated place as captain of the guard was appointed Sir Walter Ralegh. Though it was an honorary position – carrying, instead of a salary, just a uniform allowance for 'six yards of tawney medly at 13 shillings and fourpence a yard, with a fur of black budge, rated at £10'[5] – its status was glittering. In practical terms it meant that its holder stood by the queen at all times, always close enough to be summoned and usually inside her ring of conversation.

In symbolic terms Walter now became the man to whom Elizabeth committed the care and protection of her body. It was his responsibility to select the corps of brave young gentlemen who graced the royal presence and who protected the monarch from poison or the assassin's knife. It was his men who served the queen's food and carried the queen's messages and who, with their captain, were at the focal point of the royal court, for Elizabeth set great store by having true Adonises attend on her. Walter had to be something of a talent spotter, rejecting on one occasion, according to Aubrey, the request of a father who wished his eighteen-year-old son to serve in the guard. 'I put in no boys', said Sir Walter. But then the father produced his son, a strapping six-footer as handsome as any of the guard. So 'Sir Walter Ralegh swears him immediately, and ordered him to carry up the first dish at dinner, where the queen beheld him with admiration, as if a beautiful young giant had stalked in with the service.'[6]

The captaincy of the guard was not the solid political appointment Walter's attempts at espionage had been aimed at, but it did bring him security of a different sort. To be given the post indicated a definite royal trust and provided a stable position removed from the rat race, while the grant of Babington estates provided Walter with resources and backing to his name which not even the most catastrophic fall from favour could take away. Men who incurred the royal displeasure might lose their offices and monopolies, but it needed an overt act of treason to get your lands confiscated. Only Babingtons and their ilk lost their estates, and in 1587 Walter Ralegh had no reason to fear that his fortunes would ever sink to that sorry state. After five years of courting royal favour he had secured a resting place.

It was not before time, for back from the war in the Netherlands had come the Earl of Essex to take Elizabeth by storm. In May 1587 Anthony Bagot wrote of the attention the queen was paying the boy who had not yet reached his twentieth birthday. 'When she is abroad, nobody near her but my Lord of Essex and, at night, my Lord is at cards, or one game or another with her, that he cometh not to his own lodging till birds sing in the morning.' In June 1587 the red-haired earl was made master of the queen's horse, a post worth some £1,500 a year in addition to the stabling and entertainment facilities that went with it, and in the very next month the tension between the new favourite and Ralegh exploded into the open.

It was high summer and Elizabeth had as usual been avoiding the plagues of London and giving her treasury a rest by being entertained at the expense of her subjects. Going on progress enabled her own palaces to be thoroughly cleaned out, and by the middle of July she was approaching North Hall, the seat of the Earl of Warwick. Essex was with her and Ralegh too, of course, as captain of her guard, but arriving at North Hall the queen discovered another, less welcome, guest. This was Dorothy Devereux, Essex's elder sister, who had a few years earlier incurred the royal disfavour by running off and marrying Sir Thomas Perrot. Elizabeth, in whom any marriage, let alone a runaway marriage, excited spinsterish reactions, took Dorothy's presence as an insult, ordering that the woman should be confined to her room – and Ralegh did nothing to cool her anger. He had his own reasons for disliking the Perrots, for back in 1580 it had been his quarrel and duel with Dorothy's husband Tom that had landed him in the Fleet prison for a week.

Essex was mortally offended, and he saw the enmity of Ralegh behind the snub administered to his sister. In the fashion he was to make peculiarly his own he upbraided Elizabeth, accusing her of insulting Dorothy 'only to please that knave Ralegh, for whose sake I saw she would grieve me in the eye of the world.'

It was an extraordinary way for a favourite, and a scarce-fledged favourite at that, to address the queen, and Elizabeth put Essex firmly in his place. She defended Walter and, as the earl wrote ruefully later, 'it seemed she could not well endure anything to be spoken against him.' It was a reaction warmly gratifying for the captain of the guard, standing just a few yards away, to hear.

But Essex would not be put down, and he was well aware that Walter Ralegh was listening to every word he said. 'I spake, what of grief and choler, as much against him as I could, and I think he standing at the door might hear the very worse that I spoke of himself.'

The earl gave Elizabeth his opinion of just what Ralegh 'had been and what he was, and . . . whether I could have comfort to give myself over to the service of a mistress that was in awe of such a man.'

Elizabeth lost her temper. If Essex wished to cast aspersions on her Walter she could do the same for Essex's mother, Lettice, a woman the queen detested. The quarrel degenerated into a screaming match from which Essex eventually retreated, to ride off sulking into the night.

'I had no joy to be in any place but loathe to be near about her when I knew my affection so much thrown down, and such a wretch as Ralegh highly esteemed of her.'[7]

The wretch Ralegh had won a handsome victory. This was the summer he was described as 'the best hated man of the world, in court, city and country', and Essex had thought to capitalize on that unpopularity. But he underestimated the firmness that the years had given to the relationship between Elizabeth and Walter. The queen might indulge her new red-headed plaything in the most extravagant fashion, but that did not imply any disloyalty so far as she was concerned to her more old established companions. Sir Christopher Hatton had been put in the shade by the advent of Ralegh, but the queen did not disown or forsake him. So now the captain of her guard, though less effusively favoured than the Earl of Essex, had reached a position in the Elizabethan constellation from which fresh rivals could not dislodge him. Elizabeth and Walter had attained a stability of mutual affection it would take more than the pressure of public opinion – or the tantrums of a mere boy – to unsettle. Ralegh did not have his political appointment, nor, after the arrival of Essex, could he be counted as the queen's lover. But he was something better. He had become her friend.

James Stuart, King of Scotland and, after 1603, of England also

Henry Howard, elevated by King James to the Earldom of Northampton

Edward Coke, raised by James to be Chief Justice of England

Opposite: Henry, Prince of Wales, until his death in 1611 King James's heir

Ralegh's bitterest enemy,
Count Gondomar, Spanish
ambassador to the court of
King James

Ralegh's closest friend,
Henry Percy, ninth Earl of
Northumberland, painted
after Walter's death by
Anthony Van Dyck

❧ 14 ❧

The Munster Colony

When Elizabethans talked of colonies and of foreign planting they thought first not of the New World and Virginia but of Ireland – and Sir Walter Ralegh was no exception. Though history has rightly given him the credit for recruiting North America into the English speaking world, his settlements there were significant for their ambitions, not their permanence. It was in Ireland that he founded the plantations that, in solid territorial terms, made his most substantial contribution to the extension of England's overseas empire.

He had left Ireland at the end of 1581 and the contact he re-established with it in 1586 was the fruit of the royal favour he had gained in the five intervening years. On 27 June 1586, in the same busy summer that Ralph Lane returned from America and Don Pedro Sarmiento de Gamboa was brought back captive to England, royal letters patent named Sir Walter Ralegh as head of a group of West Countrymen who would colonize the southern Irish counties of Cork and Waterford – the lands of the Earl of Desmond who had led the rebellion that Ralegh had helped put down in 1581. Desmond had been captured and executed in November 1583 and as Ralegh profited from the treason of Babington, so now he benefited from Desmond's misdeeds.

But Burghley and Walsingham, the privy councillors given special responsibility for this troublesome area, saw the resettlement of southern Ireland as more than a matter of rewarding royal favourites. They wanted to make sure that Munster, devastated by the rebellion and by English reprisals, should not only be secured against the threat of future insurrection and foreign assistance, but should also become self-sustaining and profitable. It should be able to pay from its own resources for the garrisons needed against the possibility of another Smerwick intervention by foreign Catholic troops, while yielding in addition some solid dividends – taxes

– as compensation for the decades of English investment in the area. In this context Walter Ralegh took on a particular significance for he was the man who had been, and still was, attempting a similar enterprise on the other side of the Atlantic.

The links between American and Irish planting were substantial. It was in colonizing Munster back in the 1570s that Ralegh's kinsmen, Gilbert and Grenville, had learnt the lessons that both intended, but only one managed, to apply in the New World, and the roots of both the distant and the closer colonizations lay in the West Country. It was from Bideford, his home port, that Grenville had sailed with his Roanoke relief expedition in the spring of 1586, and, from the same port and its neighbours on the north Devon coast, it was but a brief voyage to the inviting estuaries of Cork, Kinsale, Waterford and Youghal (see map p. 36).

The strategy that Burghley and Walsingham formulated for settling southern Ireland, furthermore, drew on the ideas Walter Ralegh was developing about Virginia. Military strength was obviously important but, as Ralegh had come to recognize, establishing a garrison alone was not enough. It was just as vital to sink into the soil of the colony a self-sustaining society whose primary interest would lie not in what it had left back in England but in its survival in a foreign context.

When the going got difficult it was many times easier for settlers to return to England from Munster than from Virginia, so a significant number of the colonists must be given a definite stake in the land they worked. The proposal was that men like Ralegh – 'undertakers' – should take over huge blocks of land and people them with entire cross-sections of English society: gentlemen, freeholders, tenant farmers, craftsmen, shopkeepers, servants and labourers. The native Irish would be rigidly excluded, and the hope was that entire families which worshipped in Anglican churches, which produced children who went to Anglican schools and who thought of themselves first and foremost as inhabitants of Munster rather than as émigrés from Devon, would create on the other side of the Irish Channel a little England.

The difference from the American schemes of settlement was that Elizabeth's government actively involved itself in Munster – indeed the whole colony depended upon state organization and support. So although Walter Ralegh, as an undertaker, was given by royal grant the opportunity of private enrichment in Ireland as in Virginia, he did not have to finance the civil administration and military protection of his estates. These were provided by the English authorities based in Dublin, and to start with they were given free. From 1586 until 1591 the undertakers would pay nothing, from 1591 until 1594 half-rates, and not until their estates had been occupied for eight years were they expected to pay the full levy.[1]

In marked contrast to the North American projects, the English Government propagandized vigorously on behalf of Irish settlement. Whereas Virginia had to rely on Hakluyt and Harriot to trumpet its praises, Munster was boosted by official circulars sent out through the justices of the peace all over England, while Government officials toured the country as travelling salesmen. They had land parcels to offer ranging from estates at £300 to smallholdings at £6, and a market they aimed at particularly was the younger sons of the gentry, well-born men without lands to their name who might well prefer the lure of Irish lands to the more doubtful dividends of foreign soldiering or the pursuit of court favour. Indeed, the very generous acreage of Munster offered cheaply to Sir Walter Ralegh was in part put forward with a view to propaganda in this direction. Coaxing well-known courtiers and celebrities to partake in Irish colonization helped add lustre to a land too often associated with mist, misery and military disaster. The government of Elizabethan England saw little solid advantage in American colonies several thousand miles distant, but the plantation of Munster was a matter of state priority.

So, in June 1586, Sir Walter Ralegh was given the lands he had fought over when first he went to Ireland as an unknown soldier five years earlier – some 12,000 acres, part of it bog and hillside, but much of it lush farming land. He was named as the head of a group of undertakers from Devonshire, Somerset and Dorset, the most prominent of whom were Sir John Clifton and Sir John Stowell, with 12,000 acres each, and they were joined later by Sir Richard Grenville and Sir Warham St Leger, the relative Ralegh had teamed up with in 1580 to sentence and execute the rebel James Fitzgerald.

Walter Ralegh himself did not travel to Munster to supervise the establishing of his new colony. It was to be a project in Virginia style. Walter would use his position at court to provide money and prestige for the venture, but then he would stay close to the source of his power, Elizabeth herself, leaving day-to-day administration to agents. He evidently had no inclination to see again Alice Goold or his own daughter who would, by now, be five years old.

His partners Stowell and Clifton, however, went over to Munster in 1586 to assist the foundation of their undertaking – only to run into difficulties which drove them rapidly back to England in disgust, relieved to hand over their shares to Ralegh, so that by August 1586 Walter had tripled his holding. The English Government had made all its grants without a proper map of the area to show exactly what land it was distributing where, and, quite apart from the complications caused by dispossessed Irish and Anglo-Irish landowners, the undertakers had started quarrelling amongst themselves over the boundaries of their grants. It was too much for Stowell and Clifton, who were quite happy to get shot of their lands to Ralegh, and after Government surveyors had worked in the winter of 1586-7 on more accurately defining his estates Walter was able, on 27 February 1587, to secure a Privy Seal warrant giving him a provisional title to no less than 42,000 acres of cultivable land[2] and probably an equal area of waste land.

It was a vast empire, and a very special privilege – a token both of royal favour and Government confidence in Walter's abilities as a colonizer – for when Burghley and Walsingham had first drawn up their Munster scheme they had laid down 12,000 acres as the maximum holding that any single undertaker was allowed to control. But this was the time when Ralegh was receiving the Babington lands and being made the captain of the guard. Though Essex, returned from the Netherlands, was taking the court by storm, Ralegh in these early months of 1587 was riding on the very crest of his fortunes. Ralph Lane and his settlers had disappointed him, but Captain John White and his 500 acre-per-man colonists were preparing another expedition for the summer that bore all the signs of making Virginia a permanent English county across the ocean. So Walter Ralegh was more than Elizabeth's principal empire builder, he was by 1587 the landowner with by far the largest single stake in England's overseas possessions.

His Irish estates were a veritable kingdom,[3] and the entire 42,000 acres was now given him at a set annual rate that was never to exceed £66 6s. 8d. Here again was special favour at work, for Burghley and Walsingham had fixed payments for other undertakers at the yearly rate of £233 6s. 8d. per 12,000 acres once the initial eight years of exemptions had expired.[4]

Nor did the favour shown Walter end with his cut-price payments, for Queen Elizabeth agreed that an extra cavalry company could be raised to protect Ralegh's settlers, and this company was headed by one Andrew Colthurst who also acted as Walter's agent and attorney for the entire settlement. So the queen was paying Colthurst for doing Walter Ralegh's work – and Colthurst did it well, labouring hard to extend his master's empire even wider. Various valuable ecclesiastical properties were acquired, Molana Abbey, north of Youghal, the Franciscan Observant and Dominican houses at Youghal and also the remainder of a lease to the manor and castle of Lismore. This latter, magnificently dominating its park and beautiful river, was intended as the capital of Walter Ralegh's Irish settlement, though, until it was completed, Youghal College, nestling cosily by the churchyard at Youghal to this day, was chosen as an administrative centre convenient to the English ferries.

In all of this Sir Walter Ralegh exhibited a singular ability in delegating his authority, for his Irish estates made progress under his agents which other undertakers could not rival, and which was not entirely because his representatives had the power of a great courtier behind them. They appear to have been men of energy, and several had experience of organizing and even participating in the Virginia voyages. Thomas Hariot came over to occupy Molana Abbey with his family after the publication of his *Briefe and True Report*, residing there for several periods until 1597. Surviving documents list an M. Butler settled with his family on the Conna Bridge River by 1589, and he was almost certainly the Michael Butler who had fought alongside Ralegh in the Irish campaigns of 1580–1 and who had commanded the *Bark Ralegh* which turned back from Gilbert's expedition of 1583. The artist John White came later to settle in Munster,[5] while if one compares the 1589 roll of Munster settlers with the names of Ralph Lane's colonists of 1585–6, one comes across several names common to both: James Mason, Thomas Hacket (or Hasket) and Thomas Allen ('Master Alleyne'). One cannot be certain, but it is logical to assume that these first Roanoke settlers should attempt to put their pioneering experience to good use in the comparatively favourable setting of southern Ireland, while we know that other names have definite transatlantic connections: John and Robert Mawle both subscribed to Gilbert's expedition of 1583, while John Achelby or Ashley came from London merchant stock associated with Sir George Peckham and transoceanic enterprise.[6]

Through 1587 and 1588 the pioneers transferred their belongings and families across the Irish Channel to Walter Ralegh's Munster lands. From administrative centres like Youghal and Lisfinny Ralegh's agents allocated their estates, making up and concluding legal agreements at a rapid rate – one surviving document alone listing twenty freehold and leasehold agreements made in the great property shareout.[7] While other undertakers got tied up in wrangles with former occupants and rival undertakers, Ralegh's little colony thrived. New tenants took over the ruined castles and manors, and by May 1589 Walter could report that he had settled on his estates 144 men, of whom at least 73 had their families with them, making a community of 300 to 400 souls, most of them from Devonshire, Dorset and Somerset. They had ploughs, farm tools and cattle to their names, were rebuilding their villages and homes and included in their number essential craftsmen – a miller, a blacksmith and a baker.[8] Ralegh was nearly half-way to fulfilling his agreement to plant 320 families in his colony, and already he was achieving Burghley's and Walsingham's objective of founding a self-sustaining community in an area England had never previously felt she could call her own. His neighbours and kinsmen, St Leger and Grenville, were also doing well in their own undertakings and, before the end of the 1580s, it looked as if the estuaries and harbours that had enticed the men of Devon to southern Ireland would soon be providing channels for a prosperous trade linking Munster firmly to the mother country.

❧ 15 ❧

The Durham House Set

The little College at Youghal, fringed with ferns in the green shade of Southern Ireland, was the headquarters of Walter Ralegh's Munster colony, but the heart of the enterprise was back in London – the towering fortress of Durham House, the inspiration of so many far flung ventures. This was the nursery in which the Virginia voyages were hatched and the listening post to which despatches from the New World were sent, the intelligence centre to which the privateering captains and pilots trained by Thomas Hariot reported. The tinners of Cornwall sent their petitions to Durham House if Walter's agents in the West seemed less helpful than they might have been. The shillings from innkeepers and wool merchants all over the country, the pennies from playing card manufacturers, all found their way to the Durham House exchequer. The rents of the Babington Estates and those manors of All Souls came here, the counting house of their new landlord, and here too came the West Country cousins fresh to the big city and anxious to draw on the favour and prestige of their famous kinsman. Durham House was a Whitehall in microcosm, a centre of administration, wealth, patronage – a palace, a court, indeed – and presiding over it all like a splendid princeling was Sir Walter Ralegh.

But if Durham House was the hub of the empire that Walter had built for himself in five years of favour, it was also his home, and to visit him there came his friends – scientists, sailors, poets, and one of the grandest peers of the realm, Henry Percy, ninth Earl of Northumberland. Queen Elizabeth allowed her favourites little free time: their pay might be guaranteed, but their holidays were not, and Sir Walter Ralegh after his appointment as captain of the guard was required to spend even more waking hours than he had previously done in the royal presence. Just the same, he found time for relaxation, and one of the men in whose company he most loved to talk and unwind was this earl, one of the grandees of the north and a descendant of the famous Harry Percy whose name he bore.

But he was no Hotspur, this tall, dark-bearded young man, for Sir Walter Ralegh did not relax with other warriors. He had had enough of campfire companionship in his youth and now preferred to occupy his hard won leisure hours with the cut and thrust of conversation in company that was artistic, intellectual or scientific. It was in this last connection that he was drawn towards Henry Percy, known both to his contemporaries and to posterity as the 'Wizard Earl', a scientific explorer who was dogged, as was Dr Dee, by the ignorance and mistrust of his contemporaries. In later years, when Walter was less prosperous, Northumberland was to help subsidize Thomas Hariot and his researches, but all he earned for that from the outside world was the taint of atheism and black magic with which Dee, Hariot and, indeed, Walter Ralegh himself came to be smeared by popular prejudice and superstition.

Like Walter, Northumberland came suddenly into his eminence by a stroke of fate that others envied bitterly. His father, the eighth earl, had been a Catholic, a born intriguer whose brother was executed for his role in the Northern rebellion of 1569 and who then himself endured two spells in the Tower in 1571 and 1582 for his own role in conspiracies on behalf of Mary Queen of Scots. As if this were not lesson enough for him, he then got involved in yet another popish plot and was despatched to the Tower for a third time. On this occasion the 'bitch', as he described Elizabeth, could not possibly extend her patience any further and the vultures gathered in gloating expectation of the vast Percy estates that would be confiscated as a result of his fall. But the eighth earl had no intention of letting the world dismember his family's rolling Border fiefdom, and so he secretly obtained a pistol and shot himself through the left breast, forestalling with his suicide, condemnation, attainder and confiscation. Thus in the sixteenth century could land and family be set above mere personal survival.

Cheating the odds and the expectations of personal profit that many had entertained, Henry Percy came into this inheritance, one of the largest fortunes in England. Apart from his northern estates he enjoyed near London the magnificent residence of Syon House, and he lavished his wealth on the very subjects that fascinated Walter Ralegh: mathematics, navigation, science, astronomy. He built up a vast library which Walter consulted and imitated: books on the arts of war and fortification, treatises from Italy and all over the Continent, journals of American voyages and explorations, works on philosophy, astrology, medicine. Sharp-eyed, alert, thirsty for intellectual excitement and novelty, it was inevitable that Henry Percy should be attracted towards Durham House. Walter Ralegh and

Northumberland were kindred spirits – and they provided a focus for other lively minds similarly unencumbered by contemporary superstitions. There was Robert Hues, the mathematician who had studied at Oxford at the same time as Hariot and who was, like Hariot, aflame with a curiosity about the earth that was both academic and practical. He worked with Hariot, noting down reams of astronomical and mathematical data, and then escaped from his papers to navigate around the world with Thomas Cavendish – another of the Durham House set who had also gone on the 1585 voyage to Roanoke. With Hariot's collaboration, Hues prepared a book, *Tractatus de Globis*, which he dedicated to Sir Walter Ralegh, and he worked under the aegis of Walter's tame businessman, William Sanderson – who seems himself to have been infected by the geographical and naviga-tion enthusiasms of Durham House. He developed a sideline with one of his clients, Emery Molyneux, in the production of cartographical globes.[1]

The inquiring spirits of Northumberland and Ralegh struck sparks in all directions. Walter Warner was another original researcher who had been one of Hariot's circle as early as 1583. His passion was medical – the circulation of the blood in the human body – and it seems likely, though it would take an expert to confirm this, that his papers contain data antici-pating the more famous theories of William Harvey about the heart, veins and arteries.[2]

Not until the foundation of the Royal Society nearly a century later was England to see such a concentration of original minds and solid scientific ability as centred on Sir Walter Ralegh and the Earl of Northumberland in the last decades of Elizabeth's reign, and it was inevitable that more conventional souls should have looked askance at the ideas bandied so freely around Durham House. The Jesuit Robert Parsons committed the popular suspicion to paper when he wrote in 1592 'of Sir Walter Ralegh's school of atheism . . . and of the conjuror that is M[aster] thereof' – the 'conjuror' he was referring to being Thomas Hariot. In Durham House, the priest alleged, 'both Moses and our Saviour, the Old and New Testament are jested at, and the scholars taught among other things to spell "God" backwards.'[3]

Father Parsons produced not the slightest evidence to substantiate his accusation, which was part of a Jesuit propaganda tract that threw mud at the reputations of all the leading figures of the Elizabethan court to discredit them in Catholic eyes, and the level of his accuracy and hysteria can be gauged from the fact that he also traduced as an 'atheist' the pious old Lord Burghley who carried a prayer book with him everywhere he went. 'Atheist' in the sixteenth century was not so much a precise descrip-tion of a man's intellectual standpoint as a blunt instrument of abuse wielded by both Catholic and Protestant in the Reformation's war of

Walter Ralegh as a young man

Ralegh's birthplace, Hayes Barton, near East Budleigh in Devon. This Victorian engraving showed the farmhouse as it was in Walter's youth – and as it remains to this day

Ralegh's half-brother, Sir
Humphrey Gilbert

The Gilbert family home,
Compton Castle near Torquay in
Devon, which has in the
twentieth century been restored to
its Elizabethan splendour by
Commander Walter Ralegh
Gilbert, a tenth generation
descendant of Walter Ralegh and
Humphrey Gilbert

Sir Walter Ralegh plans
the Virginia enterprise

Doctor John Dee

Sir Richard Grenville

Thomas Hariot

words and thus Father Parsons, having denounced Elizabeth and her entire Privy Council as atheists, was himself condemned by a Protestant counter-propagandist for his own 'impiety, irreligiosity, treachery, treason and Machiavellian atheism'.[4]

Yet in the case of Sir Walter Ralegh the charge of atheism stuck. Tales of his scientific experiments in Durham House with Thomas Hariot and the 'Wizard Earl' were to travel to Scotland and poison the mind of the future James I against him before ever that king came south to take over Elizabeth's throne and, in the twentieth century, some scholars have established a little industry producing treatises that speculate on Sir Walter Ralegh's 'School of Night' and the references that William Shakespeare might, or might not, have made to it in his play *Love's Labour's Lost*.

The essential piety of Walter Ralegh needs no special pleading or justification when his entire life is examined over its span of nearly seventy years. Animated throughout by a personal faith that was deep, genuine and orthodox, he was no secret Faustus – and nor, for that matter, was Thomas Hariot. But within that very metaphor of the enquirer who sold his soul to buy more knowledge lie the ingredients of the 'School of Night' myth. The Durham House set – Northumberland, Hariot, Hues, Warner and, for a time, Dr John Dee – were with their telescopes, love of the stars and strange scientific experiments regarded by their contemporaries as Mephistophelean by definition. They were pushing out the frontiers of knowledge and, in an age of faith, it was assumed that the price one had to pay for that was spiritual. Men who sought to analyse the mysteries of God must be working on behalf of the devil, and so a world that was already jealous of Walter Ralegh's success and offended by his arrogance found in his scientific interests a focus for their resentment.

But we do not see the real Ralegh in the envy of contemporaries and the speculation of subsequent investigators, for the testimony which counts is his own personal behaviour in religious matters and he could be surprisingly humane and tolerant. His experiences in the French Wars of Religion could not help but imbue him with a certain cynicism towards the doctrinal differences for the sake of which men were prepared in the sixteenth century to shed blood – and have their own blood shed. Yet when it came to the point, his orthodoxy was rigid. Telescopes and scientific speculation notwithstanding, he was an Elizabethan whose touchstone was absolute loyalty to the Elizabethan church. When, a few years later, he was present as captain of the guard at the execution of Oliver Plasden, a young Catholic, he demonstrated clearly the limits of his heterodoxy. The young man was kneeling on the scaffold, preparing to meet his maker when, through the baying of the crowd for blood, Walter heard him pray 'for the queen and the whole realm' and he wondered whether the loyalty of this sentiment might not hold the possibility of sparing the Catholic from his ghastly fate.

'Then thou dost acknowledge her for thy lawful queen?' said Ralegh.
'I do sincerely.'
'Wouldst thou defend her,' quoth Ralegh, 'against all her foreign and domestical enemies, if so thou were able?'
'I would,' said Plasden, 'to the uttermost of my power, and so I would counsel all men who would be persuaded by me.'

Ralegh's intervention baulked the crowd of its entertainment, but as he reasoned with the bound Catholic, people began to respond to his desire for mercy and to come round to his point of view.

'I know, good people,' said Ralegh ... 'Her Majesty desireth no more at these men's hands than that which this man hath now confessed.'
'Mr Sheriff,' said he, 'I will presently go to the court. Let him be stayed. He sayeth marvellous well ... I will presently post to the queen. I know she will be glad of this plain dealing.'

But now Richard Topcliffe, the arch torturer and scourge of the Jesuits, intervened. He was not going to let Ralegh extricate his victim so easily.

'I pray you,' saith he, 'suffer me to offer him one question, and anon you shall hear that I will convince him to be a traitor. . . . Thou sayest, Plasden,' quoth he, 'that thou wouldst counsel all to defend the queen's right, but tell me, dost you think that the queen hath any right to maintain this religion and to forbid yours?'
'No,' said the priest.
'Then thou thinkest not,' quoth he, 'to defend the queen against the pope, if he would come to establish thy religion? Speak, what sayest thou to this? I charge thee before God!'
'I am a Catholic priest,' quoth he, 'therefore I would never fight nor counsel others to fight against my religion, for that were to deny my faith. O Christ!' saith he, looking up to heaven and kissing the rope, 'I will never deny thee for a thousand lives.'
Then lo! they cried, he was a traitor, and the cart was drawn away, and he, by the word of Ralegh, was suffered to hang until he was dead; then he was drawn and quartered after their custom.[5]

Walter's humanism extended so far – but no further. He tried hard to save the life of a fellow man, but when it became obvious that young Oliver Plasden was fixed in his faith Walter Ralegh became a fanatic to equal him, and he had no hesitation in ordering his execution. Human sympathy, tolerance and intellectual enquiry were one thing, matters of established faith were another – and that applied not only to Walter himself. The base from which his Durham House friends set off on their cosmic imaginings – and to which they always returned – was the conventional bedrock of the Anglican faith. Hariot the sinister 'conjuror' set particular store by the Ten Commandments as a rule for life and, scientist or not, he explained to his doctor how he could see God working in pharmaceutical drugs and medicines.[6] Just because some sixteenth-century critics saw some contradiction between Durham House's scientific researches and the Christian faith, there is no need for us to make the same mistake.

They were modern minds but pious souls, the men who were the friends of Sir Walter Ralegh – and they were not all scientists and mathematicians. Arthur Gorges represented the other side of Walter's intellectual activities – poetry, working with him throughout the 1580s on all manner of verse. From Walter's point of view, of course, his poems were a crucial political element in his courtship of the queen, his equivalent of old Burghley's memoranda or young Essex's antics in the tiltyard. Walter, it seems, had little enthusiasm for tournaments, and that cannot have been unconnected with his experience of 'ceremonial' tiltings in France in which courtiers had, in playful joust, been slaughtered: King Henri II himself had been killed, pierced through the eye as his courtiers cheered him on.

But courtly contest aside, Walter Ralegh wrote poems for fun. He loved juggling with words as he loved playing with ideas. There was something of the crossword maniac about some of the verse he composed – most notably in the lines he wrote to be read either vertically or horizontally:

Her face,	Her tongue,	Her wit,
So fair,	So sweet,	So sharp,
First bent,	Then drew,	Then hit,
Mine eye,	Mine ear,	My heart,
Mine eye,	Mine ear,	My heart,
To like	To learn,	To love,
Her face,	Her tongue,	Her wit,
Doth lead,	Doth teach,	Doth move,
Oh face,	Oh tongue,	Oh wit,
With frowns,	With check,	With smart,
Wrong not,	Vex not,	Wound not,
Mine eye,	Mine ear,	My heart.

Mine eye,	Mine ear,	My heart,
To learn,	To know,	To fear,
Her face,	Her tongue,	Her wit,
Doth lead,	Doth teach,	Doth swear.[7]

A fanciful game, a diversion, 'Her face, her tongue, her wit,' was the result of Walter and Arthur Gorges gambolling together through their mutual technique and vocabularies. Poetry was not at this stage of Ralegh's life a matter of agonized heart searchings set down in solitude. It was something he shared with his friends – and with Arthur in particular. The two men developed their ideas together, collaborating to produce some of their poems, and playfully competing when it came to others – both writing in the same style and, indeed, in the same handwriting. It is difficult on occasions to know which of their poems was written by whom, and the trouble from the literary detective's point of view is that neither man was jealous at the other's expense. They wrote their poems for private circulation, not for publication, scrawling out their verse on manuscripts that they passed round amongst their friends – or presented to the queen. It was considered most *infra dig* for a gentleman to allow what he wrote to be distributed through commercial publication, and when in 1593 was published *The Phoenix Nest*, an anthology of verse by a group of courtiers who had been up at Oxford together, the contributions, including some by Ralegh and Gorges, did not bear their authors' names.

Though he attacked everything he attempted with professional energy and ability, Sir Walter Ralegh carefully cultivated an image as a gentleman amateur – and not accepting money for his poems was an important aspect of this. This pride, not to say snobbery, was one motive behind the satire he produced in the 1580s on a ballad of Christopher Marlowe's, 'The Passionate Shepherd to his Love'. This ditty, set to music, was one of the rages of the 1580s:

> Come live with me and be my love,
> And we will all the pleasures prove
> That valleys, groves, hills and fields,
> Woods or steepy mountain yields.
>
> And we will sit upon the rocks,
> Seeing the shepherds feed their flocks,
> By shallow rivers to whose falls
> Melodious birds sing madrigals.
>
> And I will make thee beds of roses,
> And a thousand fragrant posies,

> A cap of flowers, and a kirtle
> Embroidered all with leaves of myrtle. . . .[8]

It was a shanty that gave Marlowe the sort of commercial acclaim that Walter professed to disdain and so, for the amusement of Gorges and his other friends, he composed a retort, half facetious, half serious – 'The Nymph's Reply to the Shepherd'.

> If all the world and love were young,
> And truth in every shepherd's tongue,
> These pretty pleasures might me move,
> To live with thee and be thy love. . . .
>
> Thy gowns, thy shoes, thy beds of roses,
> Thy cap, thy kirtle and thy posies,
> Soon break, soon wither, soon forgotten;
> In folly ripe, in reason rotten. . . .
>
> But could youth last, and love still breed,
> Had joys no date nor age no need,
> Then these delights my mind might move,
> To live with thee and be thy love.[9]

Walter's reply was a private joke among friends, intended to be laughed over and forgotten. But another, more sinister significance, has since been placed on the fashion in which Walter Ralegh toyed with the verse of the scurrilous Kit Marlowe – that there was a secret friendship between the two men and that Ralegh was involved in the activities that resulted in Marlowe being summoned by the Privy Council to answer charges of atheism and blasphemy in 1593, only to be stabbed mysteriously to death before the hearing. Such a suggestion, of course, ties in very neatly with speculation about Walter's atheism, but though Marlowe knew Hariot there is absolutely no evidence – the passing insinuation of a paid informer apart – that he had any contact at all with Sir Walter Ralegh, and Walter's fun at the expense of Marlowe's nymphs, swains and fragrant posies was not the only burlesque of 'The Passionate Shepherd to his Love' written by an Elizabethan poet. William Shakespeare also parodied the ballad, and the centuries-long saga of *his* quite mythical links with Marlowe is well known.

It is safe to say that Christopher Marlowe was *not* a guest of Sir Walter Ralegh's at Durham House in the 1580s, and if the house had possessed such a thing as a visitors' book there are other names one would not have discovered in its pages either. Robert Cecil, the son of old Lord Burghley, was a near neighbour, but he was a far from close friend of Walter Ralegh. Small, crippled, introspective, the younger son picked out by his father above the family heir to be groomed for high office, he was too prudent a man to let himself be drawn towards the freethinkers of Durham House. Nor was Francis Bacon, even more canny and subtle in his effeminate way, attracted into the Ralegh orbit. Walter was too much his own master to let Bacon be his Svengali, and so Francis went off with his earnest brother Anthony to play that role to the young Earl of Essex.

Cecil and Bacon were the two sharpest minds of Ralegh's generation, less eminent than he was in the 1580s but destined with Essex and Walter to be the principal protagonists in the great drama played out through the declining years of Elizabeth's reign. Yet both men were wary of Walter, preferring to pursue their own paths to prominence and watching the activities of the Durham House set from a careful distance. Another observer from afar who was, unexpectedly, to play a crucial role in the future career of Walter Ralegh was Henry Howard, a former crony of Oxford's at the time Walter had been involved with the earl. In 1582 Howard had been held in the Tower at the same time as the father of Northumberland and for the same reason – Catholic conspiracy. Outcast by his religion he jealously watched from the fringes of high society the son of his one time fellow prisoner consorting with Walter Ralegh and his crew of scholars and stargazers – and his vitriolic pen was, in the course of time, to provide one of the most damning and poisonous condemnations of everything that Durham House stood for in sixteenth-century England.

Still, these were all shadows of the future. In the mid 1580s the sun of royal favour and promise beat warmly on Walter Ralegh and his friends, and they were all too busy with their ever-multiplying enthusiasms to worry about who or what might one day stand in their way. By the summer of 1587 all energies were being concentrated on another great venture into the New World for, though Walter had by then been lord and governor of Virginia for three years, there were actually inhabiting the colony but eighteen men at the most – the holding party of soldiers Grenville had disembarked on Roanoke the previous summer. It was time for a new and altogether more thorough initiative, the creation in the New World of a true community instead of the garrison post that Ralph Lane had tried to establish – the foundation of an actual city.

It would be known as the City of Ralegh and, as a token of its ambitions, it would sport its own coat of arms, specially designed and presented by the garter king of arms – a cross with Sir Walter Ralegh's Roebuck crest in one quarter. Heraldic emblems would dignify each of the assistants who were to rule the new community as a cross between aldermen and a board of directors, while the governor was assigned a magnificent shield in eight quarterings. Just as Munster was intended to become a permanently based English county across the seas, so the City of Ralegh was to become another Bristol, Southampton or Plymouth, a solid and prosperous trading port with all the trappings that accompanied such boroughs in the sixteenth century – not to mention families, women and children.

The plan was to land at Roanoke to pick up Grenville's eighteen men who had spent the winter there, and then sail on up the coast to found the new city of Ralegh in Chesapeake Bay, the site John White had already prospected and which Ralph Lane had selected as the safest deep water harbour for English ships. One reason for moving north was to avoid trouble from the Spaniards, who claimed the whole of North America as Florida, just as the English claimed it as Virginia. They might well by now have discovered the position of the Roanoke settlement. 'Your best planting,' Hakluyt advised Ralegh at the end of 1586, 'will be about the bay of the Chesapeans.'[10]

William Sanderson was willing to continue his financial support, Hariot was working enthusiastically on his *Briefe and True Report*, and John White was very happy to act as the governor of the new city and to take with him across the Atlantic his daughter Eleanor and her husband Ananias Dare. The basic principle of the venture was the same as that of the Munster settlement, that the participants should have a firm and permanent stake in the enterprise, and on 7 January 1587, Sir Walter Ralegh formally chartered White and twelve others to be the 'governor and assistants of the City of Ralegh in Virginia' – the first municipal corporation in North America's history. Apart from White only one of the assistants, the pilot Simon Fernandez, had been to Virginia before, but, unlike the principal members of Ralph Lane's 1585 settlement, these were men prepared to risk their lives, families and possessions for the sake of the new city: Roger Baylye, Ananias Dare (White's son-in-law), Christopher Cooper, John Sampson, Thomas Steevens, William Fulwood, Roger Prat and James Prat, Dionyse Harvie, John Nichols and George Howe, these were the founding fathers, all but three of whom (Fulwood, Nichols and James Prat stayed in England to bring out relief supplies) paid in full the high stake they had wagered.

Eighty-nine men, seventeen women and eleven children were to found the new city – fourteen families, all of reasonably well-born English and Irish stock, with two of the ladies, Eleanor Dare, the governor's daughter and Margery Harvie, the wife of Dionyse, both pregnant. So this indicated the serious settling priorities of the adventurers, together with the fact that, for all Richard Hakluyt's talk of silver mines, there were no foreign mineral experts brought along as there had been in 1585. Walter Ralegh, as lord and governor of Virginia, remained the overall head of the venture, contributing his money and retaining ultimate authority, but this was no privateering syndicate interested in the quick profits of a trading post or garrison. The City of Ralegh was to be a settlement in the full sense of the word.

❧ 16 ❧

The City of Ralegh

The seriousness with which the citizens of Ralegh took their colonizing responsibilities was shown by the fleet that sailed out of Plymouth harbour on 8 May 1587. There were no spare warships for dallying in the Caribbean, just Governor White's flagship, the 120-ton *Lion* – probably the same *Red Lion* or *Lyon* of Chichester that Cavendish had sailed in in 1585 – and no more of an escort than a flyboat and a pinnace. The colonists intended to sail straight to Virginia and get down immediately to the task of settlement. Captain Stafford, one of Ralph Lane's lieutenants, commanded the pinnace, Edward Spicer, who had never previously crossed the Atlantic, captained the flyboat and as master of the *Lion*, theoretically subordinate to White, was Simon Fernandez. Manteo, by now a most Anglicized Indian, was sailing across the Atlantic for the fourth time and it was intended that he should take over Roanoke in Ralegh's name after the settlers had moved on north to Chesapeake.

Following the route Walter Ralegh had laid down, the *Lion* headed south-west from Devon for the Caribbean which it reached in five weeks. For three days the planters went ashore to enjoy the tropical fruit and fresh water of the Leeward Islands – which must have been a pleasant relief after more than a month cooped up with salt meat and brackish water. But some of the party picked from the trees 'a small fruit like green apples' which burnt their mouths and made their tongues swell – the poisonous manchineel against which Columbus had first warned – while between White and Fernandez broke out the first of several quarrels about the best place to pick up salt and live fruit trees for planting in Chesapeake. In the end they sailed up towards Virginia without the supplies they had sought, White recording ever more acrimonious comments about Fernandez in his log, which is the only surviving record of the voyage.[1]

On every single one of the three trips he piloted, with Barlow and

Amadas, with Grenville and Lane and now with White, the Portuguese seems to have annoyed his English commanders intensely and to have had set against his name responsibility for a whole catalogue of disasters, the worst of all being the grounding of the *Tyger* in 1585. On the other hand, he was repeatedly selected to take charge of navigation in waters that were still largely uncharted, and he never made any secret of the fact that his main interest lay not in colonial planting but in privateering. Whatever aspersions White might cast on Fernandez's ability and loyalty, the Portuguese certainly won the total respect of the crews he commanded – and some of the criticisms made of him must be put down to the frustration that a White or a Lane felt on board ship, theoretically in supreme command but in practice in the hands of this self-confident and self-willed foreign seaman.

Off Virginia came the next clash, for cruising along the flat and similar-looking lagoon banks of the Carolina coast, Fernandez decided they must be near Croatoan. In fact, they were still a hundred miles or so south of that island, and, after two days fruitlessly searching for an inlet, the pilot had to admit he had been wrong. Moving on up the coast, the *Lion* and its two little escorts were nearly wrecked on Cape Lookout, another error which White put down not to the treacherous nature of the coast but to 'the carelessness and ignorance of our master'. Then, arriving finally at Roanoke on 22 July 1587, came the most decisive clash of all, for Fernandez, insisting that it was by now too late in the year to move up to Chesapeake, ordered that all the colonists and stores be unloaded on the site of Ralph Lane's old settlement. White, faced with the support that Fernandez had whipped up for his plan among the sailors and settlers, could only note lamely 'it booted not the governor to contend with them'.

John White was certainly a great artist, but as a leader of men he was less proficient, and his half-hearted surrender and shifting of responsibility for the location of his settlement onto the shoulders of his pilot effectively undermines many of his criticisms of Fernandez. For Walter Ralegh had given clear instructions that his settlers were to stop at Roanoke only to pick up Grenville's holding party and put down the Indian Manteo. Then they should proceed north to Chesapeake. Once the colonists had arrived on Virginian soil, White was the undisputed commander-in-chief of the venture with the responsibility for carrying out these orders to the letter. But he did not behave like a commander-in-chief.

In the event it would seem that the decision to stay on Roanoke and not move north that season was the best that the circumstances would permit. When Fernandez complained 'that the summer was far spent', he was probably thinking of the Spanish plate fleet due to arrive in the Azores in

August or early September, but, privateering apart, it was also true that the second half of July was a late date to start planting crops for the autumn. By the time the colonists had reached Chesapeake Bay and got sufficiently organized to start cultivating, most of August would be past, and with it the hopes of a harvest that year. On Roanoke, furthermore, were still standing the houses, though not the palisade, of Ralph Lane's colony, so the menfolk need waste little time erecting shelter for their families before starting work in the fields. With women and children in the party, it was prudent to err on the side of caution, and, most decisive of all, there was on Roanoke no sign of the eighteen men Richard Grenville had left on the island the previous year. Any fears White may have had about the unknown dangers of Chesapeake must have been magnified by the indications that Grenville's little holding party had come to an untimely end.

Once Manteo had been able to re-establish contact with local Indians – Wingina's followers had all left Roanoke – it was discovered what had happened. The eighteen Englishmen, under the command of two Barnstaple mariners Coffin and Chapman, had scarcely settled on Roanoke in the summer of 1586 when they were ambushed by a war party of braves twice their number who smoked them out of their huts and then set upon them as they staggered out confused and defenceless – the very strategy Wingina had planned to adopt against Lane. A few of the soldiers got away in a boat to take refuge down near Port Ferdinando and Hatarask Island, but by the summer of 1587 all trace of them had disappeared. They had either been murdered there, starved, or possibly drowned at sea in an attempt to sail south and take refuge with the Spanish.

The fate of the holding party did not augur well for their successors. Only a week after White's settlers had landed and while they were still busy repairing houses and carving out fields, George Howe, one of the assistants with a particularly fine coat of arms, was set upon by a party of Indians while fishing for crab about two miles from the settlement. His body was discovered pierced by no less than sixteen arrows, while his skull had been beaten in with a club. It was clearly time for the new settlers to win over at least one group of neighbouring Indians to friendship, since the hope of peace with all had been ruled out by the clashes between Lane and Wingina.

On 30 July 1587, Governor White, Captain Stafford, Manteo and a score of men set off for Croatoan, where Manteo's mother came from. The natives' first reaction was to flee from the white men, but calling to them in their own language Manteo coaxed them to a parley which ended with them 'embracing and entertaining us friendly'.

White invited the chief to come up to Roanoke for a meeting in a week's time so that on 8 August 1587, the seal could formally be set on an agreement of peace and cooperation between red skin and white.

But such a precise date meant little to men used to measuring time by the movement of the heavens and the seasons, and on 8 August 1587, there was not a sign of an Indian party on or approaching Roanoke Island. So reacting with the same jumpiness as Grenville back in 1585, White decided that friendliness had failed and that he must act to revenge the murder of assistant Howe, not to mention the destruction of the holding party commanded by poor Coffin and Chapman. With an armed guard he crossed over to Wingina's old village and, finding it full of Indians, ordered his men to open fire. One Indian was killed before it was discovered that these natives were not, in fact, anything to do with Wingina but the friendly Croatoans who were proceeding in a leisurely way to the planned conference. They had stopped off to gather stores of corn, tobacco and pumpkin that they had found in the deserted village, and it was fortunate that their goodwill enabled them to overlook White's hastiness. But the mutual suspicion – and the death – that the misunderstanding had engendered ruled out wholehearted cooperation between settler and Indian.

Back on Roanoke, White and his followers took comfort in European rituals. On 13 August 1587, Manteo was christened and formally installed as 'Lord of Roanoke and Dasempunkepenc' – Dasempunkepenc being the village where the English had fired on the friendly Croatoans. It was simpler to import the feudal system to the New World and invest Manteo as Walter Ralegh's vassal than to come to terms with the realities of coexistence with the native inhabitants.

Five days later, on 18 August 1587, everybody in the City of Ralegh had still greater reason for celebration, for on that day Governor White was presented with a healthy new grand-daughter, the first European child to be born in North America outside the Spanish Empire, and 'because this child was the first Christian born in Virginia, she was named Virginia'. Then a few days later Margery Harvie presented young Virginia Dare with a playmate, and the babies were both christened by Governor White who, in the absence of a chaplain, presided over the colony's religious devotions. The Virginians were settling down and their little colony seemed to be thriving. All their supplies for a year had been brought ashore together with White's books, maps, pictures and his fine suit of ceremonial armour; there was the artillery that had been intended for the Chesapeake fort, and the colonists had also been able to cut down good stocks of timber that could be sold – or used for publicity purposes – back in England by their supreme commander who liked to make presents of the products that his colonies exported. He gave the Earl of Northumberland, his scientific friend, a bed made of fine red Virginia cedar.

It was time for the *Lion* to set sail for England to tell Walter Ralegh that his settlers were well founded, if not in the precise geographical situation that he had selected. Fernandez was anxious to be gone, and there was a definite need for one of the assistants to return to England and galvanize activity for a relief expedition in the spring. William Fulwood, John Nichols and James Plat, the three assistants who had not sailed, could be presumed to be organizing reinforcements with Ralegh, but they would need someone who had seen the colony in action to tell them what supplies were particularly necessary. Salt, for example, had proved hard to obtain on Roanoke, and there was a need for more livestock. Christopher Cooper was persuaded to go back with Fernandez, but then he changed his mind. Ananias Dare and Dionyse Harvie were unwilling to leave their wives and new-born babies, and all the other assistants seem to have considered themselves so well established that they were anxious to stay through the winter. On 22 August 1587, they urged White to make the sacrifice himself. The governor was, after all, the most prestigious representative that the new City of Ralegh could send back to Sir Walter.

But White was reluctant to go. He had taken on the job of governor and felt it reflected poorly on him to desert his post after only a month. He had had little time to do any sketching, and he was worried about who would look after his own home on Roanoke. Not until the assistants had reassured him on that account and, on 25 August 1587, given him a certificate setting out his reluctance and their insistence on his departure, did he agree to go.

A fierce storm had driven Fernandez and the *Lion* out to sea, but on 27 August 1587, Governor White was able to embark on the expedition's flyboat – he evidently did not want to spend the best part of two months on the Atlantic with the Portuguese – and set sail. He left his colony healthy, happy and full of confidence for its first winter in Virginia, comfortably housed with 'a high palisade of great trees, with curtains and flankers, very fort-like', right around their homes. Their plan was to establish themselves there firmly, and then, perhaps in the following year, 'they intended to remove 50 miles farther up into the mainland', either to Chesapeake or else inland up the Albermarle Sound where Ralph Lane had prospected in 1585 and noted the fertility of the soil. They had several small boats to help transport themselves about Pamlico Sound, and also the pinnace that had sailed across the Atlantic with the *Lion* and which, recaulked, was eminently oceanworthy. Governor White looked forward to returning with succour to his post the following spring and to greeting again his friends, daughter and grand-daughter Virginia. She would be one year old.

But the governor barely got back to England alive. An accident to a capstan, one of whose bars broke to injure a dozen sailors 'so sore that some of them never recovered' virtually incapacitated the flyboat's crew of fifteen. Not until the vessel had limped across the Atlantic to the Azores did Fernandez transfer sailors from the *Lion* to help the five fit men who had avoided mishap, and then he left the flyboat to find her own way back to England while he cruised round the Azores looking for prizes. A wild Bay of Biscay storm then caught poor Governor White in his miniscule craft until, on 16 October 1857, seven weeks out from Virginia with only 'stinking water, dregs of beer and lees of wine', the crew expecting 'nothing but by famine to perish at sea', a strange harbour was sighted. It might have been Spanish or enemy French for all the suffering sailors knew, but they sailed straight into it, to discover they were in Ireland, at Smerwick, that town of such significance in Sir Walter Ralegh's past. Though Governor White, despite his troubles, got straight onto a horse to bring medical help from the nearby town of Dingle, the flyboat's boatswain, steward and boatswain's mate all died. White had to find another ship, the *Monkie*, to take him to Marazion near St Michael's Mount in Cornwall, and thence he travelled overland to arrive at Portsmouth on 8 November 1587. The *Lion* had arrived there three weeks earlier prizeless and in as miserable a state as the flyboat. Disabled by sickness and death the crew had been unable to beat into the harbour and, forced to anchor outside, 'all might have perished there, if a small bark by great hap had not come to them to help them'.

Still, these sad adventures apart, it was on the whole good news that Governor White could bring Sir Walter Ralegh, and Ralegh responded promptly to White's list of supplies needed on Roanoke. The assistants' confidence in their governor was justified, for at his entreaty Walter 'forthwith appointed a pinnace to be sent thither with all such necessaries as he understood they stood in need of, and also wrote his letters unto them, promising that a relief expedition should be with them the summer following'.

But that summer following was the summer of 1588, the great crisis year in the reign of Queen Elizabeth 1. Bad weather delayed the pinnace bearing Ralegh's letters from sailing until the spring, when the large relief fleet promised to the colonists in Ralegh's letters was also ready – the *Tyger* and other vessels being collected at Bideford by Sir Richard Grenville. And then, at the end of March 1588, the Privy Council intervened and ordered Grenville 'to forbear to go on his intended voyage'.

The settlers on Roanoke Island would have to tighten their belts and do their best to survive through the summer of 1588 without help or even news from Sir Walter Ralegh, for King Philip of Spain's great Armada was threatening the survival of England itself. The comfort of distant colonies would have to wait on the salvation of the realm, and that depended on every single ship which could sail into the Channel – the *Tyger*, the relief fleet, and even that little pinnace with its letters of good cheer from Sir Walter Ralegh. The good cheer was badly needed at home.

❧ 17 ❧

The Armada

The vessel that led the English navy against the great might of the Spanish Armada was Sir Walter Ralegh's – a graceful, deadly warship bristling with three banks of guns set low in her waist to rake the enemy's waterline. The *Ark Ralegh* had been built in 1586 as the flagship of Walter's privateering fleet and a model of what a modern fighting vessel should be. She was quite the most advanced English warship of her age. She had four masts instead of the usual three, and her main masts carried above the normal main and top-sails additional furls of canvas – topgallants that could be struck by the newfangled system John Hawkins had introduced. She was a galleon, built with a fine projecting beak and a square transom stern in which two cannon were mounted on either side of the rudder.

When in 1587 the queen had given Walter Ralegh the lands of the traitor Babington and symbolically surrendered herself into his hands as captain of her guard, he had returned the gesture by giving her the nation's finest fighting vessel. And rechristened the *Ark Royal*, Ralegh's pride became the flagship of Elizabeth's navy from whose masts fluttered the English flag, the royal standard and the ensign of the lord admiral who sailed in her. 'I pray you tell Her Majesty from me,' said Lord Howard, 'that her money was well given for the *Ark Ralegh*' – though Elizabeth had, in fact, paid nothing for the ship – 'for I think her the odd ship in the world for all conditions; and truly I think there can be no great ship make me change and go out of her.'[1] Even if Walter was not to sail in person against the Spaniards, his loyalty, patriotism and honour would be borne into the very thick of the battle by the ship he had himself built.

Elizabeth had crucial work on shore for her favourite to execute. In November 1587 Sir Walter Ralegh was appointed to the council of war charged with preparing England for the great challenge facing the nation. The sea confrontation with the Armada would largely take care of itself.

Apart from the new *Ark Royal* and the other capital ships of the line there were dozens of privateers like Ralegh's *Roebuck*, heavily armed, manoeuvrable and manned by experienced crews who could guard the Channel. England's great vulnerability was her land defences. A chance wind could well land the Spanish army – or part of it – anywhere on the English coast between Lands End and the Wash, and while English sailors had been, through privateering, involuntarily training for Armageddon for years, the ordinary English levies with their longbows, pikes and billhooks were no match for the Spanish stormtroopers hardened by decades of Continental campaigns.

Ralegh's special responsibility was the coast of Devon and Cornwall. But in these winter months he ranged far beyond the counties where his writ as vice-admiral ran. He travelled up round the ports of Essex, Suffolk and Norfolk as far as Kings Lynn, noting down the details of coastal fortifications and the gaps that needed filling. East Anglia was particularly vulnerable, for though the Spanish navy would be sailing up the Channel from the south-west to pass by the coast of Devon and Cornwall, the bulk of the Spanish army was in the Netherlands and could quite easily be ferried across to Harwich or the Norfolk beaches. Walter drew up a list of priorities, the harbours and castles which needed most urgent reinforcement, and personally advised the Norfolk authorities on the best way to secure their coastline.

Then he headed back south to Dorset, lobbying the Privy Council for several banks of heavy cannon to strengthen Portland and Weymouth. The Spaniards might well pick on the middle of England's underbelly for their landing, reasoning that Devon and Cornwall involved too long a march to London, while the Home Counties were too solidly defended. Ralegh argued that first priority should be given to deep water harbours, for it was quite impossible to defend every foot of beach where the enemy might land, and no invasion could succeed in the long term without a port in which Spanish ships could safely unload supplies for their army. 'For to invade by sea upon a perilous coast, being neither in possession of any port, nor succoured by any party, may better fit a prince presuming on his fortune than enriched with understanding.'

Twenty years later, when he wrote that summary of his strategy, Walter was forced to admit that King Philip of Spain was not, in fact, a prince enriched with understanding – and that he was quite capable of landing the entire Spanish army on the exposed shingle of Beachy Head or Dungeness. But in 1587 Ralegh's tactics of concentration were the only practicable ones, given the paucity of English resources and time available. In between the main strongholds would be watchguards and beacons ready to warn of a landing, and, taking a leaf from the book of the Irish guerrillas, preparations were made to devastate the countryside between any beachhead and London.

Plymouth was Ralegh's primary responsibility, for there were his head-quarters as vice-admiral and there too was the harbour that was closest to Spain. So plans were laid for several thousand men levied from Devon and Cornwall to converge on the port.

But down in Devon at Christmas 1587 Walter found open disaffection, with the city of Exeter refusing to make any contribution. It was the old problem of local resentment at bearing the main brunt of the national effort, and it took careful work by Ralegh's JPs to 'induce the inferior sort to whatsoever shall be thought necessary for Her Majesty's safety and their own defence.' In January 1588 Walter was cajoling the stannary parliament at Lostwithiel to contribute generously, so that in 1588 Cornwall made a more impressive military return than it had ever before achieved: 5,560 men, 1,395 shot, 633 corselets, 1,956 bills and halberds, 1,528 bows, 4 lances and 96 light horse.[2]

Ralegh's efforts were demonic – and he did not forget his more distant duties. He managed to slip over to Youghal to carry out some administra-tive responsibilities there – and he did his best for his hundred colonists in Virginia. He wrote a pompous letter to his half-brother Sir John Gilbert who was supposed to be enforcing the Privy Council's stop on shipping leaving English waters:

Sir,
Hearing of late that there is little regard taken of the general restraint made heretofore by the lords of the council of shipping and mariners, but that every man provideth to go to Newfoundland and other places at their pleasure ... I thought good therefore to put you in mind to have special care that none pass without special order from the lords of the council. . . .
Your loving brother, W. Raleigh

[But his postscript was in quite a different tone:]
P.S. Such as I acquainted you withal, to whom I have given leave, you may let them steal away.[3]

Ralegh's official orders were one thing, in other words, and his private interests quite another. So despite the decree which had prevented Grenville from setting off on his relief expedition to the City of Ralegh in Virginia, John White, in two small ships, pinnaces of no more than 30 tons was now allowed to 'steal away' from Bideford on the same mission.

But Captain Arthur Facy, the admiral of this two vessel fleet, was more interested in privateering than in relieving anxious colonists and he picked a fight off La Rochelle with a couple of French warships over twice his size. He was forced to surrender and was lucky to limp back home with his ships and crews looted but living.

Once again poor John White had suffered from the clash of interests between prize-taking and pioneering. He would not see his granddaughter that summer. He got back to the West Country on 22 May 1588, in the very same week that an army of priests in Lisbon were hearing the confessions and giving communion to each one of the 30,000 warriors Pope Sixtus v had blessed for the conquest of England.

On 19 July 1588, the great Spanish crescent was sighted off the Isles of Scilly, and Ralegh's beacons flared down the coast. The long months of preparation and waiting had come to their testing point. Ralegh's guns and levies were waiting in Plymouth as Lord Charles Howard, followed by his two score fighting ships, sailed out to do battle in the *Ark Royal*. The mayor, corporation and citizens of Plymouth had a grandstand view of the two fleets converging. But the Spaniards, some 120 sail all told, were not yet prepared to turn and fight, and Walter's fortifications were not put to the test, for the enemy were aiming higher up the coast. Ralegh's troops marched eastwards after them heading for Portland, the Solent and the Isle of Wight, but the Spaniards did not make for land there either. Day after day and night after night they kept moving steadily up the Channel while Howard, Drake and their ships were quite content to cannonade and harry them ever eastwards until, off Calais one week later, the confrontation came. There the Armada stopped. To continue any further would have meant losing contact with the troops waiting in the Low Countries, while the south-west wind that had blown the two fleets up the Channel would have pushed the would-be invaders out hopelessly into the North Sea.

It was here that Sir Walter Ralegh became an actor in the drama which he had followed, until this point, frustratingly cooped up by his shore responsibilities. Now that the danger to the west and south was past he could join the fleet, and in the small hours of Sunday, 28 July 1588, he set foot on his old flagship with a message for Lord Howard from the queen. Having chased and harassed for a week the lord admiral was now 'to attack the Armada in some way, or to engage it if he could not burn it'.

Yet there was no need to tell Lord Charles Howard or Sir Francis Drake what to do. That very night blazing fireships had been set to drift among the anchored Spanish galleons and, panicking, the enemy captains had cut their cables and run before the wind out into the North Sea. The regiments of Parma could never now be escorted across to England. The invasion threat was dead.

As dawn broke on the morning of Monday, 29 July, the three rows of the *Ark Royal*'s guns tore into the *San Lorenzo*, one of the great galleons that had gone ashore, while Drake, Hawkins and Frobisher took their ships within 'half a musket shot' of every fleeting Spaniard they could catch, firing broadsides so that the high castles were blown to splinters and blood began to run out of the scuppers. As Ralegh wrote scornfully:

> Their navy, which they termed invincible ... were by thirty of Her Majesty's own ships of war, and a few of our own merchants ... beaten and shuffled together, even from the Lizard in Cornwall, first to Portland ... from Portland to Calais ... and from Calais driven with squibs from their anchors, were chased out of sight of England, round about Scotland and Ireland.
>
> Where, for the sympathy of their barbarous religion, hoping to find succour and assistance, a great part of them were crushed against the rocks, and those other that landed, being very many in number, were notwithstanding broken, slain and taken, and so sent from village to village, coupled in halters to be shipped into England.
>
> Where Her Majesty, of her princely and invincible disposition, disdaining to put them to death, and scorning either to return or entertain them, they were all sent back again to their countries, to witness and recount the worthy achievements of their invincible and dreadful navy.

The sarcasm was merited. As the Armada medal struck to commemorate the victory stated, 'God blew with His winds and they were scattered'. Certain courtiers who, like Ralegh, had spent the crucial days of the week-long battle on land, ventured to criticize Lord Admiral Howard for letting the Spaniards drift as far as Calais. He should have closed with them far earlier, they said. But Ralegh appreciated the wisdom of the lord admiral's tactics and has defended him pungently to posterity:

> There is a great deal of difference between fighting loose, or at large, and grappling. The guns of a slow ship pierce as well and make as great holes as those in a swift. To clap together ships without consideration belongs rather to a madman than to a man of war. .... The Lord Charles Howard, Admiral of England, [had] been lost in the year 1588 if he had not been better advised than a great many malignant fools were that found fault with his behaviour. The Spaniards had an army aboard them and he had none; they had more ships than he had, and of higher building and charging; so that, had he entangled himself with those great and powerful vessels, he had gravely endangered the kingdom of England.

Ralegh's was the most apposite contemporary summary of the Armada epic and of the English strategy, and for all that he had scarcely played the part of a Howard, a Drake or a Hawkins, Walter was justified in taking personal pride and a certain credit for the fact that the Spaniards, despite their 'so great and terrible ostentation . . . did not in all their sailing round about England so much as sink or take one ship, bark, pinnace or cockboat of ours or even burned so much as one sheepcote of this land.'[4]

Part 3

❧

1588-92 Fall

The best of men are but the spoils of Time, and certain images where-with childish Fortune useth to play – kiss them today and break them tomorrow – and therefore I can lament in myself but a common destiny.

Sir Walter Ralegh

❧ 18 ❧

The Summer's Nightingale

The defeat of the Spanish Armada marked the high spot of Queen Elizabeth's reign. There were triumphs to come, but it was definitely a turning point, a climax after which the old intensity of events was never again to be recaptured – and 1588 marked a watershed for Walter Ralegh as well. He had great exploits of privateering, war and exploration to look forward to; his finest poems and all his prose works were still to be written; he was within a few years to receive his beautiful and vast estates located around Sherborne in Dorset; and ahead of him, too, lay the whole new dimension that marriage and a family were to bring. But 1588 was definitely the conclusion of the meteoric stage of his career, the end of the half dozen years into which he had brilliantly compressed fame, wealth, favour and glory, the years which had made his name and turned a tenant farmer's son into the glittering colossus that overshadowed his age and posterity as well. After 1588 the soaring projectory flattened out.

The rise to favour of Robert Devereux, Earl of Essex, was the most noticeable reason for this slowing down, and it was the cause of many changes in the next thirteen years, in the history not only of Sir Walter Ralegh but of England as a whole. For since the funeral of Sir Philip Sidney the previous year, the red-haired earl had deliberately bid for and won that dead hero's role as England's champion knight, the bright young Galahad that popular mythology needed to offset the ageing glamour of the queen, and though Ralegh had made a gesture towards playing the same game by composing an elegy to the dead Sidney whom he praised as the 'Scipio, Cicero and Petrarch of our time', he had to admit that he scarcely knew the young man whose death he was lamenting.

> . . . I, that in thy time and living state,
> Did only praise thy virtues in my thought. . . .
> With words and tears now wail thy timeless fate.

137

There was about the entire 'Epitaph upon Sir Philip Sidney Knight' a melancholy that stemmed not so much from sorrow at Sidney's youthful promise cut off in its prime, as from Ralegh's awareness that, now in his mid-thirties, he himself could never hope to rival the fresh vigour of a Sidney or an Essex.

> There didst thou vanquish shame and tedious age,
> Grief, sorrow, sickness and base fortune's might,
> Thy rising day saw never woeful night,
> But past with praise from off this worldly stage.

These are the best lines in the poem, but their power springs from envy, not from mourning.

It was envy which inspired in the dying months of 1588 another fierce quarrel between Ralegh and Essex. The two men met almost daily at court, and almost always in the presence of the lady who so dearly loved to set the one against the other. When one suitor gave her a present, a poem perhaps, she would use it to inflame the jealousy of his rival. She was always testing, nudging away at the limits of the affection offered to her in an attempt to extend her emotional suzerainty, and the strain this imposed on her menfolk was severe. Tension would swell up inside them to explode in quarrels, flaming rows over the most trivial disagreements, fierce verbal threats and duels that could, on occasions, go beyond words – and so it was that after the epic months of the Armada saga, Ralegh and Essex found themselves at loggerheads and resolved to settle their differences in a duel which the Privy Council, only with great difficulty, prevented.

Both the protagonists and the Council contrived to keep talk of the quarrel from the queen, but Elizabeth knew exactly how her rival favourites were feeling. She thrived on such competitions of affection, and continued to encourage them with a capriciousness whose capacity to infuriate seemed deliberate. After the Armada triumph she made Essex a Knight of the Garter, even though he had done nothing to approach the solid labours of Ralegh, and then the following year, when Essex went off to fight bravely, if somewhat ineffectively, in Portugal with Drake, it was Walter Ralegh, just an investor in the expedition, who received the token of royal favour – a fine gold chain bestowed as a pledge of Gloriana's true affection. Sir Roger Williams, the wild Welsh warrior who was Essex's mentor, remarked angrily that *he* deserved the chain as much as Ralegh, but that sort of bluntness cut no ice. The Privy Council ordered that a prize taken on the expedition and disputed between Williams and Ralegh's captains should go to Ralegh.

Now it was that Walter wrote his cutting little verse that poked derision

at the noise and commotion the Earl of Essex made in the wooing of
Queen Elizabeth:

> Our passions are most like to floods and streams.
> The shallow murmur, but the deep are dumb. . . .
> They that are rich in words must needs discover
> That they are poor in that which makes a lover.[1]

Essex was a brook that babbled, while the waters of Walter ran quiet and
deep. Overflowing with words, Essex lacked stability of affection, and
Walter was glad in the summer of 1589 to get away from all the uproar
the earl caused. He went off to visit his estates in Ireland, but even in his
absence the tittle-tattle of court pursued him, for there were not wanting
gossips to explain his departure in terms of his rivalry with the queen's
new young favourite. 'My Lord of Essex hath cashed Mr Ralegh from
court and hath confined him to Ireland,' wrote Francis Allen triumphantly
to Anthony Bacon. Ralegh indignantly refuted such suggestions. 'For my
retreat from court,' he told his cousin George Carew, 'it was upon good
cause, to take order for my prize'[2] – presumably the prize he had disputed
with Williams.

But Walter did protest too much – certainly in the opinion of Sir
William Fitzwilliam, the lord deputy of Ireland. From his castle in Dublin
Deputy Fitzwilliam had conceived a deep jealousy of the fiefdom Ralegh
was carving out down in the south, shipping over his West Country
cronies, rebuilding Lismore Castle as a palace, reclaiming land, and
winning agricultural renown with his tuberiferous innovation, the potato.
So in the disputes and law suits which arose as native Irish and older
settlers tried to regain the lands that Ralegh was parcelling out to his
colonists, Fitzwilliam began taking the side of the petitioners against the
new arrivals, confident that Walter no longer possessed the influence in
London to take issue with him. Incursions into Ralegh's land intensified
as squatters discovered that the lord deputy would back up their claims
against the royal favourite, and late in 1589 Walter, furious, wrote to
Carew:

> If in Ireland they think that I am not worth respecting they shall much
> deceive themselves. I am in place to be believed not inferior to any
> man, to pleasure or displeasure the greatest. . . .
>   When Sir William Fitzwilliam shall be in England, I take myself far
> his better by the honourable offices I hold, as also by that nearness to
> Her Majesty which still I enjoy, and never more.[3]

Walter was quite right. He was not in disgrace, he held all his offices
and, far more important, he retained his nearness to the queen. But times

had changed just the same. Ralegh now had to share his intimacy with the queen with young Essex, and that in itself represented a dilution of power. In the summer of 1589 there were important matters to attend to in the running of his Irish colonies, and so in travelling to Ireland to see to them Walter had certainly not been 'chased' by the earl from court. But neither can the summer progresses of 1589 have been an appealing prospect to Walter with the knowledge that at every halt Essex would be there bounding round Elizabeth like a puppydog, demanding, sulking – and even provoking perhaps yet another scene like the row at North Hall over his sister Dorothy or the quarrel and near-duel of the previous autumn. To escape to the college at Youghal and the green summer meadows of the Blackwater valley represented a welcome release for Walter and to that extent his retreat *was* prompted by the Earl of Essex. Life with Elizabeth was no longer the comparatively uncomplicated experience he was used to. He was listless and weary. He was feeling his age.

> Like to a hermit poor in place obscure,
> I mean to spend my days of endless doubt,
> To wail such woes as time cannot recover,
> Where none but love shall ever find me out.[4]

Melancholy was a fashionable mood. It was the other face of the Renaissance. But Walter's sadness went deeper than mere fashion. He was tired not so much physically as spiritually. He had drained the hedonistic cup of court life to the lees and was still thirsty. He was thrown back on himself 'like to a hermit poor'. Neither in disgrace, nor any longer in the ascendant, Walter was in a limbo, and in his uncertainty he turned to poetry that was rather more thoughtful, and far less fanciful, than anything he had previously written. As the man caught sight of new horizons so did his verse:

> Like truthless dreams, so are my joys expired,
> And past return are all my dandled days;
> My love misled, and fancy quite retired,
> Of all which past, the sorrow only stays.[5]

Ralegh called that sonnet 'Farewell to the Court'. It was a symbolic title, for his farewell was a spiritual rather than a physical matter. He could not afford to be a hermit poor, since his economic future was mortgaged to the queen and depended upon his participation in public life – which meant attendance at the court. But after nearly a decade dancing attendance on Elizabeth, Walter Ralegh obviously realized that there were more things in heaven and earth than a courtier's life could embrace, and in the summer of 1589 he was intent on finding them.

One of his neighbours in Ireland who lived some thirty miles further up the River Blackwater was the poet Edmund Spenser who had been at Smerwick Fort with Lord Grey of Wilton at the same time as Ralegh. We do not know whether the two men met then, but that had scarcely been an occasion for the sort of intellectual friendship which the poets now struck up. Spenser was in 1589 working on *The Faerie Queene*, the epic poem which Sir Philip Sidney and the Earl of Leicester had both sponsored, and one day in that summer of 1589 Ralegh went to seek him out. In *Colin Clout's Come Home Again* Spenser provides a delightful description of the encounter between the poet and the poet-courtier. He recreates in the arcadian convention that was his hallmark the moment when Ralegh came upon him by the Blackwater:

> One day . . . I sat (as was my trade)
> Under the foot of Mole, that mountain hoar,
> Keeping my sheep amongst the cooly shade,
> Of the green alders by Mulla's shore.
> There a strange shepherd chanced to find me out,
> Whether allured with my pipe's delight,
> Whose pleasing sound yshrilled far about,
> Or thither led by chance, I know not right:
> Whom when I asked from what place he came
> And how he hight, himself he did yclepe
> The shepherd of the ocean by name,
> And said he came far from the main-sea deep.[6]

'The Shepherd of the Ocean' – a fine title for Ralegh, wreathed in an irony which Walter may not have grasped, for when it came to oceanic matters he was indeed the shepherd rather than the sheep. He tended to gather his flocks together and send them out on the waters rather than venture himself.

Walter obviously flattered Spenser in the full, open fashion of which he was a master:

> He, sitting me beside in that same shade,
> Provoked me to play some pleasant fit;
> And when he heard the music which I made,
> He found himself full greatly pleased at it.

But Walter had not travelled up the Blackwater simply to sit at Spenser's feet and listen to extracts from *The Faerie Queene*. He had verses of his own that he wanted expert opinion on:

141

Yet, aemuling my pipe, he took in hand
My pipe (before that aemuled of many),
And played thereon (for well that skill he conned),
Himself as skilful in that art as any.
He pip'd, I sung; and when he sung, I piped;
By change of turns, each making other merry,
Neither envying other nor envied –
So piped we, until we both were weary.

For all its archaism, *Colin Clout's Come Home Again* is an exciting fragment of literary history: a rare piece of journalism, it describes the meeting
of two immortals and, through its pastoral conceits, gives us some insight
into the preoccupations of two fine minds at a specific moment of time.
Ralegh, apparently, made no secret of his disenchantment with life at the
court of Queen Elizabeth:

His song was all a lamentable lay
Of great unkindness and of usage hard,
Of Cynthia, the Lady of the Sea,
Which from her presence faultless him debarred,
And ever and anon, with singults rife,
He cried out, to make his undersong,
'Ah, my love's queen and goddess of my life!
Who shall me pity, when thou dost me wrong?'[7]

How like Walter to speak his mind straight out to this comparative
stranger! Spenser had obviously struck a sympathetic chord in him. We
can easily picture the dark-bearded Walter gesticulating violently beside
the Blackwater in the green shade of the alders, expounding to his new
friend all he disliked about life in London and what was wrong with its
focus, the whimsical, ageing queen. And on the basis of what Spenser
wrote we can guess with some precision which poems Walter chose to
declaim. 'A Secret Murder' sums up Ralegh's position in 1589 precisely:

A secret murder hath been done of late,
Unkindness found to be the bloody knife,
And she that did the deed a dame of state,
Fair, gracious, wise as any beareth life. . . .
You kill unkind; I die, and yet am true;
For at your sight my wound doth bleed anew.[8]

In the last line, referring to the popular superstition that a corpse bleeds
when its murderer is brought before it, Walter tried to explain the effect
that Elizabeth was coming to have on him. She had displayed no overt

signs of displeasure, so the murder he complains of was indeed 'secret' and her weapon was nothing sharper than a dilution of kindness – Walter now had to share her affections with another. But simply to be in Elizabeth's presence was now to be reminded of times that never again could be, and Walter was wounded by that to the quick:

> Sought by the world, and hath the world disdained
> Is she, my heart, for whom thou dost endure. . . .

> Steer then thy course unto the port of death,
> Since thy hard hap no better hap may find,
> Where when thou shalt unlade thy latest breath,
> Envy herself shall swim to save thy mind.[9]

This was melancholy with a vengeance – melodrama even, to talk of steering a 'course unto the port of death' because life at court was not as comfortable as it once had been. Walter needed the companionship of Spenser, if only to persuade him to take himself less seriously and, through poetry, Spenser succeeded. Walter Ralegh was not noted for his sense of humour, least of all in his brooding verse, so it was a real triumph that, when *The Faerie Queene* was published, it was prefaced by two complementary sonnets, one by Ralegh to Spenser and one by Spenser to Ralegh that were monuments of wit and playfulness. The affection both men felt for each other was transparent. Ralegh declared that Spenser's poem to *The Faerie Queene* surpassed Petrarch's famous sonnets to Laura, the models on which Renaissance sonnets were based, and even made Homer look to his reputation. Spenser responded in a similar vein: he paid Walter the sincerest compliment possible. He wrote dedicatory sonnets at the beginning of *The Faerie Queene* to a dozen Elizabethan worthies: Walsingham, Hatton, Burghley, the Earls of Oxford, Northumberland, Essex and Ormonde, Lord Admiral Howard, Lord Hunsdon, Lord Grey of Wilton, Lord Buckhurst and Sir John Norris: each worthy was presented with a formal sonnet. But to Ralegh, Spenser gave the warmest, most generous and, quite simply, the best poem of all, 'To thee, that art the summer's Nightingale.'

Spenser had much to thank Ralegh for. Walter had returned to England at the end of 1589 taking Spenser with him to introduce him to the queen, and Elizabeth, flattered by the compliment that *The Faerie Queene* paid her, granted its author a pension of £50, despite Lord Burghley's disapproval. 'All this for a song?' the old lord treasurer exclaimed.

Ralegh could pride himself on playing a major role in procuring the publication of one of English poetry's greatest epics, and he personally had derived a certain benefit from his friendship with Spenser, for he returned from Ireland nursing a little epic poem of his own, the subject of which – 'fair Cynthia' – Spenser had alluded to in his dedicatory sonnet.

As goddess of the moon, the sole queen of the heavens, Cynthia represented a neat deification of Queen Elizabeth, for the sun, the usual symbol of royalty, was too masculine a comparison to make, and the moon, furthermore, controlled the tides, so that 'Cynthia' became a complimentary riposte to 'Water'. With this somewhat convoluted connection in mind, Ralegh decided that he would entitle his epic *The Book of the Ocean to Cynthia*, using the image that he had tried out before in a sonnet in which he had addressed the moon goddess by her alternative name, Diana (born on Mount Cynthus the lady had a choice of titles).

> Prais'd be Diana's fair and harmless light,
> Prais'd be the dews wherewith she moists the ground;
> Prais'd be her beams, the glory of the night,
> Prais'd be her power, by which all powers abound.[10]

That had been a straightforward poem of courtly homage. Now, in 1589, Ralegh had something far more grandiose in mind – a ten or twelve thousand line saga split into a dozen books – and it may well have been to get Spenser's advice on the rather special problems of versifying on such a scale that Walter had gone up the Blackwater to Kilcolman in the summer of 1589, for in *Colin Clout's Come Home Again*, Spenser specifically mentioned 'Cynthia, the Lady of the Sea'.

But *The Book of the Ocean to Cynthia* is one of the unsolved mysteries of Ralegh's life. For though Spenser talks specifically on more than one occasion about a great verse epic written by Walter Ralegh on the subject, and though there are other contemporary references to 'Sir Walter Ralegh's Cynthia'[11] as if some definite corpus of verse existed, we today only have five small fragments preserved by chance among the Cecil papers at Hatfield House. One section is classified, in Ralegh's own handwriting, as being from the Eleventh Book of the Cycle, another from the Twelfth, but what happened to all the other books – or whether, in fact, Ralegh even wrote them, we do not know. The fragments we do possess are ragged and hasty, more the impetuous jottings from which an epic enterprise is built than extracts from the polished, finished whole. They date, so far as can be deduced, from the middle and late 1590s, so do not relate to the Irish summer of 1589, and the most plausible hypothesis is that the project was never completed, and that the *Book of the Ocean to Cynthia* was another offspring – and victim – of Walter's ever-vaulting ambition that was continually leaping off into new adventures before the tasks he had originally set himself were finished. It is difficult to see into

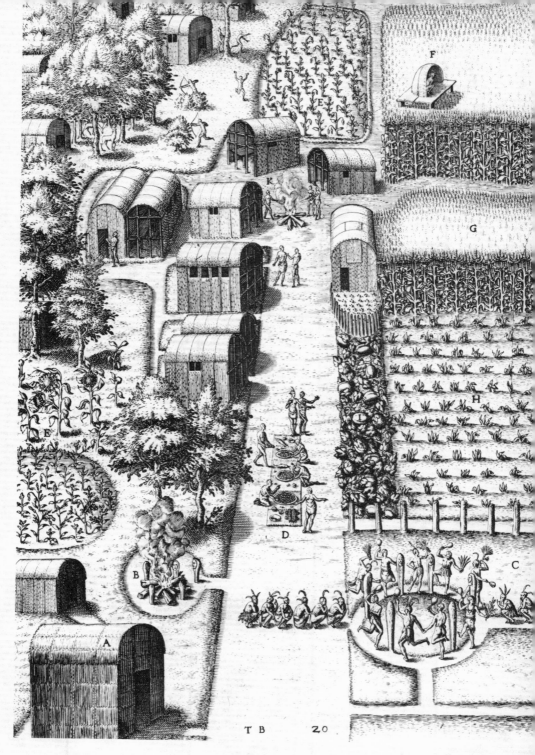

An Indian village drawn by John White. *A* indicates the hut in which the chiefs were buried; *B* the idols in the village praying ground; *C* the recreation area where the Indians gathered to dance; *D* the feasting area; *E* the tobacco crop beside a ring of sunflowers; *F* a scarecrow; *G* the maize crop, and *H* maize seedlings; *I* the pumpkin patch; *K* the communal cooking area for feasts; *L* the river, the source of the village's water

White's drawing of the Indians eating maize sodden in a meat or fish stew –
their standard diet

The Indians make a dugout canoe by burning out the inside of a tree trunk,
having burnt and not axed the tree to the ground. Note the Indians' shaven
heads. All these drawings were turned into engravings by Theodore de Bry
and published in the illustrated edition of Thomas Hariot's *Briefe and True
Report of the New Found Land of Virginia*

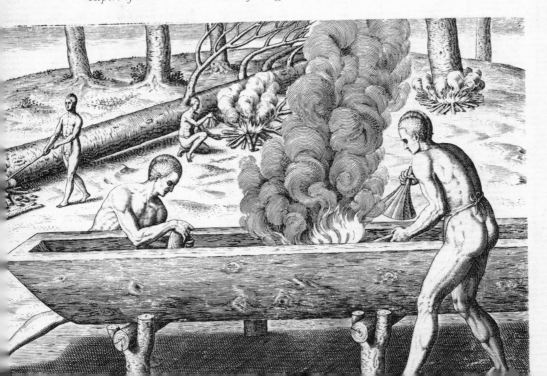

ELIZABETA D. G. ANGLIÆ. FRANCIÆ. HIBERNIÆ. ET VERGINIÆ
REGINA CHRISTIANAE FIDEI VNICVM PROPVGNACVLVM
Immortalis honos Regum, cui non tulit ætas   *Queis ipsa tantum superant reliqua omnia regna,*
Ulla prior, veniens nec feret ulla parem.   *Quantum tu maior Regibus es reliquis*

Elizabeth I, 'Queen, by the grace of God, of England, France, Ireland and Virginia'.

Bess Throckmorton, a portrait
painted after she had become
Lady Ralegh

Walter Ralegh in the Armada
year, 1588, when he was in his
mid-thirties. Behind him *(top
left)* is the moon, emblem of
his goddess Cynthia – Queen
Elizabeth I

which part of his career even Sir Walter Ralegh could have squeezed the creation of over 10,000 lines of epic verse.

He certainly had little time for either the poetic or the real life Cynthia after his return from Ireland in 1590 and 1591. For by then his heart was dedicated to another goddess.

❧ 19 ❧

'Now Serena, be not coy . . .'

'Love', 'desire' and 'passion' had long been the coinage in which the poems of Walter Ralegh dealt, but his wooing had been expedient and his seduction political. The romance, the genuine emotion in the words, had been debased by the purpose for which they had been employed, the flattery of a sovereign by a subject. The sexual allusions of Ralegh's verse had concealed the essence of his relationship with Elizabeth which was chaste: at one level the companionship of lively minds, the enjoyment of shared memories and tastes, at another the tension between a beggar and benefactor. A genuinely sexual component was lacking and, at the profoundest level, so was any element of total personal commitment. Elizabeth could not afford to give herself entirely to anyone, while Walter's personal inclinations were also spread over a wide horizon of different friendships. For sexual release he resorted to the 'Swisser Swattering' that John Aubrey described so graphically.

But in the late 1580s and early 1590s a new and refreshing sensuality transformed the previously platonic verse of Sir Walter Ralegh. No longer did he write poems to be declaimed publicly in the presence of the queen and her court, but he composed private entreaties, low, urgent appeals overflowing with a passion he had never before betrayed on paper. He described the object of his desire with a sexual directness that was almost shocking when compared to the polished purity of his verses to the queen:

> Her eyes he would should be of light,
> A violet breath and lips of jelly,
> Her hair not black not over-bright,
> And of the softest down her belly.[1]

Gone are the metaphysical conceits and contractions of Ralegh's other poems. A vibrant, basic driving force flows through the rhymes as Walter unashamedly revels in the lips, hair and belly of his mistress:

Now Serena, be not coy,
Since we freely may enjoy
Sweet embraces, such delights
As will shorten tedious nights . . .
Let's then meet
Often with amorous lips, and greet
Each other till our wanton kisses
In number pass the days Ulysses
Consum'd in travail. . . .[2]

After ten years of theatrical royal courtship and casual sexual encounters, 'love', 'desire' and 'passion' had evidently taken on a new meaning for Sir Walter Ralegh.

The object of his affections was a soft, deceptively gentle-looking beauty called Elizabeth Throckmorton, who had been sworn as one of the queen's maids-of-honour in her twentieth year back in 1584. She and Walter had been moving in the same circles and seeing each other frequently for some time, but it was not until the early 1590s that Ralegh's verse took on the fresh tone that indicated the depth of his feelings for her. Sir Walter Ralegh was in love, and that love was to have the most far-reaching consequences so far as every aspect of his life was concerned.

We have a good idea of what Walter looked like when he met Elizabeth Throckmorton – his own Bess – for he commissioned a portrait of himself in the Armada year, 1588. In the top left-hand corner is a small moon, the Goddess Cynthia, and his clothes are all of black and white, the colours of Elizabeth. But the man himself is no moon-struck ethereal lover of the Virgin Queen. Ralegh looks tough, self-confident and matter-of-fact, with more than thirty years of experience very definitely stamped on the firm cast of his features. His double-pearl earring does not gild effeminacy but on the contrary brings out his dark Celtic virility. Beneath his curling moustache his lips are full and sensuous. He has bulk, solidity, texture – a quality of rawness which is disconcerting and which his piercing stare makes even more unsettling.

How did Bess Throckmorton react when that gaze was turned on her? We know that she succumbed, that she accepted Walter's invitation to 'enjoy sweet embraces, such delights as will shorten tedious nights' but we know too that she was no silly maiden surrendering helplessly to the blandishments of the great Sir Walter. She had a will and spirit of her own – a mind that Walter loved her for – and her energy and originality survive to this day in the spelling of her letters, turbulent to the point of eccentricity, but redeemed to comprehensibility by a charming phonetic logic: 'I assur you trewly I never desiared nor never wolde desiar my lebbarte [liberty] with out the good likeing ne advising of Sur W.R.'[3]

Bess Throckmorton had a delicate chin, a high forehead, pouting lips and misty almond eyes which made her one of the ornaments of the Elizabethan court, but for all her beauty she was far from empty-headed. She was to prove herself a wife who stood steadfastly by her husband and a mother who fought fiercely for her children, and her grit was in evidence from the first.

She had come to court back in 1584 at an inauspicious time, only a few months after her cousin Francis had been executed for his involvement in a Babington-like Catholic conspiracy to kill Elizabeth and place Mary Queen of Scots on the throne. But though his plot bore the Throckmorton name, it did not smear the family reputation, for Bess was the daughter of Sir Nicholas Throckmorton, Queen Elizabeth's first ambassador to Paris, while her brother, Sir Arthur, was a good and faithful courtier. In his diary, we can read how Sir Arthur worked on his sister's behalf until, on Sunday 8 November 1584, he could record with satisfaction: 'I came and dined at Hampton Court. My sister was sworn of the Privy Chamber'.[4]

Well might Sir Arthur feel relieved, for his sister had been a financial burden on him. £500 set aside for her marriage portion had been put out in the hope of providing some sort of regular income, but it had been lost irrecoverably[5] and all she had left as a dowry was a farm down in Mitcham.[6] So prestige apart, Bess's admittance to the ranks of the queen's maids-of-honour was an occasion to be celebrated. Henceforward she would be a charge on the royal household's budget and Sir Arthur would not have to worry so much about marrying her off.

But if Bess Throckmorton's admittance to Queen Elizabeth's Privy Chamber lifted the problem of her matrimonial future from her brother's shoulders, it posed special problems for the lady herself and for Walter Ralegh when he came to pay court to her. For Queen Elizabeth guarded the virtue of her ladies with a fierceness that verged on paranoia. She treated every smirch on their purity as though she herself had been despoiled, regarding herself as being *in loco parentis* to her maids-of-honour. Living constantly in the royal presence involved frequent contact with favourites like Sir Walter Ralegh and Robert, Earl of Essex, but what happened to any lady who dared to give herself to one of these men was vividly demonstrated soon after Ralegh returned from Ireland. For in 1590 Robert Devereux paid court to Frances Sidney, the daughter of Sir Francis Walsingham, the spy-catcher. The widow of Sir Philip Sidney, she was a quiet, unobtrusive lady, who, of all possible mates, represented the least threat to the relationship between the earl and his queen, but when Elizabeth heard of the couple's secret marriage she was beside herself with fury, banishing Essex from the court until she could get over her annoyance.

This was a sobering warning to Walter Ralegh who was at that time courting on his own account and revelling in his mistress's 'violet breath and lips of jelly'. He was playing with fire and the sight of his enemy getting burnt could only serve to remind him of the risks he was running himself.

So Walter and Bess's love affair had, by the very nature of the positions each held in Queen Elizabeth's entourage, to be secret, and this in itself tells us something of the strength of the feelings that swept the couple away, for both of them were mature individuals – Walter was in his late thirties, Bess her late twenties – and both were quite aware of the enormous risk they were running. Both from comparatively humble backgrounds, they had much to lose if they offended Elizabeth, and they realized what they might suffer if they followed through the emotions that directed them towards each other. But pursue love they did, laughing to scorn the risks they ran – and enduring, in due course, the consequences of their passions with a fortitude which bore witness to the depth of their love.

Bess Throckmorton, both in herself and in the events she provoked, represented a crucial stage in the transformation of Sir Walter Ralegh, the education which changed a spoilt and one-dimensional dilettante into a fully mature man capable of genuine feeling. The queen's favourite became a woman's husband, and in crossing the great gulf between those two roles, Sir Walter Ralegh became a different person, a rounded human being. The dissatisfaction he had come to feel with existence at court crystallized, and in Bess Throckmorton he now discovered the new dimensions he sought. As his sonnets like 'A Secret Murder' and 'Like to a Hermit Poor' had demonstrated, he was tired of the charade of paying court to Elizabeth, and he was tired too of the casual physical release which constituted the extent of his relations with the opposite sex. He was sated with 'affection' and was thirsty for 'love' – and it was love, not affection, that Bess gave him, as he explained in verse. Though 'Swisser-swattering' had its pleasures:

> Desire attained is not desire,
> But as the cinders of the fire –
> As ships in ports desired are drowned,
> As fruit once ripe, then falls to ground,
> As flies that seek for flames are brought
> To cinders by the flames they sought. ....
> As if wild beasts and men did seek
> To like, to love, to choose alike. [7]

Walter himself had been guilty of the very fault that he castigated in his final couplet: he had confused physical attraction with true love. But his courtship of Bess Throckmorton swayed his life – and his poetry – onto more authentic tracks. He came to see animal passion, and political philandering, for what they were.

It is Arthur Throckmorton's diary that provides us with the most reliable traces of Bess and Walter's romance. Their love affair, the creation of two hearts and spirits, was by its nature a private thing. Out of sight of Elizabeth – and the rest of the court – they met and made love, sharing together snatched moments of passion that grew into undying love. Then in the high summer of 1592 Bess conceived, and what had been a secret could be hidden no more. Poor Arthur Throckmorton, rightly worried by the consequences that could flow from his sister's liaison with the queen's favourite, noted down anxiously the sequence of events. When he was particularly worried he resorted to French – a flimsy disguise – and it was in that language that, on 19 November 1592, he scribbled down '*le jour quand je savoye le mariage de ma soeur*'[8] (the day when I came to know of my sister's marriage).

How long before that date in 1592 the wedding took place remains a mystery. It would seem likely that they went through some secret ceremony in the autumn of 1592 soon after they discovered that Bess was pregnant, and then broke the news to brother Arthur after the event. It has been suggested that the couple might have married secretly as early as 1588, but the impossibility of the captain of the guard concealing such a liaison with a royal maid-of-honour for over four years at the Elizabethan court rules out so premature a date: the speed with which the gossips latched onto the affair after 1592 demonstrated the efficiency with which such juicy titbits of information would get rooted out.[9]

Sir Arthur Throckmorton was evidently agitated. More serious considerations aside, he had no little difficulty in spelling his new brother-in-law's name, trying both Rawlley and Rayley before settling on Raelly in his journal. At the end of November 1592 he had an interview with Walter, and then, with Christmas coming up, he went to some trouble and expense to curry royal favour with a couple of expensive presents for the queen: a waistcoat purchased for £9 on Christmas Eve and two ruffs costing £5 and presented on New Year's Eve. Would such peace offerings placate the royal wrath? Only time would tell.

In the meantime Walter prepared himself for what was obviously a major turning point in his life. His marriage and the child Bess was carrying could not help but alter his life-style. Were the queen, when she found out about his love match, to take his behaviour hard, he could expect a substantial loss of income and prestige, perhaps even banishment from court. Were Elizabeth, after an outburst of displeasure, eventually to resign herself to the new state of affairs, life would still be very different in Durham House with a wife, baby, nursemaid and all the trappings of domesticity intruding upon the camaraderie of his bachelor existence. Whichever eventuality occurred – and Walter, from his behaviour, obviously anticipated the latter – it would involve a change of pace, a slowing down.

It was not an inappropriate alteration for a man approaching forty to make, but it was a change none the less, and Walter was now becoming increasingly conscious of his age. The onward march of age consuming youth, the years relentlessly pursuing each other to destroy the promise that went before, this was the melancholy theme that was coming to haunt him more and more – paradoxically at the very moment when his love for Bess was providing him with ever more vigour and youth. The seriousness of the emotions she aroused stimulated other profundities:

> Oh cruel Time, which takes in trust
> Our youth, our joys, and all we have,
> And pays us but with age and dust,
> Who in the dark and silent grave,
> When we have wandered all our ways
> Shuts up the story of our days.[10]

Walter Ralegh was to take up that last verse again on the night before his death and, with the addition of two lines, create for himself a memorable epitaph. The solemnity was there, even in the throes of sexual passion, waiting for Walter to turn to it again in his last moments.

Deep currents were flowing inside the gilded courtier who, after more than a decade of favour, was approaching the first great climacteric of his career. Most men experience but one such climax – if that; Walter Ralegh was to live through three, each one more testing than the previous one and each one drawing out of him even finer qualities which owed their increased strength to his previous challenges. Even as Walter invited his Serena to 'be not coy' he thought on 'conquering Time'. He was, in Elizabethan terms, on the threshold of middle age, no longer the casual young adventurer who had left Alice Goold to fend for herself and her daughter ten years earlier. He was embarking on marriage and fatherhood with all that that implied for his relationship with Elizabeth, and as well as his new responsibilities, there were one or two old ones too which he still had to worry about.

✥ 20 ✥

The Lost Colony

id it occur to Sir Walter Ralegh in the summer of 1590, when he was so shortly himself to become a father, that little Virginia Dare, the grand-daughter of Governor John White, should, if she were in good health on the other side of the Atlantic, be getting ready for her third birthday? There should by now on Roanoke Island in Pamlico Sound be a veritable community of expatriate Englishmen, women and children, cultivating their fields, drying, perhaps, some tobacco leaves for sale to fashionable English courtiers, developing their own patterns of commerce with the local population and building their own special tissue of social practice and customs.

Whether or not Ralegh thought particularly about young Virginia Dare – and if he did not, her grandfather John White can have thought of little else – he was concerned about the fate of the colony that bore his name. The Armada and the cancellation of the relief expeditions of 1588 had been a great disappointment, but there was no obvious reason why the colonists should not have been able to survive through that summer and then, with a good harvest, live snugly through the winter following. In fact, a Spanish patrol ship had in June 1588 been despatched up the coast as far as Chesapeake Bay by the governor of Florida to examine the English settlement that posed a potential threat to Spanish power in the Caribbean. And, almost a year after Governor White had left for England, at just about the same time that the 1588 relief ships should have been arriving, the Spaniards sighted the City of Ralegh and noted down the existence of a shipyard, a sloop and every sign of activity.[1]

No one in England knew about this report at the time, of course, but it accorded with general expectations. In March 1589, the Company of the City of Ralegh was augmented by a group of nineteen men who injected fresh capital into the enterprise in return for shares in the colony and perpetual freedom of trade without taxes or customs within the territories colonized under Ralegh's patent.[2]

It must have seemed a fair deal to Governor White who accepted its terms on behalf of the colonists and, in truth, the new partners were prestigious. They included Thomas Smythe, the famous Customer Smythe, who administered the customs of London to his own considerable profit, and also his son, another Thomas, who was later to play a prominent role in the East India Company and in the Jacobean settlement of Virginia.

Those true friends to colonization, William Sanderson and Richard Hakluyt, undertook in this new enlarged organization the roles of liaison officers with Ralegh who, having sunk heavy investments of both time and money into Virginia, was pleased to have his burden lightened. He retained his overlordship and his general responsibility for the colony's activities,[3] maintaining his patent and rights to establish other colonies, but he reserved to himself and to his own heirs only one fifth of all the precious metals that might be found.

Walter was, in essence, withdrawing somewhat from the Virginia venture. For nearly a decade he had been the spirit of the enterprise. But by 1589 he was devoting more time to poetry, there were the prospects of marriage in the offing, he was developing an interest in Guiana and the city of El Dorado that the Spaniard Sarmiento de Gamboa had told him of, there was his Irish colony, and, too, there were the intimations that he might not always be Queen Elizabeth's most favoured son. Whatever his personal inclinations, it was only right to hand the hundred men and women who were risking their all for the City of Ralegh into the care of a wealthy and respected corporation comparatively immune to the fluctuations of royal caprice.

In Ireland for a good part of 1589 Walter did not throw himself with his customary abandon into the task of succouring the colonists of Roanoke Island, but when, in February 1590, there was an embargo, in anticipation of a Spanish attack, placed on ships leaving England's ports, he acted swiftly through William Sanderson to secure an exemption for John White to sail with his supply fleet and on 20 March 1590, the governor finally got away from Plymouth in a little fleet of three ships.

It was almost inevitable, of course, that these ships should be privateers, and that the admiral of the little fleet, Abraham Cocke, should have accepted the inconvenient task of ferrying Governor White to Virginia solely as a device to secure exemption from the general shipping embargo. But William Sanderson and Thomas Middleton had also equipped two other vessels under a Captain Spicer to carry relief supplies to the City of Ralegh, and once Cocke had done the privateering he wished to in the Caribbean, the ships met up off Cape Tiburon, Haiti, and set sail northwards. On 15 August 1590, they anchored off Port Ferdinando in five fathoms of water and to their delight saw smoke rising over Roanoke Island. The next morning, 16 August 1590, the English fleet hoisted out two little boats and, in anticipation of meeting the worthy corporation of the City of Ralegh, both Captains Cocke and Spicer joined Governor White in the landing party. They spotted on the way to Roanoke that smoke was also rising from Hatarask Island and, wondering if the colonists might have moved there, turned aside to investigate. They found nothing and with darkness falling decided to go back to their ships and set out again next morning.

But 17 August 1590 proved a black day indeed. For a north-east wind was blowing in against an ebb tide and raising fierce breakers that capsized Captain Spicer's boat. Toppled out into the cold water and probably wearing heavy armour, Spicer and six of his rowers were drowned. It was an ill omen, and it was only with great difficulty that Captain Cocke and John White persuaded their sailors to continue to Roanoke which, after the disaster, they did not reach until nightfall.

There on Roanoke Island, in the lurid flicker of a forest fire, came the most affecting moment in all the long years that Walter Ralegh struggled to plant an English city in America. As Governor White later wrote with touching simplicity: 'We let fall our grapnel near the shore, and sounded with a trumpet and call, and afterwards many familiar English tunes of songs, and called to them friendly. But we had no answer.'[4] There was no answer because there was in that Roanoke forest no one to recognize the English songs and hymns that Governor White and his little band sang plaintively into the thin night air, and next morning the landing party discovered that the smoke they had presumed to be rising from the City of Ralegh was, in fact, caused naturally by the sun burning up dried grasses and rotten trees. Then they walked on to the site of the settlement that White had founded only to leave three years earlier, and came across fresh native footprints, as well as the beginning of a word carved on a tree 'CRO'. The colonists' palisade and cabins were all overgrown with grass and weeds and pumpkin creepers, and on a post nearby was carved 'in fayre Capitall letters' the full name CROATOAN. Governor White had agreed with the colonists before he left that, if they should move to a new settlement, they should leave the name of their destination carved on Roanoke, and that, if they had been compelled to depart in adverse circumstances, then they should carve as well a Maltese cross beside it.

There was no cross carved. But other sights were definitely depressing. Cocke's sailors found five chests broken open, obviously by Indians. Three of them belonged to White himself, torn apart to expose to the elements the personal possessions he had left against the day when he would return to govern the colony. There were his precious books, their pages ripped from their covers to moulder and curl. The fine framed maps and pictures he had intended to adorn the walls of the governor's mansion were all 'rotten and spoyled with rayne' and, most poignant of all, his grand suit of armour specially transported across the Atlantic to be worn on ceremonial occasions, lay in the sand 'almost eaten through with rust'.

Returning sadly to their ships White and Cocke agreed that they would sail south to Croatoan Island next day to see if the colonists were there as their carved sign indicated. But that night a storm blew up and tore away all but one of the ship's anchors. It was now impossible for the vessels to stay moored off Roanoke or to moor off Croatoan either, and White had reluctantly to agree to a direct voyage south. After wintering in the Caribbean, some repairs – and, of course, some prizes – it would be possible to return to Croatoan in the spring to search thoroughly.

But the weather frustrated this unlikely-sounding plan, for the wind blew up so strongly from the north-west and west that the relief fleet had no choice but to be driven out into the Atlantic and to head for England, where they arrived before the end of October 1590.

What happened to Walter Ralegh's lost colony remains a mystery to this day. The evidence of the carving and the absence of a cross suggests that the settlers moved to Croatoan Island in good order, though the unfinished CRO could indicate some haste. Manteo had friends and relatives on Croatoan and, if the Spanish report of activity on Roanoke in June 1588 is reliable, the spring of 1589 seems the most likely date of the move, possibly after a winter of some severity. Since Croatoan was right on the coast and some thirty miles down the route that relief ships would take up from the Caribbean, it offered better lookout facilities than Roanoke. The chests which poor John White found split open so savagely had been carefully buried along with heavy cannon, cannonballs and iron bars so, transportation difficulties apart, the colonists could not have been expecting an unfriendly welcome in their new home.

But whether the hundred Englishmen, women and children actually reached Croatoan and what happened to them there if they did, we do not know, for there were no more serious attempts to search for them in the sixteenth century. The new shareholders in the corporation of the City of Ralegh appear to have found other, more profitable outlets for their risk capital, and even Governor John White seems to have resigned himself to the loss of his family, hopes and plans.

Only Sir Walter Ralegh, despite the special problems that the declining years of Elizabeth's reign brought him, made any real effort to look for his colonists, and then somewhat belatedly. He tried to sail past Virginia on his way home from Guiana in 1595 and he despatched Samuel Mace in 1602 to search Croatoan Island – to no avail. It was an end to the enterprise less worthy than its beginning, and in 1625 Francis Bacon published in his essay 'Of Plantations' a judgement on the venture with which it is difficult to disagree. He did not mention Walter Ralegh or Virginia by name, but he did go to some lengths to point out the danger of expecting rapid profits from such a plantation, the need to choose the very best sort of personnel to man it, and the futility of trying to seduce the natives with trifles 'instead of treating them justly and graciously' – summing up his argument with the damning indictment: 'It is the sinfullest thing in the world to forsake or destitute a plantation once in forwardness; for besides the dishonour, it is the guiltiness of blood of many commiserable persons.'[5]

No single man tried so hard as Sir Walter Ralegh to establish an English-speaking nation in the New World in the sixteenth century and his efforts provided a fine example to more successful emulators in later years. Yet, in the last analysis, his planting of Virginia cannot be said to have occupied the centre of his attention for very long. It was an aspect of his quenchless intellectual curiosity. It was a subdivision of his maritime business activities. It was one weapon among several in his campaign against Spain. It was one of his many ambitions and quests for power – and the men and women who committed themselves to the City of Ralegh undoubtedly suffered from not possessing the full and undivided energies of the man after whom their settlement was named. He was the butterfly and they were the moths. He fluttered on – and they were burned.

But what, in fact, did happen to them? The settlers of the Jamestown colony of 1607, who were naturally curious about the fate of their predecessors, could find no solid traces of their whereabouts, but they were told stories about the white people's assimilation with Indian tribes, and this explanation of what happened to the Lost Colony seems the most likely one, unless it be that the colonists, despairing of ever being succoured by White and Ralegh, set out to sea in their pinnace and all perished in a storm. For Ralph Lane's history of misunderstanding with the local population had been continued by John White before he left in 1587, and, despite the good offices of Manteo, the colonists were probably attacked at quite an early stage by hostile Indians. Though the menfolk would have been slaughtered, the women and children would almost certainly have been spared and incorporated into the Indian community, intermarrying and adopting willy-nilly the lifestyle of their savage masters. There are, in fact, in the present day Robertson County of North Carolina survivors of a tribe of Indians called the Croatoans whose language incorporates incongruous words of Elizabethan English. Some of them have fair hair and blue eyes – and some even carry the same surnames as Sir Walter Ralegh's lost colonists.[6]

❧ 21 ❧

The Revenge

Although in 1591 Sir Walter Ralegh was wooing his Bess with some of his finest poetry, it was an example of his prose which became in this year his first publication. As a gentleman amateur he was always to keep his verse a private matter, particularly when his theme – his love for Bess – made anonymity essential. But his first work of prose, though initially veiled for form's sake, brought him as a writer very much into the public eye. What he wrote was a stirring adventure story which became the best seller of the year and which stands to this day as one of the classics of one genre in English literature.

Walter can even be credited with adding a whole episode to the popular history of Britain, for his tale was of Sir Richard Grenville and the last fight of the *Revenge*, an event of not the slightest strategic significance in the long naval war between England and Spain, but plucked from obscurity by Ralegh's dramatic prose to stand confidently in our Island Story alongside the singeing of the king of Spain's beard and the defeat of the Spanish Armada. Had not Sir Walter Ralegh rushed forward in 1591 to act as his cousin's bard even as the news of the *Revenge*'s destruction reached England it is doubtful whether this costly, pointless and totally avoidable defeat would have been accorded quite the glamour that it has.

Writing in London as the reports flowed home, Walter managed to inject into his prose the impression that he was an actual participant in the battle, and his interest was certainly more than incidental, for he had been named in January 1591 vice-admiral of the fleet with which Lord Thomas Howard was to attack the Spanish treasure fleet in the Azores, and it was only when Queen Elizabeth changed her mind and ordered him to stay at home that his cousin Richard Grenville took his place. Grenville had been Walter's surrogate in the voyages to Virginia and now he went in his stead to the Azores, while also in the squadron for good measure was that stout warship the *Bark Ralegh*.

Though Bess Throckmorton can hardly have complained, Walter himself must have been bitterly disappointed at Elizabeth's ban on his sailing, for this vice-admiralship would have been his first active command in the sea war, and the chances of both fame and profit looked high. So weak were the Spaniards that King Philip had actually ordered his silver fleet in 1590 not to risk the voyage from the West Indies across to the Azores, so if the English managed to remain off those islands in force they could, in 1591, look forward to the arrival of two treasure fleets.

The English strategy was to have two small but strong and mobile squadrons lying in wait for the prey they anticipated capturing with ease. One would patrol the Spanish coast. The other would prepare an ambush further out in the Atlantic, off the Azores, which would be the Spaniards' first landfall after the West Indies, and it was with this squadron of about a dozen vessels that Sir Richard Grenville sailed as Ralegh's substitute in the *Revenge*.

But in 1591 the English made a mistake which not all subsequent chroniclers of these years have avoided either. They underestimated Spain's power of recovery after the Armada débâcle. Though English privateers brought home in 1590 the greatest haul of captured Spanish vessels ever – ninety, one for every day of the high summer's campaigning season – this was not a sign that King Philip was capitulating. He was retrenching, rather, and retrenching intelligently. Learning the lessons of the Armada he had ordered twelve new galleons to be built on the English model, low and snug in the water, guns bristling from their bellies and with the towering superstructures that had made the Armada galleons topheavy drastically reduced. These twelve capital ships were to be known as the Twelve Apostles and they were built quickly and well. The largest of them all, the *St Philip*, was completed and launched with remarkable speed, the *St Barnabas* soon joining her, and these were among the score of prime fighting ships which, in the summer of 1591, were despatched to deal with Lord Thomas Howard and his squadron lolling arrogantly off the Azores.

By the end of August 1591 Howard had been at sea for six months, which represented the limit of the average sixteenth-century ship's endurance. By the end of that time cracks between the timbers would need caulking and, far more important, the ballast would need changing, since those parts of the hold of a Renaissance vessel not taken up with ammunition and supplies were filled with sand, shingle and pebbles to maintain the ship's stability. Into this ballast flowed much of the filth of the ship – drainage from the decks, leftover food, vomit, and often, incredibly in view of the open ocean all around, sewage, for it was not always appreciated that there was a connection between the 'pestilential funkes' which began to rise from the bilges after a few months at sea and that scourge of naval health, typhus – ship's fever. As microbes and rats multiplied beneath the decks there would be nothing for it but to beach the ship, empty the ballast, wash out the vile-smelling interior of the hold with vinegar and then to load up again with fresh, clean shingle. It was while Lord Thomas Howard and his squadron were engaged in precisely this distasteful task of 'rummaging' on the sparsely inhabited island of Flores at the far west of the Azores group in August 1591 that they heard of the approach of the Spanish fleet – and not the slow treasure fleet which they were expecting but a veritable armada fresh from the coast of Spain, far superior in both numbers and firepower to their own little handful of leaking vessels manned by plague-shattered crews.

Lord Thomas Howard quite rightly decided that discretion was the better part of valour and ordered his ships out to the open sea. But such a retreat was too simple and less than honourable for Sir Richard Grenville, who had been a little late shifting the sick among his crew back from shore to the *Revenge*, and who now engaged the entire Spanish fleet in the suicidal battle which became the subject of Sir Walter Ralegh's vivid and masterful prose.

It was not simply out of family loyalty that Walter wrote, indeed he may even have been commissioned to take up his pen as a government spokesman. For as news of the catastrophe reached England – the *Revenge* was the only English warship to be captured by the Spanish throughout the very many years of the naval war – rumour put a poor construction on the withdrawal of Howard and even suggested that Sir Walter Ralegh might challenge him on his return for leaving his kinsman alone to the mercy of the Spaniards. So Ralegh himself was the ideal man to put out the Government's side of the story, and it is a measure of Walter's skill that while immortalizing one of the more obstinate and fractious of his relatives, he succeeded in remaining true to the facts of the case as well. Drawn from interviews with eyewitnesses and *Revenge* survivors carried out by himself and the Privy Council, together with other semi-official letters and reports, Ralegh's *Report of the Truth of the Fight about the Iles of Acores this last Sommer* – rushed off the presses in pamphlet form and circulating all over England within a matter of weeks – was a triumph of journalism: fresh, dramatic, analytical and accurate.

The acid test is his reconstruction of the moment when the master of the *Revenge* explained to Grenville how, by turning and going around the Spanish ships, he could rejoin the English fleet in safety. 'But Sir Richard utterly refused to turn from the enemy, alleging that he would rather choose to die than to dishonour himself, his country and Her Majesty's ship.'

Ralegh indulged in no special pleading on his cousin's behalf: 'But the other course had been the better and might well have been answered in so great an impossibility of prevailing. Notwithstanding, out of the greatness of his mind, he could not be persuaded.'

Grenville was not left in the lurch, in other words. He could easily have escaped with the rest of the English fleet, but he chose to pick a fight – and Walter Ralegh made it clear that the choice was Grenville's and Grenville's alone. The great *St Philip* was the first to attack him with her broadside of thirty-three guns 'three tier of ordnance on a side and eleven pieces in every tier'. For a whole afternoon, much of the night and all the next morning the bombardment continued.

All the powder of the *Revenge* to the last barrel was now spent, all her pikes broken, forty of her best men slain, and the most part of the rest hurt. . . . The Spanish were always supplied with soldiers brought from every squadron, all manner of arms and powder at will. Unto ours there remained no comfort at all, no hope, no supply either of ships, men or weapons; the masts all beaten overboard, all her tackle cut asunder, her upper deck work altogether razed and in effect evened, she was with the water but the very foundation or bottom of a ship, nothing being left overhead either for flight or defence. . . .

Now came the ultimate gesture, only slightly marred by the inconsistency of Ralegh's previous statement that all the gunpowder was exhausted 'to the last barrel'.

Sir Richard, finding himself in this distress . . . commanded the master gunner, whom he knew to be a most resolute man, to split and sink the ship, that thereby nothing might remain of glory or victory to the Spaniards . . . and persuaded the company, or as many as he could induce, to yield themselves unto God and to the mercy of none else. . . . The master gunner readily condescended and divers others, but the captain and master were of another opinion and besought Sir Richard to have care of them. . . .

Against the helplessly wounded Sir Richard's 'greatness of mind', and to the infinite distress of the master gunner who 'would have slain himself with a sword had he not been by force withheld and locked into his cabin', the *Revenge* was surrendered on generous terms. For two or three days the Spanish admired their strange adversary as he sank towards the grave, cheerfully crunching up the glasses in which they gave him wine, according to one Dutch account, until the blood ran from his mouth, then swallowing the splinters without flinching – such is the borderline between bravery and madness. Then, after his death, there arose a storm which shattered the victorious Spanish fleet, killing hundreds, showing, said Ralegh, how it 'pleased God to fight for us and to defend the justice of our cause against the ambitious and bloody pretences of the Spaniard who, seeking to devour all nations, are themselves devoured'.

As for the suggestion that Lord Thomas Howard might have done more to help Sir Richard Grenville, Ralegh concluded that it would have 'ill-sorted or answered the discretion and trust of a general, to commit himself and his charge to an assured destruction, without hope or any likelihood of prevailing, thereby to diminish the strength of Her Majesty's navy to enrich the pride and glory of the enemy.'

Thus did Sir Walter Ralegh propagandize on behalf of both his kinsman and authority, and though for a century now it has been Alfred Lord Tennyson's commemoration of 'the fight of the one and the fifty-three' that has been the most venerated shrine to this extravangantly futile episode of Elizabethan history, it is Walter Ralegh who built the true memorial to Richard Grenville. Francis Bacon is usually credited with establishing the rhythms and style of modern English prose, but in Ralegh's brief account of the last fight of the *Revenge* was born, half a dozen years before the publication of Bacon's Essays, a direct and forceful mode of literary expression that strides clean through the convolutions of the established Elizabethan written word.

Ralegh's pamphlet made him the toast of the court at the Christmas celebrations of 1591, and in the very next month, January 1592, he received a New Year's present of outstanding generosity – a ninety-nine-year lease from the crown of the fine castle at Sherborne in Dorset and the rich manors surrounding it.

It was a jewel of a reward, but it did not come entirely out of the blue, for Ralegh had been trying for some years[1] to obtain this country seat so conveniently located half-way along the road between London and the south-western ports of Plymouth and Falmouth. On each of his frequent business trips between the capital and the west he rode past the fine twelfth-century castle and ranged the deerpark nestling beside it in Sherborne's delicate limestone valley. The castle had been built by one of the great medieval fighting bishops, Roger of Sarum, and now in the sixteenth century it still belonged to his less powerful successors in the See of Salisbury.

The prospect of the great Sir Walter Ralegh covetously surveying the lush green acres belonging to a mild and toothless bishop suggested to Sir John Harington a biblical parallel, and in his *Nugae Antiquae* he tells of Ralegh, riding up one fine day from the West Country to London, this castle being right in the way, he cast such an eye upon it as Ahab did upon Naboth's vineyard, and once above the rest being talking of it, of the commodiousness of the place, and how easily it might be got from the bishopric, suddenly over and over came his horse, that his very face, which was then thought a very good face, ploughed up the earth where he fell.[2]

The story of proud Ralegh's 'very good face' ploughing up the earth of Sherborne must have been a most popular one in sixteenth-century England, for even though, after the Reformation, there could be little justification for an Anglican bishop already amply endowed with living accommodation enjoying a wealthy and fortified palace like Sherborne, there was no more justification either for a courtier already amply endowed with royal favour receiving such a plum. Adrian Gilbert, an astrologer and rather a toady, said that Ralegh's rapid and intimate contact with the Sherborne earth betokened possession not misfortune, but it took some time for his prophecy to come true.

Queen Elizabeth had no objection to robbing her bishops. In fact, she rather enjoyed it. The problem at Sherborne was to find a bishop meek enough to consent to being robbed. So for three years the bishopric of Salisbury lay vacant while a candidate was sought who might be willing to resign Sherborne to Ralegh, and when the right man was found Walter got a manor from the See of Bath and Wells thrown in for good measure. The Bishop of Bath and Wells had had the indiscretion in his old age to get married, an indulgence Queen Elizabeth deeply resented in a cleric, especially in a bishop and even more in an old one. As a ransom the old man had to consent to the rich lease of Wilscombe Manor being presented to Walter to make up with the Sherborne lands a veritable little Ralegh empire in Dorset.

Well might Walter present his queen with a fine jewel worth £250 for finding a bishop willing to lease out Sherborne at £360 a year. Both the cost of the jewel and the rent were small prices to pay for such a magnificent castle and the extensive estates which became for the next decade one of the great joys of Ralegh's life. If his roots were in Hayes Barton and his magnificence in Durham House, his favourite haunt soon became Sherborne. He lavished all his reserves of time and money on getting the old castle repaired and then, across the river, he had plans drawn up for a smaller, modern, more comfortable and intimate residence set in the midst of ornamental gardens and leading directly into the deer park where he could engage in the pastime of all true country gentlemen, the chase.

Sherborne meant more to Walter Ralegh than just a rural retreat. He regarded it as his home, an organic, natural base to be enjoyed not alone but in the company of a total family: wife and children, servants and relatives, the foundations, in fact, of a dynasty – and this was the irony of Queen Elizabeth's gift to her favourite in January 1592. For the pregnancy of Bess Throckmorton, who had since the previous November been known to a growing number of friends as Bess Ralegh, threatened ruin to the very happiness that Sherborne offered Walter Ralegh as a family man, and in this connection the curse pronounced by a former bishop of Salisbury, St Osmund, took on a gruesome relevance. For St Osmund had promised destruction to any who alienated the estates of Sherborne from his bishopric, and the lay successors of Ralegh at Sherborne laughed at his warning to their cost: three died on the scaffold; two died in prison; a sixth was murdered. And Walter himself was to discover more quickly than any of them how effective the curse of the old holy man could be.

❧ 22 ❧

'In the Walls Captived'

The brief note for 19 November 1591, recording in Arthur Throckmorton's diary that his sister Bess had married Sir Walter Ralegh, was the beginning of a remorseless sequence of events. Bess's pregnancy and the arrival of Ralegh's first legitimate child meant that the spring and summer of 1592 would be a testing time. The secret would come out and the queen's anger would be terrible, and so through the winter months of 1591-2 the main participants in the drama prepared for the coming trial in their respective fashions.

Having done his best with his fine Christmas and New Year's gifts to the queen to establish a credit balance in the royal favour, Sir Arthur Throckmorton turned his attention to his hen house. As if searching for some portent in their gestatory activities, he noted down how his white hen, dun hen and blue hen laid eggs at night on 13, 14 and 16 January respectively, and then in February he wrote urgently to his new brother-in-law. Bess's time was approaching. Visibly pregnant and only a few weeks away from giving birth she had had to retire from court.[1]

Walter himself, meanwhile, was also away from court, though his absence was less discreet. The sound and fury that he was generating indeed had all the character of a diversionary manœuvre, for he was down at Chatham working night and day to prepare a naval expedition intended to take him out onto the high seas at precisely the moment that Bess was expecting her baby. He would be out of the country when his first legitimate child arrived.

Having taken the decision to stand by Bess, Walter was scheming desperately to soften the blow that the discovery of his love would deal to his relationship with the queen. If he could contrive to carry out some exploit abroad and return home with fame and profit, it would be difficult for the queen not to pardon him. So in the winter of 1591-2, as Bess's pregnancy advanced, Walter threw himself into the organization of an expedition to accomplish what Lord Thomas Howard had failed to achieve the previous year, the capture of the king of Spain's treasure – and also, incidentally, to avenge the defeat of Grenville and the *Revenge*. The enterprise had been organized on a joint-stock basis, with the queen contributing two ships and £3,000, George, Earl of Cumberland six vessels, London citizens two, Carew Ralegh one and Walter one also.

But though Walter's contribution in ships was small, he was the expedition's moving spirit and major shareholder, for he had invested almost all his capital and borrowed a large sum – over £10,000[2] – to get the fleet manned and equipped. So deep had he dug into his pocket, that he had had to ask the Government to pay him for the *Ark Ralegh* which he had presented to the queen's navy before the Armada, and he was duly reimbursed with £5,000 for the ship. He was in sole command of the fleet, but the expedition took longer to organize than he had anticipated and then, probably about the time that Bess, on 28 February 1592, went to lie in at her brother's Mile End house and await her accouchement, Queen Elizabeth changed her mind. Yet again she decided that her Walter should not risk his life on the high seas and that someone else must take his place, on this occasion Sir Martin Frobisher.

Walter's carefully laid strategy seemed in ruins, but there was one chance of escape which he could snatch at. His replacement as commander, Sir Martin Frobisher, was a stiff-necked martinet, who was not at all popular with the sailors, many of whom had been attracted by the prospect of following Walter Ralegh in person, and so it was eventually decided that Walter would travel with the fleet as far as the coast of Spain in order to help his substitute play himself into his command.

But clever little Robert Cecil smelt a rat. Sir Walter was too hasty, uncharacteristically anxious. People had been talking. There were rumours to the effect that he had contracted a secret marriage with one of the ladies-in-waiting, while Bess Throckmorton had been absent from court for a suspiciously long time. So Sir Robert wrote to Sir Walter a probing letter, and Sir Walter replied with a gross and palpable falsehood:

> I mean not to come away, as they say I will, for fear of a marriage and I know not what. If any such thing were, I would have imparted it unto yourself before any man living; and therefore I pray believe it not, and I beseech you to suppress what you can any such malicious report. For I protest before God, there is no one on the face of the earth that I would be fastened unto.[3]

It was a shameless lie and, worse, a foolish one. For Robert Cecil was not a man easily deceived, nor one who forgave easily when he was, and for Ralegh to compound his deceit by enlisting Cecil's help 'to suppress what you can' of the rumours circulating was the height of impudence.

But this letter was the essence of the man. An ordinary mortal might have confessed to Cecil's suggestions weakly, humbly or with dignity, might have tried to evade the issue, or might simply have made a curt denial.

Yet Walter rejected the simple reply. He blustered, he elaborated. Instead of one lie he told many. He even burdened himself with an unsolicited obligation he was bound to fail in – that of telling Cecil the truth about his marital situation 'before any man living'. It was a typically grandiose effort – pure Ralegh and the reason why so many men distrusted him. Vices that others concealed, he displayed proudly.

On 29 March 1592, with Walter still away, came the fateful entry in Sir Arthur Throckmorton's diary: 'My sister was delivered of a boy between 2 and 3 in the afternoon. I writ to Sir Walter Ralegh and sent Dick the footman to whom I gave him 10s,'[4] and less than a fortnight later, on 10 April 1592: 'Damerei Ralegh was baptised by Robert, Earl of Essex and Arthur Throckmorton and Anna Throckmorton.' Essex was a strange godfather – on the face of it the most unsuitable possible, for no one had a better political motive for disclosing the news of Walter's indiscretion to the queen. But Arthur was a friend and client of Essex, and the earl, who had suffered cruelly himself just two years earlier from the discovery of his own secret love match was, for all his faults, a warm-hearted and generous young man. Ralegh's romantic dilemma was a weapon that it was beneath the earl's honour to stoop for. They were both knights jousting for the same favour – and both suffering under the same tyranny.

There was reason too, and characteristic arrogance, behind the archaic name with which the infant Ralegh was christened – Damerei. For John Hooker, the West Country genealogist whom Walter had hired to dignify his family tree, had come up with the information that the Raleghs were descended from the Plantagenets through the marriage of Sir John de Ralegh to the daughter of Damerei Clare,[5] and so baby Damerei was turned into a living symbol of the Ralegh's connection with the blood royal – a dangerous parallel to make at a dangerous time.

Nor was his new wife keeping her head down, for on 27 April 1592, young Damerei was put out to a wet nurse while Bess went back to court to resume her place among the queen's maids-of-honour as if nothing had happened. Her impudence was the equivalent of her husband's lies to Robert Cecil, if not worse, for the lady she was hoodwinking was infinitely more irascible – and more powerful – than Burlegh's dispassionate, intelligent son.

Sir Walter, meanwhile, was down in the West Country about to put to sea and on 6 May 1592, he sailed from Falmouth. But if he had hoped to slip quietly away from England for a period, his plans were foiled, for a royal order came for him to return immediately, and though he stayed with his ships until they had safely reached Spain at Cape Finisterre, the tone of Elizabeth's summons brooked little delay. By the middle of May Walter Ralegh was back in Plymouth and the game was up. By this time the secret of his love was a secret no more.

With the possible exception of the Earl of Essex no courtier of Queen Elizabeth's was more fiercely subjected to the scrutiny of public attention than Sir Walter Ralegh. Informers would pick on the most circumstantial detail to weave into malicious gossip, and, so far as Walter's romance was concerned, the evidence became daily less circumstantial. On 11 May 1592, Sir Arthur Throckmorton had had an interview with Henry Carey, Lord Hunsdon, who as lord chamberlain was responsible for the maids-of-honour and on 19 May the marriage settlement between Walter and Bess was formalized after Throckmorton had negotiated with Sir George Carew representing Ralegh. On that same day Sir Arthur paid Lady Ralegh's nurse fourteen weeks wages at 2 shillings a week – 28 shillings, and on 21 May 'the nurse and the child came hither' – to Arthur's house at Mile End. A week later Sir Walter was back in town and 'the child and the nurse went to Durham House'. Ralegh was obviously keen to see his son and apparently felt little concern about the attention that the baby's presence at Durham House would attract.

By now the queen's officials were enquiring into the whole affair and Lord Chamberlain Hunsdon had already taken a statement from Sir Arthur Throckmorton's wife Anna, Damerei's godmother. On 31 May Sir Robert Cecil took Walter Ralegh into custody and then allowed him to return to Durham House where Sir George Carew, Walter's cousin, became an informal sort of jailer. On 3 June it was Lady Ralegh's turn to be detained – by Lord Chamberlain Hunsdon who asked Sir Arthur Throckmorton for a statement, which he made on 10 June.

But here is a mystery. Though the secret liaison between Walter Ralegh and Bess was the talk of London, and though Elizabeth's agents, Cecil and Hunsdon had actually arrested the couple, the queen herself made no public comment on the behaviour of her favourite. There was no outburst of wrath as there had been when Essex married secretly, and Elizabeth was content for the moment for the delinquents to suffer nothing severer than mild house arrest. Not for another two months, until the beginning of August 1592, did Elizabeth react publicly, and in the middle of this strange lull, on 27 June 1592, her gift of Sherborne Castle and its estates to Ralegh[6] was formally confirmed.

What was she thinking? She was certainly not indifferent to the couple's action. It touched her very closely, and her long weeks of indecision were a token of the friendship that she felt for Sir Walter Ralegh – a fine gauge, indeed, of precisely what sort of emotions he aroused in her. Had she felt for him less, she would have wasted no time in punishing him. Had she felt for him more, as she felt for Essex, alternately enraged and entranced by him, she would also have reacted on the spur of the moment.

But her relationship with Sir Walter Ralegh merited more careful handling. He was an old friend, and in 1592 she had few enough of them. Leicester had died in 1588, Walsingham in 1590 and Hatton, her besotted bell-wether, in 1591. With the exception of old Burghley, whose days were numbered, Sir Walter Ralegh was the one close companion left from the stirring days of the 1580s when clever Robert Cecil and temperamental Robert Essex had been but youths on the periphery of events. Those two men were to be the opposing poles of her reign's declining years, and in the context of their rivalry Walter Ralegh represented a personal ally who could stand by her – and between them. Her long-matured friendship with him was not something to be cast aside lightly. And so she waited. Walter's deception was unkind, but it was not the end of the world, and if he could acknowledge his fault it could, with time and understanding, be overcome. The formal confirming of her gift of Sherborne Castle to him showed that, in the long term, Walter could look forward to continuing friendship and favour.

Yet although Queen Elizabeth's silence was an olive branch extended, with as much humility as a queen could show for over two months to a friend too important to be cast aside in an access of fury, Sir Walter Ralegh did not respond to the royal gesture, for swept off his feet by his love affair and the intrigue surrounding it, he had manœuvred himself into a position from which his terrible pride would not let him retreat. Like a schoolboy he had been caught out badly and could not bring himself to admit it. As he had blustered to Cecil rather than acknowledge the truth, so now he omitted to apologize to Elizabeth. His pride, the fatal arrogance that damned him in the eyes of almost everyone except the queen, now soured his relationship with her as well.

Nor was it only Walter's arrogance that provoked punishment. His Bess had a spirit of her own – like had attracted like – and, in the weeks while Queen Elizabeth's judgement was suspended, Walter's wife made no effort to mitigate the consequences of her deception. Her behaviour, indeed, indicated that she was as unrepentant as her spouse, and so Queen Elizabeth waited in vain for either of the couple to come to her to beg forgiveness.

Sir Walter Ralegh's proud heart was, if anything, prouder in these weeks of waiting than ever before, for though found out in his appalling falsehoods to Cecil, he now had the gall to write to Sir Robert, claiming his help against the activities in Ireland of Sir William Fitzwilliam – Cecil's own cousin. Sir William had again been taking advantage of the cloud over Walter's fortunes to nibble away at the Ralegh estates in Munster as he had done in 1589. 'It is a sign how my disgraces have passed the seas,' complained Ralegh. 'So I leave to trouble you at this time, being become like a fish cast on dry land, gasping for breath, with lame legs and lamer lungs.'[7]

To make some human gesture of contrition simply was not Walter's way. He had for ten years played the part of proud Ralegh, and he could not change now. He was a player to the core of his being with the player's ultimate inability to convince. He had passed the point where his audience would suspend their disbelief – and this made particularly ill-judged his one attempt to display some regret to Elizabeth. Hearing one day in July that the queen was due to land at Blackfriars he went up to his little turret room in the battlements of Durham House and:

> having gazed and sighed a long time at his study window, from whence he might discern the barges and boats about the Blackfriars Stairs, suddenly he brake out into a great distemper, and sware that his enemies had of purpose brought Her Majesty thither, to break his gall asunder with Tantalus' torment. . . .
> And as a man transported with passion, he sware to Sir George Carew that he would disguise himself and get into a pair of oars to ease his mind but with a sight of the queen; or else, he protested, his heart would break. But the trusty jailor . . . flatly refused to permit him. . . .
> Upon this dispute they fell out to choleric outrageous words, with striving and struggling at the doors . . . and, in the fury of the conflict, the jailor had his new periwig torn off his crown.

The witness of this strange charade was the poet Arthur Gorges.

> At last they had gotten out their daggers, which, when I saw, I played the stickler between them, and so purchased such a rap on the knuckles as I wished both their pates broken.
> And so with much ado they stayed their brawl to see my bloodied fingers. . . .

Gorges set down his account of the incident in a long letter to Sir Robert Cecil dated 26 July 1592,[8] in an attempt to prove that 'Sir W. Ralegh will shortly grow to be Orlando Furioso if the bright Angelica persevere against him a little longer'.

But that fanciful reference to the book Sir John Harington had translated the previous year betrayed Ralegh's hand in the artifice, and the postscript to Gorges' tale – written out on a little slip of paper and affixed to the letter with wax so it could be pulled off easily before being passed on to the queen – destroyed the whole strategem entirely: 'If you let the Queen's Majesty know hereof, as you think good, be it. . . .'

Devising such tricks, and threatening to resort to mindless violence, scarcely exhibited true remorse. If that was the best Walter could do it was not good enough, and the buzz of court gossip heightened. One anonymous letter writer with a talent for innuendo seems to have had a working knowledge of Walter's poetry:

S.W.R., as it seemeth, have been too inward with one of Her Majesty's maids. All think the Tower will be his dwelling, like hermit poor in pensive place, where he may spend his endless days in doubt. It is affirmed that they are married; but the queen is most fiercely incensed, and, as the bruit goes, threateneth the most bitter punishment to both the offenders. S.W.R. will lose, it is thought, all his places and prefer-ments at court, with the queen's favour; such will be the end of his speedy rising, and, now he must fall as low as he was high, at the which many will rejoice. I can write no more at this time, and do not care to send this, only you will hear it from others. All is alarm and confusion at this discovery of the discoverer, and not indeed of a new continent, but of a new incontinent.[9]

One can almost hear the malicious chuckle of Sir Edward Stafford as he wrote to Essex's Anthony Bacon, on 30 July 1592. 'If you have any-thing to do with Sir Walter Ralegh, or any love to make to Mistress Throckmorton, at the Tower tomorrow you may speak with them.' Just over a week after that prediction was made it was proved well founded. '*Ma Soeur*,' wrote Sir Arthur Throckmorton on 7 August 1592, resorting to French again '*s'en alla a la tour et Sir W.Raleigh*'. So Queen Elizabeth had finally acted. She was forced into a course she had hoped to avoid, and it was Elizabeth's resentment at that as much as her anger at Walter's original deception that made her punishment, when it came, so severe.

The queen went off on her summer progress leaving the lovers to sweat out the plague-ridden weeks of August in the Tower. Did Walter Ralegh realize quite how serious his plight was? The tone of the letter he despatched to Robert Cecil scarcely suggests it:

My heart was never broken till this day, that I hear the queen goes away so far off – whom I have followed so many years with so great love and desire, in so many journeys, and am now left behind her, in a dark prison all alone . . . I that was wont to behold her riding like Alexander, hunting like Diana, walking like Venus, the gentle wind blowing her fair hair about her pure cheeks, like a nymph; sometime sitting in the shade like a goddess, sometime singing like an angel, sometime playing like Orpheus.[10]

That list of garbled similes was intended for the eyes of the queen, but its facetiousness was aimed at a woman whose anger was coquettish, who had punished him in play. It was not the letter of a man who acknowledged the deep offence he had caused, and the verse Walter composed after his confinement was equally lacking in remorse.

> My body in the walls captived
> Feels not the wounds of spiteful envy,
> But my thralled mind, of liberty deprived,
> Fast fettered in her ancient memory,
> Doth nought behold but sorrow's dying face.
> Such prison erst was so delightful
> As it desired no other dwelling place,
> But time's effects, and destinies despiteful
> Have changed both my keeper and my fare.
> Love's fire and beauty's light I then had store,
> But now close-kept, as captives wonted are,
> That food, that heat, that night I find no more.
> Despair bolts up my doors, and I alone
> Speak to dead walls, but those hear not my moan.[11]

There was self-pity in those lines, but very little self-reproach. The great days of Sir Walter Ralegh's court career were ended, but it was some time before he could bring himself to admit how and why that end had come. He had risen proud like Lucifer, and now, like Lucifer, he must fall and learn to live with what had brought him down.

23

Madre de Dios

Walter Ralegh was released from the Tower of London rather more rapidly than he – or Queen Elizabeth – had expected. For on 8 September 1592, exactly a month after Walter and Bess had been imprisoned, an East Indian Carrack, the *Madre de Dios*, was brought into Dartmouth by the English fleet that Ralegh had organized and had hoped to sail with. She was a floating castle with no less than seven decks towering one above the other, a crew of over six hundred men, and a cargo of immense value – the richest privateering prize captured by English sailors in Queen Elizabeth's reign – and her arrival in port provoked an orgy of looting, embezzlement and waste. Dartmouth and the West Country were in chaos. 'To bring this to some good effect,' wrote Sir John Hawkins in desperation to Lord Burghley, 'Sir Walter Ralegh is the especial man,'[1] and so out of the Tower, though still with a guard, came the especial man to create some order in the ports and among the people who were especially his own.

The capture of the *Madre de Dios* had been a vindication of the strategy that Walter Ralegh had devised. While Martin Frobisher cruised with his squadron along the coast of Spain, occupying the patrols which had caught Howard and Grenville unawares the previous year, Sir John Borough, Frobisher's deputy lay in wait off the Azores with the rest of the fleet including Ralegh's *Roebuck* and the ships of George, Earl of Cumberland. On 3 August 1592 he sighted a huge carrack, not a Spanish ship from the Caribbean but a Portuguese vessel which had come across the Indian Ocean and round Africa all the way from the East Indies. To the English her origins were immaterial – Portugal was, in any case, little more than a province of Spain – and the first ships to open fire were Ralegh's *Roebuck* and Borough's *Foresight*, a royal warship. The battle ended with the Earl of Cumberland's men boarding the carrack to discover in her hold the most fantastic booty: 537 tons of spices, 8,500

hundredweight of pepper, 900 hundredweight of cloves, 700 hundredweight of cinnamon, 500 hundredweight of cochineal, 59 hundredweight
of mace, 59 hundredweight of nutmeg, 50 hundredweight of benjamin,
15 tons of ebony, two great crosses and another large piece of jewellery
studded with diamonds, alongside chests overflowing with musk, pearls,
amber, calicoes, drugs, silks, ivory, tapestries, silver and gold.[2] It was
more than a king's ransom – half a million pounds worth of treasure,
according to Sir John Hawkins, treasurer and controller of the navy.

But by the time the final reckoning came to be made back in London
there was only £141,200 plus the precious stones and the ship itself left to
be shared out among the investors – for the Earl of Cumberland's men
had started pillaging the ship the moment they boarded it and though Sir
John Borough had taken charge of the prize for the return voyage to
England, the scent of its priceless cargo seemed to waft across the waters
as it arrived in Dartmouth so that in no time the port was a St
Bartholomew's Fair. Men came by horse and ship from all over the West
Country, and down from London rode jewellers and merchants with
ready cash for the bargains of a lifetime. Thomas Myddleton made a big
killing and privateers like John Watts and Abraham Cocke were much in
evidence.[3] Sailors were trading pieces of amber for tankards of ale.

Sir Robert Cecil was the man the Privy Council chose to restore law and
order and, more important, to retrieve from the free-for-all the share of
the booty the queen was entitled to as one of the shareholders in the
expedition. But little more than 5 feet tall, puny and deformed, Cecil
was scarcely the man to bring order to carousing mobs of seamen, and so
Sir John Hawkins' 'especial man' was released from captivity to help
discipline the looters. 'If I meet any of them coming up,' swore Ralegh, 'if
it be upon the wildest heath in all the way, I mean to strip them as naked
as ever they were born, for it is infinite that Her Majesty has been robbed
and that of the most rare things.'

It was infinite too that Walter himself had been robbed, and his release
on the queen's business seemed to give him an unlooked for opportunity
to safeguard his own. Robert Cecil, who could sniff out the looters he met
on the way by the perfumes in which they were soused, was infected with
the fever of the great auction. 'My Lord, there never was such spoil!' he
wrote back to London in amazement, estimating there were 'above two
thousand buyers hard at work! . . . Fouler ways, desperate ways, no more
obstinate people did I ever meet with.'[4]

When Walter Ralegh arrived Cecil's wonder increased. 'I assure you,
Sir, his poor servants, to the number of 140 goodly men, and all the
mariners came to him with such shouts and joy as I never saw a man more
troubled to quiet them in my life.' Walter was back among his own and

Robert Cecil, who had only seen him in a court setting, was impressed. When Walters' half-brother Sir John Gilbert greeted him it 'was with tears on Sir John's part', and Cecil had to admit that Walter's standing, 'I do vow to you before God, is greater among the mariners than I thought for.'

In any other context Sir Robert Cecil cared not a fig for what ordinary sailors thought. Walter Ralegh was welcome to his mariners' cheers. But down in Dartmouth in the autumn of 1592 Walter's particular strengths were the qualities that the task in hand called for, and so the two ill-sorted men pulled valiantly together in harness re-establishing order and retrieving for the queen a surprising amount of her booty. Back to London Walter sent a note to Lord Burghley with some flattering comments on the efforts of the old lord treasurer's son.

> I dare give the queen £10,000 sterling for that which is gained by Sir Robert Cecil's coming down: which I protest before the living God, I speak of truth, without all affection or partiality, for (God is my judge) he hath more rifled my ship than all the rest.[5]

Though written in an attempt at jest those last words were true. With the seamen and hucksters being the principal gainers from the *Madre de Dios*, the shareholders in the expedition took their profit from Sir Walter Ralegh. Never formally charged before being thrown in the Tower, Walter was never formally fined, simply deprived now of the dividends which could have rebuilt Sherborne Castle, re-ordered his Irish estates and financed in addition the expedition to Guiana and El Dorado that was coming to be one of his ambitions. After Walter Ralegh had laboured honestly down in Dartmouth in the autumn of 1592 under the impression that every pearl or bale of silk he snatched back from the profiteers represented an addition to the common pool from which he would share, Queen Elizabeth stepped in at the end of the year to allocate the takings in a fashion that bore no relationship to the sums the various shareholders had staked.

Walter and his associates, notably his brother Carew, whose joint investments had totalled £34,000, were reimbursed £36,000, which made no allowance for the interest charges on the £11,000 Walter had borrowed, nor for the ships they had risked, notably the *Roebuck* which had first attacked the *Madre de Dios*. 'Besides', complained Ralegh, 'I gave my ships' sails and cables to furnish the carrack and bring her home, or else she had perished.'[6]

£36,000 was a particularly galling sum in that it was exactly the same as that awarded to George, Earl of Cumberland who had only staked £19,000 in the expedition and whose ships had, in the opinion of Sir

John Borough, allowed the *Roebuck* and the *Foresight* to bear the brunt of the attack and had then taken advantage of their exhaustion to nip in at the end of the battle and start plundering. Ralegh was incensed that instead of returning to Dartmouth, Cumberland's ships had made for Plymouth, Portsmouth and even Harwich where they could unload their loot without being taxed by the royal commissioners.[7]

Nor was this the end of the inequity, in Walter's opinion, for now the London merchants who had had their arms twisted by the queen to put up £6,000 unwillingly, received back £12,000. 'I that adventured all my estate,' objected Ralegh, 'lose of my principal, and they have double. I took all the care and pains, carried the ships from hence to Falmouth and from thence to the north cape of Spain; and they only sat still and did but disburse £6,000 out of the common store, for which double is given to them and less than mine own to me.'[8]

But it was Elizabeth, who had risked just two ships and £1,800, who took the lion's share of the *Madre de Dios'* spoils – 50 per cent of the proceeds, some £80,000. 'Fourscore thousand pounds is more than ever a man presented Her Majesty as yet,' wrote Walter to Burghley before he seriously imagined that Elizabeth might actually take for herself anything like that amount. 'If God have sent it for my ransom, I hope Her Majesty of her abundant goodness will accept it.'

Walter had pronounced his own sentence. However unfair the distribution of the profits of the *Madre de Dios* might appear in normal joint stock terms, the only loser on the venture was Ralegh himself, and there was a solid and obvious reason for that. Walter was indeed lucky, in the circumstances, that Elizabeth had punished him out of money he had never possessed, that she actually paid back his capital, and that she did not force him to dig into his own resources or give Sherborne back to her. Men had paid far higher prices for the royal displeasure, and Queen Elizabeth was extremely displeased.

When his work in the west was completed, Sir Walter Ralegh went back to the Tower. The *Madre de Dios* had been the very success he had worked and hoped for to wipe away Elizabeth's anger at his marriage, but the coup won him no dispensation. The capture of such treasure might have helped to calm Elizabeth's annoyance at his secret love-making, but his real offence, his deep, stubborn, unbending pride – this was a fault it was to take him five long years to purge.

Part 4

❈

1592-7 Disgrace

Sir Walter Ralegh was one that Fortune had picked out of purpose, of whom to make an example, or to use as her Tennis Ball ... for she tossed him up and out of nothing, and to and fro to greatness, and from thence down to little more than to that wherein she found him, a bare Gentleman.

Sir Robert Naunton, 'Fragmenta Regalia'

❧ 24 ❧

Sherborne

Queen Elizabeth was merciful. She decided to release Walter Ralegh and his Bess from the Tower of London in time for them to enjoy the Christmas of 1592 at liberty. But they could not celebrate the festival at court, nor join in the New Year celebrations that were the high point of the Elizabethan social round, for that life was now behind them. Down to the country they must go fortunate, at least, to have been given the castle and estates of Sherborne, – and more fortunate still to have been allowed to keep them. Through the long years of disgrace this Dorset home was to become the new centre of their world, the focus of energies previously devoted to public life. Sir Walter Ralegh the courtier and man of affairs was to become Sir Walter Ralegh the squire.

His new rural home, an authentic, working fortress, was in a remarkable state of preservation, with its fine turreted gatehouse and its soaring keep groined with strong dog-toothed arches. 'There be,' wrote Leland in his *Itinerary*, 'few pieces of work in England of the antiquity of this that standeth so whole', and Walter promptly set about embellishing the 400-year-old building to his tastes. But it was to the south of the castle, to the gardens on the other side of the river, that the Raleghs came most strongly to be drawn. Although in the eighteenth century Capability Brown was to dam the River Yeo to create a flat crescent of water, it is still possible to recapture the delight of walking in the park that Walter and Bess Ralegh knew and loved so well – 'the greatest refreshment to the spirits of man', as Francis Bacon wrote in his essay on gardens – and it was in these gardens, on the site of a little hunting lodge, that Walter decided to have a new home built to mark the beginning of a new stage in his life.

It looked rather like a pepper pot, the Raleghs' up to date residence, on which work started in 1593, and it was quite the most imposing palace for miles around. Each of its brick walls which rose to a graceful double-curved gable was pierced by almost a dozen lead-paned windows – very new-fangled indeed – but each of the house's four corners bulged out into a hexagonal buttress echoing the old-fashioned fortified turrets on the looming castle across the river. Instead of battlements, the roof was a forest of chimneys and heraldic beasts, stone Ralegh Roebucks squatting proudly, scanning the estates their master owned, and formal gardens ran across the little valley to connect the old palace to the new. In their centre, the river was just partially dammed to provide, in the middle of the promenade, a little pool – not the stagnant sort of pond that Bacon condemned for 'making the garden unwholesome and full of flies and frogs', but one whose 'water be in perpetual motion, fed by a water higher than the pool' – a source of 'great beauty and refreshment'. In this delightful setting Walter had planted flowers, trees and shrubs brought back from abroad by sailors who knew of his interest in exotic flora and fauna. Thomas Hariot was to be a frequent guest at Sherborne and it must have been a particular pleasure for him to wander through Ralegh's park – the closest approximation Elizabethan England possessed to the modern Kew Gardens.

Bess Ralegh had written during her captivity in the Tower 'wee ar trew in ourselfes I can asur you' and the two years following Walter's disgrace were the proof of that. This was in many ways the happiest period of the Raleghs' marriage when, resigned to their fate, the couple threw themselves into building a quiet family future together. We hear no more of baby Damerei who, we must presume, succumbed to the rigours of sixteenth-century disease or, more probably, to sixteenth-century medicine. But in these early months of 1593 was conceived the son who, on All Saints Day 1593, in the church of Lillington near Sherborne, was to be christened with his father's name that affection shortened to 'Wat'. The arrogance of poor Damerei's royal nomenclature was not repeated – Walter's fall marked the beginning of a re-education of the old Ralegh – and when another son came, a dozen years later, he was to be christened after his uncle Carew who, in these Dorset years, was a frequent visitor at Sherborne.

Walter's life-style became altogether more rustic as his elder brother introduced him into the society of his county friends. It had been as Walter's protégé that Carew had taken over the governorship of Portland Bill on the coast and the wardenship of Gillingham Royal Forest that nestled up into the corner of Dorset which separated Somerset from Wiltshire; but now it was Walter who was beholden to Carew for taking him under his wing. He came to be on close terms with local luminaries like Sir George Trenchard and Sir Ralph Horsey, two landowners who were deputy lieutenants of the county; he went out hunting and hawking with local farmers like John Fitzjames, one of the worthies of Sherborne, and he was able to spend more time with relatives like Charles Thynne, a nephew of his living over at Longleat, and Adrian Gilbert, his half-brother.

Adrian, in fact, became at this time Walter's right-hand man in the elaboration and beautification of the Sherborne estate, the chief surveyor and architect as it were, devoting much of his energies during the next half dozen years to the 'making and planting of his [Walter's] walks and gardens'.[2] He made a good job of it and earned quite a name for himself as a landscape designer, for Robert Cecil was later to commission him to lay out water courses in his new park at Theobalds and to stock them with fish and fowl.[3] But Adrian was in due course to fall out with Walter, suing his half-brother in 1610 for £4,653, a sum made up of alleged debts dredged from a vindictive memory that extended as far back as a loan of £10 'when Sir Walter Ralegh first went to the court' and covering also £700 of his own money that he claimed to have spent on the Sherborne improvements. Adrian was the odd man out of Katherine Champernowne's five sons, a dabbler in astrology and alchemy who kept to himself and who nursed resentment against his more extrovert and successful brothers with their quartet of knighthoods won by their own merits.

Walter's other choice as an agent at Sherborne turned, in the long term, equally sour, though in the 1590s he worked as a resourceful servant of the Raleghs. John Meere had been the reeve for the Bishop of Salisbury when the church owned Sherborne, and Walter saw the advantage of recruiting him to his own service. He should have taken warning, however, from the fact that Meere had been found guilty of clipping coin, so that Walter had to get the man out of prison before he could take up his duties. Within ten years Meere was actively working against Ralegh in Sherborne, even having the gall to refuse to accept dismissal and disputing the authority of the bailiff Walter eventually appointed in his place.

Still, this was a comparatively minor and far from unusual inconvenience in the life of a sixteenth-century country gentleman. Walter enjoyed the role of a squire. It was, after all, the style of existence his father had attempted but, as a tenant, had never totally achieved. For all his seafaring connections and ambitions, Walter derived deep satisfaction from the land, just as Francis Drake returned from the ocean to establish himself on his own patch of West Country soil. Walter spent his days riding to hounds or with falcons, passing his evening at home or drinking and talking in the homes of other squires like Ralph Horsey and George Trenchard. He took a pride in his parkland, gardens, orchards and the new woodlands he had planted – even though he held the estate on a lease and not a full freehold, and he took a parochial interest in local government affairs, the search for Catholic priests, the ever-present need to maintain local levies and the coast defences. He still held his West Country offices, the wardenship of the stannaries and the vice-admiralship of the west and exercised those in a leisurely fashion – being out of favour he was less pestered by the Government or by suitors hoping for his patronage – and privateers continued to scavenge the shipping lanes on his behalf, though now he had neither the credit nor the burning inclination to organize big expeditions in the old style.

But Walter Ralegh was no ordinary squire and the circumstances of his enforced retirement could not help but give him food for thought. The question he had to decide was the degree to which he would continue to guide himself by the interests that had been his lodestars for so long – the pursuit of royal favour, and intellectual enquiry. About the latter there could be no argument. Exploration, debate, discovery, these flowed in Walter Ralegh's bloodstream. He could no more stop wondering about new lands, new concepts, new experiences than could Thomas Hariot or Henry Percy, Earl of Northumberland – both of whom stood by Walter throughout his disgrace with unwavering steadfastness: Walter went on seeing them just as he went on writing verse – and, indeed, took advantage of the peace of his rustic retreat to write more poems than ever.

But the pursuit of royal favour was a less obvious option. Queen Elizabeth expected that her Walter would fight to regain his closeness to her. He retained his royal offices, and had only been suspended, not dismissed, from his duties as captain of the royal guard. He still enjoyed his income from the monopolies Elizabeth had bestowed on him. So if he cared to throw himself once more into the maelstrom of Elizabethan court life, Sir Walter Ralegh could anticipate some sort of restoration of his former greatness. Elizabeth might never again entrust him with the intimacy taken for granted in the months before his fall, but she would forgive much.

The trouble was – as the poems Walter Ralegh wrote at Sherborne indicated clearly – that the prospect of forgiveness and restoration was less than inviting to the former favourite. Walter had paid a price for his greatness at court, a spiritual price, and reflecting on what he had achieved in his years of favour he could not help wondering whether it had all been worthwhile. He had learnt to be a courtier, but at the expense of the genuine emotion and love he experienced with Bess. He had sacrificed much in the service of the queen. He had, from one point of view, wasted ten years before discovering the fulfilment that every brainsick couple discover when they love and marry young, and he poured out his resentment in verse:

... skill that's with so many losses bought,
Men say is little better worth than nought.
... yet henceforth I may know
To shun the whip that threats the like again.[4]

Once bitten, twice shy. Walter looked back on the life he had lived with
Queen Elizabeth and did not like what he saw. Their relationship had
been 'brought forth in pain and christened with a curse'.

And you, careless of me, that without feeling,
With dry eyes, behold my tragedy smiling,
Deck your proud triumphs with your poor slave's yielding
    To his own spoiling.
But if that wrong, or holy truth despised,
To just revenge the heavens ever moved,
So let her love, and so be still denied,
    Who she so loved.[5]

This was hardly poetry for the eyes of the queen, to beg heaven, as
Ralegh did, to curse Elizabeth's affections so that they would be rejected
by whoever she turned them on – just as she had 'with dry eyes' beheld
his own sadness smilingly. It was a rejection, a turning of the back on
memories that were too bitter to be recalled without pain. Both in content
and in style the poem was the very opposite of the political compliments
Walter had paid to Elizabeth for so many years. It was most impolitic,
positively dangerous, and yet now, for the first time since his juvenile
sally on George Gascoigne's behalf in 1576, Walter took steps actually to
get 'My first born love unhappily conceived' published along with other
poems that he had composed with Arthur Gorges. *The Phoenix Nest*
anthology came out during 1593 and provided Ralegh with a platform for
his diatribes against Elizabeth. His name did not appear beneath his own
verse, so it was a veiled renunciation, but it was a renunciation none the
less, and one that the fallen favourite could count on the queen and her
courtiers reading and understanding.

Yet Walter Ralegh did, as so often, protest too much. There was
genuine feeling behind his anger, but there was as well the shadow of the
actor, the theatricality he was never to shake off. As Elizabeth had
acknowledged by her reluctance to pronounce sentence upon Walter's
deception of her, there was more to his friendship with the queen than
coquettishness or infatuation. Their twelve years together could not be
shrugged off by whipping up the weeping mask. Reality was more complex
than that, and so, whatever Walter might spit out as he dashed off his
bitter, melancholy poems of 1593, he had to admit that there was an

element of dishonesty in his rejection of Elizabeth. He had to acknowledge his own foolishness in destroying his relationship with the queen in so cavalier a fashion, and this meant that, alluring though his retreat to Sherborne might be, he must eventually tread the boards of Whitehall, Hampton Court, Greenwich and Nonesuch again.

There were obvious economic reasons why Walter should try to recapture royal favour and the bounty that flowed from it. There was, too, his pride that spurred him to recapture all the eminence he once possessed. But it was a personal impulse deeper than either of those motives which drove Sir Walter Ralegh from his disgrace in 1593 and 1594 back towards his queen, and the vehicle for his impulse was, as ever, poetry – though on this occasion its form was more ambitious than anything he had previously attempted: the great epic he had discussed with Edmund Spenser beside the Blackwater River in 1589, the *Book of the Ocean to Cynthia*.

The scope of the saga was the truest homage he could pay to what the queen had meant to him in the past and what she might come to mean again. If he were to write twelve books he would be able to log the twelve years of their relationship:

> Twelve years entire I wasted in this war,
> Twelve years of my most happy younger days;
> But I in them, and they now wasted are,
> Of all which past the sorrow only stays.[6]

The years to write first were the freshest, the eleventh and the twelfth, and so in 1593 and 1594 Walter began scribbling down notes for the eleventh and twelfth books, unconnected jottings which could be joined up later and polished into the finished and complete monument. There were echoes of former lines he had written, some deliberate – the line 'of all which past the sorrow only stays' was reproduced word for word from 'Farewell to the Court' – others the haphazard consequence of dashing off hundreds of verses without systematic revision. *The Book of the Ocean to Cynthia* as it has come down to us in Ralegh's own handwriting is a feverish, unlicked piece of work, possibly because Walter wished the turbulence of his verse to convey to Elizabeth the distress he felt, more probably because he scarcely got more than ankle-deep into the enterprise before he left it in 1594 with only 500 lines in Book 12 completed. But he painted a shrewd portrait of his Cynthia:

> So hath perfection, which begat her mind,
> Added thereto a change of fantasy
> And left her the affections of her kind,
> Yet free from every evil but cruelty.[7]

Both fantasy and cruelty were at the very core of Elizabeth's nature – the former necessary for her psychological survival, the latter for political durability – and Walter never fully realized the health-giving natural qualities of both characteristics.

He told of his foreign ventures and how, on almost every occasion, Elizabeth had called him back:

> To seek new worlds for gold, for praise, for glory,
> To try desire, to try love, severed far,
> When I was gone, she sent her memory
> More strong than were ten thousand ships of war
> To call me back. [8]

He painted his own emotions in disgrace, and in doing so managed to achieve a sensitivity that set *Cynthia*, for all its rough edges, far above the more polished but less genuine efforts of his youth. The melancholy of this fragment is contagious, alive with the freshness that could have made the *Book of the Ocean* his greatest work, and showing too the confused and uncompleted imagery beyond which the epic never progressed:

> My days' delights, my springtime joys, fordone,
> Which, in the dawn and rising sun of youth,
> Had their creation and were first begun,
> Do in the evening and the winter sad
> Present my mind which takes my time's account,
> The grief remaining of the joy it had.
> My times that then ran o'er themselves in these,
> And now run out in others' happiness,
> Bring unto those new joys and newborn days.
> So could she not, if she were not the sun,
> Which sees the birth and burial of all else,
> And holds that poor with which she first begun,
> Leaving each withered body to be torn
> By fortune and by times tempestuous,
> Which, by her virtue, once fair fruit have borne,
> Knowing she can renew and can create
> Green from the ground and flowers, even out of stone,
> By virtue lasting over time and date,
> Leaving us only woe, which like the moss,
> Having compassion of unburied bones
> Cleaves to mischance and unrepaired loss,
> For tender stalks. . . . [9]

It was evocative, haunting verse, breaking in many places away from sixteenth-century conventions in an effort to explain not what Walter should have felt, but what he really did experience. But for that very reason Ralegh abandoned the great enterprise scarce started, for when, in the last analysis, he came to examine what he really felt for Queen Elizabeth he was compelled, willy-nilly, to compare it to the love with which he burned for Bess – 'a durable fire in the mind ever burning, never sick, never old, never dead, from itself never turning'. Consumed by such a love he could not consecrate himself for months, if not years, to the creation of an epic dedicated to a relationship which, however warm and important, occupied second place in his consciousness.

So Walter abandoned his *Book of the Ocean to Cynthia* and wrote instead a sequence of questions and answers to explore the nature of his affections for the two women in his life, basing it on the popular ballads about pilgrimages to the shrine of Our Lady of Walsingham, one of the principal holy places of pre-Reformation England:

> As you came from the holy land,
> Of Walsingham,
> Met you not with my true love
> By the way as you came?
>
> *How shall I know your true love*
> *That have met many one*
> *As I went to the holy land*
> *That have come, that have gone?*
>
> She is neither white nor brown
> But as the heavens fair,
> There is none hath a form so divine
> In the earth or the air. . . .
>
> *What's the cause that she leaves you alone*
> *And a new way doth take;*
> *Who loved you once as her own*
> *And her joy did you make?*
>
> I have loved her all my youth,
> But now old, as you see,
> Love likes not the falling fruit,
> From the withered tree.

Know that love is a careless child
And forgets promises past,
He is blind, he is deaf when he list
And in faith never fast. . . .

But true Love is a durable fire
In the mind ever burning;
Never sick, never old, never dead,
From itself never turning.[10]

Walter Ralegh was a proud man. Just turned forty, he did not enjoy admitting that his youth had been wasted and had left him a 'falling fruit from the withered tree'. He was a complex spirit, and in the depths of his disgrace, he resolved to prove that he had not frittered away the high summer of his life. He would fight back, regain royal favour and show that he was not defeated. Queen Elizabeth had cast her spell on him as she had cast it on Leicester, Essex and so many others. Sir Walter Ralegh knew, indeed, no other way to live but in pursuit of the favour of the Faerie Queene.

But the lessons of his new love and his old friendship were not forgotten. Though Walter Ralegh was in the last decade of the sixteenth century to rise like the phoenix from the ashes of his humbling, he rose a more noble and more rounded man, and that was because of his love, marriage and the trials that had attended it. Sir Walter Ralegh, the brash young royal favourite, had been a worthy subject for gossip and tall stories swapped by his contemporaries. Sir Walter Ralegh, the older, sadder husband and father was the stuff of which more enduring tales are told.

※ 25 ※

Parliament Man

The legend of Sir Walter Ralegh was partly the product of his own lifetime, but it also owed much to the two generations that immediately succeeded him – to the men who created the Civil War and the English Revolution; Pym, Eliot, Milton and Cromwell. What they thought about Ralegh has had an effect on his reputation that has lasted to this day, for they saw him as a precursor of themselves, one of the great worthies of England who championed the principles for which they went to war with the king – and this interpretation took its roots in his period of disgrace in the mid 1590s.

The men who were to idealize Sir Walter Ralegh were revolutionaries, but they were also reactionaries, harking back to the golden age of Gloriana when monarch, parliament and people lived harmoniously together. The yeomen of England were their heroes to whom, they thought, the Tudor monarchs had lent an attentive ear. Their villains were James and Charles, the first two Stuart kings who, with their unnatural ideas, had upset the Tudor scheme of things and set government against people. Sir Walter Ralegh fitted into this mythology as a symbol of the golden age who survived into the Stuart era to fall foul of the foreign dynasty's newfangled ways and to provide in his life, death – and, above all, in his *History of The World* – a defiant reproach to the absolutism that the parliamentarians took up arms to defeat.

This view of English constitutional development under the Tudors and Stuarts manipulated historical truth for its own ends: sixteenth-century Englishmen certainly did not regard Sir Walter Ralegh with his privileged wealth and power as the symbol of all that was healthy and just in the Elizabethan body politic. Still, the idealization was a fair reflection of the role that Ralegh was to play in the reign of James I, and it reflected too the contribution to parliamentary affairs that he made during the reign of Elizabeth. Liberated by his disgrace from the need to toe the government line in the parliament of 1593, Walter struck chords that the likes of John Hampden were to echo a third of a century later. Coming up to Westminster in that year as the squire of Sherborne rather than the favourite of the queen, Walter made a series of independent-minded speeches that were to lay the foundation of his posthumous reputation as a 'parliament man'.

His changed status was reflected by the constituency he represented. In 1586 Walter had been senior knight for the county of Devon. Now he was just a humble burgess representing St Michaels, an obscure Cornish pocket borough with only a handful of electors. Sergeant Harris, a Devon lawyer, called in the foreign policy debate for a formal declaration of war to make it possible to attack the French Catholics who, in Brittany, were providing bases for the Spanish navy, and Walter Ralegh backed him up strongly. A pathological hatred of the Spaniard was the most dominant of all his political emotions and he considered that, five years after the Armada 'the time is now more dangerous than it was in '88'.[1] This undying mistrust of Spain – eloquently displayed in his pamphlet on the last fight of the *Revenge* – was to bring Ralegh into direct conflict with the foreign policy of the first Stuarts, and thus to win the sympathy of the Stuarts' domestic opponents.

Oliver Cromwell came to echo what Ralegh had to say about the Dutch when the question of foreign merchants selling their wares in England was discussed. 'The nature of the Dutchman is to fly to no man but for his profit', declared Walter, opposing the suggestion that some sort of special relief might be offered to Dutch merchants trading in England. They might be our co-religionists, fighting against Spain, but they needed no special help when it came to economic survival. 'The Dutchman by his policy hath gotten trading with all the world into his hands',[2] he stated – a sour yet shrewd foretaste of the time when Calvinistic English merchants were to discover that their bitterest enemies in the world were Calvinistic Dutch merchants.

When it came to levying taxes, the voice of Ralegh also expressed sentiments prefiguring seventeenth-century cries for social justice. Men so poor that their annual taxable income was assessed at only £3 should be exempted, he proposed, and the amount lost made up by increasing the tax paid by those more comfortably off – 'the £3 men to be spared, and the sum which came from them to be levied upon those of £10 and upward'.[3]

Most sympathetic of all to the modern ear, Walter spoke out strongly in support of disentangling the law from the sphere of personal religious belief. A new bill to enforce religious conformity proposed severe measures for dealing with Catholic recusants – taking children away from their parents to be educated under official supervision, forbidding recusants to go more than 5 miles from their family home – and harsh punishment, too, for Puritans who persisted in organizing their own forms of worship: first offenders would spend three months in jail, second offenders would lose an ear, and a third offence would be punished with permanent banishment from the country.

Legislation designed to regulate a person's beliefs was, said Walter, a very dangerous thing. 'What danger may grow to ourselves if this law pass, it were fit to be considered. For it is to be feared that men not guilty will be included in it. And the law is hard that taketh life and sendeth into banishment, where men's intentions shall be judged by a jury and they shall be judges what another means.'4

It was not that Walter supported extreme Puritans nor their rights to freedom of worship. Indeed they deserved 'to be rooted out of the commonwealth'. But the law should concern itself not with intentions that were a matter of speculation but with solid evidence, and the law would look an ass indeed if it tried to despatch 20,000 Puritans from the kingdom. As one with not a little experience of foreign expeditions he could testify to the difficulties – and expense – of embarking just a few hundred.

Puritanism, of course, was one of the core elements of the English Revolution and Sir Walter Ralegh's defence of puritanism was to be remembered by the revolutionaries. With his Low Church roots and implacable anti-Catholicism, Walter stood on the side of the angels in the eyes of his immediate posterity. He had intervened in 1591 together with the Earl of Essex to save the life of John Udall, a noted Calvinist who had publicly advocated the need for radical Church reform, coaxing Udall into swearing loyalty to 'Her Majesty's happy government', thus preventing bloodshed – as he had tried, but failed, to save the Catholic Oliver Plasden.

But Walter's efforts on Plasden's behalf provide the corrective to any view that he was a special champion of the Puritans. He stated firmly in the Parliament of 1593 that he regarded attemps to alter church discipline as 'mutinous' since they implied that the organization of the state should also be subverted. He was unwilling to 'make windows in men's souls', but he was just as unwilling to tolerate any attempts to alter the status quo of the Elizabethan constitution.

Walter had worked hard as the burgess for St Michaels, but the weeks in Westminster had been a strain. After parliament broke up in April 1593 he travelled back to Sherborne via the spa at Bath where he stayed for a time to take the waters and rest – to his great displeasure. 'I am worse for the Bath, not the better', he complained. He was over forty now, entering the grey-haired stage of life when more than a few of his contemporaries took to skull caps and walking sticks – though that would never be Walter's style. His only concession to the pursuits of middle age was his hunting – and even that involved some energetic riding through the fields and woods around his new home, looking down from the lip of the Yeo valley at the masons and carpenters at work on the former hunting lodge rising across the river from the old castle.

Sir Walter Ralegh was removed, for the moment, from all the exertions of court life, but he had more than enough to keep him fully occupied. There were his lush estates in Ireland where masons and carpenters were also creating a residence on his behalf – and in June 1593 his commitments in Munster brought him up to London once again. When Walter had been over to Ireland in 1589 he had not spent all his time discussing epic poetry with Edmund Spenser. He had also set up with an Englishman named Henry Pyne a flourishing export trade in timber – mainly timber from Walter's own woods around the Blackwater River. Ralegh's royal favour had secured a special licence for this trade so that Pyne could sell to any foreign customers he could find without taking account of the normal export restrictions – and some most eager customers were the Spanish. In three years Pyne succeeded in exporting to the Spanish islands of the Canaries and Madeira – very poorly provided with timber – no less than 340,000 barrel staves for making wine casks.

The objection to this commerce, that England was throughout these years engaged in the most bitter war with Spain, held less weight in the sixteenth century than it would today. Many English merchants imported from Spain sherry, Madeira and other sweet wines – in hogsheads doubtless made of Ralegh's staves from the Blackwater – and this trade continued steadily throughout the years of the war. Common was the toast drunk by loyal Englishmen in sherry on which King Philip had taken his profit. Good drink was not to be forgone merely for the sake of a war.

Yet if that was the viewpoint in the taverns of London, Lord Deputy Fitzwilliam in Dublin took a more rigid stand. He was in the very front line of the confrontation with international Catholicism and, consumed as ever by his crusade against Sir Walter Ralegh, he now took advantage of Walter's fall from grace. Alleging that heavy planking suitable for shipbuilding was going to Spain, and that Henry Pyne was providing a channel of communication between Irish Catholics and Catholic agents on the Continent, Fitzwilliam got all further timber exports from the Ralegh estates stopped, arrested Pyne and transported him to London to be examined on charges of treason.

Ralegh could no longer rely on the queen to help Pyne, but that did not prevent him speaking vigorously to the Privy Council. He denied the export of anything but barrel staves to the Islands – there was no proof that heavy shipbuilding planks had been cut – and he denied too the allegation of intelligence with the enemy. The Council concurred and the charges against Pyne were dropped. As for the ban on trade with the Spanish islands, Ralegh pointed out that a capital investment of some £5,000 had been made in saw-mills and other plant on his estates and that the timber industry on the Blackwater provided work for over two hundred workers – most of them English settlers. The timber was sawn up at Mogeely where Pyne was tenant of the castle, then dragged by horses to the Blackwater where it was floated downstream to Youghal. It was just the sort of enterprise envisaged when the Munster settlement had first been mooted by Walsingham and Burghley, yet as a result of Deputy Fitzwilliam's action there were now great quantities of timber cut and rotting on the ground. The export trade should be resumed – and the Privy Council, with some delay, agreed with Walter once again, permitting Pyne to sell barrel staves to the Atlantic islands, Bordeaux and La Rochelle, but not to metropolitan Spain.

It was a battle satisfyingly won without any royal assistance, but, as always in Irish affairs, it was by no means the end of the war. The squabbles between Ralegh and Lord Deputy Fitzwilliam paled into insignificance beside the popular discontent which was growing in Ireland through the 1590s and which finally exploded in the great uprising of 1598. In 1594 Walter devised a scheme to send fifty Cornish miners to Munster to exploit iron ore that had been discovered on his lands, and in 1595 he licensed the erection of iron mills that could use his timber as fuel for smelting. But the 1598 rebellion and the four years of war that followed it swept away the whole basis of the Munster colony, and Ralegh, losing money heavily, was very happy first to lease and then to sell off all his Irish estates before the end of Elizabeth's reign. The Munster plantation became a chapter in his life like Virginia – conceived with great promise, commenced with great energy and concluded in anti-climax. In each case the difficulties and handicaps were, to be fair to Ralegh, formidable. Few others even tackled them in the sixteenth century, and no one defeated them. But it cannot really be said that Walter went down fighting.

Adversity induced a contradiction of reactions in Walter Ralegh. For a time he would lash out and battle fiercely against his fate – as he did when he stood up for Henry Pyne in front of the Privy Council and as he was to fight his way back into Elizabeth's favour. But then he would sink into brooding melancholy – as he did for periods in 1593 and 1594 when he composed his bitter poetry against Elizabeth and abandoned the *Book of the Ocean to Cynthia*. Though happy at Sherborne with Bess, through her pregnancy and the birth of young Wat, Walter dreamed of escape from England altogether and, his Virginia ventures having proved abortive, he concentrated his fantasies on the strange land that Sarmiento de Gamboa had told him of where the Indian chieftain bathed in gold dust – El Dorado.

As this interest grew more and more consuming, so too did another of the key friendships that was to run through his life and stand alongside his love for Bess and his relationships with Hariot and Northumberland as the foil to his aloof public persona. Lawrence Keymis was his new friend's name, a fellow enthusiast in the quest for El Dorado and a former fellow of Balliol who was probably introduced to Walter by Thomas Hariot. Keymis became, indeed, to Guiana what Hariot had been to Virginia – Walter's organizer, lieutenant and propagandist, crossing the ocean when Walter could not to explore and report on his behalf.

Through 1593 and 1594 Walter's eyes and thoughts turned more and more towards Guiana and the dream of El Dorado. But before he could pursue it, he had to pause to cope with the consequences of one other facet of his restlessly enquiring mind.

❧ 26 ❧

The School of Night

One summer evening in 1593 towards the end of Bess's pregnancy, Sir Walter Ralegh went out to dine with George Trenchard and a group of the other friends he had made in Dorset – his brother Carew, Ralph Horsey, John Fitzjames of Sherborne, and two ministers, Mr Whittle, the Vicar of Fortnington and Ralph Ironside, the Vicar of Winterbourne. Ironside quite fancied himself as a theologian, and after dinner Sir Walter Ralegh gently baited him with some of the old philosophical queries to which theology has never been able to provide a logical answer.

The occasion of the debate was some scandalous after dinner conversation on the part of Carew, whose coarseness Sir Ralph Horsey gently reproved with the Latin tag *Colloquia prava corrumpunt bones mores* (evil words corrupt good morals). Boorish or not, Carew understood the Latin, and asked the local theologian precisely what danger he was incurring by indulging in such 'loose speeches'.

'The wages of sin is death', replied the Reverend Ralph Ironside primly.

Carew made light of this wet blanket of a text, asking the Reverend Ironside not just to throw out quotations but to explain precisely what he meant, since death is 'common to all, sinner and righteous'.

The vicar explained that he was referring not to the death of the body but to the death of the soul.

'Soul!' said Carew Ralegh, 'what is that?'

With another comment intended as a conversation stopper the Reverend Ironside snapped that men should spend more time worrying about how the soul could be saved and waste less energy investigating what it might possibly be made of.

But this was not good enough for Sir Walter Ralegh, who insisted that the minister should give a proper answer to his brother Carew's question. 'I have been', said he, 'a scholar some time at Oxford, I have answered

194

under a Bachelor of Arts, and had talk with diverse; yet hitherunto on this point – to wit, what the reasonable soul of man is – have I not by any been resolved.'

This led to some trading of definitions out of which the Reverend Ironside emerged triumphantly brandishing 'a spiritual and immortal substance breathed into man by God, whereby he lives and moves and understandeth, and so is distinguished from other creatures.'

'Yes, but what is that spiritual and immortal substance breathed into man, etcetera?' said Sir Walter.

'The soul' answered the Reverend Ironside.

This circular argument struck Ralegh as just plain nonsense. John Fitzjames interjected with Aristotle's definition of the soul, *ens entium* – how many Sherborne farmers could manage that today? – a definition which, said the Reverend Ironside, the Christian Church would endorse. 'God was *ens entium*, a thing of things, having being of himself and giving being to all creatures.'

'But what' persisted Sir Walter Ralegh, 'is this *ens entium*?'

Coming round full circle again the vicar could only lamely repeat, 'It is God.' At which Sir Walter gave up, asking that grace should be said for the end of the meal.

'For that,' he said, 'is better than this disputation.'

It is a rare privilege to be able to eavesdrop on a private conversation held the best part of four centuries ago. One can imagine sitting at the table, watching the nimble Sir Walter keeping one step ahead of the ponderous Reverend Ironside, and reading the record of that Dorset summer evening's talk, one is struck by how modern the spirit of Sir Walter Ralegh was. His scepticism struck the tone of the Age of Reason, and that is why his arguments have been preserved for posterity to savour. For it seemed to some, and obviously to the Reverend Ironside, that Sir Walter Ralegh's attitude smacked of impiety, and in March 1594 the Court of High Commission – the Church of England's tribunal for maintaining religious orthodoxy – directed that the conversation that evening around the dinner table of Sir George Trenchard should be the subject of a formal enquiry to be held nearby at Cerne Abbas.

Religious conformity was taken at this time to be the touchstone of national unity, and the heterodox were not treated gently. Francis Ket, the tutor of the playwright Christopher Marlowe, had been burned at the stake in 1589 after being found guilty of atheism, so the suggestion of blasphemy imputed to Sir Walter Ralegh was not one to be taken lightly, especially as this was not the first time that he had incurred the displeasure of sanctimonious men. There was that allegation of the Jesuit Parsons that Sir Walter Ralegh ran a 'school of atheism', and the Reverend Ironside's annoyance at being worsted in his after dinner argument at George Trenchard's chimed with all the suspicions attached to Walter's patronage of men who probed the heavens with strange glasses.

More dangerous still was the mistrust aroused by Walter's passion for overseas exploration, in which, of course, John Dee and Thomas Hariot both assisted him. It was a common accusation that atheists 'impudently persist in it that the late discovered Indians are able to show antiquities thousands [of years] before Adam'[1] – words that struck a chill through all true believers, for sixteenth- and seventeenth-century faith depended on a chronology derived from a literal interpretation of the Old Testament which set the adventures of Adam and Eve a few thousand years before the birth of Christ. To retail stories about Red Indians whose traditions went back much further and which did not include, say, the story of a massive flood, was plain atheistical. So Sir Walter Ralegh's reputation as an explorer of the New World was, in sixteenth-century terms, as much a claim to notoriety as to fame – a two-edged sword.

Chronology aroused the bitterest arguments in the England of Sir Walter Ralegh. Mathematicians like Dee and Hariot, for example, had demonstrated that England should adopt the Gregorian calendar in place of the existing Julian system. The Julian calendar was inaccurate and differed extraordinarily from the Gregorian dating in Europe. English and European months ran smoothly together side by side, Christmas and the end of December being celebrated simultaneously on both sides of the Channel, but English (Julian) years were dated from 25 March, so that for the best part of three months after 1 January England maintained that it was still, say, 1593, while Europe had moved on to 1594, as we would today.

It was nonsense, and confronted with its inconvenience the bureaucrat got the better of the conservative in Lord Burghley. He caused to be drafted a proclamation 'declaring the causes of the reformation of the calendar and accompting of the year, hereafter to be observed, to accord with other countries next hereto adjoining'.[2] But the proclamation stayed in draft, for the 'countries next hereto adjoining' adhered to a false religion. The Church of England assessed the reformed calendar by its origins not by its accuracy and decided it 'would rather be wrong than be Roman'.[3]

Such was the climate of opinion in which Walter Ralegh bantered so lightly with the Reverend Ironside, and the three-day investigation held into his religious beliefs at Cerne Abbas in the spring of 1594 confirmed the dangerous power of rumour. Although there was not a single solid piece of evidence produced of real impiety on the part of Sir Walter Ralegh himself, the Commission listened gravely to every morsel of gossip and suspicion presented to it about Ralegh and his friends. Two or three witnesses maintained that Sir Walter was 'suspected of atheism'. Hariot too was 'suspected of atheism'. He had, apparently, 'brought the Godhead in question and the whole course of the scriptures'. Carew Ralegh was said to have argued provocatively with clerics and had, on one occasion after he and Sir Walter had requisitioned a horse from a vicar who remonstrated that he needed the animal to travel to preach a sermon next day, jestingly retorted that 'his horse should preach before him'.[4] There were complaints against two local protégés of Walter's, a Mr Thynne, probably Charles Thynne, the nephew of Ralegh living at Longleat, and Thomas Allen, the lieutenant of Portland Castle, a rough soldier Walter had met in Ireland in 1580–1. Thynne was alleged to have said that divine providence did not extend to all creatures, while Thomas Allen was accused of tearing pages out of his bible to dry his tobacco, of swearing 'that if God were in the bush there he would pull him out with his boots' because a downpour of rain had spoiled his hawking, and of corrupting his servant Oliver with his ideas. Oliver had, apparently, shocked two good wives of Lillington by informing them that Moses had enjoyed the company of fifty-two concubines.[5]

Such was the tittle-tattle to which the judges of the High Commission listened for three days, most of it served up by clerics and parish officials of the diocese Walter Ralegh had so deeply offended by seizing Sherborne. Of fifteen witnesses, eight were priests, four were churchwardens and only three had no traceable connection with the church – except, of course, that they worshipped in church at least once a week. The great bulk of evidence was casual hearsay, and the credence to be accorded it was well illustrated by the Curate of Motcombe:

He hath heard that Sir Walter Ralegh hath argued with one Mr Ironside at Sir George Trenchard's touching the being, or immortality of the soul, or such like, but the certainty thereof he cannot say further, saving asking the same of Mr Ironside upon the report aforesaid, he hath answered that *the matter was not as the voice of the country reported thereof*, or to the like effect. [My italics.][6]

This was the heart of the matter. 'The voice of the country' did not correspond to the truth, and even the offended Reverend Ironside had to admit it. More than a little malice and jealousy had been involved in the calling of the Cerne Abbas Commission and in the scraping together of so many unsubstantiated smears. It was fortunate for Ralegh that the men who heard the evidence were not as prejudiced as the clerics who produced it: a cross-section of the local establishment, they included Walter's friend the deputy lieutenant, Sir Ralph Horsey, who had actually been present at the dinner party that caused all the trouble, John Williams, sheriff of Dorset and nephew of Sir George Trenchard, and Francis

Hawley who, as vice-admiral for Dorset, held the same position and interest in privateering that Ralegh held in Devon and who was also a good friend of both Horsey and Trenchard. The other two commissioners, Thomas Viscount Bindon and Dr Francis James, an ecclesiastical official, may have been less kindly disposed towards Walter, but with the moonshine presented to them they were not in a position to take the matter further. The allegations against Sir Walter Ralegh's piety were dropped – officially.

Yet the gossip continued and 'atheist' became a stigma that branded Ralegh to the end of his days. There is, in fact, some evidence that he was the victim of a deliberate campaign to blacken his reputation. The facts about the conspiracy revolve around the poem 'The Lie' which has conventionally been attributed to Sir Walter Ralegh's pen. Its irreligious contempt for established society, and its cynical refusal to hold anything sacred have been interpreted as the logical continuation of Ralegh's more melancholic poems, and its famous reference to the royal court glowing like wood that is so rotten it has become phosphorescent is taken to chime with Walter's disgrace and retreat to Sherborne. 'To give the lie' to anyone was to deliver a mortal, final insult, effaceable only with death, and the bitter rancour of every verse, deeply shocking in its day, has been seen as positive proof of Walter Ralegh's godlessness:

> Go soul, the body's guest,
>   Upon a thankless errand,
> Fear not to touch the best,
>   The truth shall be thy warrant.
> Go, since I needs must die,
>   And give the world the lie.
>
> Say to the Court it glows
>   And shines like rotten wood,
> Say to the Church it shows
>   What's good, and doth no good:
> If Church and Court reply,
>   Then give them both the lie. . . .
>
> Tell zeal it wants devotion,
>   Tell love it is but lust,
> Tell time it metes but motion,
>   Tell flesh it is but lust:
> And wish them not reply,
>   For thou must give the lie. . . .[7]

The fact that Walter Ralegh never put his name to this poem means, of course, no more than his refusal openly to acknowledge any of the verses in *The Phoenix Nest*. But there are other indications that 'The Lie' was not the work of his pen. Nowhere, not even in his Lady of Walsingham dialogue, did he approach the cynicism of: 'Tell love it is but lust', a simplistic adolescent saw which bears no relationship to what we know of Walter's emotional maturity nor of his intellectual sophistication. And the style of the entire poem, with its crude and repetitious rhyme, was unlike anything else that Ralegh wrote.

This makes it hardly surprising that four of the earliest manuscript versions of 'The Lie' attribute its composition not to Ralegh but to a Dr Richard Latworth, a cynical Puritan who was a fellow of St John's College, Oxford, and one of the manuscripts is actually entitled: 'W R farewell made by d:Lat'.[8]

In other words, 'The Lie' was a not poem written *by* Walter Ralegh but a poem *about* him as the supreme exemplar of the ways of the world which Dr Latworth disliked and denounced so savagely. Three of the four manuscripts follow 'The Lie' with two other poems. One begins:

> Go, Echo of the Mind,
> A careless truth protest.
> Make answer that *so raw a lie*
> No stomach can digest. [My italics.]

Another version actually turns 'so raw a lie' into 'rude Rawly', and another ends up:

> Such is the song, such is the author,
> Worthy to be rewarded with a halter.

The rhyme of this last line would equally well be served by 'Such is Sir Walter'.[9]

It is these additional poems that caused many contemporaries – and subsequent scholars – to connect Walter Ralegh's name with 'The Lie', quite ignoring the implausibility of the poem's style and content, and quite ignoring, too, other poems of Richard Latworth that *were* written in that same bad-tempered simplistic vein:

> Earth what art thou?
>   A point, a senseless centre.
> Friends what are you?
>   An age's trustless trial.
> Life what art thou?
>   A daily doubtful venture.[10]

It was the pen that wrote *these* lines that wrote 'The Lie' and the notoriety that Latworth's poem gave Walter was both unfounded and unfair, for just a few weeks after the Cerne Abbas investigation of March 1594 came a true illustration of Ralegh's religious attitudes. Down in Chideock near Bridport was captured in April 1594 a priest trained by the Jesuits, Father John Cornelius, and Walter's friends, the Dorset deputy lieutenants Sir George Trenchard and Sir Ralph Horsey, brought him back to Trenchard's house (the scene of the now notorious dinner party), for cross-questioning.

So soon after the Cerne Abbas affair Ralegh might have been expected to demonstrate his religious zeal and reliability, but the very opposite was, in fact, the case. One evening he fell into conversation with Cornelius and

passed the whole night with him alone that he might have certain doubts resolved; nor would such a man [as Ralegh] rest contented with mere questions and doubts, but would go into matters more deeply. He was so pleased with the father's conviction and reasoning and with his modest and courteous manner that he offered to do all he could in London for his liberation, and this although the father had gently reproved him for his mode of life and conversation.[11]

This story comes from a Catholic account of Father Cornelius's life, but it was quite in character for Walter, if he encountered an interesting stranger, to sit up until the small hours, probing the man's ideas and beliefs and testing out his own. Cornelius sounds to have had a stronger line in argument than the Reverend Ironside, and Ralegh's indifference to public opinion echoes that of his mother back in the 1550s when she went to comfort Agnes Prest on the night before her burning.

But it was also quite in character for Walter to behave as he did in the second part of this story (from the same Jesuit source). Having been taken up to London to be tortured, Father Cornelius was sent down to Dorchester to be tried. Ralegh could be no help to him. The priest was duly sentenced to death and Walter Ralegh was in charge of the execution. But as Father Cornelius, standing on the gallows ladder with the rope round his neck, took advantage of his right to make his peace with the world, it seemed to Walter that the Jesuit was presuming on the privilege and was making a speech that threatened to turn into a piece of popish propaganda. Walter tried to stop him several times from speaking, and then, when the priest persisted in declaiming, had the gallows ladder pulled away from under him so that poor Father Cornelius was strangled in mid-sentence. His body jumped and choked on the rope until he was almost senseless and then he was, on Walter's orders, cut down, disembowelled, castrated, beheaded and cut in four. His head was placed on the pinnacle of St Peter's Church in Dorchester High Street and the four quarters of his body stuck up to greet travellers through the gates of the town.

There we have the religious faith of Walter Ralegh displayed to its full extent. A sincere and rigorous intellectual, he kept an open mind towards new ideas and questioned old ones. He could plumb the depths of another man's soul and his own. Earnestly discussing points of faith and personal conviction, this satisfied one of his profoundest passions. And then, when the treason of that other man had been established by a court of law, he organized the spiking of his fellow debater's head on the pinnacle of the nearest church – Walter Ralegh saw no contradiction in this.

Sir Walter Ralegh was a curious man, a brave man not afraid of people or ideas that frightened others and made others mistrust him. But it is evident both in his life and his writings that just as surely as he could envisage no England without a monarch, so he could envisage no world without a God, and no man without the personal grace and salvation extended by Jesus Christ. Sir Walter Ralegh was certainly a sceptic, but a sceptic who asked questions the more firmly to believe, not to doubt. 'The mind in searching causes,' he wrote, 'is never quiet until it comes to God, and the will is never satisfied with any goodness until it comes to the immortal goodness.' That was his credo, no matter what the gossips said.

❧ 27 ❧

The Dream of El Dorado

We may laugh at men who chase rainbows, who seek fame
or wealth where reason tells us none can be. They seldom
find their crock of gold. But they can sometimes find
themselves, discovering fulfilment simply in the act of
searching, and so it was with Walter Ralegh in 1595, the mid-point of his
disgrace, when he set out to discover a land where men bathed in oil then
powdered themselves with gold dust – El Dorado.

The legend was an old one – and not impossibly implausible. Pizarro
had discovered in Peru a fantastic and wealthy civilization hidden high in
the Andes. Cortez had located a similarly astonishing society in Mexico.
Both the Incas and the Aztecs possessed fabulous treasures – and yet it was
a constant disappointment to their Spanish conquerors that they could
never discover the great mines from which they assumed that the gold
ornaments they looted must have come. The conquistadores were, in fact,
pillaging storehouses stocked over centuries from many sources, but if
Montezuma and Atahualpa could rule over their concealed cities, it was
not too far-fetched to assume that there might be a third great emperor
hidden in some South American mountain or lake, nor that his empire
should be the source of the gold that tapestried the walls of the Inca
Palace of the Sun.

There were clues to indicate where this empire might be. Between the
mouths of the Orinoco and Amazon rivers stretched a tropical jungle
where few white men had set foot – Guiana, and the natives of this land
talked of a city which they called Manoa, lying somewhere deep in the
Orinoco basin. It was a city they feared, whose ruler, they said, was
fabulously wealthy, and there was also a white man who told how he had
penetrated the jungle to the magic city and who died swearing to his
confessor to the truth of the wealth he claimed to have seen.

His name was Juan Martinez, who, as munitions master of a Spanish exploratory party, had sailed up the River Orinoco to where it joins the Caroni river. The expedition camped at the confluence of the streams, and one of the Spanish ships lost its anchor – which Ralegh was to come across when he sailed to the same spot at the end of the century. The course of the Caroni appeared to run straight out of the jungle heartland where the city of Manoa lay hidden, but the Spanish explorers got no further, for their entire powder store exploded. To advance further without ammunition was unthinkable and so the expedition turned back, but not before punishment was inflicted on the man held responsible for the catastrophe.

The master of munitions, Martinez, was marooned as a scapegoat in an open canoe without food or arms and for days he drifted through the jungle beneath the blazing sun becoming slowly crazed with heat, hunger and solitude.

Natives found him at last. They had never seen a white man before and they carried him, he said, into the jungle, passing from settlement to settlement until, eventually, they came to the borders of the kingdom they called Manoa. At this point Martinez was blindfolded, and he was taken on for another fifteen days, seeing nothing. When the blindfold was removed the Spaniard found himself before the gates of a marvellous city. So vast was it, he claimed, that he walked from noon until dark and then, next day, walked again from sunrise to sunset before he came eventually to the palace of the emperor.

This was the home of the Inca who bathed in turpentine and then had gold dust blown on his body through hollow canes. Martinez confirmed the legend and went one better. Every year, he said, the men who governed El Dorado for the Inca would gather with their chief for a celebration in which the fine powdered gold was blown onto their bodies as well, so the palace was full of men glittering and 'shining from foot to the head'. The emperor, furthermore, had very little contact with any metal that was not precious. All his tableware was gold and silver, and so were all the pots and pans in his kitchens. He had ropes, chests and troughs of gold and silver, and, said Martinez, he had 'a garden of pleasure' in which he had reproduced in gold or silver life-size models of everything that lived or grew in his country. There were flowers, herbs and trees all wrought of precious metal – fishes, animals and birds of 'an invention and magnificence until then never seen'.

When it was time for Martinez to leave, the emperor graciously allowed him to take away samples of the wealth of El Dorado to prove that the city was no dream and the traveller, miraculously transformed from a hopeless castaway to a man of substance and property, struck back through the jungle in the direction of civilization. But his story had an unhappy ending, for once he left the protection of El Dorado, Martinez was set upon by natives who relieved him of all his fabulous gifts except for 'two great bottles or gourds, which were filled with beads curiously wrought'.

These gold beads and an unshakable faith unto death were all that Martinez could show for his tale, but it was enough for Sir Walter Ralegh. Once he had heard the Spaniard's story – passed on to him by Don Sarmiento de Gamboa, the grandee he had captured in 1586, El Dorado became a wraith that he would follow to his grave. He had had little time actually to investigate the tale in his years of favour; but just as disgrace gave him more leisure for his poetry, so in the long months he spent down in Sherborne in 1593 and 1594, he began to dream with an ever fiercer intensity of the city and ruler whose wealth would do so much to win back the favour of the ruler nearer home. If he ever paused to consider how much faith could really be placed in the babblings of a man lost for months in a tropical jungle, his own dreams soon cast them aside. He did not simply believe, he was certain, and men who spoke to him or read his writings about El Dorado found themselves assuming that Ralegh must have been there himself to have the gold dust blown over him.

Nor was he alone in his conviction. Richard Hakluyt had realized the strategic and colonial significance of Guiana for some time and, back in 1584, when he and Ralegh had been trying to inject more purpose into the queen's wayward enthusiasm for Virginia, he had mentioned the alternative to a North American settlement:

> All that part of America eastward from Cumana unto the river of St Augustine in Brazil containeth in length along the sea side 1,200 miles. In which compass and tract there is neither Spaniard, Portingales nor any Christian man but only Caribs, Indians and savages. In which place is great plenty of gold, pearl and precious stones.[1]

This vast natural wealth would make an English privateering base self-sustaining, able both to drive a wedge between Brazil and Peru and to menace the entire Caribbean.

Then, in 1586, the captured Spaniard, Don Pedro Sarmiento de Gamboa, had had his strange dealing with Ralegh and had told him not only of the wanderer Martinez, but also of a wealthy old Spaniard who believed fiercely in El Dorado and who was searching for it at that very moment. This explorer, Don Antonio de Berreo, had come out to the Caribbean after his sixtieth birthday in order to supervise some of his wife's colonial properties, had heard the legend and was seized by it as remorselessly as Ralegh. He devoted himself to the quest, and made three expeditions into the Guiana jungle. He collated all the accounts he could discover of men who had sought the gilded city, and worked out a definite location for it – in the remote Guiana Highlands. He lacked the men to make a full-scale attack on this fortress, so in his mid-seventies, he built a base camp on the island of Trinidad. Corking up the mouth of the Orinoco, this island was a good place from which to observe any travellers sailing into the river.

Ralegh made it his business to discover as much as he could about Berreo. The possibility of a scrap with a Spaniard made the prospect of mounting an expedition to South America that much more appealing to him, and he could, furthermore, argue that there were reasons for exploring Guiana, whether or not all tales of treasure proved true. For it was the only substantial area of tropical America not occupied by the troops of Spain or Portugal and it was a privateering base *par excellence*. Ships sailing up the river inland could threaten settlements along the Spanish Main from the rear, while ships sailing out into the Caribbean could plunder the sea that Spain had once hoped to call her own. The prevailing easterly trade winds, which meant a direct and convenient voyage from England, made it difficult for a Caribbean-based war fleet to undertake reprisals and, indeed, the great necklace of islands we today call the Windwards and Leewards was left almost uncolonized by Spain, largely because the trade winds made for difficult access from the main Spanish settlements.

By 1593 El Dorado had become fixed in Walter Ralegh's mind as one of his guiding stars. A topic which had once been an occasional diversion now took control of him. He talked to potential backers and anyone who would listen. Apart from all the attractions the project possessed in its own right, it seemed the most inviting way back to his old court offices – not the most politic route – Elizabeth in old age was not one for knight errant gestures, but in the circumstances the best that Walter Ralegh could manage. He had certain standards of personal dignity he could not compromise – and his gambler's streak. There were obviously safer ways to please the queen than embarking on a wild goose chase across the ocean, but what excitement did the alternatives possess? The odds against finding El Dorado were long, but they did at least involve the chance of scooping the pool, and Walter Ralegh always played for the top stakes. It was one cornerstone of his character – his Sampson's hair.

Lady Ralegh was worried. The tranquillity of the little world she and Walter had built themselves at Sherborne was being broken in upon by this strange tropical obsession. Her husband was off whipping up support in London among prospective investors and partners. He had less and less time for her and their baby son Wat. Walter was in a daydream, forever planning and scheming about the strange corner of a distant continent that seemed likely to leave her a widow and Wat an orphan. The great Sir Robert Cecil was one of the men Walter had approached for help, and so, to Sir Robert Bess wrote, begging him to turn Walter's energies in other directions:

> I hope you will rather draw Sir Walter towards the east than help him forward towards the sunset, if any respect to me, or love to him, be not forgotten.

But her entreaty was in vain, and Sir Robert Cecil invested in the Guiana voyage as did Lord Admiral Howard, who contributed a ship, *The Lion's Whelp*.

Before the expedition proper sailed there was a reconnaissance. Ralegh's privateering captain, Jacob Whiddon, a cool customer not scared of sailing unescorted into Spanish waters, was sent off to inspect the Orinoco in 1594, and on Trinidad, as expected, he found Antonio de Berreo guarding the delta like a cat over a mouse hole. The Spaniard appeared to make the English scouting party welcome, supplying them with food and water, but he was as obsessed with El Dorado as Ralegh was and also as devious. He got some Indians to lure Whiddon's crew ashore and ambushed them. Eight men were killed, and Whiddon hoisted anchor immediately for England.

The reconnaissance was not a waste of time, however. Whiddon had been able, Hariot-style, to secure the services of an Indian who came back to London to learn English so that he could act as an interpreter for the main expedition, and the English had rapidly discovered that most of Trinidad's natives bitterly hated Berreo and the Spaniards, and that the same was probably true on the mainland itself. All the Indians had, furthermore, been most happy to satisfy the Englishman's enquiries as to the existence of El Dorado. They had certainly heard of it they said, and of its fabulous wealth.

That was hardly surprising, since every ship searching for the treasures of the Orinoco must have called in at Trinidad, and the natives soon learned the best way to please their curious foreign visitors. Still, Whiddon's information was sufficient justification, in Ralegh's opinion, to request Letters Patent permitting him officially to explore on the queen's behalf – and he duly received them, though hardly in the glowing terms to which he had been treated in the past.

He was to Elizabeth no longer 'trusty' or 'well-beloved', as he had been when commissioned to colonize Virginia ten years previously. Now he was just 'our servant Sir Walter Ralegh'. Still, he was empowered to take possession of any territories not already in the possession of a Christian king, and was instructed to annoy and enfeeble the king of Spain and his subjects in any way he cared. He could, furthermore, capture any trading ship that trespassed within what he considered to be his domain.

So, with that last provision, Walter Ralegh was back in business again as a privateer, and the Westcountrymen rallied round him eagerly. There was Humphrey Gilbert's son, John, Grenville's son, John, and another of the Gorges clan, Butshead. The great pirates were keen to join in. Amyas Preston and George Somers both asked if they could join the party, while George Popham and Sir Robert Dudley, Leicester's son, agreed to meet up with the expedition in Trinidad. Some hundred and fifty men, crews apart, would sail on five ships, and remembering the shallow rivers of Virginia, Ralegh converted a Spanish galley that one of his privateers had captured into a scouting boat. This was placed under the command of Lawrence Keymis, the Oxford don who was by now so mesmerized by all things Raleghian that he was devoting all his geographical and mathematical talents not to abstract tutorials but to Walter's explorations.

It was February 1595 when the expedition set off. After more than a dozen years as an armchair admiral commissioning and dispatching explorers by the score, the Shepherd of the Ocean was finally risking his own life and health to cross the Atlantic for the first time and take his chances among the swamps and Spaniards of the Orinoco delta. When he arrived off Trinidad, he set about reconnoitring the Spanish positions and the Trinidad coast, inspecting the great pitch lake and noting another strange sight – oysters lodged on mangrove roots. If shellfish could grow on trees and lakes could bubble black tar, why should there not be a king nearby who powdered himself with gold dust? Local natives confirmed the legend and they also complained bitterly of Spanish cruelties. Berreo had, apparently, attempted to demonstrate his authority by capturing five of their chiefs and fettering them with one long chain. The wretches had been tortured and were now staked out starving to death while burning bacon fat was dripped on to their bodies.

Ralegh was to make much of Spanish harshness towards the natives of both Trinidad and Guiana. When he returned to the area as a failing old man over twenty years later, there were still Indians who remembered his kindness to them. But at the beginning of April 1595 his concern was not so much with the bacon-burnt native chiefs, as his suspicion of Berreo and the possibility of Spanish reinforcements being sent to the island. 'To leave a garrison at my back', he wrote, which 'daily expected supplies out of Spain, I should have savoured very much of the ass', and so he lost no time in eliminating that threat to his rear. Gathering together his little band of men he led a vigorous assault on the fort of St Joseph, killed the unsuspecting Spanish guards, burned the town and captured Berreo along with a Spanish sailor, Captain Jorge. It was like the old days again, the risk and excitement of real battle Walter had not tasted since he had been in Ireland and France over fifteen years earlier.

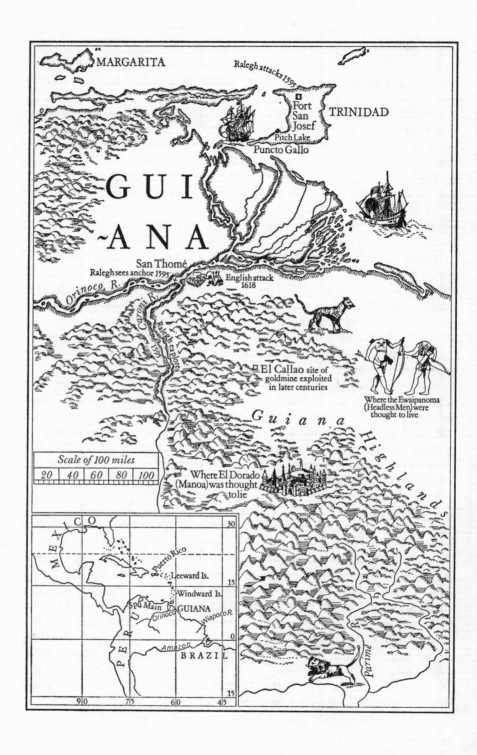

MARGARITA

Ralegh attacks 1595

Fort San Josef

TRINIDAD

Pitch Lake

Puncto Gallo

G U I

~A N A

San Thomé
Ralegh sees anchor 1595

English attack
1618

Orinoco R.

Caroni R.

Ralegh explores 1595

□ El Callao site of
goldmine exploited
in later centuries

Where the Ewaipanoma
(Headless Men) were
thought to live

G u i a n a   H i g h l a n d s

Scale of 100 miles

| 20 | 40 | 60 | 80 | 100 |

Where El Dorado
(Manoa) was thought
to lie

M E X I C O

Puerto Rico

Leeward Is.

Windward Is.

Sp. Main

GUIANA

Orinoco

Wiapoco R.

P E R U

Amazon

B R A Z I L

Parime R.

30

15

0

15

90   75   60   45

The staked-out chiefs had their chains struck from them and were reunited joyfully with their people, but Walter was scarcely vindictive towards their captors, treating Berreo and Jorge as honoured guests, wining and dining them lavishly. He wanted to hear about El Dorado – and the Spaniards duly obliged. Jorge talked of a silver mine on the Caroni River, and Berreo was happy to confirm the existence of Manoa. But it was a long way off, he warned, and the Orinoco flowed with dangerous swiftness in the spring. There would be few inhabitants in the riverside settlements and any expedition now would founder through lack of supplies.

Ralegh and his captain, Whiddon, had solid reasons for mistrusting Berreo. But the old Spaniard, delighted though he might have been to discourage Ralegh, was not inventing the problems that any penetrator of the Orinoco was likely to encouter – as the English were soon to discover.

Still, for the moment Ralegh busied himself with consolidating his rear guard. Ever since Drake, some twenty years earlier, had allied with the Cimaroon natives of the Panama Isthmus, Englishmen had been hopeful of enlisting local Indian help against the Spanish Empire. Now Ralegh had the chance to put the idea into practice. The Trinidadians helped him build a fort at Icacos Point, brought him supplies and politely paraded for this energetic white man's little ceremony to mark the annexation of their island. A pole was erected bearing the arms of the Queen of England, and Ralegh made a speech explaining how his lady Ezrabeta Cassipuna Acarewana (Elizabeth the great princess) would be their friend and protect them against the Spaniard. He showed them a picture of this virgin who, he explained, was the great *Cassique* (chief) of the North and who had more Cassiqui under her than there were trees on Trinidad.

The chiefs were most impressed, and one of them agreed to go off with John Douglas, the master of Ralegh's ship, to help locate a suitable route into the Orinoco delta. Douglas returned reporting that they had discovered 'four goodly entrances, whereof the least was as big as the Thames at Woolwich' but that the water was shallow, 6 feet deep at the most. As anticipated, the sea-going vessels would have to be left off Trinidad, and the expedition continue in small open boats. The old Spanish galley could take sixty, *The Lion's Whelp* boat and wherry held twenty between them, Captain Calfield's wherry ten more, and Ralegh's barge another ten, and so, in these cockleshell open craft, one hundred brave Englishmen rowed off in search of El Dorado.

✿ 28 ✿

Up the Orinoco

There was in Walter Ralegh much of the carpet knight. Not without reason did he have the reputation of a braggart, eternally claiming more than he could ever perform, over-eager to take credit he did not thoroughly deserve. But now, in May 1595 at the mouth of the Orinoco, in his helmet, breastplate and sticky West Country cloth, he performed all that he had promised. The extravagant courage of the man is remarkable – as is that of the hundred Elizabethans who followed him in their open rowing boats into the heart of tropical America. How many people today would, of their own free will, entrust their lives for a month to a wooden skiff meandering through the swamps of the Orinoco Delta?

> In the bottom of an old gallego which I caused to be fashioned like a galley, and, in one barge, two wherries, and a ship's boat of *The Lion's Whelp*, we carried 100 persons and their victuals for a month in the same, being all driven to lie in the rain and weather, in the open air, in the burning sun, and upon hard boards, and to dress our meat, and to carry all manner of furniture in them, wherewith they were so pestered and unsavoury, that what with the victuals being mostly fish, with the wet clothes of so many men thrust together and the heat of the sun, I will undertake there was never any prison in England that could be found more unsavoury and loathsome, especially to myself, who had for many years before been dieted and cared for in a sort far differing.[1]

It was hard going for a man turned forty who had grown soft-bellied with easy living. A manuscript work of the time, which some have attributed to Ralegh, lists the sort of rations Elizabethan sailors would stock up with in tricky circumstances like these: beer, hard biscuit, butter, cheese, pickled herrings, smoked herrings, dry sprats, oil, vinegar,

210

mustard and onions. Ralegh's party can have had little opportunity to cook, and that they returned so healthy after a month in such insalubrious and taxing conditions is a testimony to Ralegh's leadership – and his medical wisdom.

They had a long haul before they even reached the Orinoco, 'for we had as much sea to cross over in our wherries as between Dover and Calais, and in a great billow, the wind and the current being both very strong.' And the delta itself was a tangle of water courses and dead-ends.

All the earth doth not yield the like confluence of streams and branches, the one crossing the other so many times, and all so fair and large, and so like one to another, as no man can tell which to take. And if we went by the sun or the compass, hoping thereby to go directly one way or other, yet that way also we were carried in a circle amongst multitudes of islands and every island so bordered with high trees, as no man could see any further than the breadth of the river.

These Elizabethans had crossed the Atlantic Ocean and the Caribbean Sea to find themselves lost in a deadly Hampton Court maze. They had a pilot, a young Indian they called Ferdinando whom they had captured with his brother but neither were of much use as they came from further down the coast. The expedition 'might have wandered a whole year in the labyrinth of rivers' had they not, on 22 May 1595, spotted a small dug-out rowed by three local Indians. Ralegh urged on his barge, and, with his eight oarsmen pulling furiously, was able to overtake the canoe.

The Indians came from a local tribe – a very local tribe indeed, as it turned out. For all their friends and relatives had been hidden in the riverside bushes watching the chase. They appeared friendly and, attracted by the prospect of some local food and wine, Ferdinando went ashore with his brother. But once separated from their white companions the two boys were set upon viciously. They wriggled free of their captors to be pursued by a hunting party through the woods, and Ferdinando's brother arrived at the boats to pant out the story of the chase. Luckily some of the Indians in the canoes the English had captured were still with the white explorers, so Ralegh promptly laid hands on one of them, an old man, and made obvious the fate he could expect if any harm befell poor Ferdinando, still running desperately through the woods. The old man began shouting to the bank, warning his fellow tribesmen that his life was in jeopardy. But by now the Indians' bloodlust was up. They had put dogs on the scent of their prey and it was only with extreme agility – and good luck – that Ferdinando saved his own life, and the old hostage's. He swam to Ralegh's barge 'half dead with fear'.

The old hostage's life proved well worth the saving. For though he was sometimes as perplexed as Ferdinando by the drowned swamps of the delta, he was able to lead the Englishmen inland with some success.

Flora and fauna interested Ralegh. He was amazed by the colours of the jungle birds, 'some carnation, some crimson, orange-tawny, purple, green, watchet [a shade of blue] and of all other sorts both simple and mixed'. But his company's main interest was in the nutritional value of any wildlife they could shoot. After only three days in the oppressive humidity of the jungle their spirits were flagging. The current seemed to be growing stronger against them almost hourly. The Indian pilots promised every morning that the journey's end was just a day's rowing away – on Ralegh's orders – but every nightfall they found themselves no nearer El Dorado or anything resembling it. Bread supplies dwindled to nothing and their drink was almost all used up so that 'the thick and troubled water of the river' looked like becoming their last resort.

> The further we went on [wrote Ralegh], our victual decreasing and the air breeding great faintness, we grew weaker and weaker when we had most need of strength and ability ... so as we were brought into despair and discomfort, had we not persuaded all the company that it was but only one day's work more to attain the land where we should be relieved of all we wanted, and if we returned that we were sure to starve by the way, and that the world would also laugh us to scorn.

Was it this last spur to his pride, the fear of being ridiculed once again at the distant court of Queen Elizabeth, that drove Walter Ralegh, faced with disaster within days of setting out so hopefully, to snatch at a desperate hope suggested by their old Indian pilot? There was, he claimed, a village nearby with friendly inhabitants who would give the English all the fresh food and drink they required – 'bread, hens, fish and of the country wine'. But it could only be reached by a stream too small for the galley to penetrate. The expedition must divide in two, half remaining in the main river with the galley, the remainder striking off up the side stream. There was no need for the foraging party to take any food, said the old man, for, if they left at noon, they could be back at the galley loaded with provisions by nightfall.

As the little party got further and further into the jungle, Ralegh began to realize that the situation had all the ingredients of a trap.

> When we had rowed three hours, we marvelled we saw no sign of any dwelling, and asked the pilot where the town was. He told us a little further. After three hours more, the sun being almost set, we began to suspect that he led us that way to betray us, for he confessed that those Spaniards that fled from Trinidad ... were joined together in some village upon that river.

But Ralegh had no choice except to go on. There was certainly no food and drink along the banks they had passed until then.

> When it grew towards night, and we demanding where the place was, he told us but four reaches more. When we had rowed four and four, we saw no sign, and our water-men, even heart broken and tired, were ready to give up the ghost, for we had now come from the galley nearly forty miles.

If only to placate his men, Ralegh would dearly have loved to murder the old Indian:

> and if we had known the way back again by night, he had surely gone, but our own necessities pleaded sufficiently for his safety. For it was as dark as pitch, and the river began so to narrow itself, and the trees to hang over from side to side, as we were driven with arming swords to cut a passage through those branches that covered the water.

The last meal they had eaten had been at eight that morning – a small breakfast, 'and our stomachs began to gnaw apace'.

This is a fine piece of story telling by Ralegh, taking the reader with him up the dark creeper-infested river, the Englishmen straining desperately in the moist night air for a light, a sound, that might be their goal – or might be the last warning that their Spanish enemies would give before slaughtering them and leaving their bodies to rot in the jungle. And then incredibly, in the midst of fear and gloom, 'about one o'clock after midnight, we saw a light, and, rowing towards it, we heard the dogs of the village'.

Safety! The Indians were as friendly and hospitable as the old pilot had promised and loaded the white explorers with bread, fish, drink and chickens. Next day the Englishmen joyfully coasted back the way they had advanced so uncertainly, discovering in daylight that the river banks they had been so fearful of rolled down from a beautiful, almost soft country-side. It was a relief to English eyes to look out over parkland, 'the grass short and green, and in divers parts groves of trees by themselves. . . . And still as we rowed, the deer came down feeding by the water's side, as if they had been used to a keeper's call.'

The only thing to mar the enjoyment of this Arcadian scene was the exuberance of one of the native bearers who leapt into the river for a swim – and was promptly devoured by a crocodile. There were in the river, said Ralegh, several thousands of these ugly blunt-nosed reptiles – which he called Lagartos. It was a sobering little tragedy, but soon forgotten since the victim was only a native and because, reunited with the galley in the main stream, the English made next day a discovery that restored much of the original faith which their jungle meanderings had dissipated.

Looking for land to make a fire and cook a meal, Captain Gifford caught sight of four dug-out canoes to which he immediately gave chase. Two escaped, but the others made for the bank, their occupants vanishing into the trees leaving for the English a vast store of bread. When Ralegh landed with search parties he stumbled over the very evidence he had travelled these thousands of miles to seek:

> As I was creeping through the bushes I saw an Indian basket hidden. It was a toolkit dropped by a metal refiner containing quicksilver, saltpetre, and divers things for the trial of metals and also the dust of such ore as he had refined.

Wildly excited Ralegh shouted out that he would pay £500 – a vast and impossible sum – to the soldier who could drag from the woods the white man that had dropped this basket, for it had looked to Ralegh as though three Spaniards had been in the canoes. This suspicion was confirmed by the Indian pilots whom the English did catch up with, but the Spaniards themselves got away. Still these pilots were useful, for one of them knew exactly where the Spaniards had been searching for gold and had further-more a fair idea of the success they had met with. He told Ralegh all he knew – and it sounded as if some most profitable workings existed very close by. Treasure was but a mile or so away.

At this point the modern reader expects Ralegh and his men to get out their spades and start digging. Certainly the contemporaries who read his account – and particularly the investors who had risked their own money in the hope of profit – must have expected the explorer to grasp this opportunity definitely to establish the plausibility of the dream on which he had staked his reputation. But Walter did not –and one can sense in the style of his writing his anxiety to explain away his failure.

He claims, with typical unsubstantiated audacity, that the canoe that got away was definitely loaded down with 'a good quantity of ore and gold'. But he then tries to imply that the object of his expedition was not so much to bring back gold as to sniff out sites and workings from which gold *might* be brought back in the future. One cannot imagine that he had proposed anything so half-hearted to the men he had urged to part with their money, but still, warming to his theme, he side-steps vigorously:

> I thought it best not to hover thereabouts, lest if the same had been perceived by the company there would have been by this time many barks and ships set out, and perchance other nations would also have gotten of ours for pilots.

His ordinary sailors might, in other words, go back to England and sell their knowledge of the treasure's whereabouts to the highest bidder – perhaps even to the Spaniards.

One can imagine Sir Robert Cecil, at least, reading this excuse and pointing out that the untrustworthiness of his followers was something that Ralegh should have thought of when first he recruited them, not at the moment when the expedition's goal appeared to be within reach.

'I could have returned a good quantity of gold ready cast', wrote Ralegh high-mindedly, 'if I had not shot at another mark than present profit.' But what is the moral distinction between present profit and future profit – sparing something, the better to loot it later – and what about Walter's obligation to bring back some dividends for the men who had risked their money with him?

It could be suggested, of course, that Walter Ralegh was reluctant to start digging for gold because the local evidence for its existence was much thinner than he subsequently pretended. But the simplest explanation of his failure is the influence of the hostile environment on both him and his party. El Dorado was supposed to be located in the still distant Guiana highlands, not in this steamy delta that was in flood. And the river was rising alarmingly: 'all the branches and small rivers which fall into the Orinoco were raised with such speed as, if we waded them over the shoes in the morning outward, we were covered to the shoulders homeward the very same day.' The onslaught of the elements was frightening. What might happen to the boats on the swelling tide if the expedition went into the jungle digging for gold? The safest course seemed to be to press on out of the swamps into the main stream where, with plainer sailing and the sniff now of some sort of treasure in the nostrils, the party might proceed more smoothly. They had already been gone from their ships for the best part of a fortnight.

Once out of the delta, things did go more smoothly. 'On the fifteenth day we discovered afar off the mountains of Guiana to our great joy.' The highlands of El Dorado were in sight at last! Another Indian canoe was caught up with, and, once the natives got over their apprehension that these bearded white men might be Spaniards, they brought the Englishmen fish and turtles' eggs 'which are very wholesome meat and greatly restoring, so as our men were now well filled and highly contented both with our fare and the nearness of the land of Guiana which appeared in sight.' Next morning the local chief brought more supplies, including fresh fruit, gratefully supping, in return, a bottle or two of Spanish wine which Ralegh offered him, and inviting the whole party back to his village. The expedition was taking on a most civilized character. Some of the English captains were developing a taste for the local beverages and they were glad of an opportunity to carouse and become 'reasonable pleasant'. In the village the English found, too, a couple of other chiefs resting in hammocks and being refreshed with little cups of wine ladled from a vast twelve gallon container by their womenfolk.

One of these chiefs had a wife who greatly took Sir Walter's fancy. 'In all my life I have seldom seen a better favoured woman. She was of good stature, with black eyes, fat of body, of an excellent countenance, her hair almost as long as herself, tied up again in pretty knots.' This physical beauty was presumably enhanced by the fact, which Sir Walter did not mention in his account for the Virgin Queen, that the lady was stark naked.

With a new guide, an experienced old pilot from this friendly village, the Englishmen made fast progress up the main stream of the Orinoco itself – some 30 miles wide at this point, estimated Ralegh, making allowance for the large islands around which the river flowed and on which the party camped for its overnight stops. Ever sanguine, Ralegh noted that the rocky banks of the river had 'a blue metalline colour, like unto the best steel ore, which I assuredly take it to be', and as further evidence that the local inhabitants would render to English prospectors help they would give to no other, he describes at length all they told him about the *curare* poison they used on their arrows, a secret 'that in all this time there was never Spaniard either by gift or torment that could attain to the true knowledge'. The only salvation was, apparently, to abstain rigorously from all drink, for any victim quenching his thirst

endureth the most insufferable torment in the world and abideth a most ugly and lamentable death, sometimes dying stark mad, sometimes their bowels breaking out of their bellies, and are presently discoloured as black as pitch, and so unsavoury as no man can endure to cure or to attend them.

Not a pleasant end, and one to which Ralegh's alleged cure was, in fact, a far from effective antidote.

After a week on the Orinoco's main course, the English reached an important milestone, the junction of the Orinoco and Caroni rivers where, in a sort of harbour, Ralegh saw a great Spanish anchor which he presumed to have been left by the Spaniards in whose company the legend-sowing Juan Martinez had been master of munitions. Here, the English were graciously received by the local chief, a venerable old fellow – Ralegh set his age at 110 – called Topiawari. He came to meet his visitors bringing fresh provisions, especially pineapples, 'the princess of fruits that grow under the sun', and bearing as presents some miniature parakeets and an armadillo 'which seemeth to be barred all over with small plates some what like to a Renocero' (rhinoceros). With such a fantastic beast alive in front of him, it did not seem unreasonable to believe the other legends that Walter Ralegh was to hear in the next few days about the surrounding countryside. There were living on a branch of the Caroni River, apparently,

a nation of people whose heads appear not above their shoulders; which though it may be thought a mere fable, yet for mine own part, I am resolved it is true. . . . They are called the Ewaipanoma: they are reported to have their eyes in their shoulders, and their mouths in the middle of their breasts, and . . . a long train of hair growth backward between their shoulders.

What about the Amazons, those mythical female warriors after whom the great river to the south-east was named? It appeared that they too were alive and well and very well known to certain local chiefs who, once a year, would meet with them. The ladies would 'cast lots for their valentines' and then, for a month, feast, drink, dance and make love non-stop. If, as a result of this annual bacchanalia, any Amazon conceived and bore a son she would send him back to the chief she presumed to be the father, but daughters were kept to be reared in the 'cruel and bloodthirsty' ways of the female warriors, their fathers being rewarded with an expensive present and an invitation to return to the following year's festivities. In a land of poisoned arrows and naked wives it did not sound an impossibly far-fetched tale, and there was some sort of evidence as well for the story – green, jade-like stones which were produced by the Amazons and exchanged for gold. 'Of these I saw divers in Guiana, and commonly every king or cassique hath one, which their wives for the most part wear, and they esteem them as great jewels.'

But the most important legend of all was El Dorado. This was the question on which everything depended, and pointing to the mountains towering high in the west, Ralegh asked old Topiawari who lived there.

He answered with a great sigh . . . that he remembered in his father's lifetime . . . that there came down into that large valley of Guiana a nation from so far off as the sun slept (for such were his own words) with so great a multitude as they could not be numbered nor resisted, and that they wore large coats and hats of crimson colour, which colour he expressed by showing a piece of red wood, wherewith my tent was supported; and that they . . . had slain and rooted out so many of the ancient people as there were leaves in the wood upon all the trees, and had now made themselves lords of all.

These were the supermen of the lost city Ralegh had come to conquer, and Topiawari told how these crimson-clad strangers had built a great town at the foot of their mountains 'at the beginning of the great plains of

Guiana that have no end. And that their houses have many rooms, one over the other.' Their king was so jealous of his kingdom where the sun slept that he had 3,000 men constantly under arms to defend his borders.

The quest would not be easy, but it now seemed more than ever to Ralegh a real one. As he moved on up the Caroni River he met another chief who confirmed Topiawari's story, adding that these crimson-clad men 'abound in gold' and that, if the English could ally with certain local tribes, there was a good chance of invading the highland kingdom to 'satisfy ourselves with gold and all other good things'. It was on this river, the Caroni, moreover, that Captain Jorge, Berreo's lieutenant, had said that there lay a most profitable silver mine. So the best thing seemed to be to split up into small reconnaisance parties. Captains Thynne and Grenville were sent off with one party to survey the river by land, moving towards the lands of a tribe said to be immediate neighbours of the Guianan Empire. Captain Whiddon and eight shot were sent off to prospect for mineral stone, while Ralegh himself struck off overland with Captains Gifford and Hancocke to inspect what looked to be a vast pall of 'smoke that had risen over some great town'. It turned out to be spray rising high from a succession of thundering waterfalls 'every one as high over the other as a church tower, which fell with that fury, that the rebound of waters made it seem as if it had been all covered over with a great shower of rain'.

The cross country walking had tired Ralegh badly. He said he could not go on any further 'being a very ill footman', but his companions persuaded him onwards – and he was to be glad that they did, for his painful exercise was rewarded by a vision of the most heavenly little countryside, a veritable promised land that needed but nymphs and shepherds to convince him that he had discovered Arcadia.

I never saw a more beautiful country, nor more lively prospects, hills so raised here and there over the valleys, the river winding into divers branches, the plains adjoining all fair green grass without brush or stubble, the ground of hard sand easy to march on either for horse or foot, the deer crossing on every path, the birds towards the evening singing on every tree with a thousand several tunes, cranes and herons of white, crimson and carnation perching on the river's side, the air fresh with a gentle easterly wind, and every stone that we stopped to take up promising either gold or silver by his complexion.

These stones, littering the prospect of Croesus' wealth casually over the landscape, were the most seductive vision of all. The explorers fell on their knees, tearing at the spar with their diggers and fingers, unable to believe the treasures sprinkled around them like daisies for the picking.

They tore out all they could to bear back in triumph to the main party – to discover that the other patrols had already returned and, miraculously, had also picked up samples of rock that seemed to promise solid ore in the earth below. 'Captain Whiddon and our surgeon, Nicholas Millechap, brought me a kind of stone like sapphires', and when Ralegh showed these to the Indians they said that they could show him a mountain studded with them in 'very large pieces growing diamond-wise'. On the way home a few weeks later, Ralegh was to be told by a Spaniard to whom he showed his samples of spar 'that it was *El Madre del Oro,* and that the mine was further in the ground'.

It was all too good to be true – the triumphant conclusion to long months of faith and courage. Ralegh had not reached the city of El Dorado, but that could wait. He had discovered a land where 'the sun covereth not so many riches in any part of the earth'. He could go on, but the expedition, after four weeks of tense travelling, seemed to have reached a natural conclusion. Some of Topiawari's more hotheaded followers expressed themselves eager to join with the English in an attack on the crimson-clad men of the highlands, suggesting as booty 'their women for us and their gold for you'. But the mood of the party was not for further adventures. It was time to go home. Everyone was tired of wearing the same shirt for weeks on end, even if the ever more frequent rains meant that it got 'thoroughly washed on his body for the most part ten times in one day' – everyone, that is, except for two, Francis Sparrow, a servant of Gifford's, and Hugh Goodwin, Ralegh's cabin boy. Topiawari was keen for his son to go back to England with the expedition, and these two adventurous young men were anxious to stay with the Indians, learn their language and to discover more about Guiana.

So one day in June 1595, Sparrow and Goodwin waved goodbye to the boats and companions that had brought them so many miles to this isolated and unknown spot lost in the South American jungle. Goodwin, just a lad in his teens, was to stay there, learning the native tongues so thoroughly that when Ralegh returned to the Orinoco some twenty years later, he scarcely spoke a word of English, and Sparrow was eventually captured by the Spaniards and sent back to Europe, sadly proving totally unable, when he came to set pen to paper, to recapture any of the excitement that these two Robinson Crusoes had lived through. Ralegh's talent with words was all too rare among the sixteenth-century explorers.

The journey back down the Orinoco was an anti-climax. Lawrence Keymis was sent off with a small party to search for a gold mine that was reported along the way, but he did not find anything, and back in the salt water of the estuary 'there arose a mighty storm' which almost destroyed the little craft that had served so well in the river currents. It seemed for an hour or so that, having triumphed over the worst that the jungle could do to them, these seafarers were to be destroyed by the very elements they knew best. But dawn rose to find them still safely afloat and in sight of Trinidad, which they rounded to find their ships at anchor 'than which there was never to us a more joyful sight'.

Before setting course for England Ralegh led his ships in raids on three Spanish settlements along the Spanish Main, sacking two of them, and then went on to meet up with Captains Preston and Somers and prowl off Cuba in the hope of taking home a truly rich prize. He had brought back from Guiana only tokens of wealth – nothing to pay for even half of the expedition's expenses. But the Spanish treasure galleons stayed safely inside Havana harbour. Then, troubled by that occasional blot on his conscience, the lost colony he had always promised to succour, Walter Ralegh toyed with the notion of a trip north to Virginia. But adverse winds and crews more than anxious to get home relieved him of the obligation. By September 1595 he was in England again – to discover the sceptical claiming that he had not crossed the ocean at all. Sir Walter Ralegh had spent the last nine months, so the story went, skulking in an obscure cove in Cornwall.

❧ 29 ❧

'The Discovery of Guiana'

I t was hardly a hero's welcome. As well as the stories that Walter Ralegh and his crew had been hiding in Cornwall, there were claims that the ore samples he so proudly produced had come originally from Barbary. What proof was there that they had been dug from the soil of South America? One officer of the mint, at the instigation of a London alderman, even declared that, wherever they came from, the ore samples were totally worthless – fool's gold. Ralegh's stories of armadillos, Amazons and headless warriors were too much of a piece with the fantastic conceits associated with his name already and some of the men who had scrabbled gems from the turf of that luscious pasture near the Caroni River confirmed the general disbelief, for they refused to believe Ralegh's warnings that many of the stones they had kept were worthless, and that some diamonds they had found in Trinidad were only marcasite. They bore them proudly to the assayers, only to be disappointed and to add their own bitter testimony to the common scorn.

There was only one remedy. Since the assays of the ore samples that he set most store by were just encouraging rather than conclusive, Ralegh must justify himself in writing, and so, in a matter of weeks, he dashed off *The Discovery of the Large, Rich and Beautiful Empire of Guiana with a Relation of the Great and Golden City of Manoa*. Its narrative excitement was compulsive, but it was more than an adventure story. It was a work of propaganda on behalf of all Ralegh had hoped for in his months of exploration:

Guiana is a country that hath yet her maidenhead, never sacked, turned, nor wrought; the face of the earth hath not been torn, nor the virtue and salt of the soil spent by manurance, the graves have not been opened for gold, the mines not broken with sledges nor the images pulled down out of their temples. It hath never been entered by any army of strength, and never conquered or possessed by any Christian prince.[1]

The Discovery was an instant success and despite the lack of solid evidence Ralegh could produce for all his claims, his imperialist ambitions struck a chord in many, George Chapman, the poet, for example:

> Guiana, whose rich feet are mines of gold,
> Whose forehead knocks against the roof of stars,
> Stands on her tip-toes at fair England looking,
> Kissing her hand, bowing her mighty breast,
> And every sign of all submission making,
> To be her sister and the daughter both
> Of our most sacred maid.[2]

Shakespeare's imagination was stirred also. Othello scared Desdemona with talk of

> ... the Cannibals that each other eat,
> The Anthropophagi, and men whose heads
> Do grow beneath their shoulders,

and in *The Tempest* Gonzalo made a similar allusion.[3] The whole of that latter play, in fact, owes its theme to the vividness with which Renaissance travellers like Ralegh recreated the strange lands they had visited. It is certainly plausible to trace Milton's images of the Garden of Eden to the countryside Ralegh described where 'the deer came down feeding by the water's side, as if they had been used to a keeper's call'. In *Paradise Lost* Adam has a vision of the furthermost ends of the earth:

> Rich Mexico, the seat of Montezume,
> And Cuzco in Peru, the richer seat
> Of Atahualpa, and yet unspoiled
> Guiana, whose great City Geryon's sons
> Call El Dorado.[4]

Not for the first or last time Ralegh became a best-selling author: one Dutch edition, two Latin and four German within five years, and a score of successive English, Dutch and French editions throughout the seventeenth century.

But paper success was a poor substitute for the accolade Ralegh most desired – royal approval. He prayed for Guiana that the 'King of all kings and lord of lords will put into her heart which is lady of ladies to possess it' – but He did not. Queen Elizabeth remained unmoved – and it cannot be said, in all honesty, that history has proved her wrong for not grasping the imperial opportunity which Walter offered her. At the end of the nineteenth century, it is true, Venezuelan Guiana could boast at El Callao the world's largest output of gold. But only in comparatively modern times has it proved possible to master the rivers that hampered Ralegh's activities and would sorely have jeopardized the survival of any sixteenth-century colonists foolhardy enough to act on his exhortations to occupy the area. Sugar, rice, bauxite and timber – British Guiana's modern exports – are comparatively slow earners and could not have made an Elizabethan colony self-sufficient.

Still, Ralegh's speculations as he looked at the metallic blue stones of the Guianan river banks have been endorsed by the massive modern steel plant erected where the Orinoco and Caroni rivers join, where the Englishman found that great Spanish anchor and where he talked for long hours with old Topiawari about the crimson-clad men of the mountains. Though his prophecy that 'I shall yet live to see it an English nation' did not come true in his lifetime, it was fulfilled for at least one period in the British Empire's history, and, more magical still, the memory of the bearded knight who served a virgin queen lived on among the thatched villages of the Orinoco delta, so that when, in 1604, some Dutch explorers beached there, they discovered friendly natives rushing towards them shouting 'Anglee, Anglee!' Sir Walter Ralegh's wraith survived to haunt the men of the swamps and jungles, the legend of a saviour from the Spaniards, a once and future king like King Arthur – except that, unlike King Arthur, Sir Walter Ralegh was definitely to return to the dark trusting people who hallowed his memory.

❀ 30 ❀

Cadiz

After nearly five years of disgrace – the best part of one in the Tower and the best part of another in the swamps of Guiana – Sir Walter Ralegh seemed as far away from royal forgiveness as ever. From revelling in rustic seclusion at Sherborne, he had become restless and frustrated. As time went by he travelled down to the West and up to London more and more. He strained ever harder to catch royal attention, Privy Council attention – *any* attention. The spirit that loved to strut upon the public stage gripped him ever more irritably – but to no avail. The Earl of Essex provided Queen Elizabeth with the courtly companionship she enjoyed, whilst, in the council chamber, old Burghley was grooming his crippled son Robert to take his place. Walter's attempts to influence national policy so far as Guiana was concerned had, to put it kindly, been noted.

But, foreign colonization apart, there was another passion of Walter's that was of enduring relevance to the national interest – the sea conflict with Spain, and it was in this direction that Ralegh, even as he was scribbling furiously to complete his account of his travels in Guiana, began to occupy himself. He had no doubt about how Spain should be dealt with: a hard, uncompromising blow to the body was called for. It would advance England's national interest, and there was, of course, the matter of family honour. Walter still sought some triumph to set against the destruction of Richard Grenville and the *Revenge*.

The trouble was that Queen Elizabeth had never shared Sir Walter Ralegh's capacity for that sort of indignation and it was one of her strengths that she knew the limitations of resentment. The queen, complained Ralegh, 'did all things by halves, and by petty invasions taught the Spaniard how to defend himself . . . which, till our attempts taught him, was hardly known to himself.'[1]

Only a few weeks back from Guiana, in November 1595 Ralegh wrote in alarm to the Privy Council. The Spaniards, he had been told, were forming a fleet to carry reinforcements to the Irish rebels. Would the queen grant a small sum for him to send a swift pinnace down the Spanish coast to reconnoitre? Or would the Privy Council organize some really substantial retaliation?

The first suggestion kindled little enthusiasm, but the invasion idea fell on ground already well prepared. The Earl of Essex and the lord admiral themselves wanted to be done with half-measures and to launch a full-blooded invasion on the Spanish mainland, an Armada in reverse. English ships, they planned, would carry English soldiers to the beaches of Spain, and an excellent place to disembark would be Cadiz, Spain's great harbour just outside the Mediterranean. It would be as if the Spaniards sacked Plymouth or Chatham, and it was, furthermore, the port where the treasure fleets from America anchored.

The scheme appealed very much to Walter. Having set out for Guiana 'in the winter of my life' he had got back to England 'a beggar and withered'. If he could not find his gold in El Dorado he was all in favour of seeking it nearer home, and he was not alone in hoping for another *Madre de Dios*. Even the queen shared that particular optimism – and there were other unusual advocates besides. Old Burghley advised an offensive. The likely dividend, he felt, justified the investment.

So in the spring of 1596, ninety-six English ships were equipped for an attack on Cadiz that summer, and an invitation sent to the Dutch to send a further twenty. Sir Francis Vere was called back from the Continent to organize the 10,000-strong army that was to land, and, as advisers to the two principal commanders – Essex and the lord admiral, Charles Howard – a council of war was selected, including not only Lord Thomas Howard, the lord admiral's brother, but, his privateering and exploratory activities finally recognized by a naval command, Sir Walter Ralegh.

It was a great opportunity, and Walter grasped it firmly. Guiana had proved a disappointment so far as the battle to regain Elizabeth's friendship was concerned. Cadiz would be the turning point. Walter's particular duty in the preparations was to round up men and supplies in the London area, for there was a lumbering fleet of victuallers to be gathered together, and the queen's ships needed crews which would have to be pressganged. It was a most unpalatable task loaded onto Ralegh, but he took it on with resolution. 'As fast as we press men one day, they ran away another and say they will not serve,' he complained to Cecil early in May 1596, but he got the men just the same.

He spent the spring of 1596 almost constantly in skiffs on the Thames travelling from captain to captain of his transport fleet. 'I cannot live to row up and down every tide from Gravesend to London' he wrote to

Borough, the controller of the navy, asking him to crack an official whip to make the pressed supply captains a little more cooperative. Ralegh was so seldom in his headquarters that a messenger sent from Cecil had to ride for hours through the muddy Kent lanes before he found the rear admiral 'in a country village, a mile from Gravesend, hunting after runaway mariners and dragging in the mire from alehouse to alehouse'. Sir Walter scribbled off a quick note to be carried back to London. 'Sir, by the living God, there is no king nor queen nor general nor anyone else can take more care than I to be gone.' Then he was up in the saddle again, off to the next beer shop to whip away from some village green men to fight in the broiling high summer of southern Spain.

It was hard work, but it was good to be, once again, back in the mainstream of affairs. Walter toiled with all his old fiendishness, writing on one day to Robert Cecil no less than four letters.[2] He was slipping again into the mantle of a man who mattered, putting up a Puritan friend for an Irish bishopric, begging special treatment for a kinsman who had incurred the royal displeasure, pushing forward an Exeter fellow for a position in the cathedral there. 'Sir, I beseech you for my sake, because it standeth much on my credit, to favour the suit.'[3]

All the hard work had some effect. The tone Ralegh's fellow organizers adopted towards him became less patronizing and when all the ships and men had finally been gathered together for the trip down the channel to Plymouth, only to be delayed yet again by a contrary head-wind that sprang up, Essex wrote to Ralegh a charming letter of thanks and sympathy:

> Your pains and travail in bringing all things to that forwardness they are in, doth sufficiently assure me of your discontentment to be now stayed by the wind. Therefore I will not entreat you to make haste ... but I will wish and pray a good wind for you.
>
> And when you are come, I will make you see I desire to do you as much honour, and give you as great contentment as I can. For this is the action and the time in which you and I shall be both taught to know and love one another.[4]

It was a gentle, boyish touch on the earl's part to admit their past quarrels so naturally. To be a brother-in-arms loomed high on the list of Essex's romantic priorities. And Walter, too, had a yearning for such a straightforward relationship even if, in his heart, he knew what potential misunderstanding lay between them.

His reception, when he did finally arrive in Plymouth on 21 May 1596, proved it. Tempers there were short, for Elizabeth had been blowing hot and cold. 'The queen wrangles with our action for no cause but because it is in hand', complained Essex. The Spaniards had been attacking Calais just across the English Channel and Elizabeth had refused to commit her troops to a relieving sortie until it was too late. Then she had suggested to Essex and Howard that she might recall them and entrust the Cadiz enterprise to commanders of lesser rank. An explosion of protest from the whole council of war in Plymouth put an end to that, but when Ralegh arrived from London, there were those who suggested that he had put that particular idea up to Elizabeth to win command for himself, and at dinner that evening a furious quarrel broke out between Francis Vere and Ralegh. The issue between them was precedence: whether Vere, as marshal of the army, could issue orders to Ralegh while at sea, and the dispute widened with the sailors and soldiers present taking their respective sides. Conyers Clifford, as a soldier, took Vere's part, and Arthur Throckmorton, Bess's brother, spoke up fiercely for Ralegh. Indeed, he spoke so fiercely and violently that he was cashiered on the spot for his aggressive insults. Clifford and Vere were his senior officers.

It was Essex who patched up the quarrel. He seems to have realized how overwrought everyone was by the weeks of preparation, and to have made allowances accordingly. Arthur Throckmorton was quietly reinstated, and the argument forgotten in the bustle of preparations for departure.

Everyone was glad to be off on 3 June 1596. Ralegh was commander of one of the five squadrons into which the 120 vessel-strong fleet was divided, and he was sailing in the *Warspite*, a new galleon with two decks and forty guns with a name that was to grace British naval vessels for centuries and to earn fame as recently as 1940 at Narvik. It was not his own ship, but the queen's, one of the two brand new vessels she had supplied for the expedition. The other was *Due Repulse*, Essex's flagship. Both had been designed by Drake.

When the great white arc of English sails came over the horizon off Cape St Vincent on 15 June, 1596, after less than two weeks sailing, the Spaniards were taken completely by surprise.

The Cadiz fortress was in the middle of being repaired, with great gaps in its walls, and the English soldiers when they landed found the tools the Spanish workmen had dropped in terror as the invasion fleet drifted into the bay.

Just before the English fleet came over the horizon they had captured a little merchantman, an Irish barque bound for Waterford whose captain told the lord admiral that there was a fleet of fifty or sixty rich-laden merchant ships in the harbour, a pack of some twenty galleys, and only a handful of ocean-going warships. Battle – and booty – seemed certain.

'Lord God!' wrote the lord admiral's doctor, 'what a sudden rejoicing there was! How every man skipt and leapt for joy, and how nimble was every man to see all things were neat, trim and ready for the fight.'

That merchant fleet must not escape. It was not a treasure fleet, but it was laden down low in the water with supplies for the settlements along the Spanish Main. It bore Spanish America's imports for a whole year, and there were rich naval supplies as well. So Ralegh was assigned a dozen vessels to sweep a dragnet between the main English fleet and the shore, lest the Spanish merchantment should take advantage of the main battle to sneak off through the beach shoals.

It meant that Ralegh might, if he captured any of the merchant fleet, get first crack at rich pickings that the English had scarcely dared dream of, but it also meant that he was not present at the council of war, which, out in the centre of the bay, decided on the strategy of attack – and a poor strategy it was. The Spanish merchantmen were now huddling inside Cadiz harbour, but instead of driving hard into the obvious prey, it was decided instead that Essex should land troops to the seaward side of the town.

The weather, fortunately, put a stop to this – at some cost. As the heavily-armoured soldiers slithered down into the skiffs that were to land them on the beach, the breeze stiffened, whipped up waves and capsized two of the landing craft. Immobilized by their heavy armour the soldiers were helpless and, screaming horribly, nearly a score of men drowned.

It was at this point that Ralegh's squadron rejoined the body of the fleet. The Spanish merchantmen were now obviously tucked deep into the harbour and Ralegh was for sailing straight into Cadiz bay. The English had an overwhelming superiority and should use it to assure the soldiers an undisturbed landing in the quiet waters of the harbour. To risk the troops through the waves on to an open beach was pointless – and the sea battle would still have to be fought.

Sir Walter Ralegh had never actually experienced a massed sea battle in his life before. He had seen action as a soldier in France and Ireland. He had been worsted in the scrap he fought in the queen's *Falcon* in 1568, and he had helped sweep up the Armada. But Cadiz caught him, in his mid-forties, never having actually sailed in mass formation, slogging it out, broadside to broadside while Essex, on the other hand, had sailed on Drake's Portuguese raid in 1589 and so had some experience to back up the superiority bestowed by his earldom.

But to Ralegh, as he rejoined the main body of the fleet after the tragic fiasco of Essex's attempted landing through the Atlantic breakers, this all mattered not a jot. The moment he came close to the *Due Repulse* he had himself rowed over and, on the quarter deck, in front of all Essex's officers, gave the young man a dressing down for attempting to land in such conditions. Essex replied with some restraint in the face of Ralegh's arrogance that he was acting on the orders of the whole council of war. If Ralegh knew better he should upbraid the lord admiral – and Ralegh did just that. He was working himself up into a fever of excitement. He was rowed through the swell to Charles Howard's ship, persuaded him to call off the sea-side landing for an assault inside the bay, and, jubilant at his triumph, cried out to Essex on the *Due Repulse* 'Entramos! Entramos!' – 'We're going in!' The soldiers on the *Due Repulse* gave back a cheer and young Essex tossed his gay plumed hat into the air. High above the deck the wind caught it – and blew it out into the sea.

It was hardly proper, and quite unexpected, but Ralegh had effectively taken command of the whole enterprise. It was partly the commonsense of what he suggested, but his triumph was essentially one of personality. He had stood on Essex's quarterdeck and outshouted the earl and then he had done the same to old Charles Howard. With his dark eyes aflame and swaggering from ship to ship, he was irresistible, riding one of those great waves of confidence that have swept him out of history and into legend. Many men did brave things at Cadiz in 1596, but all drew some inspiration from Walter Ralegh. Nothing could stand in his way.

By the time Essex's ships and soldiers were reorganized for the new strategy, it was afternoon. At Ralegh's suggestion, the whole fleet hove to, ready to attack at dawn next day, 21 June, and as the sun rose it was Ralegh's ship the *Warspite*, which led the English fleet into the bay.

It was a colourful affair. Howard, Essex and Ralegh were dressed as though they were off to present Elizabeth with her birthday gifts, and Ralegh, in particular, strutted the deck of the *Warspite* like a peacock. The others had glory to capture, but he had revenge to seize as well, for one of the four great galleons protecting the merchant fleet in the harbour owed to the Raleghs a special debt. It had been the guns of the *St Philip*, flagship of the admiral of Spain, that had blasted to destruction Ralegh's cousin Richard Grenville, and now that the galleon which had sunk the *Revenge* off the Azores was cooped in the harbour of Cadiz, Ralegh was saving his fire for her, 'being resolved', he said 'to be revenged for the *Revenge*, or to second her with mine own life'.

From the fort of Cadiz the Spanish batteries plopped cannonballs down onto the English vessels proceeding into the harbour. Snipers tried to pick off the English captains who, like Ralegh, disdained to hide their rank in drab attire. Two centuries later, and only a few miles away, Horatio Nelson was to exhibit the same flamboyant pride with less fortunate consequences. But Walter Ralegh, his guns still quiet as his ship glided silently forward, decided on a still more extravagant gesture. He gathered on deck the musicians who, in an age before ship's wirelesses and foghorns, were a crucial part of a fleet's communications system. They raised their trumpets to their lips and, when the fort's guns next salvoed, they blasted forth a discordant chorus, and responded to each blast with ever more derisive buglings. The Earl of Essex hurled another hat into the sea.

Walter Ralegh's excitement was more sardonic for he was faced with a ticklish problem, whether to heave to and swap broadsides with the Spanish galleons or to take the *Warspite* right up to the enemy ships and board them.

The trouble was that he was under the strictest orders not to risk one of the queen's ships in such a fashion. No amount of heroism would compensate in Elizabeth's eyes for the financial loss involved in having one of her expensive men-of-war destroyed, and so Walter Ralegh dropped anchor. Aflame with revenge he might be, but burnt into his mind even deeper than the memory of Grenville's fate was the pain of the humiliation administered by the lady for whom he was now risking his life. If disgrace had taught Walter Ralegh nothing else it had taught him prudence.

But the Earl of Essex could not understand what was going on. He had his *Due Repulse* brought up to the *Warspite*, so that, no longer moving targets, the two vessels caught a nasty battering. Ralegh jumped into a skiff and was rowed over to Essex's flagship. Would the earl back him up and grapple right into close quarters with the Spaniards? 'I would board with the queen's ship', said Ralegh, 'for it was the same loss to burn or sink, for I must endure the one.'[5] It was a needless query to put to Essex. Anything Ralegh dared, Robert Devereux would dare better, so whatever happened in this battle, Ralegh had one ally for the battles which might occur when he got home. The queen's favourite would protect the queen's ship – and her captain. A strange moment for politicking – but there were stranger politickings to come.

Ralegh's sally for moral support had not taken thirty minutes, but as he scrambled back onto the *Warspite* he discovered his lieutenants seething. While they had lain at anchor the other English ships had manœuvred themselves into the honour of leading the van of the fleet. Sir Francis Vere had pushed his *Rainbow* forward, and then the *Nonpareil*, with the two Howards on board, had gone even further ahead. It was not a matter of strategy but of comic opera precedence.

But Ralegh could play that game as well as the next man. He weighed anchor, slipped past Vere and then swung round to block the *Rainbow*'s passage. It brought him under still fiercer Spanish fire and he did not, for a time, realize how Vere was retaliating – the *Rainbow* had got a rope onto the *Warspite* and was using this to pull herself nearer.

What nonsense! Ralegh had the rope cut, weighed anchor finally, and moved on into the Spaniards. He steered straight at the *St Philip*, and the guns which had pounded the *Revenge* into splinters now poured their punishment at the *Warspite*. The battle was reaching its climax. The four great galleons were all that stood between the English and Cadiz. Heaving and swaying from the recoil of their guns firing all to one side, they blocked the channel. The Spanish shot ripped through the *Warspite*'s sails and wood and rigging. The noise of their guns grew louder. Peering through the smoke from his own cannon Ralegh could see the Spaniards on their ships, and he must have looked especially hard at the men on the *St Philip*, the crew going furiously about the very same tasks which had destroyed his cousin. After five years and many thousand miles of voyaging only a few yards of water separated Walter Ralegh from this ship that owed him so much.

But he was not to have the pleasure of collecting his debts in person, for the shot was flying thicker and faster, and suddenly a cannonball smashed into the deck by his feet. An agonizing pain struck through his leg and looking down he saw blood and his calf 'interlaced and deformed with splinters'.[7] Unable to stand he collapsed onto the deck. It was an ugly wound that was to haunt Walter Ralegh for the rest of his life, for he would never walk straight again, limping until the day he died.

His only immediate consolation was that his more fortunate comrades – no one was killed by the Spanish guns and many escaped without a scratch[8] – were also to be denied the pleasure of tackling the Spaniards hand to hand, for the great galleons cut their cables, drifted aground and were deserted by their crews. Lying on the *Warspite*, having his wound dressed, Ralegh watched the Spanish ships 'tumbling into the sea heaps of soldiers, so thick as if coals had been poured out of a sack in many ports at once; some drowned and some sticking to the mud'.

Now the Dutch ships moved in for the kill. Schooled in the vicious reprisals of the Netherlands fighting, their soldiers jumped into skiffs, drew their swords and prepared to slaughter any Spaniards who did not drown. Their prey were helpless, many burnt horribly by the fires that had broken out on board the galleons, 'very many hanging by the ropes' ends by the ships' sides, under the water even to the lips; many swimming with grievous wounds, stricken under water, and put out of their pain'. The *St Philip* and the *St Thomas* exploded, strewing flaming debris everywhere. 'If any man had a desire to see Hell itself', wrote Ralegh later 'it was there most lively figured.'

Did the sight of the *St Philip* exploding satisfy Walter Ralegh? Or did the pain of his own wound nag him into an humanity which had not been conspicuous at Smerwick Fort? Whatever the reason, he moved quickly to set English flyboats between the advancing Dutch and the poor Spanish wretches thrashing in the water. The Netherlanders had, after all, scarcely risked their lives to an extent which justified their taking others, and then, racked by pain, Ralegh had himself rowed ashore and borne on a litter through the streets of Cadiz. It was less a matter of pride than of plunder, for the English soldiers and sailors were ransacking the city, and he who did not, in these first few hours, capture for himself plate, jewels or a wealthy merchant he could ransom, could expect to pick up little of value next day.

But the sack of Cadiz was too much for an invalid. Though Essex got the churches protected, in the streets the soldiers went berserk. Ralegh's litter bearers were jolted, his wound was searingly painful and he had ruefully to go back to the *Warspite* with no plunder worthy of the name.

The town of Cadiz was very rich in merchandise, in plant and money [he complained with some bitterness when he got home]. Many rich prisoners [were] given to the land commanders so as that sort are very rich: some had prisoners for sixteen thousand ducats, some for twenty thousand and, besides, great houses of merchandise. What the generals have gotten, I know least; they protest it is too little. For my own part, I have gotten a lame leg and a deformed. For the rest, either I spake too late or it was otherwise resolved. I have not wanted good words and exceeding kind and regardful usance. But I have possession of naught but poverty and pain.[9]

Ralegh was especially bitter because, nursing his wound back on the *Warspite*, he could see what the other commanders, roistering in the town, forgot. If the value of Cadiz could be reckoned in hundreds of thousands of ducats, the value of the great merchant fleet, still untouched less than a mile away, was a matter of millions. The ships, quite defenceless, were clustered together in Port Royal on the opposite side of the harbour. At daybreak next morning Ralegh sent his nephew Sir John Gilbert with his brother-in-law Sir Arthur Throckmorton, to ask permission of the lord admiral, Essex and Vere to enter Port Royal and seize the fleet.

But Cadiz was still a hectic place, with money and men to organize, and the merchants who owned the vessels were anxious to cut their losses. They had sent a deputation to the English commanders offering two million ducats ransom if they could sail off their cargoes unharmed. That, of course, only increased the English appetite. If it was worth the merchants' while to pay that much to get away, their ships must indeed be valuable, and this was only an unofficial offer, made secretly by the merchants without consulting the Spanish royal officers. The English decided to wait and bargain for a higher ransom.

It was a grave and expensive miscalculation, for no representative of King Philip would compound the humiliation of Cadiz's capture with sordid hagglings over mere merchants' property. Orders went out for the great fleet to be fired at once and scuttled.

Poor Ralegh! When he had heard of the merchants' clandestine bartering he had been all for seizing the ships and discussing the price afterwards. Now he had to lie on the *Warspite* watching pillars of smoke billow from the ships whose wealth was that of a squadron of *Madre de Dioses*. Twelve million ducats was said to be the value that the merchants themselves had put on the fleet when they had been working out their ransom money, and the scuttling bankrupted them all. South American trade was practically halted for a year. It was a sacrifice of gigantic, foolish proportions. But it did – at a price – sour the English triumph.

Essex and the lord admiral consoled themselves with mutual congratulations at the honour their conquest had won them. Bemoaning the money sunk at the bottom of Cadiz harbour seemed ungracious in the ceremonies of triumph that followed. After a grand banquet in the Friary of St Francis, Essex and Howard dubbed over sixty of their followers knights, prodigally diluting an honour Elizabeth had been jealous in preserving, but Ralegh nursed his resentment and his wound on board the *Warspite*, and was heartily glad when after ten days of junketing it was decided to leave Cadiz. Essex had a scheme for holding Cadiz as a permanent English garrison from which raiding squadrons could sail out to harass the homecoming Spanish treasure fleets, yet Ralegh had no time for it. He wanted to get home and the whole expedition was similarly inclined.

It later turned out that it might have been possible for the English to waylay some Spanish treasure ships if the Earl of Essex's advice had been followed, but no one in England blamed Walter Ralegh for arguing as he had. His reading of the circumstances and mood of the English fleet had been precise, and he had done more than enough finally to claim what he had worked so hard to win. The long years down in Dorset, the *Book of the Ocean to Cynthia*, the arduous months in Guiana, and his desperate exploits in Cadiz harbour had all, in the end, paid off. Sir Walter Ralegh had earned the forgiveness of Queen Elizabeth, and his five years in the wilderness were at an end.

Part 5

❀

1597-1603 Favour Regained

It is reported of the women in the Balear Islands, that, to make their sons expert archers, they will not, when children, give them their breakfast before they had hit the mark. Such was the dealing of the queen with this knight, making him to earn his honour, and by pain and peril to purchase what places of credit or profit were bestowed upon him.

Thomas Fuller, 'History of the Worthies of England'

❀ 31 ❀

Reconciliation

On 1 June 1597 Sir Walter Ralegh was, after five years of disgrace, received at court by Queen Elizabeth I. The queen could never forget completely how her Walter had deceived her, but she could see that he had worked hard to be forgiven. So she received him 'very graciously, and gave him full authority to execute his place as captain of the guard, which immediately he undertook, and swore many men into the places void', wrote Rowland Whyte, the courtier, who appreciated the significance of the reconciliation. It was an attempt to re-establish one of the vanished certainties of a court in which Elizabeth could remember herself at ease. 'In the evening he [Ralegh] rid abroad with the queen, and had private conference with her; and now he comes boldly to the Privy Chamber, as he was wont.'[1]

The Earl of Essex went off for a day or so to inspect the fleet at Chatham, for he would not trust himself to witness the reconciliation. But he was as responsible for it as anyone – more than anyone, in fact, with the exception of the queen's new secretary, Burghley's son Robert Cecil, for it was part of a wider reconciliation which involved all three of the men who loomed over the declining years of Elizabeth: Essex, the established favourite, Ralegh, the now restored favourite, and Robert Cecil, the careful shopkeeper whose store was England.

The three men needed each other, and it was Cecil, the man who realized this most clearly, who was the architect of their loose triumvirate. He was only just in power, more apprehensive than he need have been about Elizabeth's favour. A cripple ever conscious of the golden physiques of Essex and Ralegh – though Ralegh, since Cadiz, walked with a limp – Cecil was anxious to harness to his chariot the young charger and the older warhorse. He knew his father's hold on life was tenuous and he could sense the tensions which the last years of Elizabeth's reign were to bring: it was the men who stood close around the queen who would have the power to help her successor to a smooth accession and who would be rewarded by that successor's gratitude. It was too early for young Cecil to stand alone, so he would stand with the two men who, in their different ways, were the obvious heavyweights of the waning century.

The three were moving towards each other in any case, for Essex, whom the public lionized as the hero of Cadiz, was anxious to repeat his success with another naval enterprise against the Spanish mainland and treasure fleets. After his experiences with Walter in the heat of battle he could see that Ralegh was the very man to breathe fire into such an expedition, and Cecil, with his reputation for prudence, could contribute powerful advocacy if he chose to endorse the project to the queen.

There were solid reasons why Burghley's son should find it expedient to move away from the peace policy which his father had long championed, for it had been while Essex was away that Cecil had benefited from his absence to win the secretaryship, and now he had an equally lucrative position in sight – the chancellorship of the duchy of Lancaster.

So on 18 April 1597, an unexpected dinner party was held at Essex House in the Strand. The earl played host to Robert Cecil and Walter Ralegh, a triangular gathering that would have seemed impossible a year or so earlier and that was to be but a bitter joke in a year or so's time. It had been noticed how the three men had been seeing an unusual amount of each other in the months of February and March, and this supper together set the seal on a definite agreement: Essex could have his expedition; Cecil could anticipate an absence of competition when he moved for his next court office; and Ralegh could count on the support of Cecil, and no opposition from Essex, in his pursuit of royal forgiveness.

Less than six weeks later Walter was back at the queen's side again, and he was to stay there for the next five and a half years until her death. Both of them were older, Elizabeth in her mid-sixties, Walter his mid-forties, and in their age lay an important reason for their reconciliation. For the queen was more out of touch than she had ever been with her realm and people – Walter was as out of touch as ever – and their reunion held for both of them an element of nostalgia, a turning of the back upon the dangers threatened from outside.

Walter's deception of his queen in 1592 had been one of the great disillusionments of Elizabeth's later years and one that she could never forgive, so Bess Ralegh, once a member of her most intimate entourage, could never again be received at court. But that reminder of past deceit aside, Queen Elizabeth was anxious to recapture the joy of her dozen years with Sir Walter Ralegh, and there were many moments in the evening of her reign when it seemed, with her captain of the guard by her side, laughing and playing the old games of conversation and wit, that the old certainties of the 1580s, the high Elizabethan years, had been recaptured.

Walter Ralegh himself was as ready as she was to escape into imagination and memory, and this was to prove as disastrous for him as the penchant for intrigue which had landed him in trouble in 1592. But while the Indian summer lasted, he enjoyed it. Durham House became again his own little court and to it flocked the old friends: Gorges, Carew, Northumberland, Hariot and his Guianan lieutenant, Lawrence Keymis. Hariot had grown closer to Northumberland during the years of Walter's disgrace and, at about this time, transferred himself formally to the earl's patronage, accepting a retainer and moving the centre of his studies from Durham House to Syon House. But this implied no cooling of friendship with Ralegh – there was between Walter and Northumberland no question of yours and mine – and the bonds uniting the band of enthusiasts remained as firm as ever. The principal difference from the grand old days of the 1580s was the importance that Guiana had come to assume as the focus of Walter Ralegh's overseas interests. Lawrence Keymis now played with his charts and notes the role that Hariot and Hakluyt had played for Virginia, for Keymis had been back to the Orinoco in 1596 to follow up Walter's explorations and to produce for publication at about the moment of his patron's return to favour a *Relation of the Second Voyage to Guiana*.[2] With Guianan Indians stalking swarthy and proud just as Manteo and Wanchese had walked before them in the entourage of Sir Walter Ralegh, the spirit that Hariot had kindled in the exploring of Virginia remained alive in the new South American interest.

But there was one important difference, for though an element of wishful thinking had always been associated with the exploration of Virginia, it had never been the principal driving impulse. While paying lip service to prospects of treasure and easy wealth, Hariot had always kept the enterprise tethered firmly to reality.

But that was not the case with El Dorado. The quest had started as the pursuit of a chimera, and it continued – and ended – in the same fanciful fashion, for Keymis lacked the rigorous intellectual discipline with which Hariot could rein in his patron's exuberant optimism. Sir Walter Ralegh was convinced there was gold in Guiana and so Keymis, too faithful a follower, agreed that he must be right, even though his follow-up voyage had unearthed no positive evidence. So the mirage remained dangling in front of Walter Ralegh, a fatally flawed jewel forever tempting him to reach out and risk all. The time would come when he would be prepared to gamble disastrously – but in 1597 he was too busy re-establishing himself in the rhythm of life at court.

It was refreshing to occupy the centre of the stage once again. When rumours had filtered back from Cadiz that Sir Walter Ralegh had been drowned it was a matter of national concern, for he had become one of the principal stars in the Elizabethan constellation. When he fell ill a few years later his survival was considered important enough to merit a special parliamentary motion of sympathy, and from 1597 onwards his name started appearing again in all the goings-on of courtly life. He was gambling late one night in the Presence Chamber long after the queen had gone to bed, playing primero with the Earl of Southampton. The squire of the body that night asked him to pack up the game and go home and, when Walter ignored him, threatened to 'call in the guard to pull down the board'. The Earl of Southampton lost his temper but Walter, an older man, quietly packed up his money and went off to bed. His duelling days were over.

A new friend Walter made at this time was Henry Brooke, the heir of Lord Cobham, the warden of the Cinque Ports. He was a wealthy young man with a pleasant turn of wit which amused Elizabeth as much as it did Ralegh. Somewhat indolent and wayward, and unreliable under stress, he was a fairweather friend – but a powerful one. When the Brookes had taken exception to the fun that William Shakespeare poked at their fat ancestor, Sir John Oldcastle, they forced the playwright to change the character's name to Sir John Falstaff. Henry's father, Lord Cobham, held an influential position at court, he was a privy councillor,[3] and Henry hoped for a similar status in the future – as did Sir Walter Ralegh. The Brookes were a useful family to have on his side, and when old Lord Cobham died in the summer of 1597 Walter naturally supported Henry's nomination to the wardenship of the Cinque Ports in succession to his father. Henry Brooke was the brother-in-law of Cecil who, therefore, had a yet stronger reason for supporting his candidacy, but the secretary appears to have been more circumspect in his advocacy than Ralegh, wanting to avoid a confrontation with the Earl of Essex who, he rightly anticipated, would have his own ideas on who should get the position. Sir Robert Sidney was the man for the job in the earl's view, or, if Sidney were thought too lowly or inexperienced – as Sidney himself considered – then Essex would put his own name forward for the post. The earl was mortally offended when Elizabeth blandly gave the Cinque Ports to Ralegh's new friend Henry Brooke, and his resentment threatened the whole basis of Cecil's carefully patched entente.

So the little secretary devised an evening at the theatre to which on 6 July 1597, he invited both Essex and Ralegh with the intention of soothing the tensions between them, and the soirée proved a great success. The secretary's choice of play was an odd one, though, *The Tragedy of*

Walter Ralegh and his eldest son
Wat, a portrait painted in 1602,
when Wat was nine

The new castle at Sherborne built
to Walter Ralegh's specifications
during the 1590's across the river
from the original Norman castle.
This modern drawing shows
Ralegh's home as he saw it. The
Digby family, who were given
Sherborne by James I after
Walter's condemnation, and who
have held the castles and estate to
this day, added wings to each of
Ralegh's corner towers to give the
building an H-shaped plan

Robert Devereux, Earl of Essex, who increased his sway over Queen Elizabeth during Ralegh's disgrace

Below left: Robert Cecil, later Earl of Salisbury, who also came to the fore during Ralegh's disgrace

SERO SED SERIO

Right: Sir Walter Ralegh, the hero of Cadiz. The map behind him shows him leading the English fleet to capture the town – but he rests on a walking-stick. As a result of the injuries he received in the battle, Ralegh was to limp for the rest of his life

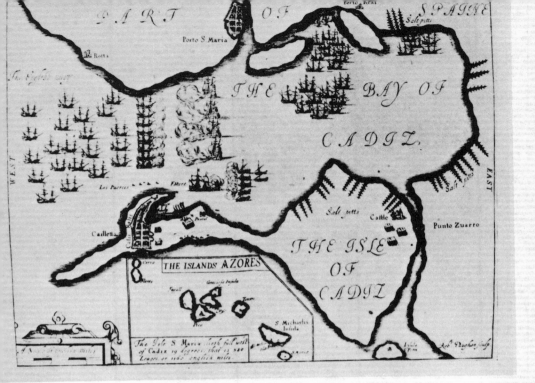

The English navy
captures Cadiz, a
contemporary map.
Behind the four great
'Apostle' galleons shelters
the Spanish supply fleet
intended for South
America

Henry Brooke, Lord
Cobham, became one of
Ralegh's close friends
after Walter returned
from Cadiz

Richard II, the story of a monarch's deposition by a martial subject. Cecil was not to know that this would be the play Essex's followers were to get specially staged on the night before their rising – but Ralegh saw the point. Thoroughly steeped in all the subtleties of court intrigue – and savouring them with all his old relish, he wrote the secretary a conspiratorial letter to thank him for the night out, remarking pointedly on how 'wonderful merry' Cecil's choice of play had made the earl.

It was a summer for patching up old quarrels. When Sir Francis Vere arrived back from the Netherlands, Essex brought him and Ralegh together to heal the rancour caused by the previous year's squabblings in Cadiz harbour. 'He would needs have us shake hands,' wrote Vere later, 'which we did both the willinglier because there had nothing passed between us that might blemish reputation.'

Vere had brought with him some 1,200 experienced musketeers to make up to 6,000 the number of troops going on the voyage to Spain which Ralegh, Essex and Cecil had proposed and to which Elizabeth had agreed. The triumph of Cadiz would be followed up with another body-blow to the Spanish mainland – a raid on one of Philip's northern ports, the Groyne (Finisterre) or Ferroll. The fleet was to be around a hundred strong, its nucleus being seventeen royal ships, among them two of the great Spanish 'Apostles' captured at Cadiz and refurbished since then in accordance with English ideas of seamanship. The Dutch were contributing twenty-two men of war which would sail in one squadron, Essex would have another, Thomas Howard a third, and Ralegh the fourth, sailing on the *Warspite* again with Sir Arthur Gorges as his captain. Having Gorges with him made the venture quite a family affair: Sir Ferdinando Gorges was to be sergeant-major to the whole force and Sir George Carew would be Walter's vice-admiral in the great *St Matthew*.

The preparations had been thorough, but winds blowing up the Channel kept most of the ships bottled in their different ports of origin for weeks, unable to sail south-west to the Plymouth rendezvous, and by the time the ships had struggled down past Sandwich to Weymouth, the food and drink intended to last into Spanish waters were seriously depleted. Then a storm that blew up on the last stage of the voyage across Lyme Bay showed that many of the men levied into the royal fleet just were not sailors at all 'but men unserviceable, taken up by the press-masters in mariners' clothes, that know not one rope in the ship'. The press-gang bosses, complained Essex, were filling the queen's navy with men who had never been on a boat in their lives. There were wholesale dismissals and this proved fortunate for the survival of the English flotilla when the voyage began, for scarcely had it set sail on 10 July 1597, with Ralegh and his squadron bringing up the rear, than it was buffeted by fierce winds.

In the expedition's very first night out of port, Walter Ralegh became separated from the main fleet, dawn breaking on 11 July to reveal him alone at sea with just the *Bonaventure* of his own squadron and the *St Matthew* and the *St Andrew*, the two Spanish vessels. Determined to catch up fast, Walter set on a course for Finisterre – only to run into seas and winds that grew higher and higher, whipping into one of those tempests for which the Bay of Biscay is famous. It was more than an evening's squall. It grew fiercer and fiercer as day succeeded night, to be followed by day again. Each new dawn broke on skies more lowering and waves more savage than had seemed possible twenty-four hours earlier. Continual lightning flashes replaced the sun and shed an eerie, demoralizing light on the heaving little boats. The buffeting smashed open the bulkhead of the *Warspite* and ground the bricks of the galley's oven to powder. After days working ceaselessly without sleep, fully grown men fell to their knees crying helplessly.

Ralegh had never suffered anything like it before. Though rightly considering himself an old sea dog, he had not logged up actual hours at sea on the scale of a Drake or a Hawkins. So after resisting all that the elements could hurl at him for a week he turned his ships back north and ran for home, to discover, to his immense chagrin, that he had been the first of the queen's captains to capitulate. The rest of the fleet was still battling it out over the horizon. He promptly dashed off a letter to Cecil reconjuring all the beastliness of the storm, and endeavouring not to betray too abjectly the need he felt to excuse himself. Then the very next day, Essex came limping into Falmouth, his flagship holed and leaking badly, thoroughly depressed by the chaos that had beset his first great command.

Ralegh entertained him to dinner in his cabin on board the *Warspite* and the two men took stock of the situation. The squadron under Sir Thomas Howard had not returned. Had it been wrecked? The answer came a day or so later, for Howard, who had, back in 1591, weathered the tempest that destroyed the Spanish fleet lying round the hulk of the captured *Revenge*, sent a despatch to report that he had ridden out the storm and had sailed on to await the rest of the fleet off Corunna. There he was cruising provocatively, trying to tempt out the Spanish ships to give battle 'if their hearts served them' – which they did not.

His exploit put Ralegh and Essex on their mettle, and the two of them worked feverishly to put their ships out to sea before Howard tired of waiting for them. But though they re-equipped within a week, and were ready with a 'nimble fleet, dispestered from our worst sailors, undefensible ships and superfluous number of men', all set to head for Corunna, the winds were against them. Day after day they lay in Plymouth, beside themselves with impatience until, on 31 July 1597, Lord Thomas Howard and his tempest-tossed squadron sailed into the harbour on the very same brisk wind that was bottling Ralegh and Essex against the side of the quay.

The whole strategy of the venture would have to be recast. The frustrating weeks of delay had eaten dangerously into the supplies and the morale of the soldiers intended for the land assault on the Spanish, while Thomas Howard's reconnaissance seemed to indicate that the Spanish fleet was in no fit condition to put to sea. So another attack in the style of the Cadiz invasion seemed both risky and pointless. Rather than destroy a few ships which could not possibly threaten the English coast, should not Ralegh and Essex attempt a Drake-style raid on the Spanish treasure fleet as it came back laden from the New World either in the Azores or, perhaps, in the Caribbean itself? Ralegh and the earl rode up to London to urge on the queen the attractions of the venture in the light of the changed circumstances.

But Elizabeth was adamant. Drake and Hawkins had lost their lives – and her money – attempting the same sort of exploit two years previously. She sympathized with her admirals' difficulties, but a trip to the West Indies was out of the question. A compromise must be reached and so, in the end, it was agreed that the expedition's first objective must remain an attack on the Spanish warfleet, however small it might be, in the port of Ferroll. But this attack need only be carried out with fireships rather than by troops, and the English fleet could then, if it were fit to do so, move on the Azores to see what havoc it could wreak there.

So on this new basis the refitted fleet was towed out of Plymouth on 17 August 1597, in search of a breeze to carry it south. But Essex's last action before embarking had been to dismiss all the soldiers attached to the fleet so that the enterprise could not help but be an exclusively naval one – and this was a clear indication that the main objective of Essex and Ralegh was now the Spanish treasure fleet, not the mainland. For there was no serious possibility of an expedition lacking both infantry and artillery tackling the land defences of a Spanish harbour. The queen's specific instructions were being ignored. 'Whatsoever pretences and speeches were given out of that matter', wrote Arthur Gorges, 'both our general and the wisest of his council of war did well enough know that the Groyne (Corunna) or Ferroll were then no morcels fit for our mouths.'

It was a dangerous and short-sighted way to deceive Elizabeth, for if the gamble did not work she would be merciless. Perhaps Ralegh calculated that Essex would receive the brunt of her anger since he was the commander. But Walter should have paused to reflect on how Robert Cecil would react, for the trick which Essex and Ralegh were now playing was at the expense of the secretary even more than at that of the queen.

Robert Cecil had stood up to be counted on the two adventurers' side. He had lent his own voice and reputation to all the expense and risk that the expedition involved. Slyly to recast their entire strategy behind his back was hardly the way to repay him for his support, and the enmity of so astute a politician was a dangerous thing to incur – as Cecil demonstrated as soon as he suspected that Essex and Ralegh might be ganging up against him. He started playing on the rivalry that the two great competitors for royal favour had always felt for each other, deriding in his private letters to Essex 'good Mr Ralegh, who wonders at his own diligence, because diligence and he are not familiars' – and reinforcing this implication of slothfulness by picking out individual instances of alleged inefficiency: 'Your rear admiral [Ralegh] . . . making haste but once in a year to write a letter by post, had dated his last despatch from Weymouth, which I know was written from Plymouth.'

There were many criticisms one could make of Walter Ralegh, but lack of energy was not one of them. It was a strange game to play, and, wary of Cecil, Essex's uncle Sir William Knollys wrote to warn his nephew against the treachery of such devices: 'If we lived not in a cunning world, I should assure myself that the secretary were wholly yours. I pray to God it had a good foundation and then he is very worthy to be embraced. I will hope for the best, yet will I observe him as narrowly as I can. But your lordship knows best the humour both of the time and the person.'

Knollys was wrong. His nephew did *not* know the true nature of Robert Cecil – and neither did Sir Walter Ralegh.

❧ 32 ❧

Walter's Will

Before he left for the Azores Walter Ralegh had made a will.
It was witnessed on 10 July 1597, the very day that the full
expedition had set sail, only to be shattered by the tempest
that caused him with Essex to recast the entire strategy of their
venture. It cannot have been the only will that Ralegh made in his life,
but it is the only one that has survived to our day, clean and heavy, on
thick cream parchment, bearing Walter Ralegh's signature and the
remains of a vast seal.

Its greatest interest is its reference to Walter's illegitimate daughter –
'My Reputed Daughter begotten on the body of Alice Goold now in
Ireland' – to whom was left 500 marks (£331 13s 4d) from the sale of his
privateering ship, the *Roebuck*,[1] but there were other bequests, and the
document also provides a unique inventory of Walter's worldly goods
at the end of his disgrace. He always complained that he sacrificed most
of his wealth to the war effort against Spain – in which he included his
privateering and colonizing activities – and his will of 1597 confirms that
claim.

After he had made proper provision for Bess and one or two minor
gifts to friends and servants, he wished his estate to pass undiminished
to his sole son and heir, four-year-old Wat, and he bequeathed just
two groupings of land – his estates in Cork and Waterford, which, after
the great Irish uprising of the following year were to become of only
notional value, and the lease on Sherborne and its adjoining manors.
There was no London property Walter could leave, since his occupancy
of Durham House was in the gift of the queen and it was not his to
bestow. But he did pass on his interest in 'Spilmane, Her Majesty's
Jewellers House', a property whose lease he held near Durham House,
while his other principal gift was his patent for the sale of wine and
licensing of vintners, the cornerstone of his fortune.

He left instructions that his debts should be settled with debts. Hopeful of recouping Bess's marriage portion loaned in her childhood to the Earl of Huntingdon and unpaid since 1572, Walter set aside that sum together with £500 owed him by the Earl of Derby to meet all his outstanding commitments, while his principal financial legacy was the profits from the sale of the *Roebuck*. That was, apparently, the only vessel left from his once extensive privateering fleet. Oddments of clothing, plate, furniture, books and jewels made up the residue of the estate.

Thomas Hariot was remembered kindly. He was to receive £200 from the sale of the *Roebuck*, £100 a year from the patent of wines, some books and furniture from Durham House and, a nice touch for a sober mathematics lecturer, 'all such black suits of apparel as I have in the same house'. Arthur Gorges, now Walter's companion in arms on the Azores voyage was, appropriately, to receive Ralegh's 'best rapier and dagger', and on Laurence Keymis was bestowed another £100 from the sale of the *Roebuck*.

Those were Walter's truest and closest friends. To his brother-in-law Arthur Throckmorton, the patient diarist, he left 'my best horse and my best saddle with the furniture'. To another Throckmorton relative, Alexander Brett from Somerset, he left 'my long black velvet cloak now in my wardrobe in Durham House', and these two kinsmen, together with George Carew and Hariot were to be the overseers of the estate if Walter were to die before young Wat attained his majority. Adrian Gilbert and John Meere, Walter's Sherborne assistants who were still, apparently, on good terms with him, also received small gifts.

But the most interesting aspect of Walter Ralegh's will is not the small bequests that it included, but all the lands and property that it did *not* mention. There is no mention of the leases Walter was granted in the halcyon days of his favour on the estates belonging to All Souls College; none of the lands that the traitor Babington had forfeited to him were any longer in his possession; the Ralegh privateering fleet that had once been such a source of profit was broken up, the *Roebuck* being the sole survivor, and there was no mention of the capital of over £30,000 that had been involved in the *Madre de Dios* affair. Sir Walter Ralegh was in 1597 a much poorer man than he had been at any time since the early 1580s.

Where had his fortune vanished? His new house and gardens at Sherborne had obviously swallowed up a lot of money. Guiana had cost a fortune and earned nothing, and Cadiz, for all its glory, had not recouped the investment Ralegh put into it. Since his fall from grace Walter had obviously had to sell off many of his assets and tighten his belt, and his will is the gauge of all his complaints about wasted substance and virtue ill-rewarded. They were true, and he was looking to the Azores to set his finances on a firmer footing once again.

❧ 33 ❧

The Azores

Sir Walter Ralegh had been wise to make his will in 1597, for the vicious storms which had broken up his original expedition against Spain lingered, and they had not disappeared when the reconstituted fleet set sail again. Off Cape Ortegal Ralegh and his squadron were struck by a tempest as ferocious as any they had experienced after their first departure, and Walter suffered again from the inadequacy of the Spanish prizes in his charge. The *St Andrew* lost her foremast in the gale and the *St Matthew* her bowsprit and foremast. Then, about thirty miles off the Spanish coast, Ralegh's own mainyard snapped and the *Warspite* began wallowing helplessly in the Atlantic rollers. To avoid disaster without a mainsail his only hope was to run before the wind, a brisk easterly which took him down towards Lisbon, one of the pre-arranged rendezvous points for the expedition. Meanwhile Essex's flagship had sprung a most desperate leak, so that he had to remain where he was, off Cape Finisterre.

Between these two poles, the admiral off the north of the Spanish coast and the rear admiral off the south, the rest of the English fleet gravitated, and when the storm calmed the Earl of Essex discovered that about thirty ships, twenty of whom were West Country privateers, were no longer with him.

Essex was a suspicious fellow at the best of times, and he surrounded himself with cronies who were even more paranoid. They suggested that the disappearance of Walter Ralegh and such a significant number of pirates was the fruit of a conspiracy – and their suggestions nurtured the doubts about Walter that Cecil's letters had sown in Essex's mind before the fleet's departure. Was the Ralegh strategy to creep out into the Atlantic, ambush the treasure fleet and gain for himself all the honour and profit? It sounded a plausible allegation.

On the other hand, the disappearance of Ralegh was in Essex's own interests, for it provided him with the perfect excuse to call off the inconvenient commitment to attack Ferroll. With his fleet at less than full strength he had no choice but to sail south with his responsibility for that obligation absolved. So when he did meet up again with Ralegh off the Azores, on 15 September 1597, his suspicions were not at first apparent. He was, said Gorges, 'the joyfullest man living'. Walter and the earl dined convivially together, Essex 'protesting he never believed we would leave him, although divers persuaded him to the contrary'. The two men were now exactly where they had hoped to finish up: lying in wait for the unsuspecting treasure fleet from the West Indies, with all the English ships, men and resources unharmed by any involvement in an unprofitable mainland port.

But their harmony did not last. The English fleet was anchored off Flores, and since Ralegh's ships needed provisioning, Walter asked if his men could go ashore to fetch fresh food and water. Essex, his own vessels recently supplied and watered, was anxious to be off in search of the treasure fleet, so he decided to leave Ralegh to catch him up. All evening Ralegh's men worked at ferrying fruit, meat and drink from shore to ship when, quite unexpectedly at midnight, an urgent despatch arrived from Essex. Ralegh's squadron was to leave Flores at once and set sail for Fayal, one of the central islands, where Essex and his ships would be waiting for them. They could carry on with their watering there.

By dawn Ralegh was approaching Fayal to find, to his total mystification, not a trace of Essex or the rest of the fleet. Precisely where he was will never be known. Essex offered no explanation at the time or later, and one can only presume that, acting on some new information or a hunch, he veered off to another part of the Azores archipelago in the hope of catching the treasure fleet, totally omitting to tell Ralegh anything about his change of plan.

So the rear admiral waited patiently with his ships off Fayal while the guns of the fort there loosed cannonades against him. His sailors, and particularly his privateers, watched with dismay as the inhabitants fled from the town bearing their valuables up into the hills. But Ralegh refused to attack. He expected Essex to appear at any moment, and, having just avoided an unpleasant misunderstanding with his commander, he was disinclined to risk any action that might be misinterpreted. Two Portuguese swam out to the English ships with exact information on the strength and disposition of the fort, and it was obvious that Ralegh could take it easily with the forces at his disposal. He had no need to wait for reinforcements. But still he held back and for the rest of the day his ships just lay in front of the town.

Another whole day and another whole night the English ships waited for the Earl of Essex to appear and then, frustrated beyond all measure and burning to attack, Ralegh summoned a council of war. His orders as rear admiral expressly forbad him to launch any offensive without the consent of the commander-in-chief, but the incredible circumstances and the fact that several of the captains with him were followers of Essex made him hope that a unanimous vote for a landing would break the impasse. Yet these captains following the lead of Sir Gelli Meyricke and Sir Christopher Blount, two of Essex's chief lieutenants, refused to budge until their leader appeared, and since Ralegh knew Meyricke and Blount to be the very men who had done their best to poison the earl's mind against him in the previous weeks, he felt compelled to yield to their demand to wait another night. But by the fourth day, with the horizon as bare as ever, he had had enough. He upped anchor and, followed by his West Country privateers, sailed out of the bay, leaving Meyricke, Blount and their cronies obstinately floating in front of Fayal.

Rounding a headland that hid him from the town, Ralegh found himself facing a verdant countryside that could obviously provide his ships with all the water and fresh supplies they needed and he decided to land. His orders had been to re-provision at Fayal. But as his long boats approached the shore a detachment of Spanish soldiers appeared and opened fire. To turn the other cheek now was impossible, so with 260 men behind him Ralegh headed for the beach. There were awkward reefs, and the concentrated Spanish salvoes raking the water scared some of the sailors so much that their rowing lost its vigour. But Walter furiously shouted at them what Gorges daintily described as 'disgraceful words' and then, seeing that his oaths were of no avail, ordered his own watermen to head straight at the rocks, leaping into the surf as soon as the bows splintered into the reef. Two of his boats were crushed as the waves smashed them on to the rocks, but all except a few men managed to scramble through the wreckage and the musket fire.

> And so [relates Gorges], clambering over the rocks and wading through the water we passed pell mell with swords shots and pikes. . . . Thereupon the Spaniards began to shrink, and then seeing us to come faster upon them, suddenly retiring, cast away their weapons, turned their backs and fled.[1]

It was a splendid little victory, won against an entrenched body of soldiers twice as numerous as the English. The credit had to go to Ralegh's bravery as he limped cursing through the surf, and there was better still to come. The town of Fayal was but 4 miles away over the headland, and Walter's blood was up. Wearing no armour but his neck-piece he led his small company to within musket range of the fort

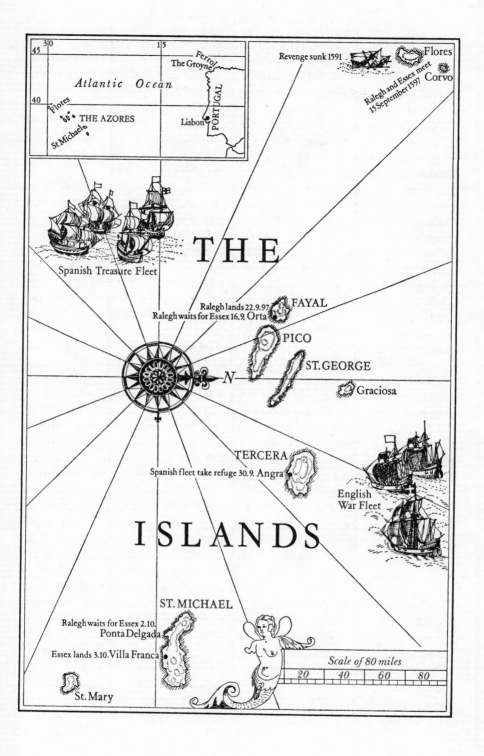

Atlantic Ocean

30 | 15
45
The Groyne
Ferrol
40
Flores
THE AZORES
St.Michael
PORTUGAL
Lisbon

Revenge sunk 1591
Flores
Ralegh and Essex meet
15 September 1597
Corvo

THE

Spanish Treasure Fleet

Ralegh lands 22.9.97.
Ralegh waits for Essex 16.9. Orta
FAYAL

PICO
ST.GEORGE

Graciosa

N

TERCERA
Spanish fleet take refuge 30.9. Angra

English
War Fleet

ISLANDS

ST. MICHAEL
Ralegh waits for Essex 2.10.
Ponta Delgada
Essex lands 3.10. Villa Franca

St. Mary

Scale of 80 miles
20   40   60   80

controlling the road into the town. Someone had to creep forward to reconnoitre the best route for attack, and there was but one man for the job – Ralegh. As in Cadiz harbour, Guiana and Ireland, Walter was showing that, whatever his strategic and political failings, he could be a very brave man.

Pausing only to put on a helmet and cuirass, he crept with a few followers among the low loose stone walls which the guns of the fort were bombarding. Poor Gorges was struck in the leg, and bullets shot several holes through Ralegh's sleeves and breeches.

Then with the correct attack route plotted, the offensive went in smoothly. The Spaniards fled yet again before Walter Ralegh's personal onslaught, and Fayal was his. All that remained to be taken was the high citadel overlooking the town, which was left until morning.

But it was while this final attack was being prepared next day – five days after Ralegh had first sailed into Fayal bay – that the Earl of Essex appeared at last with his ships, tired and frustrated by the fruitlessness of whatever mission he had been engaged upon. To discover that Sir Walter Ralegh had, in his absence, achieved the only significant triumph to light the expedition's aimless weeks of wanderings upon the sea, was galling news, and when Gelli Meyricke and Christopher Blount told him how they had reminded Ralegh of the prohibition against preceeding without the commander's orders, and how the West Countryman had gone off with his pirate friends just the same, Essex exploded in righteous indignation. Ralegh's offence merited immediate court martial – execution even.

Messengers were sent to summon the miscreant, but there was no need, for Walter was already on his way to his admiral's flagship, anxious to tell Essex all about his exploits and expecting congratulation. It was only when he reached the deck of the *Repulse* that the truth hit him. Down in the commander's cabin Essex bluntly charged him with his offence – for which the penalty was death – and if the melodrama of the situation amused Ralegh, he had no time to show it. Essex was a dangerous youth when roused and Walter had to put his arguments to him quickly. The main point was that, though it was indeed an offence for any ship's captain to 'land anywhere without directions from the general', Ralegh was not a ship's captain. He was 'a principal commander under your lordship' and therefore not subject to that particular regulation – and Ralegh further pointed out that he had, in literal terms, simply followed his superior's orders which were to reprovision and water at Fayal. So Essex could do nothing, and in the last resort it was Essex's own failure to inform his rear admiral of his own activities for the best part of a week that constituted the real offence. The earl had attempted to snare Ralegh with a technicality, only to have the tables turned on him.

But Essex still smarted at his indignity. He came ashore to rest and gave orders that all the military officers who had taken part in the attack on Fayal should be cashiered. Walter now felt that his own honour was engaged. He could look after himself, but his officers had no redress, so he showed he could ride a high horse as well as Essex, swearing he was prepared to set his squadron in line and fight it out unless the earl counter-manded his cashiering order. The third of the English admirals, Lord Thomas Howard, had to work hard to heal this new breach between his fellow commanders, persuading Essex to accept an apology and then coaxing Ralegh to utter the necessary form of words. 'And so,' wrote Gorges, 'all things after a little dispute came to a quiet end.'

The treasure fleet was still expected any day from the west. Its objective would be the island of Tercera, roughly in the centre of the Azores, where the Angra Road provided what Ralegh in his *History of the World* was to describe as a harbour whose guns provided virtually impregnable cover for any ships anchored beneath them. Once the Spanish reached the Angra Road they were safe, so the obvious English strategy was to lie in wait outside it or to patrol the routes that the galleons must pursue from the west. But now Essex adopted another of his strategies which could not be adequately explained at the time or since. He gave the order for the English squadrons to sail *east*, leaving Angra and its approaches open and unpatrolled for the Spanish treasure ships to sail into and unload at their leisure – as they did only three hours after the earl's ships had left.

In mitigation of Essex's apparent stupidity, one must say that neither Ralegh nor Howard, his two squadron leaders, appear to have questioned his tactics. Perhaps some report arrived to the effect that the Spanish fleet, suspecting an ambush, were working round to approach from the east or else to slip away directly to Spain, or perhaps, after all the tantrums they had just soothed, Ralegh and Howard felt it prudent to avoid another confrontation that might result from opposing Essex's policy. If that was the case, then their prudence proved expensive. For in the small hours of Michaelmas Day 1597, the Spanish galleons sailed tight under the guns of the Angra Road and the dockers there were hard at work getting their cargoes stored deep inside the Tercera fortress by the time Essex returned from his wild goose chase to the east. The earl was wild to attack Tercera itself immediately and make the Angra Road English. But Ralegh and Howard knew better and their opinion prevailed. The last hope of salvaging some profit from the expedition was to sail to the easternmost island of St Michael, land there and use it as a base for a blockade which could cut the treasure fleet off from the Spanish mainland. It would be a long drawn out business, but there was some slight chance of success.

But reconnoitring the landing at St Michael provoked yet another altercation between Ralegh and Essex, for Sir Walter set out to survey the beach in a flyboat. Essex, as his superior officer, indignantly called him back and took his rear admiral's place in the little patrol craft, sneering at Ralegh's warning that he should take his helmet and breastplate with him, for there were Spanish musketeers lining up along the shore. Shouting pointedly from the boat that he would not deign to give himself protection that his watermen did not possess, Essex spurned the armoured Sir Walter in front of the entire English fleet.

This final enterprise was as ill-starred as all its predecessors, for deciding from his ostentatious reconnaissance that St Michael was too strong to be taken by frontal assault, Essex decided that he would sail under cover of night round the headland to the east and make a landing near the town of Villa Franca. Ralegh should stay with his squadron in front of St Michael, making every pretence, with occasional cannonades and much trumpeting and drumming, of launching a full-scale assault. With this decoy distracting the garrison, Essex could then lead his men to take the town from the rear.

Next morning Ralegh's men began their charade, the watches straining for a sight of Essex's standards appearing over the hills behind the town. In vain. The enterprise was a repetition of the Fayal fiasco. All day Ralegh waited for his commander to appear, then all night and again the following day. Once again Essex had altered his strategy without bothering to inform his rear admiral. The countryside around Villa Franca had proved so fertile, and the land attack on St Michael had seemed to Essex's lieutenants so unpleasant that a council of war had persuaded the commander to dig himself in. Essex made no effort to communicate with his subordinate – and Ralegh's captains had no doubt that that was because his officers wanted to keep the plunder of Villa Franca for themselves.

When a huge Spanish galleon came round the headland to the west, though, it looked as if Ralegh and his squadron were to receive the reward that their patience deserved, for the 2,000-ton vessel – it was a rich East Indian carrack – was cruising straight towards them, having no means of guessing that the ships waiting in the same anchorage for which she was steering were English: they looked like any fleet of King Philip's, for Ralegh's squadron contained several Spanish prizes and a swarm of Dutch vessels. Yet in the event it was one of these Dutch vessels that gave the game away, disobeying Ralegh's order to strike flags and hold fire until the last possible moment. The captain weighed anchor and sailed straight for the carrack, firing a cannonade into her at the very moment that she was about to enter the bay and be trapped. Thanks to the warning, the Spanish captain was able to change course just in time, drive his craft on to the beach and set fire to its cargo, molten molasses pouring out of the wreck and turning the surf to steam that blew in the faces of the Englishmen trying hopelessly to steer their longboats close enough for salvage.

Ralegh could not be blamed for the debacle, and if Essex had carried out his part of the attack on St Michael, there would have been English soldiers waiting on the beach to arrest the crew and cargo. So when the order finally came for the rear admiral to bring his ships round to enjoy the fresh food and water of Villa Franca, it was in a bitter mood that Ralegh and his captains weighed anchor. With winter gales approaching and some of Ralegh's squadron leaking so badly that they had to stow their cannon in their holds, it was time to go home. Sir Walter was never to take to the sea again as a naval commander, nor was there much point in his ever again pretending that he could be a close or a true friend to Robert, Earl of Essex.

❧ 34 ❧

The Essex Revolt

Sir Walter Ralegh landed in St. Ives at the end of October 1597, but he had little time to savour the pleasure of being back in the West Country, for the coast was in uproar. The very same wind that had blown his leaking ships back to England had been propelling a great armada of Spanish galleons up the Bay of Biscay. King Philip of Spain, on his deathbed, kept alive only by his daughter blowing liquid food down his throat, had determined on one last swordthrust at the heart of the English Jezebel. Over-ruling his captain's objections that the late autumn departure of the expedition would doom it to certain destruction, the palsied king told his admiral 'that he would hang him at his wife's neck' if he did not set sail at once. The last armada was to do more than scour the Channel of English ships. It was to land in Falmouth and turn that town into a base through which Spanish troops could march to subdue Plymouth, Bristol, London and the whole damned heretic country.

The Privy Council frantically recalled English troops from France and mobilized the southern counties. Essex arrived in Plymouth and promised to beat off the Spaniards 'though we eat ropes' ends and drink nothing but rainwater'.[1] Then he rode off to London to hurry up supplies and money, leaving Ralegh to organize the defence of the West as lieutenant general. And Walter was just about to set about organizing the land forces under his command when the great crisis deflated as rapidly as it had blown up. A captured Spanish flyboat reported that the armada had been struck and scattered by a storm, and other news confirmed that King Philip's final fling had suffered the end his own sailors had always predicted that it would in the savage tempests of late October.

It was for England a relief none the less welcome for being forseeable, but it raised an ugly question. Why had the country had to rely for its salvation on the forces of nature rather than on the expensive fleet commissioned specifically to destroy this latest armada before it could sail out of Ferroll harbour? As Elizabeth and Cecil probed into Essex's excuses for ignoring the Spanish mainland and his lame account of his actions in the Azores, they found much to criticize. Rowland Whyte was one of the many courtiers who charted the favourite's falling stock, noting that the queen 'is not pleased with his service at sea, and that his proceedings towards Sir Walter Ralegh in calling his [Ralegh's] actions to question before a council of war is misliked here'.[2]

Ralegh, fortunately, somehow escaped censure for the expedition's failure to attack the Spanish ships in Ferroll, but he came less lightly out of his next entanglement with Essex, which involved, as so often with the earl, an affair of honour. Elizabeth had taken advantage of his absence in the Azores to raise Lord Admiral Charles Howard, Lord Thomas's brother, to the earldom of Nottingham. It was an action sufficient in itself to inflame Essex's jealousy, but the queen had carefully embellished it so as to throw her favourite into a paroxysm of pique, for not only did the patent explaining why she had given out this rare honour mention the triumph of Cadiz for which Robert Devereux considered himself to be primarily responsible, but Howard was also made lord steward of the parliament about to meet, so that in all the public ceremonies at Westminster he would take precedence over all the other earls – Essex among them.

In dudgeon the favourite stalked off to Wanstead where he barred himself in his room, swathing himself in layers of cloaks and blankets, ostensibly on the pretext that he had a cold. It was the reaction of a child, but his absence created a certain void in the affairs of the court that might prove embarrassing in the presence of a French embassy which was due shortly to visit London. The French were most partial to taking advantage of such rifts, and Essex was a personal friend of Henri IV.

So Ralegh, eager to play the statesman, came forward with a diplomatic suggestion. Essex should be given the vacant position of earl marshal, a rank which held precedence over the lord steward. Howard would keep his earldom, but Essex would march more prominently into parliament, and with such a mandarin victory Essex was more than content.

But the new Earl of Nottingham had been looking forward to lording it at Westminster at Essex's expense and did not take kindly to Walter's initiative. Now it was his turn to turn his back on the court in a huff, and just before the 1597 Christmas celebrations he stumped off to his home in Chelsea, cutting himself off from the world with the same excuse that his rival had used – illness. His sulks would have been comical had they not proved more durable than Essex's moods, for, never very friendly towards Ralegh, Lord Admiral Howard was now to nurse a grudge and to blame Walter ever afterwards for spoiling his coup over Essex.

Precedence was the cause of several rows in this December of 1597. At the same time that Sir Walter Ralegh was helping to sort out the caste quibblings of Essex and Howard, he was sitting in the House of Commons, as befitted the owner of Sherborne Castle, as the senior knight for Dorset. Going with a committee of fellow MPs to confer with the Lords, he was compelled, along with the other Commons' representatives, to stand uncovered before the representatives of the Lords – who remained seated with their hats on – and Ralegh exploded at the 'indignity' of the situation. He harangued the House of Commons on the presumption of the Upper House in treating his committee like servants and he moved a motion demanding an explanation. With such gestures was the reputation of a 'parliament man' built up.

But that was a rare burst of energy for, aged forty-five and having had precious little opportunity to rest from his tiring months at sea, Walter took the winter of 1597–8 easily. He went once again to Bath, this time with Bess, to recuperate. She had had little time to see him the previous summer and autumn – and the general concern for the great man's health was gratifying. The Privy Council sent a special message to hope that the waters there would act on his strained constitution with their renowned efficacity, and the speaker of the House gave his half-brother Adrian Gilbert, the member for Bridport, permission to miss some committees and debates and go down to visit the invalid. Relaxing in the spa only a few hours away from Sherborne, Walter was able to take a stage further the improvements and additions he wanted to make to his Dorset home, and more builders moved in the following year, continuing their reconstructions until 1601.

But it was not in Ralegh's nature – or interests – to remain away from the centre of affairs for long, and at court the Earl of Essex was whipping up a whirlwind. In a Privy Council meeting called in July 1598 to discuss the appointment of a new commander for Ireland, Essex maliciously proposed Sir George Carew for the job. The Irish under Hugh O'Neill, Earl of Tyrone, had been sweeping through the English plantation putting their foreign occupiers to rout and to subdue the rebels would be a difficult and lengthy task which the earl did not want for himself nor for any of his followers – hence his nomination of Ralegh's cousin. There had even been talk of Walter himself being given this very hot potato to handle. No one was keen to suffer all the risks that prolonged absence from court and an intractable military campaign involved. It was the sort of job to wish on one's enemies and rivals, but to say this, as Essex did, in the presence of the queen herself, was to exhibit a mentality hardly worthy of a jealous page-boy, let alone a member of the royal council confronted with a national emergency. Elizabeth lost her temper and Essex responded with an ugly face, then turned his back on her.

Losing control of herself, the old queen rose and struck her churlish favourite with all the strength she could summon. Essex whirled round, his hand on his sword, bellowing that he would not have accepted such an insult from King Henry's hands and he would not tolerate it from hers. The new Earl of Nottingham had to step between the queen and favourite for fear of further violence.

It was a dangerous, unprecedented confrontation from which no good could come. As old Burghley had said, pulling out his Bible after a very similar outburst of Essex's in council and waving the 55th Psalm under the earl's obstinately jutting jaw: 'Bloodthirsty and deceitful men shall not live out half their days'.

In the event, that summer of 1598 was to mark the end of Lord Burghley's days, but he had certainly lived out his full term. Elizabeth went to his bedside, cradling his tired, failing head in her lap and feeding him gently with a spoon, and when the news of his death reached her, on 5 August 1598, she withdrew to her own rooms to weep sadly alone. He was almost the last of the great generation: Leicester, Mildmay, Walsingham, Hatton, Frobisher, Drake, Hawkins – they were all gone now. Only Sir Walter was left to reminisce with on the grand old days of the 1580s.

Ralegh was certain he would be elevated at last to the Privy Council. Burghley's death left a gap which had to be filled, and Essex's increasing instability left a gap of a different sort. Walter seemed to be in line for the vice-chancellorship of the duchy of Lancaster, or possibly an even higher position at the exchequer, and he was sure that his careful cultivation of Robert Cecil would now pay dividends. Cecil and Ralegh, said the common rumour, 'do infinitely desire to be barons and they have a purpose to be called unto it'.[3] The two men had a common interest against the ever swelling power and ambition of Essex, for they needed to stand together against the day when the young earl over-reached himself.

But the little secretary, now, after his father's death, more obviously than ever Elizabeth's first minister, was not the friend Ralegh thought. In the year that Robert Cecil died, 1612, Francis Bacon was to write and publish his essay *Of Deformity*. A dispassionately cutting analysis, of an insight too coldly accurate for Ralegh to match, the little character sketch embalmed the personality of the hunchback secretary in a mixture of pseudo-psychology and malice. Deformed persons, said Bacon, resent the trick they feel nature has played on them: they are 'void of natural affection'. Denied strength and masculine attractions, the cripple has to forge himself sharper weapons to triumph in the battle of life. His apparent feebleness disarms others, putting them off their guard – and that was certainly true of Walter Ralegh's attitude towards Cecil.

When Bacon's essay appeared Ralegh had spent nearly ten years in the Tower of London, and the essay explained to him then, if he had not realized it before, that if there was one single man to blame for the misfortunes that shadowed the last years of his life, it was the crippled secretary he had numbered among his closest friends. He had been too trusting, giving of himself without reserve – as when the secretary's wife, Lady Elizabeth had died in 1597:

> I had rather be with you now than at any other time, if I could thereby either take off from you the burden of your sorrows, or lay the greater part thereof on mine own heart. . . .
>
> It is true you have lost a good and virtuous wife, and myself an honourable friend and kinswoman. But there was a time when she was unknown to you, for whom you then lamented not. She is now no more yours nor of your aquaintance, but immortal, and not needing or knowing your love or sorrow.[4]

At the heart of the letter Ralegh set a little jewel of homespun theology. The mind of man, he wrote, 'is that part of God which is in us', so the more we allow sorrow to overwhelm the natural reason of our minds, then the more we cut ourselves off from God: 'Sorrow draws not the dead to life, but the living to death'.

The death of Lady Elizabeth left motherless small children, relatives of Ralegh, and when he and Bess saw that the eldest boy, Will Cecil, was not well, they took him down to Sherborne to benefit from the country air. There he lived as one of the Ralegh family, Walter writing to his father to tell him how stoutly the lad was eating and digesting his food. Will seemed drawn to Bess almost as a second mother, and he struck up with Walter an affectionate and playful relationship which must have been difficult to establish with his grey, hard-working little father:

> Sir Walter, we must all exclaim and cry out because you will not come down [to Sherborne]. You being absent we are like soldiers that when their captain are absent, they know not what to do: you are so busy about idle matters. Sir Walter, I will be plain with you. I pray you leave all idle matters and come down to us.[5]

Those 'idle matters' were the great concerns of state over which Will's father worried day after day, and from which Walter was to suffer for not worrying sufficiently, for Sir Walter Ralegh was, in essence, an overgrown schoolboy. Boisterous, devil-may-care and thoughtless, consumed by the interest of the moment rather than by any long term goal, open and forceful in his pleasures and his irritations, quick to anger and quick to forget, it is easy to see why he got on so well with children like Will Cecil – and why men like Will Cecil's father mistrusted him. Could Walter Ralegh really sustain the concentration which Renaissance statesmanship demanded? Was he not, in the last resort, a dilettante? He was an ornament to any court or military expedition. But was that a reason to move heaven and earth on his behalf? To secure Walter the position he desired – a seat on the Privy Council, some sinecure like the duchy of Lancaster or a peerage – Cecil would have his work cut out cajoling an ageing queen to forget deep burnt memories of betrayal and calming the anxieties of a score of powerful courtiers and councillors who all had their own reasons for feeling jealous of a uniquely unpopular figure. And all for what? To elevate Walter to honours for which there were other more suitable candidates, who might be smaller human beings but who were, with their more limited horizons, probably better men for the job.

So the vacancy that old Lord Burghley's death caused on the Privy Council went in the end to George Talbot, sixth Earl of Shrewsbury, who had served so solidly as Mary Queen of Scot's jailer, and Walter Ralegh did not win the peerage or the vice-chancellorship of the duchy of Lancaster that he had hoped for. He had to be content with the governorship of the Channel Islands, a militarily important but politically insignificant position which he received in 1600. But in order to assuage Sir Walter Ralegh's hurt pride, Robert Cecil commissioned memoranda from him on subjects in which he had specialist knowledge – Ireland, for example, where the situation had deteriorated alarmingly since Essex's melodramatic confrontation with Elizabeth. The ambush and slaughter of some 2,000 English soldiers at the Yellow Ford across the Callan River on 14 August 1598 had proved the signal for a ferocious uprising under Tyrone. The English settlers fled for their lives to Dublin, Edmund Spenser leaving his Kilcolman estate to be utterly destroyed by fire, Ralegh's 100 colonists at Tallow in Munster flying, too, without firing a shot. In London Cecil and the Privy Council reluctantly laid plans for the Earl of Essex to lead an expeditionary force of unprecedented size and crippling expense against Tyrone – but Ralegh had an alternative suggestion. The assassination of William the Silent by agents of Philip 11 had brought the revolt of the Dutch to the point of collapse. It would be altogether cheaper and quicker, Walter argued, to deal with Tyrone in a similar fashion. 'It could be no disgrace if it were known that the killing of a rebel were practiced, for we see that the lives of anointed princes are daily sought, and we have always given head money for the killing of rebels, who are evermore proclaimed for a price.'[6]

Ralegh could play the Machiavel with gusto. The following year he was to send another memo to Cecil with an even more blood-chilling prescription – on this occasion aimed at the Earl of Essex himself, who had led the English army around Ireland with unrelieved incompetence and had then deserted his post. In September 1599 the earl had returned secretly to England with a small gang of swordsmen and had broken into the queen's bedchamber uttering threats against Cecil and Ralegh. For this insolence Essex was placed under house arrest, the queen unwilling to bring him to formal trial, the Council reluctant to release him. Ralegh's way out of the dilemma was direct: when a snake was underfoot, why spare it to turn its poison on those who had once had it at their mercy? He wrote to Cecil: 'If you take it for a good counsel to relent towards this tyrant, you will repent it when it shall be too late. His malice is fixed, and will not evaporate by any of your mild courses.'[7] Walter Ralegh knew how little credit to expect for kindnesses shown to the Earl of Essex. The earl, he told Cecil, would ascribe any mercy he might be shown 'to Her Majesty's pusillanimity, and not to your good nature. . . . The less you make him, the less he shall be able to harm you and yours. And if Her Majesty's favour fail him, he will again decline to a common person.'

Apologists for Walter Ralegh have seized on this last sentence as proof that their hero wished nothing more sinister than Essex's removal from court and the royal favour. But this is only one stage in the argument. If Essex were to continue his fall from royal favour, Sir Walter argued, then the earl would 'decline to a common person'[8] and, deprived of the queen's protection, would thereafter be at Cecil's mercy.

What should Cecil then do if that happened? This is the point of the letter. Ralegh cites three examples in which noblemen were put to death and their heirs took no revenge on the men who had secured their fathers' destruction. 'I could name you a thousand of these.' If Essex were eliminated, 'his son shall be the youngest earl of England but one, and, if his father be now kept down, Will Cecil [Cecil's son and heir] shall be able to keep as many men at his heels as he, and more too.' With this talk of bodyguards for future generations, Ralegh was clearly thinking in terms of a blood feud between families following Cecil's elimination of Essex. 'If the father continue, he will be able to break the branches, and pull up the tree, root and all. Lose not your advantage.'

Nowhere in his note did Ralegh say in so many words that Essex should be murdered or executed. To that extent the letter was ambiguous. Walter was not so foolish as to spell out on paper such a hostage to fortune, for sixteenth-century letters so often ended up in hands other than those for which they were intended. But his reference to Essex's son becoming 'the youngest earl of England but one' was susceptible to only interpretation and, in the light of what was to happen the message was not unrealistic. The Essex revolt was, in 1601, to cost more lives and threaten royal power with far more force than the ripples or waves that the judicious murder or execution of Essex would have caused in 1599 or 1600.

Still, Sir Walter Ralegh should not be given the credit for too much foresight, for his letter to Cecil stemmed as much from personal hatred as from any special political wisdom. His emotional reaction to the favourite who had replaced him was of no higher stamp than the envy and anger which was to push Essex into revolt. Pique and personal enmity flowed as bitterly as ever between the two men. Before the earl had gone off to Ireland, a tournament had been held to celebrate the birthday of Elizabeth in November 1598, and Ralegh dressed his royal guard in orange plumed hats and orange favours – an almost identical hue to the tangerine in which the Earl of Essex loved to livery his retainers. When the earl got to hear that the captain of the guard proposed to parade his small handful of followers in this fashion, he made preparations accordingly. Ralegh and his men were in position round the queen when Essex suddenly exploded into view with a vast orange clad army of followers, swamping both the royal guard and the entire tournament. Elizabeth saw the point and did not like it, calling off the ceremonies before they had finished – and thus between assassination plots and sartorial squabbles, did the tensions of late Elizabethan court life flicker towards the death of the lady from whose life they took their meaning.

The Earl of Essex's paranoia was the consuming theme of Elizabeth's final years. From his catastrophic Irish campaign he had written letters home accusing Walter Ralegh and his friend Henry Brooke, Lord Cobham of poisoning her mind against him. When there was a scare in that summer of 1599 that a Spanish fleet was sailing up the Channel, and when Walter Ralegh, as vice-admiral, set about organizing defence forces with his customary energy, friends of Essex said that the invasion report had been concocted as an excuse to raise an army against the earl. Acolytes like Gilli Meyricke and Christopher Blount were once again whipping their master up into a frenzy of suspicion. The earl 'hath been somewhat crazy this week' wrote one newsletter writer in February 1600, and the following month he described the deposed favourite as 'quite out of his mind'.[9] 'His speeches of the queen,' wrote John Harington, 'becometh no man who has *mens sana in corpore sano*.'[10] In the earl's imagination was beginning to form the phantom of an enormous conspiracy of which he and

Elizabeth were to be the prime victims – a Spanish plot to subvert the state – a plot that could justify Essex taking the law into his own hands and overthrowing the Privy Council.

Ralegh was the prime mover in the scenario Essex devised, the man who controlled Cornwall and could guarantee the Spaniards a safe beach-head. He had recently been given the governorship of Jersey, so he could provide a staging post for their armada, and Essex read a sinister meaning into a recent trip Walter had made to inspect and improve the fortifications that were his responsibility. Henry Brooke, Lord Cobham, must also be in the plot, thought the earl, for Ralegh had worked hard to gain for him the control of the Cinque Ports – another key strategic post.

There were, in fact, certain circumstantial details that appeared to confirm the Earl of Essex's suspicions. Walter Ralegh was indeed at this time becoming more friendly than ever with Lord Cobham whose easy-going hedonism woke echoes of the young Walter: the two men, like a couple of schoolboys, 'stole over' to Dunkirk in the summer of 1600 to catch a flavour of the land war between Spain and the Netherlands and to recapture for Walter memories of his own battletrain youth on the Continent; Cobham was an amusing companion who had time for Walter – unlike the busy Cecil – and, as a peer of the realm, he seemed a useful ally to enlist against Essex. But the sinister interpretation that the earl now put on the Ralegh-Cobham friendship was as ridiculous as the aspersions he cast on Cecil. The secretary was selling England to Spain, Essex maintained, with the help not only of Ralegh and Cobham but a whole crew of clients: there was Cecil's brother, the second Lord Burghley who was president of the north, George Carew, the president of Munster – a Cecilian creature and Ralegh's cousin for good measure – and that inveterate enemy of Essex's the new Earl of Nottingham, Charles Howard, the lord admiral.

The only evidence for Essex's tissue of fantasies were the undeniable facts that all these men did hold positions of great strategic or political significance, and that none of them held any love for Essex. But as for intriguing with a foreign power, it was Essex, not his opponents, who was guilty of that, for the earl was pouring all his fears into secret letters to James VI, inviting the Scottish king to intervene to guarantee his accession to the throne of England and to deal with the traitors working on behalf of the Spanish king.

In this hidden and treasonable correspondence were sown the seeds of doubt that were to prejudice James's mind so strongly against Sir Walter Ralegh before ever he met the man, for if the Earl of Essex was supporting the Scottish king's claims to the English throne then Essex's enemies, especially Ralegh, must be James's enemies. Cecil was later to do favours for James that more than eradicated any suspicions Essex may have planted, but neither Ralegh nor Cobham did anything actively to disprove what the earl stated so confidently. And as a token of the faith James placed on Essex's accusations he decided to send an embassy down to London with the official task of discussing the succession with Elizabeth, and with the secret mission of coordinating plans for action with the earl.

But by the time that embassy arrived, the Earl of Essex was dead. One Sunday morning, on 8 February 1601, Sir Walter Ralegh rowed out into the middle of the Thames to meet and talk with his cousin, Sir Ferdinando Gorges. For weeks Essex House in the Strand had been the venue of unruly gatherings, swordsmen riding in from Wales and Puritan preachers haranguing the crowds with strange doctrines which appeared to sanction the deposition of monarchs. The previous evening, as a Saturday night celebration, roistering followers of Essex had paid Shakespeare's company at the Globe to stage a special performance of *Richard II*, and, led by Sir Gilli Meyricke and Sir Christopher Blount, had applauded loudly the scenes in which King Richard had had his crown and throne taken from him. The message was obvious. 'Know you not,' Queen Elizabeth once asked, 'that I am Richard?'

Worried to hear that among this rebellious rabble was his own kinsman, the governor of the Plymouth Fort, Ralegh sent a message asking Ferdinando Gorges to meet him at Durham House. But on Essex's instructions Ferdinando refused, saying he would meet Walter instead in an open boat in the middle of the Thames off Essex stairs. So, on this cold February Sunday before church, the two cousins jostled their rowing boats alongside each other on the flowing tide.

Walter told Ferdinando that there was a warrant issued for his arrest and urged him, both as a kinsman and superior officer, to go straight back to his fort in Plymouth lest he find himself locked up in the Fleet Prison.

'Tush, Sir Walter,' replied Gorges, obviously as confident as the rest of the little army in Essex House that the capital was theirs, 'this is not a time to talk of going to the Fleet. Get you back to the court, and that with speed, for my Lord of Essex hath put himself into a strong guard at Essex House, and you are like to have a bloody day of it.'[11]

Then a fusillade of shots rang out. From Essex House Christopher Blount was attempting to shoot Ralegh – that was the extent to which the situation had got out of hand. A boat containing four armed men moved off from Essex Stairs and headed towards the two cousins in midstream. There was clearly no time for further argument and Gorges pushed Walter's boat away towards the opposite bank, warning him that this February Sunday was likely to see the 'bloodiest day's work that ever was'.

Walter headed straight back to the court to add his own reports to the intelligence coming in from all sides. A deputation of privy councillors had gone to read the Riot Act at Essex House and been arrested as hostages. It looked as though the rebels could march on Whitehall and it was obvious what the captain of the queen's guard must do. Ralegh spent 8 February 1601 getting his men and the palace ready to defend Elizabeth to the death.

But his precautions proved unnecessary, for though Ferdinando had assured Walter that there were in Essex House '2,000 gentlemen who had resolved that day to live or die free men', the actual number at the Earl's back was nearer 200. Gorges had said that the purpose of the rising was to reform the way in which men like Ralegh abused the queen's authority and favour, but when the crowds of Londoners wandering through the City after the Sunday sermon at St Paul's Cross were told of the great Spanish plot that Essex had uncovered, most of them kept on walking home for their lunch.

'For the queen, for the queen! A plot is laid for my life!' shouted Essex, crying out that Ralegh and Cobham had tried to murder him and that they were planning to hand over the throne of England to Spain. But the citizens of London did not rush for their arms – and Sir Ferdinando Gorges was quick to see that the *coup* was doomed. He sidled away from the ever more feverish earl, took a quick boat back to Essex House and there released the privy councillors held as hostages since that morning.

The arrests, trials and executions that followed reaped a rich harvest of Ralegh's enemies. It can have been no hardship for Walter to see to his death Sir Gilli Meyricke who had slandered him so frequently and Sir Christopher Blount, another of Ralegh's persistent detractors was also sentenced to be executed. But Blount somewhat redeemed himself in his last days. In answer to a question from Cecil during his examination he acknowledged that neither he nor Essex had really believed that Ralegh and Cobham were plotting their destruction: 'it was a word cast out to colour other matters', and when, on the scaffold saying his prayers, Blount was cut short by the impatient sheriff, Ralegh, present as captain of the guard, told the sheriff to let the condemned man finish his confession in peace.

'Is Sir Walter there?' asked Blount, and then he called out for the whole crowd to hear. 'Sir Walter Ralegh, I thank God that you are present. I had an infinite desire to speak with you, to ask your forgiveness 'ere I died, both for the wrong done you, and for my particular ill intent towards you. I beseech you forgive me.'

'I most willingly forgive you,' replied Walter seriously, 'and I beseech God to forgive you and to give you His divine comfort.'

The end of Essex himself did not pass off so happily for Walter. When Ralegh was sworn in to give his account of his early morning meeting with Gorges in the middle of the Thames, the earl laughed loudly, 'What booteth it to swear the fox?' Ralegh, said Essex, should be made to place his hand on a large folio Bible rather than a small testament – to emphasize the size of his alleged perjury.

Through his duties as captain of the guard, Ralegh had to be present at the execution of his enemy. He stood close to the scaffold anticipating that Essex might want to say something to him as Blount had done – and that proved to be the case. Essex was to try before his execution to make amends to Ralegh and Cobham, saying he knew them to be 'true servants of the queen and state'. But Sir Walter Ralegh was not present at this moment of repentance on the part of the defeated earl, for detecting hostile murmurs to the effect that no man should stand so close to his mortal enemy at such a time, he withdrew to the armoury where he could witness the execution unseen. So he did not hear, and he had no chance to respond to the condemned man's desire to be reconciled with him.

Some men who saw Ralegh as he went home to Durham House after the execution on that Ash Wednesday in 1601 said that his face looked sad and gloomy. But a much more improbable tale about Walter was generally circulated and believed with more readiness. Ralegh, it was said, had smoked and joked as his enemy's head was cut off. He had contrived the earl's death, said public opinion, and having achieved it he gloated openly over his triumph. It was a slander which was to haunt Sir Walter Ralegh to the end of his days.

✤ 35 ✤

The End of a Lifetime

I n his *History of the World* Sir Walter Ralegh was to write that whatever the virtues and kindnesses of Alexander the Great, men were always to say of him, 'But he killed Calisthenes,'[1] and throughout the closing two years of Elizabeth's reign, men were to hang the same reproach around Ralegh's neck:

> Essex for vengeance cries
> His blood upon thee lies,
> Mounting above the skies,
> Damnable fiend of hell,
> Mischievous Matchivel![2]

Popular ballads were merciless in their savagery:

> Ralegh doth time bestride:
> He sits 'twixt wind and tide
> Yet uphill he cannot ride,
> For all his bloody pride.
> He seeks taxes in the tin:
> He polls the poor to the skin:
> Yet he swears 'tis no sin.
> Lord, for thy pity![3]

The Earl of Essex was accorded in death a loyalty he could never command in life, for the destruction of his extravagant promise was a parable of the times, a token of the decay that was gnawing at the world of Gloriana, and at Elizabeth herself. 'Sweet England's pride is gone', went the dirge,

> Though the Law strict course of justice kept,
> The most and best of all sorts wept.

The queen herself sobbed bitterly whenever she was reminded of her dead favourite, and even James of Scotland took it upon himself to describe the Earl of Essex as 'my martyr', which meant logically that Sir Walter Ralegh was his persecutor.

Robert Cecil, though more responsible than any single man – with the exception of Essex himself – for the earl's tragic downfall, somehow managed to avoid too much opprobrium for his own role in the affair. He knew that Ralegh was not to blame for Essex's sad end, but he also knew that what mattered now that England had crossed the threshold of the seventeenth century was the judgement passed by the king over the border, and that there was little interest to be gained, either from James or from popular opinion, in championing a man as reviled as Ralegh.

The sad thing about Walter, at this time when the opinion of others was so crucial, was his feckless indifference to popularity. In a more politic man that insensitivity would have been a strength, but in conjunction with his irredeemable obstinacy it was to prove an Achilles heel. In the parliament of 1601, for example, sitting in the honourable position he had regained as the senior knight for the county of Cornwall, he spoke in favour of the Government's unpopular proposal to extract the unprecedented number of four full subsidies from the taxpayers. Then, having attempted to ingratiate himself with the Privy Council to which he still hoped to be appointed, he cancelled out the dividends of his loyalty by attacking Robert Cecil for suggesting that men should, in the national interest, be prepared to sell everything they possessed: 'neither pots nor pans, nor sidh nor spoons' should be spared to save queen and country', the secretary had said.

'I like it not,' retorted Sir Walter, 'that the Spaniards our enemies should know of our selling our pots and pans to pay subsidies; well you may call it policy . . . but I am sure it argues poverty in the state.'

It was a gratuitously offensive speech, for both Ralegh and Cecil were agreed on the main issue, that the poor could not be exempted from paying subsidies, and when Francis Bacon spoke to the same effect, Ralegh was once again unable to resist the temptation to criticize a potential ally. Bacon had observed unctuously that by paying their taxes, both rich and poor were happily working together in an equal yoke. 'Call you this [an equal yoke]', asked Ralegh scornfully, 'when a poor man pays as much as a rich?' It was a jibe at Bacon's complacency that was both self-evident and pointless – and, with his unnecessary attack on Cecil, it illustrated precisely why Walter Ralegh's reputation for inconstancy was of his own making. If he could turn on those he called his allies over such trifles, how could he be relied on in matters of greater moment?

He spoke intelligently on several bills. To Government proposals to regulate the uses to which farmers put their land, he pointed out as a West Countryman how futile it was to compel someone to plough up his meadows if he did not have the money to buy seed corn, or did not know how to raise it. Rather than decreeing that more pastures should be used for growing crops it was better to leave the man with his grass to graze sheep and cattle if that was what he knew best. 'I think the best course is to set it [the land] at liberty, and every man free, which is the desire of a true Englishman.' Now approaching fifty and very conscious of being an elder statesman, Walter had an almost Churchillian ability to speak for the nation – though the nation knew what a reprehensible old scoundrel he could be.

He showed the same common-sense in a speech against the export of iron ordnance. This export meant that the Spaniards had been able to get hold of good English cannon, so that their firepower could now match that of the queen's fleet ship for ship, whereas, in the past 'one ship of Her Majesty's was able to beat ten Spaniards'. That flourish of Elizabethan patriotism went down well, as did a speech in favour of parliament continuing to subsidize the maintenance of Dover harbour. But then Walter spoiled everything with another exhibition of arrogant nonchalance in a dispute over voting.

It was an old-established Commons' procedure that when a division was called, the Noes sat still and the Ayes walked out to the lobby to be counted, since each piece of legislation involved some alteration in the status quo and it was thought only proper in a conservative society that those wishing to see a change should stir themselves into overt action. Men in doubt could sit still and thus swell the voices of those defending the old order. After one particularly narrow vote – 106 Noes to 105 Ayes – someone complained that one member had risen from his seat to vote yes, only to be pulled down and kept in his seat by another, a protest which Ralegh pooh-poohed. 'Why, if it please you, it is a small matter to pull one by the sleeve, for so I have done many times.' He struck the wrong note entirely, for though every MP had tugged elbows or seen them tugged in these circumstances, the House was in a solemn mood. Such flippancy was a slander on parliament, said Cecil in pious umbrage that much applauded, and he hoped that any man whose vote could be drawn backwards and forwards, like a dog on a string, would never be returned to the Commons again.

The main issue of the session, the question that was to make this parliament the most troublesome that Elizabeth had ever known, was monopolies, and if one individual was hated above all as an example of the system's injustice, it was Sir Walter Ralegh. He took a profit on every pack of playing cards sold in England. He had once had the monopoly on the export of broad cloths. He controlled the trade in certain types of wine. As lord warden of the stannaries all tin transactions passed through his hands, and he still enjoyed that great cornerstone of his finances, the right to license – at a price to the innkeeper – all taverns to sell alcohol.

The way in which ordinary consumers had to support monopolies with inflated prices was obvious, but the real grievance which stirred the passions of parliament in 1601 was the fact that most ordinary merchants were excluded from the fruitful business of economic regulation. When, in the Commons, the list of over twenty commodities like salt and soap, all subject to monopolists, was read out, and a wag asked 'Is not bread there?' the feeling of the House was not so much that the ordinary people of England should not be taxed in this fashion, but that the closed circle of the monopolies should be widened. Bread could be added to the list if, say, the city merchants were allowed to divide the London market amongst themselves and were not shut out by royal favourites like Ralegh.

But Walter Ralegh, who had, to his credit, blushed when playing cards had been read out on the list of monopolies, was prepared to tackle the commercial moguls face to face – so far as his tin monopoly was concerned, at least, for there the argument for regulation by the crown was strong. Before Ralegh had become lord warden of the stannaries, the Duke of Cornwall had had all the county's tin production refined into ingots and stamped with his arms. He had first refusal on every hundred-weight produced and the result was that, unable to control the price of more than a proportion of their output, the tinners were at the mercy of London merchants who depressed the prices of the metal to ridiculously low levels. Profits for the Cornishmen were neglible, and the ordinary miner was lucky to take home 2 shillings a week.

But Ralegh, as he proudly told the House of Commons, had channelled all tin sales through the crown, guaranteeing the miners a fixed price that had enabled wage rates to double. He had thus helped to create spare capital which could be invested in pumps and equipment to tackle the intolerable working conditions in many of the mines: men had been working all day in water up to their knees. He could produce solid evidence to justify his tin monopoly, and he concluded with a suggestion that left the whole House speechless. He was prepared, he stated grandly, to renounce all his special commercial privileges if the other monopolists were to do the same.

It was a grand gesture in true Ralegh style. But the mercantile MPs did not want emotional renunciations by one set of courtiers simply to see the vacated privileges passed on to a different or reshuffled set of favourites. They were, essentially, attacking the patronage inherent in the royal prerogative, and it was in recognition of this that Elizabeth surrendered to their demand to review the whole system of monopolies. When they came to thank her for her graciousness, on 30 November 1601, she took her leave of them with that famous golden speech that so clearly marked the end of an era:

> Though God hath raised me high, yet this I count the glory of my crown, that I have reigned with your love . . . I was never so much enticed with the glorious name of a king or royal authority of a queen, as delighted that God hath made me his instrument to maintain his truth and glory and to defend his kingdom from peril, dishonour, tyranny and oppression. . . .
>
> Though you have had and may have many mightier and wiser princes sitting on this seat, yet you never had nor shall have any that will love you better. . . . And I pray you Mr Comptroller, Mr Secretary, and you of my council, that before the gentlemen depart into their counties, you bring them all to kiss my hand.[4]

It was an entrancing, unforgettable, but definitely final farewell to anyone who had the wit to see it. But Sir Walter Ralegh could not, or would not reconcile himself to the fact that the old order of things was vanishing – and with especial rapidity in his own case. When the Earl of Lennox approached him in 1601 on behalf of King James of Scotland to see where he stood in the event of any dispute over the accession, he responded with a formality and bumbling honesty which had long gone out of style. He was so deeply in love and in the debt of Gloriana, he replied, that it would be treason to look for favour elsewhere.

It was the response of a fool. But James took it for the retort of an enemy. He did not know the ways of the Elizabethan court and was not secure enough to give Ralegh's blunt rejection the benefit of the doubt. He was not to know that Ralegh's fault was simply that he was old-fashioned, as intoxicated as ever by his mistress Elizabeth, going without sleep and riding through the night, for example, to change his colourful costume for 'a plain taffeta suit and a plain black saddle' simply because he had discovered that the French guests his queen had asked him to look after 'wear all black and no kind of bravery at all'. He earned his brother Carew a knighthood through that sleepless night travelling as fashion's martyr, but the sacrifice he was making in reality was far more precious. He was laying his life on the altar of a goddess whose cult had always lacked a certain substance, and which now had no power at all. When he went running to Cecil to tell him proudly how he had spurned the King of Scotland's ambassador, the secretary told him, 'You did well, and as I myself would have made answer, if the like offer had been made to me.'[5]

Though Walter Ralegh was later to discover the true nature of Robert Cecil's 'friendship' towards him, he was never even to guess that the little secretary had committed himself firmly to King James months before Ralegh came to him bearing like a schoolboy the news of his dismissal of Lennox. Could not Cecil pass on this great proof of loyalty to the queen – 'what had been offered, what answered?' asked Walter. It was inadvisable, counselled the secretary, not batting an eyelid. The queen, after all, was old and suspicious and might take it amiss that Ralegh had even allowed Lennox to talk to him. She might imagine that the Scots had spotted a disloyalty in Ralegh that she had not noticed herself, and she was certain to dismiss the retold story of his loyalty as ingratiation, an attempt to 'pick a thank'. So Walter remained silent, and lost out all round. His future sovereign was offended, and his present ruler knew nothing of his faithfulness.

In the mind of King James up in Scotland, only a matter of months away from becoming the monarch of two kingdoms, the Ralegh picture was fitting firmly into place. There were Essex's old allegations against him. There was the weight of public mistrust in England. There was this first-hand and firm personal rejection of his offer of friendship, and, most powerful of all, there were the insidious and constant complaints of one man, Lord Henry Howard, whose pathological hatred of Ralegh was to poison James's mind irrevocably in a remarkable and vicious series of letters.

Lord Henry Howard did not know Ralegh well, but he had been a friend of the Earl of Oxford back in the days when Walter, not yet a favourite, had engaged in his short relationship with that earl. From that brief and mysterious episode stemmed Howard's obsessive dislike of Ralegh, but the roots of his malice derived less from any particular deed of Walter's than from a more generalized paranoia embedded in his own Howard family history. His grandfather, the parchment-faced Duke of Norfolk, gave Henry VIII two nieces as wives only to see them executed, and was then, after a quarter of a century of service, thrown into the Tower himself; his father, the Earl of Surrey, the unstable soldier-poet was also arrested by Henry VIII and executed, while his elder brother Thomas, fourth Duke of Norfolk, went to the block as well when he plotted to marry Mary Queen of Scots. Thomas paid the price in June 1572, which left Henry Howard to brood on how his grandfather, father and brother had all become victims of the Tudor dynasty. His nephew, the Earl of Arundel, was thrown into prison by Elizabeth and died there, if any further draught were needed to fill the cup of Howard bitterness.

Henry had all the weaknesses of his ill-fated family – ambition, vanity, cowardice and envy. Cut off from Elizabeth's court by these qualities and the Howard track record, he fermented his spite like a witch her potions, maliciously devoting such little credit as he had to destroying the reputations of those he envied so fiercely. When Burghley's daughter married the Earl of Oxford it was Henry Howard – supposedly Oxford's friend – who gleefully spread the rumour that she was with child by another man. Hopping cloven-hoofed round the outer fringe of Elizabethan society, he was a truly fantastic character, so cut off from reality by his jealous humours that he would have been ignored or ridiculed in more healthy times. But when, after the fall of Essex, Robert Cecil tentatively made advances towards King James and discovered that the Scottish monarch's chief correspondent in England had for sometime been this spleenful crank, Cecil realized that his personal opinion of Howard would have to be held in abeyance.

He must have been surprised that the victim that Henry Howard had selected as the prime object of his rancour was Sir Walter Ralegh. Walter had his faults and Cecil had found them out – but it was hard to recognize the Ralegh that Cecil knew in the Judas-like caricature Howard painted to the King of Scots. The royal favourite, wrote Howard to James, was a villain who 'in pride exceedeth all men alive' and ranked, indeed, 'above the greatest Lucifer that hath lived in our age'. He was a serpent who had risen to eminence with 'the soft voice of Jacob in courtly hypocrisy'. Howard informed King James as a matter of established fact that Walter Ralegh was a magician, a wizard who concocted spells and curses to keep King James from his rightful inheritance, and, if any proof were needed of how unbalanced Howard was, he named as Walter's accomplice in his demonology Lady Ralegh. She, alleged Howard, was a Proserpine, acting as a 'president' over magical sessions that were held in Durham House – a witch stirring a cauldron of ill will.

Deranged these fancies might be, but they were clever, for if one subject impassioned King James VI of Scotland it was witches and warlocks. He treated with total seriousness Howard's insinuations that Ralegh hatched charms in a coven, and believed Howard when he cited Henry Brooke, Lord Cobham and Henry Percy, Earl of Northumberland as Walter's fellow wizards. The three made up 'a diabolical triplicity, that denies the Trinity, of wicked plotters hatching treason from cocatrice eggs that are daily and nightly sitten upon'. The old atheistical smear of the Jesuit Parsons was resurrected.

Henry Howard was, of course, quite correct that Lord Cobham had become, since the fall of Essex, a friend to Ralegh as close, if not closer than Northumberland. Unreliable and weak as Cobham was, he was a wealthy man and shared many of Walter's enthusiasms. It was only natural that Ralegh should feel the need for a powerful companion at court, especially a congenial comrade like Cobham, since Robert Cecil's influence on his behalf remained apparently so ineffective.

But no new friendships could save Walter Ralegh once Cecil had realized what a monster Henry Howard had conjured up in his letters to Scotland, for it was now too late for him to change James's opinion of Ralegh. Any attempt on his part to set the record straight would invite disaster. His tender connections with the Scottish king could be destroyed almost before they were established if James – or Howard – misinterpreted his longstanding relationship with Walter Ralegh who had, willy-nilly, become overnight an albatross round Cecil's neck. Every gesture of friendship that Walter made towards the secretary could have the most disastrous consequences if reported on unfavourably by James's spies in London, and Cecil, therefore, lost no time blocking this gap in his defences: 'Let me therefore presume thus far upon Your Majesty's favour,' he wrote to James, 'that whatsoever he [Ralegh] shall take upon him to say for me [i.e. on my behalf], upon any humour of kindness, whereof sometime he will be replete . . . you will no more believe it . . . be it never so much in my commendation.'[6]

Ralegh was quite capable of clasping Cecil warmly to him in the presence of James or the Scottish ambassador, and the secretary wanted to prepare the king for that eventuality. It was expedient, he explained, that Ralegh 'shall not think I reject his freedom or his affection', so James should not assume from surface displays of friendship that Cecil could genuinely seek 'to support a person whom most religious men do hold anathema'. That, from a man who had on the death of his wife, received from Ralegh the warmest spiritual consolation was the unkindest cut of all.

Nor did the secretary confine his suddenly discovered disenchantment with Walter Ralegh to his correspondence with King James, for he was concerned that Walter's close friendship with George Carew would prove an embarrassing liability not only to Carew but, more particularly, to Carew's patron, Cecil himself. So in a series of letters to Carew, now over in Ireland as president of Munster, Cecil complained that Ralegh was forming with Cobham an Essex-like clique opposed to the true interests of the kingdom – and the Cecils. He reminded Carew of the importance of patronage: 'Believe me, he [Ralegh] shall never have my consent to be a councillor without he surrender to you the captainship of the guard.' Naturally worried that just one chance remark about all this could betray to Ralegh and Cobham the net being woven around them, Cecil warned Carew to be very careful about what he wrote to them 'for they show all men's letters to every man'. In an ostensibly impulsive burst of sentiment, he wrote, 'believe me, two old friends use me unkindly, but I have covenanted with my heart not to know it, for in show we are great. All my revenge shall be to heap coals on their heads.'[7]

Carew, whom these letters did *not* detach from Ralegh, may well have wondered when the coal heaping was due to start, for throughout 1601–3 Cecil remained on the closest of terms with the men whose downfall he was secretly countenancing. On 12 January 1603, in the closing weeks of Queen Elizabeth's reign, he commissioned from Ralegh a privateer, going fifty-fifty on the victualling expenses. The rest of the cost, he wrote, 'may be borne between my Lord Cobham and you, or for such part as any of us will not receive, let it remain upon my head.'[8] He had gone in on a similar partnership with Ralegh the previous year, and his duplicity was the greater for he was financing pirates to attack vessels of the Spanish Government with which he swore to both Elizabeth and James that he desired peace. Well might he write to Ralegh 'I pray you, as much as may be, conceal our adventure, at the least my name above any others.'[9]

Secrecy was of the essence in those years. Had James known that Cecil was not only encouraging attacks on Spanish shipping but sharing the profits with Ralegh his confidence would have been badly shaken, and if Elizabeth had discovered that her secretary was plotting her replacement, her rage could have been deadly. So Robert Cecil and his correspondents adopted a code in which numbers replaced important names: James was 30, Elizabeth 24, Cecil 10, Cobham 7, Howard 3, Ralegh 2 and Northumberland 0. The trouble was that James was so tickled to have won someone as influential as Cecil to his cause that he had great difficulty keeping the tidings to himself, and his muddled Scottish aides sent at least one secret epistle to Cecil in the same royal mail pouch as official despatches to Elizabeth – as the secretary discovered to his horror as he opened the pouch in the presence of Elizabeth herself. He only avoided disaster by telling the queen that the letter smelt so leathery it needed to be aired.

But Elizabeth's faculties were definitely waning. The end of an era was approaching for her country and, even more threateningly, for that most ardent of her suitors, Sir Walter Ralegh. For the best part of his adult life his world had revolved around Elizabeth, both in favour and in disgrace.

'How long will you remain a beggar?' Elizabeth had once asked him half in annoyance, half in jest.

'So long as Your Highness remains a benefactor,' Walter had replied, quick as a flash.[10]

He had needed no time to compose that reply, for to court the queen was second nature to him. Even in the depths of his disgrace, torn between his love for Bess and his friendship for the queen, he had been compelled to acknowledge the power that Elizabeth exerted over him. He simply had not been able to live retired in the country, immersed in his poems, experiments or schemes of exploration. He had had to return to court to win back the smiles of the woman he could not imagine ever living without.

So when all others were looking north, Sir Walter Ralegh remained an Elizabethan to the bitter end. Henri IV's great minister the Duc de Sully came over the Channel to pay Elizabeth a visit, as he imagined, incognito. Freshly arrived at Dover:

> I had scarcely entered my room, and was in the act of speaking to my attendants, when I found myself approached, behind my back, by some one who said to me 'I arrest you as my prisoner, in the queen's name'. It was the captain of her guard, whose embrace I returned, telling him I should consider such an imprisonment a great honour.[11]

Walter kept playing the old games, escorting visiting Spaniards, Frenchmen or West Country relatives around Elizabethan London and the court pointing out all the sights and explaining all the customs and ceremonies, unaware that he was acting as guide to an historical monument. While Cecil and Henry Howard wrote north, Walter entertained Cobham at Sherborne. 'I hope your lordship will be here tomorrow or a Saturday', he wrote, 'or else my wife says her oysters will be all spoilt and her partridge stale.'[12]

Robert Cecil paid a passing visit at this time to partake of Lady Ralegh's hospitality, but he was travelling on business, as always, 'and had no leisure to look abroad'. We do not know if Bess entertained the secretary with oysters and partridge, but she made him a pair of gloves – a very special present, for normally she would sew only for Walter.

It was a pity that Lady Ralegh could not always be so politic. In these last moments when every friend counted, she contrived to fall out with Cobham's new wife, Lady Kildare, whom Bess suspected of intriguing against her at court. Lady Kildare was a Howard, the daughter of the lord admiral who still nursed his resentment over Ralegh's role in his dispute of precedence with Essex, and a relative of the venomous Lord Henry Howard.

Yet another of the Howard clan, Lord Howard of Bindon, who was a Dorset neighbour of Walter's and had sat as one of the judges at the Cerne Abbas enquiry, now also enlarged the fund of Howard enmity towards the dying queen's favourite. He took John Meere's side in the disputes that the bailiff had been engaging in with Sir Walter Ralegh, procuring him a warrant to arrest the bailiff Walter had appointed in his place. With some zest Walter in his turn had Meere arrested and locked in the stocks while Walter looked on and while the people of Sherborne jeered 'Where is Lord Howard? Where is Lord Howard?'

It was a storm in a Dorset teacup, but it was hardly clever. Walter's priorities were all askew, raging that he would 'not endure wrong at so peevish a fool's hands', when there were other wrongs he should have been concerning himself with. Little Cecil was at court, never far from Elizabeth, all through the final months, and it was he who got the queen to nominate King James of Scotland as her successor. Men had seen the end coming for weeks and the post horses were prepared for the herald's ride up to Scotland. But though Walter Ralegh could read the signs as plainly as anyone, he was not with Elizabeth at the end – which came early in the morning of 24 March 1603, but down in the West Country.

Sir Walter Ralegh, that most ardent of her suitors, was later to say in a famous phrase that Elizabeth was a lady whom time had surprised. But time had not, in truth, surprised the old queen as much as it had her younger favourite – and he really had no one but himself to blame. He had made a special study of time in his poetry, so he could have little excuse for letting it catch him unawares.

Part 6

❖

1603–16 Captivity

James I slobbered at the mouth and had favourites; he was thus a Bad King. He had however, a very logical and tidy mind, and one of the first things he did was to have Sir Walter Ralegh executed for being left over from the previous reign.

Sellar, and Yeatman, '1066 and All That'

✤ 36 ✤

The New King

The accession of King James I to the throne of England in March 1603 marked the beginning of a more prosperous stage in the careers of almost all the men who had featured prominently in the last years of Queen Elizabeth's reign. Robert Cecil was given the peerage he had awaited so long and was in due course advanced to the earldom of Salisbury. Francis Bacon proceeded smoothly through the great legal offices of the land to become lord chancellor of England. Thomas Howard became lord chamberlain of the new king's household and Earl of Suffolk. George Carew was made Baron Carew and rose to become a privy councillor. The followers of the Earl of Essex were pardoned and thrived under the new régime. Henry Howard came out of obscurity to a place on the Privy Council and the earldom of Northampton, and virtually everyone flourished in a great deluge of gifts, promotions and ennoblements attending on the arrival of the new king – everyone, that is, except Sir Walter Ralegh.

To him the accession of James I came as a new stage in life, but in a cruelly different sense, for within months he was to be deprived of position, wealth and even the right to live. He had been matched to Elizabeth better than anyone had realized and only when her successor came into his inheritance was that peculiar identity remarked on. King James I and Sir Walter Ralegh were like creatures from different planets, and it was Sir Walter Ralegh who tumbled into the void that lay between them.

The contrast between the old queen's favourite and the new, thirty-seven year old monarch was so total that it could have been taken for deliberate. Sir Walter was a man of action, of exploits, a man of war, adventure and heroism. King James was a coward who wore quilted doublets, padded breeches and slept in the sweaty igloo of a dozen mattresses for fear of the assassin's knife. He was, like Cecil, physically deformed, walking with a crablike waddle, often leaning on the arm of his favourites. And those favourites were invariably male, James doting on them with extravagance that astonished before it shocked, the king nibbling their cheeks and busying his hands in the most intimate places – in public.

He smelt. His greatest concession to cleanliness was to moisten his fingers on a damp napkin, for he had a dread of water and washing which – coupled with his uncoordinated table movements, made it possible for one courtier to claim that he could tell every single meal the king had eaten for seven years from studying the stains and gobbets of dried food on his clothes.

Only at the intellectual level did James approach Walter Ralegh's stature, but again it was in a contrary fashion. His mind was an academic one, pedantic in fact, niggling over particulars rather than risking cosmic generalizations. He lacked the common touch, the grasp of practicalities, pursuing learning for its own sake rather than to discover its utility. His tutors, he was proud to say, schooled him in Latin before his native tongue.

So it was not surprising that when James and Walter Ralegh first came face to face in the spring of 1603 that the king should have attempted a pun. 'On my soul, man, I have heard rawly of thee.'[1] Nor that, according to another anecdote, there should have sprung up an instant antagonism between the two men. On James remarking that, delighted though he was with the way his new kingdom had received him, he could, if necessary, have captured it by force of arms, Ralegh replied, 'Would to God that had been put to the trial.'

'Why do you wish that?' James asked.

'Because then you would have known your friends from your foes,' answered Ralegh cryptically.[2]

Walter had come up from the West Country at the time of Queen Elizabeth's death to sign the address of loyal welcome to be sent to the new king from a sort of assembly of notables called together by the Privy Council. With Cobham he had had the indiscretion to question at this meeting the number of Scots the king was allowed to bring to England with him – but he had naturally put his name to the address.

Meanwhile James was proceeding south in triumph, welcomed with an ardour with which he was never again to be warmed by his subjects. To stem the flood of courtiers waylaying him, he issued a proclamation forbidding persons holding public office to travel north lest the Government of the nation suffer. The king would meet his new servants in London, and in the meantime they could keep at their work.

But if this proclamation was, as some whispered, a device to keep Sir Walter Ralegh at a safe distance, it was ineffective, for, said the warden of the stannaries and lord lieutenant of Cornwall, it was essential for the royal warrant in that county to be renewed, if only to forestall the unpatriotic from taking advantage of the interregnum to cut themselves free timber from the royal forests there. It was a lame excuse, but Walter rode north to Theobalds just the same to be greeted by the royal pun – and to make the cryptic remark on which so much significance could be set.

What did James think of the man of whom he had heard so little good? Before he came south he had already remarked of Ralegh and Cobham, 'We are exceeding far inamorat of them,' and he had assured Cecil, 'Your suspicion and your disgracing shall be mine.' Now the timid little king had met the buccaneer whose 'awfulness and ascendancy in his aspect over other mortals' had overawed so many. John Aubrey always maintained that 'Sir Walter was never forgotten nor forgiven' for his ambiguous comment about James knowing his friends from his foes,[3] and certainly the king's immediate reaction to Ralegh was to tell his clerk to hurry up the letters of authorization that his unexpected suitor had requested and to get rid of him.

The first token of displeasure was indiscriminate. On 7 May 1603 King James called in all monopolies for scrutiny – a blow which hit Ralegh harder than most, for the major part of his income was knocked away at a stroke. Then came the second indication of royal feeling, though again Ralegh could not claim to have been unfairly victimized. He was instructed in mid May to relinquish his position as captain of the guard, which would be handed on to Sir Thomas Erskine, the Scot who had served James in that capacity in Edinburgh. The post had always been Ralegh's special pride, the token of Queen Elizabeth's particular affection and, later, of her restoring of favour. But it was not unreasonable that the new king should want his bodyguard to be commanded by a man he knew well, especially in view of his fears of assassination. And James made some small gesture of compensation by forgoing the £300 that the crown was entitled to demand every year for the governorship of Jersey. 'Sir Walter', it was reported, 'in a very humble manner did submit himself.'

But Sir Walter, it seemed, had a death wish. When the court was on progress visiting Bess's uncle, Sir Nicholas Carew, Walter presented as a token of goodwill to the king *A Discourse Touching a War with Spain and of the Protecting of the Netherlands* – a pamphlet setting out the conventional Elizabethan rationale which justified the war against Spain. Ralegh simply did not realize that his new monarch loved neither war nor, as a champion of absolute monarchy, the Dutch rebels. He had no intention of continuing the war with Spain nor of protecting the Netherlands, and Ralegh's casual boast to the king that he, Walter Ralegh, could, if James wished, transfer the West Indies from the Spanish to the English empire was still more alarming.

Now the blows began to fall quite specifically. When crossing the border James had been asked by the Bishop of Durham if he could return to the church the London palace where Walter Ralegh lived in secular magnificence. On 31 May 1603 James made known his decision that he could, and though Ralegh protested bitterly at the short time allowed him to move, James's commissioners would allow him but three and a half weeks. Walter and Bess had to have the house emptied completely and have all their goods and chattels on the road to Sherborne by 25 June 1603.

It was a humiliating and symbolic spectacle for the possessions of the great Sir Walter Ralegh to be humped onto carts and evicted from the capital by royal bailiffs, and if any confirmation was needed that a great star was spiralling down from the firmament it came before the following month was out.

In the middle of July 1603 Walter went to Windsor to take part in the royal hunt – but he did not ride with the hounds. While he was waiting on the terrace of the castle his old friend Robert Cecil came up and told him that the king wished him to stay behind that day. The Privy Council had some questions that they wanted to put to him. So Walter went inside the palace, and there the councillors asked him what he knew of a conspiracy against the king and of communications involving Lord Cobham and the ambassador from the Spanish Netherlands. Nothing, Walter replied – but he was placed under house arrest at the end of the examination just the same. The Privy Council were not satisfied with his protestations of innocence. He knew more, they suspected, than he cared to admit, and so within a few days, by 20 July 1603, Sir Walter Ralegh was confined to the Tower of London for the second time in his life – and on this occasion he had more than a woman's indignation to assuage. The charge against him was high treason.

✿ 37 ✿

The Main and Bye Plots

There definitely was a plot. The question was whether Sir Walter Ralegh was involved in it. The principal conspirators were two Catholics, both priests, Father William Watson and Francis Clarke, who had travelled to Scotland in 1602 to ask King James whether he would, after his accession, relax the English laws against Papists.

James had been encouraging but non-committal for, uncertain of his inheritance, he was too canny to offend any section of his would-be subjects. He knew from the letters of Lord Henry Howard, himself a crypto-Catholic, how strong Papist feelings were in many parts of England, but he also knew from the letters of Robert Cecil how staunchly Protestant the bulk of the population was. So he played a double game. He assured both Henry Howard and Cecil of his devotion to their respective faiths, wrote to Elizabeth's Council calling for harsher measures against 'Jesuits, seminary priests and that rabble', but at the same time kept in touch with the pope and responded with apparent sympathy to overtures of the type made by the priests Watson and Clarke. The two men returned from Scotland under the impression that Catholics could, at the least, hope for lighter restrictions on the practice of their faith when King James came to the throne.

But events were to disillusion them, for the Scot secured his new kingdom with far more ease than he had anticipated, and he saw no need for many of the allies he had courted so assiduously from Edinburgh. 'Na, na, we'll no need the Papists noo', was the much-reported comment with which he swept aside any suggestion of more toleration for his new Catholic subjects.

Clarke and Watson felt aggrieved, and it was from their resentment at what they interpreted as a betrayal that sprang the conspiracy which was later to be known as the Bye (or Surprising) Plot – though the followers they recruited were scarcely surprising. Sir Griffin Markham and George Brooke, the brother of Lord Cobham, were almost professional malcontents who, having wasted their resources on the fringes of Elizabethan court life, had thrown in their lot with the Essex rioters and had learnt nothing neither from the fate of that conspiracy nor from the leniency with which they were subsequently treated. Anthony Copley was another impecunious swordsman who joined in the plot, the strategy of which was forcibly to seize the king and compel him to adopt a more kindly policy towards his Catholic subjects.

The absurdity of the scheme was complicated by the fact that George Brooke was the brother of Lord Cobham, and that Cobham was engaged in some dubious intrigues on his own account. Both brothers felt a personal grudge against Robert Cecil because he had in the past shown friendliness towards them – as he had towards Ralegh – which had led them both to hope for more solid favours than they had ever received, and Cobham, in addition to being friendly with Ralegh, had got involved with the son of Walter's old commander at Smerwick Fort, the young Lord Grey of Wilton. This fractious young man, who in the months leading up to the Essex revolt had pursued a poisonous vendetta against Essex's most elevated henchman, the Earl of Southampton, had conceived a bitter dislike of the new king. As an ardent Puritan, Grey felt strongly that James should grant more toleration to extremist Protestants, and though he obviously had little in common with the Catholic priests Clarke and Watson, he appeared in his bitterness and readiness for violence an apt recruit for any shady business.

The most incriminating participant in the whole muddle was Count Aremberg, the ambassador who represented the Spanish Netherlands at the English court and who was hoping to negotiate peace to end the long war between Spain and England. Lord Cobham had known Aremberg for some time and made no attempt to hide the fact, passing on to both Cecil and, later, to James, suggestions from Aremberg as to how an agreement to end the war might be reached. But, according to subsequent accusations, Cobham and Aremberg did not content themselves simply with discussing speculative peace plans: they also hatched a concrete conspiracy to remove James from the throne with the help of Spanish arms and money and to replace him with Arabella Stuart, an empty-headed girl belonging to a younger branch of the Scottish royal family.

'Many-headed' was an epithet that sixteenth-century prosecutors delighted to employ of the conspiracies subjected to the cutting edge of their oratory – especially when they were not too sure of all of their facts – and if anything deserved that description it was this complicated tangle revolving around Cobham and his brother George. When they came to

sort it out the Privy Council decided that they had discovered two conspiracies – the Bye Plot which lumped together the various attempts at
religious toleration and linked up the Catholic priests, the Puritan
Lord Grey of Wilton and the former Essex rebels; and the Main Plot,
the substance of which was provided by Cobham's efforts on behalf of
Arabella Stuart with the help of the Spaniard Count Aremberg.

It was primarily about this latter treason that Sir Walter Ralegh as a
friend of Cobham's was cross-questioned on the July day that he came to
Windsor to hunt with King James, and he strongly denied any knowledge
of dealings between Cobham and Count Aremberg. But afterwards he
reflected further. He had, as usual, said too much too fervently. Not to
put too fine a point upon it, he had lied. For though he was on safe ground
so far as Arabella Stuart was concerned – he scarcely knew the lady – he
knew as well as anyone that Cobham had been seeing a lot of Aremberg,
and he knew too that Cobham had passed on to James and Cecil certain
details of his discussions with the Spaniard. It was common knowledge.
So for Walter Ralegh, a known personal friend of Cobham's, to deny that
anything at all had passed between the Englishman and the foreign
ambassador must sound both naïve and suspicious. The Council had only
to show that one part of his denial was untrue for his innocence as a whole
to be called into question.

It was a nasty situation. The Main and Bye Plots might sound far-
fetched and comparatively harmless devices, but they did occur in 1603,
two years after the Essex Revolt and two years before the Gunpowder
Plot, both deadly serious attempts to overthrow the status quo. The Privy
Council was particularly jumpy in the months following the death of
Queen Elizabeth which had been dreaded for over a third of a century as a
signal for civil disturbance, and anyone implicated, however remotely, in
projects that threatened the new order of things, could expect rough
justice particularly if, like Sir Walter Ralegh, he had already become an
object of suspicion.

There is every reason, furthermore, for believing that Sir Walter Ralegh
was not as guiltless as he claimed to be. He almost certainly knew more
about the Main, if not the Bye Plot than he admitted to the Privy Council,
for his friend Cobham had definitely been discussing treasonable activities
with Aremberg, and it was in his nature to spill everything out to Ralegh.
So although Walter might be too level-headed to get involved in either
plot, he was guilty of not passing on immediately all that he knew to the
Privy Council. Conniving constituted treason in itself, and there is powerful circumstantial evidence that Sir Walter Ralegh *was* very well aware
that he was playing with fire. Sometime in 1602, in the final months of
Queen Elizabeth's life, he had drawn up a deed transferring his estates at

Sherborne to his son Wat. Ralegh reserved to himself a life interest in the estate, but the effect of the deed was that if, for any reason, Walter's properties were to be confiscated, Sherborne would remain in Ralegh hands, since it would no longer be legally in Walter's possession.

It was a sly device which, in an age before death duties, was not a common one and would only have been executed in anticipation of two catastrophes: bankruptcy, in which event creditors would not be able to distrain on Sherborne – or treason, when the normal attainder of a traitor's land and property could not threaten anything that was in young Wat's name. It is possible that anticipating a loss of royal favour and all the incomes that went with it, Walter foresaw economic catastrophe after the accession of James and sought to take evasive action, but it is more likely that, aware of the treasonable nature of his activities, he took steps to safeguard the welfare of his family in case his plans backfired.

In the last analysis we can, of course, only speculate about events that were a mystery to most of the people involved in them at the time, but since it is certain that Walter Ralegh knew more about Cobham's plottings than he admitted, we are left with only two explanations of his compromising behaviour. Either he intended Cobham's schemes to succeed – in which case we would expect to find him bubbling over with conspiratorial suggestions as he had been when he proposed the assassinations of Tyrone and Essex – or else he intended the conspiracy to fail and hoped, while remaining prudently detached, to bring about that failure. And here we have to hand the explanation of the whole mystery made half a century later to John Aubrey, who stated that:

> as to the plot and business of Lord Cobham, etc., he [Ralegh] being then governor of Jersey, would not fully do things unless they would go to his island [i.e. Jersey] and there advise and resolve about it; and that really and indeed Sir Walter's purpose was, when he had them there, to have betrayed the plot and have then [them?] delivered up to the king and made his peace.[1]

After the event though this explanation was, it was based on conversations with Ralegh's family who had heard Walter's own private explanation of the Main and Bye Plots. Its duplicity echoes the way in which Walter infiltrated the Oxford circle at the beginning of his court career to switch back to Leicester and Walsingham in 1579. Nothing short of a spectacular coup of this sort could possibly win for Ralegh the favour of King James and such evidence as did emerge in the course of the Privy Council's enquiries indicated such a betrayal by Ralegh. Cobham mentioned a plan to meet on the island of Jersey for no obvious reason, and Walter admitted discussing Spanish pensions and bribes with his friend.

Ralegh, in other words, was acting the role of the agent provocateur, encouraging Cobham in order to incriminate him, and his lack of scruple in doing this was of a piece with his Machiavellian actions in the past.

But once the Privy Council were on to Cobham's schemings, of course, the whole device became a deadly liability, for it implicated Walter without providing him with any means of extricating himself from the mess. He had hastily denied knowing anything at all, so any mention of his original intention would prove him to be not just a fool but, by his own admission, a liar as well. Not for the first time he had been too clever, and too hasty by half.

So when Walter came to consider his original statement to the Privy Council that he knew nothing of Cobham's schemes, he realized that he would have to change his tack, and, on the day after his first examination, he sat down to write to the one councillor he thought he could trust, Robert Cecil, a letter in which he hedged with qualifications his previous firm statement. He had noticed, he wrote, that Cobham, after calling at Durham House of an evening, had not always gone straight back to his own home but had, at least once, been rowed on to the residence of La Renzi, an agent of Aremberg's. So he suspected that Cobham had, perhaps, had dealings of some sort with Aremberg.

Ralegh's second thoughts were less than heroic. Confronted with the bloodlust of James's council he had lost his nerve. He had not said anything specific that need incriminate Cobham, yet he had given Robert Cecil a deadly weapon. Cecil did not treat Walter's letter as an explanatory note from a friend, he took it instead straight to Cobham himself – who immediately panicked. Far from reading coolly what Ralegh had written and citing in his defence the fact that both Cecil and the king knew well that he had been discussing peace propositions with Aremberg, Cobham lost his head. 'O traitor!' he cried. 'O villain! I will now tell you all the truth!'[2] and he proceeded to pour out a story of how he had indeed conducted discussions of a dubious nature with Aremberg, and how it was Ralegh who had 'procured me to this villainy'. Scarcely had he finished than he retracted all his accusations. Then later he retracted the retraction, and then finally he retracted the retraction to the retraction. But his frantic contradictions served only to discredit whatever he might protest in his own defence and in that of his friend. He had said more than enough to put Walter Ralegh in the Tower of London.

The prospect now was black indeed. Ralegh and Cobham had in their reactions to questioning compromised each other fatally, and in the context of the secret correspondence that had twisted James's opinion of them so dangerously, it was difficult to see what salvation they could now hope for.

In the Tower Walter sank into depression. The events since the death of Elizabeth fitted into a gloomy picture. He had lost in a matter of weeks his chief sources of income, his fine London house, the job that had been his greatest pride, and now he was faced with the prospect of losing his life as well. Even that was not what broke his will completely. He had been in mortal peril before and the prospect of death had on previous occasions roused in him inspiring courage. The most dispiriting prospect in the summer of 1603 was the fact that even if, by some miracle, he escaped from the fate now hanging over him, he would still be at the mercy of this unfriendly Scottish king whose favour he could never hope to win. He could never again shine at court or in any great national enterprise. The best he could anticipate was survival, probably in the country. Even when cast down by the fiercest of Elizabeth's displeasures, he had still been able to hope for forgiveness. He had known that, in the last resort, she was a friend. But he knew that James, humourless and hostile, could never be won over, and he knew too that James was younger than him – a dozen years younger. At the age of fifty-one Walter Ralegh had lost himself hopelessly in a forest more savage than any that Guiana knew.

He acted rapidly. On 21 July 1603, Sir John Peyton, the lieutenant of the Tower, had written to Cecil that Ralegh was maintaining his innocence 'but with a mind the most dejected that I ever saw'. Two days later he repeated how downcast his prisoner seemed, so that he wondered whether 'his [Ralegh's] fortitude is competent to support his grief', and then only four days later he – and Cecil – were to discover that his fears were justified, for, on 27 July 1603, while a group of privy councillors were in the Tower examining prisoners, Walter Ralegh attempted to stab himself to death. Cecil and his colleagues rushed into the wounded man's cell to find him bleeding profusely and weakly protesting his innocence.

It was a gesture of total despair, and Ralegh's reasons for it are central to any assessment of his character. He had a few days previously asked his keeper to purchase a long thin knife on the pretext that he wanted to stir his wine with it, and being denied this he had decided on a more domestic instrument of destruction. He had picked up a table knife, aimed it at his heart and thrust it into his chest. A dagger would have done the job forcefully, but the dinner knife simply bounced off a rib leaving a ragged gash which Cecil contemptuously described as a cut under the pap rather than a proper stab. The secretary clearly thought that the suicide was a sham designed by Ralegh to win public sympathy, and he accordingly did his best to ensure that news of it did not leak out.

Now if Ralegh were simply playing to the stalls, then such a charade was in keeping with his character. He was a self-conscious man, striving frequently for the sake of effect and sometimes for little else. His would-be suicide in 1603 could well be compared to the occasion a dozen years previously when he had contrived to fight George Carew in Durham House and had slashed Arthur Gorges' knuckles in an effort to win Queen Elizabeth's sympathy. He was a man of war, well used to handling weapons in the destruction of others, so why, when it came to inserting the knife between his own ribs, did he fumble? Were Cecil's suspicions not, perhaps, well justified?

We must ask ourselves, however, to what audience Ralegh was playing. He had always disdained public opinion and knew well that the ordinary people of London were delighted to see him threatened with the same fate to which they believed he had driven Essex. They would applaud his death by his own hand. Nor could Walter suppose that he might melt the hearts of the hard-faced men who sat on King James's Council with a gesture which they would all interpret with the same cynicism as Cecil. To commit or attempt suicide was, furthermore, a sin that would particularly offend the piety of the king himself. So if in July 1603 Walter Ralegh did pretend to take his own life through calculation, he did so with all the irrationality which characterizes genuine suicide attempts; and this explanation – that the great Sir Walter Ralegh sank to such depths of despair that he honestly tried to make an end of himself – is substantiated both by the testimony of his jailer, who witnessed the growing depression of his charge through the days leading up to the stabbing, and by the words of Walter himself. For there is extant a 'suicide note' of Ralegh's. Biographers have in the past dismissed the manuscript as a forgery because of its allusions to 'my poor daughter', but now that we know from his 1597 will that Ralegh did possess an illegitimate daughter, there can be no doubt that the letter was genuine. 'That thou didst also love me living, witness it to others, to my poor daughter', Walter begged his wife. 'Be charitable to her and teach thy son to love her for his father's sake.'[3]

Then sinking into a mawkish style he continued to Bess:

I am now made an enemy and traitor by the word of an unworthy man. [Cobham] ... Woe, woe, woe, be unto him by whose false hand we are lost! He hath separate us asunder, he hath slain my honour, my fortune, he hath robbed thee of thy husband, thy child of his father and me of you both! Oh God, thou dost know my wrongs, know then, my wife and child, know then, thou my Lord and King, that I ever thought them too honest to betray, and too good to conspire against!

In these meandering invocations Walter Ralegh was clearly out of control. There is a marked contrast between this hysterical sobbing and his normally stylish economy of words – but its inconsistency lay in the disturbance in Walter Ralegh's mind, not in the pen of some forger. The Earl of Essex had badly compromised his own reputation by wallowing in self-pity as he had lain imprisoned in the Tower, and now, two years later, his great Elizabethan rival revealed that he too had feet of clay – for the gilded idols who dominated the English Renaissance were volatile men. With meteoric brilliance went dark, burnt-out and tumbling reality. The contradiction lay deep within them, and now, although his light was to shine again, Walter Ralegh's spiritual extinction was abject and almost fatal.

But it also proved cathartic. The attempt to kill himself seems to have given Ralegh some kind of psychological release, for within a few days his keeper was telling the Privy Council that his prisoner appeared healed in both body and mind, and Ralegh himself was working to defeat the charges against him. He sent Lawrence Keymis to talk to Cobham to try to convince him of Ralegh's loyalty. Keymis was to explain how Walter had not, in fact, betrayed Cobham but had stood up for him in the face of Privy Council questioning, and Keymis was also to explain to Cobham a point of law which Ralegh expected to be of key importance in the coming trial – the salvation of both of them. Sir Nicholas Throckmorton, Ralegh's father-in-law, had been acquitted of treason back in the reign of Queen Mary because, although he had been a party to treasonable conspiracy, he had committed no overt action, and because there were not *two* witnesses to testify to his plottings. Statutes dating back to the reign of Edward III that imposed this numerical qualification had saved him – and Ralegh trusted to the same legal technicalities. Neither Cobham nor he were accused of any overt act of treason, and to their alleged conspiracy there could not possibly be found two witnesses.

But Walter should have studied his law more thoroughly at the Inns of Court, for, as a result of Throckmorton's escape, new and more stringent treason laws had been enacted which meant that the example of his father-in-law no longer applied, while to make matters worse, Cobham betrayed the details of Keymis's mission to the Privy Council – so the prosecution could prepare in advance a retort to the defence on which they knew Walter would be relying. They arrested Laurence Keymis, furthermore, and threatened him with torture to confirm the details they required.

The Council caught up too with another messenger Ralegh employed – the son of the lieutenant of the Tower himself, young John Peyton, who fell under the old Elizabethan's spell. The boy appears genuinely to have worked for some sort of personal reconciliation between Walter and Cobham, talking to both of them amost every day in an effort to heal the trust that had broken down between them. But he was found out, and both his father and Ralegh were punished by a neat device in which lurked the mischievous humour of Cecil, for the lieutenant of the Tower was relieved of his duties the moment it was discovered how untrustworthy his family had been, and then, in the same month of August 1603, he had bestowed upon him the governorship of Jersey which, said the king, had been 'forfeited to us' by Sir Walter Ralegh's 'grievous treason intended against us'. The legal tradition that an Englishman is innocent until he is proved guilty did not apply in matters of sixteenth- and seventeenth-century treason, and the following month Sir Francis Godolphin, high sheriff of Cornwall, was authorized to take that country's musters, 'the Commission of Lieutenancy granted to Sir Walter Ralegh being become void and determined'.

But Walter continued his labours undeterred. He won over, again through charm, the son of Peyton's replacement, Sir George Harvey, recruiting the young man to inveigle out of Cobham a letter stating honestly that he knew Ralegh to be innocent. Walter wrote a moving appeal to his friend and had it thrown through Cobham's window attached to an apple. Then when Cobham responded with a note which, though favourable, did not, to Ralegh's mind, state exactly the version of events which should be presented to the court, Walter asked for another, revised version. This second letter duly arrived, and, feeling confident finally that he had the evidence on which he could rely, Ralegh tucked it into a hidden pocket in his tunic.

To clear my conscience, satisfy the world and free myself from the cry of your blood [Cobham had written to him], I protest upon my soul, and before God and his angels, I never had conference with you in any treason; nor was ever moved by you to the things I heretofore accused you of. And, for anything I know, you are as innocent and as clear from any treasons against the king as is any subject living. . . . and so God deal with me and have mercy on my soul, as this is true.[4]

It seemed the absolute defence to whichever of Cobham's previous accusations the prosecution might produce in court. Yet, it was, in fact, as treacherous as the archaic legal technicality by which Ralegh also set so much store. For the miserable Cobham had had second thoughts after writing the note and, unknown to Ralegh, had revealed the contents of his letter to the Council. He had then composed for their benefit a further affidavit which both postdated the document that Ralegh held and contradicted the main points that it made. So once again Ralegh was relying on the surprise of a defence whose every detail was known to the prosecution and for which they had waiting a crushing rebuttal. When Cecil wrote

'Always he shall be left to the law, which is the right all men are born into', he was being ingenuous, for he knew well what justice his victim could expect.

Walter had been nearer the mark when, in his suicidal depression, he had written not only to Cecil but to the former comrades he had learnt would be his judges, Charles Howard, Thomas Howard and Lord Mountjoy, begging them to remember the welfare of his family: 'For to leave me to the cruelty of the law of England,' he wrote, 'were . . . to destroy the father and the fatherless.'[5]

To that extent, at least, Walter Ralegh knew his law.

❧ 38 ❧

The Trial

The plague went on late that year. Two thousand Londoners were dying each week. Bells tolled all day long for funerals. Infected bedding and straw were thrown out into the streets. There were even three deaths in the comparatively isolated Tower of London, and the court, as usual, took to its heels to Hampton Court, Woodstock, Winchester and Wilton. The lawyers followed, and so Sir Walter Ralegh, his fellow prisoners and the Middlesex jurors who were to decide on their guilt all travelled down to Winchester in November 1603.

If any proof were needed that King James had made a popular choice of victim it was provided by the crowds who gathered, heedless of infection risks, to curse and jeer Sir Walter Ralegh on his way to what they fervently hoped would be his doom. His escort, Sir William Waad, feared for his own life: 'It was hab or nab whether Sir Walter Ralegh should have been brought alive through such multitudes of unruly people as did exclaim against him. He that had seen it would not think there had been any sickness in London.'[1]

Waiting in Winchester was a group of men scarcely less well disposed towards Walter than the London mob – the government of England gathered to sit in judgement, anxious to prove its loyalty to its new king. Of the eleven commissioners appointed by James to try Ralegh – Cobham, as a noble, had claimed his privilege to be tried by his peers – only one, Sir William Waad, was not a member of the Privy Council or a top-ranking judge, and he was a police chief: Lord Mountjoy and Thomas Howard were two men particularly grateful for the eminence the new régime had accorded them; Robert Cecil and Henry Howard had already demonstrated what friends to Walter they were; Lord Wotton of Morley and Sir John Stanhope were lesser fry who would follow the lead set by their colleagues; while Lord Chief Justice Popham and the three other judges appointed to advise the commissioners on points of law were no less biased.

Tudor and Stuart governments no more intended the treason prosecutions they pursued to be equal trials of strength than the Romans dreamt of giving swords to the Christians on whom they loosed lions, for the spectacle was intended not to assess guilt but to proclaim it. All the privy councillors who in theory sat as impartial justices had for the weeks before the trial been employed cross-questioning the accused with a view to building up a case for the prosecution, while Ralegh was allowed no legal assistance nor even prior knowledge of the precise charges to be brought against him, which he first heard on the morning of 17 November 1603, the day of his trial. He tried to remain standing, but had soon to ask permission to sit down.

The first charge was of a conspiracy, entered into at Durham House between Sir Walter Ralegh and Lord Cobham to advance King James's cousin, Lady Arabella Stuart, to the throne. Money for this purpose was to be obtained by Cobham from the king of Spain, and Lady Arabella was said to have promised the plotters to make peace with Spain when she became queen and to tolerate Roman Catholicism.

The second charge involved a treasonable conversation between Lord Cobham and his brother George Brooke in which were used the words 'There will never be a good world in England until the king and his cubs are taken away.' The third charge concerned a book written to disprove James's claim to the throne of England and allegedly shown by Ralegh to Cobham to encourage him in his treasons. The fourth charge stated that Ralegh had incited George Brooke to start a correspondence between Arabella Stuart and the king of Spain, and the fifth charge alleged that Ralegh had incited Cobham to obtain from the Spanish envoy Aremberg money for the conspiracy (the enormous sum of 600,000 crowns).

All these indictments were based on twin presumptions that Walter Ralegh was in the pay of Spain – which made not the slightest sense in the light of his fanatical hatred of that country most recently expressed in the pamphlet that he had presented to King James shortly before his arrest – and that he was plotting to place Lady Arabella Stuart on the throne instead of King James. Yet there was no evidence produced at the trial – or discovered since – to suggest that Walter Ralegh had any treasonable dealings with this obscure lady whose unfortunate connection with the blood royal lent her a significance that neither her character nor her career justified. He had no special reason to promote her tenuous claim to the throne, and nor did his alleged accomplices the Spaniards, for their Infanta had a connection with the English crown that they considered closer than Arabella's. So whatever treason Walter Ralegh had, or had not been plotting against King James, it was not embraced by the charges that were brought against him in November 1603.

Walter pleaded not guilty to all the charges and took no exception to any members of the jury: 'I know none of them; they are all Christians and honest gentlemen; I except against none.'

What Walter did not know was that the men brought down from Middlesex had been carefully selected, sifted and changed overnight as unsatisfactory. As James himself is reported to have said afterwards, he would be sorry to be tried before a Middlesex jury.[2]

'Only this I desire,' said Ralegh. 'Sickness hath of late weakened me and my memory was always bad. The points of the indictment be many, and in the evidence perhaps more will be urged. I beseech you, my lords, let me answer every point severally, for I shall not carry all to the end.'

It was a reasonable request, yet from the prosecution's point of view it could have been the thin end of the wedge, for to examine the crown's charges one by one would have revealed their inconsistency. It was in the prosecution's interests to keep the indictments as muddled and sinister as possible, and so Edward Coke, the attorney general, was quick to object to Walter's suggestion – though his argument could not help but be a poor one: 'The king's evidence ought not to be broken or dismembered, whereby it might lose much of its grace and vigour.'

Edward Coke was to be Walter Ralegh's chief adversary on this day that he fought singlehanded for his life. About Ralegh's height, with a red face, hawk nose and piercing blue eyes, Coke was acknowledged as the greatest legal intelligence of his generation and when, in later years, he turned his abilities into paths less convenient to royal power, he established a reputation that has lasted to the present day. As a judge he was to champion the independence of the law, but as the king's attorney general he was more responsible than anyone for the travesty of justice that unrolled at Winchester on 17 November 1603. Sour, truculent and hectoring, he displayed the unscrupulous tactics he intended to employ the very moment he rose to speak. No mention of the Bye Plot had been made in the indictments which were all concerned with the 'Main', but it was with this separate and more obvious conspiracy that Coke launched his attack:

> The Lord Grey, Brooke, Markham and the rest intended by force in the night to surprise the king's court . . . purposing to open the doors with muskets and calivers. They would extort a pardon from the king and toleration for the Roman superstition. . . . Then they were going to send the lord mayor and aldermen to the Tower.

It was so much lurid hearsay quite inadmissible to the actual case before the court, but none of the judges made any attempt to check Coke's rhetoric, and it was Walter Ralegh who had to remind the jury, 'I pray you gentlemen of the jury remember I am not charged with the "Bye" which was the treason of the priests.' Coke spluttered indignantly that 'all these treasons, though they consisted of several points, closed in together like Samson's foxes which were joined in their tails though their heads were severed'.

He tried to divert attention from the unfairness of his tactics by launching into an abstruse lecture on the law of treason, bringing in the murder of Edward ii and the treasons of Perkin Warbeck, and then dragged up another charge far-fetched and quite unconnected, the conversation between Cobham and George Brooke in which had occurred the damning sentence: 'There will never be a good world in England till the king and his cubs are taken away.'

'To whom, Sir Walter,' asked the Attorney General, 'do you bear malice? To the royal children?'

Walter again put Coke in his place.

Ralegh: Master Attorney, I pray you to whom, or to what end, speak you all this? I protest I do not understand what a word of this means, except it be to tell me news. What is the treason of Markham and the priests to me?

Coke: I will then come close to you. I will prove you to be the most notorious traitor that ever came to the bar. You are indeed on the 'Main': but you followed them of the 'Bye' in imitation. I will charge you with the words.

Ralegh: Your words cannot condemn me. My innocency is my defence. Prove against me any one thing of the many that you have broke, and I will confess all the indictment, and that I am the most horrible traitor that ever lived, and worthy to be crucified with a thousand torments.

Coke: Nay, I will prove all. Thou art a monster! Thou hast an English face but a Spanish heart!

The Attorney General then proceeded to turn against Ralegh the very intelligence which Walter had just displayed, arguing that Cobham was a simple soul – 'he was never politician nor sword man' – so he could not have got involved in this conspiracy without the scheming of a conniver like Ralegh.

Coke: Now you shall see the most horrible practices that ever came out of the bottomless pit of hell. . . . Came this contrivance think you out of Cobham's quiver? No, but out of Ralegh's devilish, Machiavellian policy!

It was a dirty blow exploiting the popular suspicions of Walter's atheism. But Walter stayed calm.

Ralegh: What is that to me? I do not hear yet that you have spoken one word against me. Here is no treason of mine done. If my Lord Cobham be a traitor, what is that to me?
Coke: All that he did was by thy instigation, thou viper! For I thou thee, thou traitor! I will prove thee the rankest traitor in all England.
Ralegh: No, no, Master Attorney, I am no traitor. Whether I live or die, I shall stand as true a subject as ever the king hath. You may call me a traitor at your pleasure: yet it becomes not a man of quality and virtue to do so: for I do not yet hear you charge me with treason.

To 'thou' someone was to adopt the second person familiar, a style of speech employed by the upper classes when being patronizing to servants and inferiors, and Walter's response to Coke's gratuitous insult was dignified. It was of a piece with his stance throughout this long November day which was to be a turning point in his popular reputation. Jeered and execrated on his way to his trial, Walter 'behaved himself so worthily, so wisely, so temperately, that in half a day the mind of all the company was changed from the extremest hate to the greatest pity'.[3]

One of his finest moments came when he was allowed, despite Coke's protests, to reply to the opening speeches and to the allegations made in the first of Lord Cobham's several confessions in which the fantastic sum of 600,000 crowns was mentioned – £200,000, more than several Parliamentary taxes on the entire country could produce. Cobham's statement claimed, as Coke did, that it was Ralegh who had been the inspiration of the conspiracy, and Walter took delight in turning Coke's arguments back in on themselves. Cobham, he said:

is not such a babe as you make him! He hath dispositions of such violence, which his best friends could never temper.

But it is very strange that I, at this time, should be thought to plot with the Lord Cobham, knowing him a man that hath neither love nor following, and myself at this time having resigned a place of my best command, in an office I had in Cornwall.

I was not so bare of sense but I saw that, if ever this state was strong, it was now that we have the kingdom of Scotland united, whence we were wont to fear all our trouble, Ireland quieted, where our forces were wont to be divided, Denmark assured, whom before we were always wont to have in jealousy, the Low Countries our nearest neighbour. And instead of a lady whom Time had surprised, we had now an active king, who would be present at his own business. For me, at this time, to make myself a Robin Hood, a Wat Tyler, a Kett, or a Jack Cade! I was not so mad!

If Cobham were the hopeless creature Coke was making him out to be, in other words, and Walter the cunning partner, why should Walter be so foolish as to entrust a great plot to Cobham's care? It was all sound, undeniable common-sense. There was the graceful compliment to James's wife, Anne of Denmark, some judicious praise for Mountjoy's efforts in Ireland, and that loving, immortal homage to the dead Elizabeth, 'a lady whom Time had surprised'. As one eyewitness in the arched medieval hall later told the king, 'never man spoke so well in the time past, nor would in the time to come!'

Walter's quiet, remorseless logic continued. He had three times risked his own life fighting the Spaniards, he reminded his audience, and if he were, despite that, in Spain's pay, why would he choose this moment to betray his country? At the time of the Armada King Philip had had the power to back up the activities of a fifth column in England, but now Madrid was too weak to take advantage of the sort of treason he was accused of committing. Spain was impoverished, bankrupt, so that the king set 'the Jesuits, his imps', begging at the church doors on his behalf. He had not got six hundred thousand crowns to pay anyone, let alone Lord Cobham. What security could Lord Cobham, a foreigner, offer the king of Spain for such a fortune? Queen Elizabeth never lent money without solid security for it.

'Nay, her own subjects, the merchants of London, did not lend her money, without they had her lands in pawn for it! And to show I am not "Spanish" as you term me, at this time I had writ a treatise to the King's Majesty of the present state of Spain, and reasons against the Peace!'

It was a moving speech which made an unforgettable impact on his audience. So far as the court's verdict was concerned, Walter's cause was lost before the trial started, but when it came to his own reputation, the opinion that every one of his hearers took home of him, then he had won a glittering victory. Even a Scottish crony of James's had the good grace to admit that, 'whereas, when he saw Sir Walter Ralegh first, he was so led with the common hatred that he would have gone a hundred miles to see him hanged, he would, 'ere they parted, have gone a thousand to save his life.' The tide that had flowed out against proud Ralegh for so many years was reaching its ebb.

It was the climax of the trial. Coke had made his charges and the defendant had answered them. Which one of the two was to be believed depended on the source of the evidence they were debating – Lord Cobham. Coke maintained that Cobham had said one thing. Ralegh maintained another, and the poor jury were so confused that the foreman had had to intervene and ask for certain dates to be repeated.

The solution to the dilemma was obvious. 'My Lord,' said Ralegh, 'I claim to have my accuser brought here to speak face to face.' And now he produced the first of what he considered to be his trump cards. 'I have learned that by the law and statutes of this realm in case of treason a man ought to be convicted by the testimony of two witnesses if they be living.'

But all the precedents that Walter quoted in support of this claim were worthless as a result of the amendments to the treason laws that had closed the loophole through which Sir Nicholas Throckmorton had escaped in the reign of Queen Mary. Lord Chief Justice Popham had no hesitation in squashing Walter's involved arguments – and a modern legal historian has confirmed that he was quite right to do this.[4]

Walter then switched from argument by precedent to argument by equity. Whatever the technicalities of the law, it was surely unfair to condemn a man to death without the sworn testimony of two reputable witnesses. But once again he was on false ground, for as the Lord Chief Justice quite properly retorted, 'Equity is from the king. You can only have justice from us.' When Walter muttered 'I know not, my lord, how you conceive the law', Popham made the one remark that is his claim to legal distinction.

'Nay', he stated grandly. 'We do not conceive the law. We *know* the law.'

The other judges duly weighed in on Popham's side. Ralegh had to acknowledge his defeat, and then, as Coke read more of Cobham's statements, he made his first compromising admission. Cobham was said to have offered Ralegh 10,000 crowns.

It is true [said Walter], my Lord Cobham had speech with me about the money and made me an offer. . . . Voluntarily, one day at dinner, some time before Count Aremberg's coming over. For he and I, being at his own board, arguing and speaking violently – he for the peace, I against the peace – the Lord Cobham told me that when Count Aremberg came he would yield such strong arguments for the peace as would satisfy any man. And withal he told – as his fashion is to utter things easily – what great sums of money would be given to some councillors for making the peace: and named my Lord Cecil and the Earl of Mar.

This was a damaging admission for Ralegh to make, that he had let Cobham dangle foreign money in front of him without informing the authorities. His willingness to consider a Spanish bribe compromised his claim to be an implacable enemy of Spain, and though Walter was quite justified in alleging that James's councillors could be bribed by Spain – and this was true of Robert Cecil in particular – this was hardly the moment to make such a counter charge. His self-justification sounded casuistical:

> Now if, after this, my Lord Cobham changed his mind as to the use to be made of the money, and joining with the Lord Grey and others, has any such treasonable intent as is alleged, what is that to me? They must answer it, nor I.
>
> The offer of the money to me is nothing, for it was made before Count Aremberg's coming. The offer made to the others was afterwards.

The prosecution were quite justified in claiming 'Ralegh confesseth the matter, but avoids it by distinguishing of times,' and Lord Henry Howard, delighted to see his enemy slip a step, leapt in quickly.

'Allege me any grounds of cause why you gave ear to my Lord Cobham, as of receiving of pensions, in matters you had not to deal in.'

For Ralegh to retort, 'Could I stop my Lord Cobham's mouth?' was a poor riposte, and then was read out Lawrence Keymis's confession of how he had, at Walter's instigation, visited Cobham in the Tower to persuade him to alter his testimony against Ralegh.

Things were now going badly for Walter. To tamper with witnesses was an offence in its own right and argued less than total innocence. So with some agility, if little truthfulness, Ralegh boldly asserted that Keymis's confession was false – and, with more justice, that it had been extracted under threat of torture. This scandalized the entire court, for Protestant England cherished the baseless illusion that torture was the monopoly of Popish countries, and Lord Henry Howard lost no time in pointing out that, 'the king gave charge that no rigour should be used'.

> *The other Commissioners:* We protest, before God, there was no such matter to our knowledge.
> *Ralegh to Sir William Waad:* Was not the keeper of the rack sent for and he [Keymis] threatened with it?
> *Waad:* When Mr Solicitor and myself came to examine Keymis we told him he 'deserved the rack', but did not threaten him with it.
> *The other Commissioners:* It was more than we knew.

Walter recovered some of the ground he had lost, for the privy councillors were not convinced by Waad's explanation.

Then there was the matter of the mysterious book cited in indictment three, a volume disproving King James's title to the English throne which, according to Coke, was given by Ralegh to Cobham in order to encourage him in his treasonable activities. It was a trivial matter, for both prosecution and defendant agreed that the volume in question dated back a quarter of a century and was written to justify Elizabeth's treatment of Mary Queen of Scots. It was really a dead issue, but Walter injected some life into it by remarking casually that he had acquired it by accident from the library of a privy councillor, the late Lord Burghley. This forced Robert Cecil to his feet for, as the dead man's son, he felt called upon to offer some explanation of how the treasonable book came to be in his father's possession, and he felt also impelled to launch into a long apologia for his treatment of Ralegh. It was rare for the little secretary to be troubled by human emotions like guilt – or to display them so obviously in public.

After my father's death, Sir Walter Ralegh desired to search for some cosmographical description of the Indies which he thought were in his study and were not to be had in print. Which I granted, and would have trusted Sir Walter Ralegh as soon as any man – though since, for some infirmities, the bonds of my affection to him have been broken; and yet, reserving my duty to the king, my master, which I can by no means dispense with, by God I love him and have a great conflict within myself.

But I must needs say, Sir Walter used me a little unkindly to take the book away without my knowledge.

To hear poor Cecil's distress over the loss of a book one might have thought that he, not Ralegh, was on trial for his life, and the secretary was very careful to point out that it had been part of his father's job to collect and read all seditious literature,

. . . for whosoever should then search his [Burghley's] study may in all likelihood find all the notorious libels that were writ against the late queen, and whosoever should rummage my study, or at least my cabinet, may find several against the king, our sovereign lord, since his accession to the throne.

Ralegh then explained how there had been 'no purpose in taking that book. But amongst other books and maps it seems it was cast in. Upon sorting of the papers afterwards it came to my hand', and he went on, 'I do own, as my Lord Cecil has said, that I believe they may also find in my house almost all the libels that have been writ against the late queen.'

This was another injudicious admission, for Walter had never been given the responsibility for investigating such matters as privy councillors like Burghley and Cecil had, and Coke was quick to jump in, 'You were not a privy councillor, and I hope never shall be'.

But Robert Cecil now came to Walter's rescue. 'He was not a sworn councillor of state,' he explained, 'but he has been called to consultations.'

Walter felt entitled to complain, 'Here is a book supposed to be treasonable. I never read it, nor commended it, nor delivered it, nor urged it.'

'Why this is cunning,' exclaimed Coke.

'Everything that doth make *for* me is cunning,' retorted Walter tetchily, 'and everything that maketh *against* me is probable.'

He was correct, but that was in the nature of a treason trial. Now at the rear of the courtroom appeared the old lord admiral, Charles Howard the Earl of Nottingham, leading into the hall the lady in whose interest the entire conspiracy was alleged to have been hatched, Arabella Stuart. Nottingham shouted out that the lady had 'never dealt in any of these things', hearsay that was accepted as admissible and which the prosecution took to strengthen their case – though it somewhat diluted the consistency of the conspiracy to remove from it the one person for whose sake the plotters were supposed to have risked so much.

Then Attorney General Coke produced his one live witness, not Cobham, or Aremberg or even one of the Bye plotters, but an unknown sailor, a pilot called Dyer, who solemnly served up yet more hearsay:

Being at Lisbon there came to me a Portugal gentleman who asked me how the king of England did, and whether he was crowned. I answered him that I hoped our noble king was well and crowned by this, but the time was not come when I came from the coast of Spain. 'Nay' said he, 'your king shall never be crowned for Don Cobham and Don Ralegh will cut his throat before he come to be crowned.'

Well might Walter wax sarcastic: 'This is the saying of some wild Jesuit or beggarly priest, but what proof is it against me?'

'It shows', retorted the attorney general, 'that your treason had wings.'

Ralegh suggested to the jury that they might care to imagine themselves in his place:

Now if you yourselves would like to be hazarded in your lives, disabled in your posterities – your lands, goods, and all you have confiscated – your wives, children and servants left crying to the world; if you would be content all this should befall you upon a trial by suspicions and presumptions, upon an accusation not subscribed by your accuser, without the testimony of a single witness, then so judge me as you yourselves would be judged.

One of the many legal privileges that defendants in sixteenth- and seventeenth-century treason trials did not possess was the right to sum up

304

their case last of all, answering the various allegations made by the prosecution. But fighting desperately for his life, and not having had a chance
to produce the letter from Cobham which he believed would sweep all
the charges away, Ralegh now flouted procedure. When the crown had
finished putting its case and when everything would in normal circumstances, have been completed, Walter asked boldly: 'Mr Attorney, have
you done?'

Coke: Yes, if you have no more to say.
Ralegh: If you have done, then I have somewhat more to say.
Coke: Nay, I will have the last word for the king.
Ralegh: Nay, I will have the last word for my life.
Coke: Go to, I will lay thee upon thy back for the most confidentest
traitor that ever came to the bar.

Coke was beside himself with fury, his legal sensibilities affronted by
Ralegh's disregard for procedure, and he sat down in a huff, sulkily
refusing to say another word despite the cajoling of the privy councillors
– for Robert Cecil knew why Walter Ralegh wanted to say more, and he
knew that Coke had the letter from Cobham that would quite destroy
Walter's fondly cherished coup. Only grudgingly would Coke stand up
to rehearse his main points again, and when Walter dared to interrupt him
at one point he turned on him in a paroxysm of rage. 'Thou art the most
vile and execrable traitor that ever lived!'

Ralegh: You speak indiscreetly, barbarously, and uncivilly.
Coke: I want words to express thy viperous treasons!
Ralegh: I think you want words indeed for you have spoken one thing
a dozen times.
Coke: Thou art an odious fellow. Thy name is hateful in all the realm
of England for thy pride!
Ralegh: It will go near to prove a measuring cast between you and me,
Mr Attorney.

Once again Walter had piqued his opponent like a matador a lumbering
bull. But now Coke administered his deadly goring, for waving in the air
Cobham's latest letter, he shouted out the story of Ralegh's stratagems in
the Tower and of how Walter had had a message thrown into Cobham's
cell pinned to an apple. 'It was Adam's apple', cried Coke, 'whereby the
Devil did deceive him!' In the letter Ralegh had warned Cobham against
confiding in any priests or preachers, for it was the preacher sent to Essex
in the Tower who had betrayed all the earl's secrets – and this provided a
golden opportunity for Coke to repeat two old slanders, that Ralegh was
an atheist and that he had brought about Essex's death.

O damnable atheist! He [Ralegh] counsels him [Cobham] not to be led by the counsels of preachers as Essex was. He [Essex] died a child of God. God honoured him at his death. Thou wast by. *Et lupus et turpes instant morientibus ursae.* [Both the wolf and the foul she-bears close in on the dying.] I doubt not but this day God shall have as great a conquest by this traitor, and the Son of God shall be as much glorified as when it was said *Vicisti, Galilaeus* [You have conquered, Galilean] – you know my meaning.

Coke's audience did indeed catch his reference, for the words he quoted were of Julian the Apostate, who was for Elizabethans the prototype atheist.[5]

Yet Coke did not, in truth, need such sneers, for the testimony of Cobham's letter as it was read out was a damning indictment in itself:

I have resolved to set down the truth and under my hand to retract what he [Ralegh] cunningly got from me. . . . He hath been the original cause of my ruin. For, but by his instigation, I have never dealt with Count Aremberg. And so hath he been the only cause of my discontentment, I never coming from the court but still he filled and possessed me with new causes of discontentment.

Walter was visibly shaken by this bolt from the blue, particularly as Cobham's letter threw in for good measure the allegation that the money Walter had considered accepting from Aremberg was not to help procure peace but to betray England's foreign policy to the Spaniards. It even looked to some observers as though Ralegh might not be able to say anything more, and it was only with great difficulty that he rose to stutter, 'You have heard a strange tale of a strange man. You shall see how many souls this Cobham hath', and limply produced the letter that he had hoped would be his salvation, asking Robert Cecil to read it for him. As Cobham's brother-in-law who could certify the handwriting, Cecil did not refuse, for he knew that the note's contents could now only reinforce Ralegh's guilt, and Walter too knew that he was lost.

The jury took but fifteen minutes to reach its verdict, and Lord Chief Justice Popham pronouncing sentence, filled in with some delight the portrait of a pagan that Coke had sketched.

You have been taxed by the world, Sir Walter Ralegh, with holding heathenish, blasphemous, atheistical and profane opinions, which I list not to repeat, because Christian ears cannot endure to hear them. But the authors and maintainers of such opinions cannot be suffered to live in any Christian commonwealth. If these opinions be not yours, you shall do well, before you leave the world, to protest against them, and not to die with these imputations upon you, but if you do hold such opinion, then I beseech you renounce them, and ask God forgiveness for them as you hope for another life, and let not Heriott, nor any such doctor, persuade you there is no eternity in Heaven, lest you find an eternity of hell-torments.

So even the reputation of Walter's mathematical friend, the great chronicler of Virginia whose name had not figured once in the trial, was gratuitously dragged through the mire, and Popham did not refrain from passing judgement on other matters that had not been touched on during the long day's examination.

You might have lived well with £3,000 a year, for so I have heard your revenues to be. I know nothing that might move you to be discontented. . . .
I never heard that the king took anything from you but the captaincy of the guard, which he did with very good reason, to have one of his own knowledge, whom he might trust. . . .

If there had ever been any doubts that the whole trial was an act of political justification, Popham's final speech removed them, and, as though he had been briefed by James, the lord chief justice even saw fit to justify the king's action towards Ralegh's wine monopolies before moving on finally to pronounce the grisly sentence:

You shall be led from hence to the place whence you came, there to remain until the day of execution. And from thence you shall be drawn on a hurdle through the open streets to the place of execution, there to be hanged and cut down alive, and your body shall be opened, your heart and bowels plucked out, and your privy members cut off and thrown into the fire before your eyes. Then your head to be stricken off from your body and your body shall be divided into four quarters, to be disposed of at the king's pleasure. And God have mercy on your soul.[6]

Sir Walter Ralegh could reasonably expect that he would, as a knight, be spared the gory details of this ritualized torture. Yet that was cold comfort.

❧ 39 ❧
The Scaffold

... this is mine eternal plea
To him that made Heaven, earth, and sea,
Seeing my flesh must die so soon,
And want a head to dine next noon,
Just at the stroke, when my veins start and spread,
Set on my soul an everlasting head.[1]

Confronted with death, Walter Ralegh prepared his soul to meet his Maker, and the poem that he wrote while awaiting his execution in 1603 convincingly gave the lie to all the accusations of atheism hurled against him – most recently by Coke and Popham. Remorse descends on all of us in times of trouble, but *The Passionate Man's Pilgrimage* was not the last-minute recantation of a worried unbeliever. In its strangely Catholic confidence spoke faith born of experience and deep conviction as Walter described his soul travelling to Heaven

Over the silver mountains
Where spring the nectar fountains,
And there I'll kiss
The bowl of bliss,
And drink my eternal fill
On every milken hill.

The poem enshrined a piety which many English people in the dark winter days of 1603 were attributing to Sir Walter Ralegh for the very first time. 'Never,' wrote Dudley Carleton, 'was a man so hated and so popular in so short a time.'[2] Yet had the outside world been able to see the contortions that Walter was going through to save his skin before his execution, the general admiration would have been tempered. Brave though Walter had been in court and devout though he showed himself in his *Passionate Man's Pilgrimage*, the opportunist in him was now revealed as more ingratiating than ever. Ambitious for nothing more than his survival, he despatched a series of grovelling letters to James, to Cecil, to the Privy Council, desperately seeking the help of anyone he thought might help him. It was Ralegh the eternal paradox: chivalrous, yet counselling the assassination of Essex; plain-speaking, yet capable of the most shameless lies; proud, but now servile and totally stripped of dignity.

To Cecil he wrote:

For yourself, my Lord Cecil, and for me, sometime your true friend, and now a miserable forsaken man, I know that affections are neither taught nor persuaded. But if aught remain of good or love or of compassion towards me, your lordship will now show it when I am most unworthy of your love and most unable to deserve it.[3]

To the Privy Council he suggested: 'Let me have one year to give to God in a prison and to serve Him,' and to James himself, he simply lied: 'I have loved your Majesty now twenty years. ... Save me, therefore, most merciful Prince, that I may owe your Majesty my life itself. ...'[4]

Ralegh, before his execution date, repented of his craven beggings and told Bess to 'get those letters, if it be possible, which I writ to the lords wherein I sued for my life'. Had Walter heard perhaps of the proud note that Lord Grey of Wilton sent to James?

'The House of the Wiltons have spent many lives in their prince's service. Grey cannot beg his. God send the king a long and prosperous reign and your lordships all honour.'

Grey of Wilton was to go the scaffold with his head held high – unlike the priests Clarke and Watson. As Father Clarke was cut down from the gallows he wriggled and cursed the sheriff and his executioners and had to be pinioned screaming as the grisly rites of disembowelling and castration were administered to his already tortured body.

A week later George Brooke was beheaded in Winchester Castle yard. His brother Cobham was due to be executed the following Friday, 10 December 1603, along with Grey and Markham. Walter Ralegh would follow on Monday the 13th, and when Bishop Bilson of Winchester visited Walter to take his confession he found a Christian thoroughly prepared for death. Ralegh had regained his nerve and wrote to his wife Bess the letter that was one of the finest of all his pen's fine creations:

You shall receive, dear Bess, my last words in these my last lines. My love I send you, that you may keep it when I am dead; and my counsel, that you may remember it when I am no more. I would not, with my last will, present you with sorrows, dear Bess. Let them go to the grave with me, and be buried in the dust. And, seeing it is not the will of God that ever I shall see you in this life, bear my destruction gently and with a heart like yourself.[5]

Walter may have written few poems for his Bess, but these lines were the warmest tribute possible to his love. For over a decade the two of them had lived with the consequences of their passion for each other – and there were no regrets, except for some practical matters. Walter wished he could have provided more generously for his family:

Most sorry I am (as God knoweth) that, being surprised with death, I can leave you no better estate. . . . But God hath prevented all my determinations; the great God that worketh all in all.

If you can live free from want, care for no more; for the rest is vanity. Love God, and begin betimes to repose yourself in him; therein shall you find true and lasting riches, and endless comfort. . . .

Teach your son also to serve and fear God, while he is young, that the fear of God may grow up in him. Then will God be a husband unto you, and a father unto him; a husband and a father which can never be taken from you.

Bailey oweth me £200, and Adrian £600. In Jersey also I have much owing me. The arrearages of the wines will pay my debts. And, howsoever, for my soul's health, I beseech you pay all poor men.

The sprinkling of mundane debts and dealings among the spiritual exhortations enhances the spirit of the testament. These were the final words of a real man, not a polished poem or sermon, and Walter's strong grip on life was emphasized by his thoughts for Bess's future and re-marriage.

When I am gone, no doubt you shall be sought unto by many, for the world thinks that I was very rich; but take heed of the pretences of men and of their affections, for they last but in honest and worthy men. And no greater misery can befall you in this life than to become a prey, and after to be despised. I speak it (God knows) not to dissuade you from marriage – for that will be best for you – both in respect of God and the world. As for me I am no more yours, nor you mine. Death hath cut us asunder; and God hath divided me from the world, and you from me. . . .

I cannot write much. God knows how hardly I stole this time, when all sleep; and it is time to separate my thoughts from the world. Beg my dead body, which living was denied you; and either lay it at Sherborne if the land continue, or in Exeter church, by my father and mother.

I can write no more. Time and Death call me away.

The everlasting, infinite, powerful and inscrutable God, that Almighty God that is goodness itself, mercy itself, the true life and light, keep you and yours, and have mercy on me, and teach me to forgive my persecutors and false accusers; and send us to meet in his glorious kingdom.

My true wife, farewell. Bless my poor boy. Pray for me. My true God hold you both in his arms.

Written with the dying hand of sometimes thy husband, but now (alas!) overthrown.

Yours that was, but now not my own.

W.Ralegh

Walter was watching from a window as, on the dark grey morning of 10 December 1603, Sir Griffin Markham walked through the drizzle to the scaffold raised in the centre of the crowded courtyard of Winchester Castle. Bent and dejected, Markham looked a broken man, though he threw away a napkin that a friend offered him to tie round his eyes, saying that he could look at death without blushing. He knelt to say his final prayers and was just preparing to meet the axe when suddenly there was a commotion in the crowd and through the apprentice boys and soldiers struggled a Scottish lad, John Gibb, one of the attendants in King James's bedchamber, brandishing a warrant from his master. It was a royal order that Markham should not be executed first but should be granted two hours respite. So the poor man was led away confused, his agony prolonged.

Lord Grey of Wilton came out next to meet death with all the pride he had displayed in the letter disdaining to plead with James for mercy. An earnest Puritan, he prayed in the drizzle for a full half hour before addressing himself to the block, and then, once again, the sheriff intervened. It was the king's pleasure, he announced, that Lord Cobham should be executed first, and so back with an hour or so's grace went Grey along the path he had not thought to take again.

Lord Cobham, as he stepped out into the rain, seemed to relish King James's cat and mouse game. At his trial in front of his peers he had put up a cringing performance, but now he strode almost jauntily to the scaffold, kneeling to pray like Grey for long minutes that weighed heavy on the crowd that had now been twice baulked of blood. Ralegh was too far away to hear his former friend affirm that all his charges against Walter had been true, 'as I have hope of my soul's resurrection', but one eye-witness looked up and noted that Ralegh 'beheld the comedy played out by his companions with a smiling face'.

Comedy was the word, for Lord Cobham's execution was stayed like those of Grey and Markham, the sheriff assembling all three conspirators on the scaffold for a final pronouncement of their guilt. 'Are not your offences heinous?' he demanded. 'Have you not been justly tried and lawfully condemned? Is not each of you subject to due execution now to be performed?'

Then as, shivering in the freezing rain, the trio humbly acknowledged their sins, the sheriff suddenly cried, 'Then see the mercy of your prince, who of himself hath sent hither a countermand and given you your lives!' They were not to die! Markham was to be exiled, Grey and Cobham imprisoned. Three days earlier James had decided to spare them, but such was his sense of humour that he chose to unveil his clemency in this melodramatic and tasteless fashion.

'Ralegh, you must think', wrote Dudly Carleton, 'had hammers working in his heart to beat out the meaning of this stratagem.'[6] As the courtyard cleared, the scaffold was left there for the following Monday, dripping with rain but still to be soaked in blood. The unworthiness of James's vicious little dumb show was catching, for Walter promptly dashed off another of his begging letters to the Privy Council.

We have this day beheld a work of so great mercy, and for so great offences, as the like hath been seldom if ever known. . . . And although myself have not yet been brought so near the very brink of the grave, yet I trust that so great a compassion will extend itself towards me also.[7]

He should not have demeaned himself, for his eager plea for mercy was the penultimate act in the ghoulish scenario that James had planned so meticulously. The ultimate act was the gracious extension of the royal pardon to Walter, a contemptuous gesture that was, after Ralegh's final letter, the most bitter of all the humiliations that the new king inflicted on the old queen's favourite.

40

The Tower

The twelve years that Walter Ralegh spent in the Tower of London were the longest single period of his public life. He had enjoyed eleven years of favour, lived five years under a cloud, and then regained for just half a dozen years some semblance of his former eminence, only to be cast down again by King James I whose droll style of mercy spared Ralegh execution – but not lingering imprisonment under a sentence of death that was never removed.

It has been said that captivity in the Tower of London was the salvation of Sir Walter Ralegh's reputation, and it is true that his monumental *History of the World* together with a catalogue of other prose works were all written during his time behind bars. Yet this creative flowering only occupied the latter period of Walter Ralegh's long detention, when he was working and thinking in terms of his anticipated release. For the first four or five years of his incarceration he in fact wrote very little, though his existence in the Tower was not an uncomfortable one. He was not deprived of the refreshment of human company, and it was during his first year of captivity that his son Carew was conceived, to be born and baptised in February 1605 in the chapel of St Peter ad Vincula inside the very walls of the prison.

Bess and Walter contrived to recreate behind bars a style of existence that was a reflection, if only a pale one, of their Sherborne idyll after the fall of 1592. Walter was allotted two rooms on the second floor of the Bloody Tower with a view inwards over Tower Green and outwards on to St Thomas's Tower which looks out over the Thames. He had two staff to look after him, a serving man, Dean, and John Talbot, a young man who had trained to be a schoolmaster and who now acted as Walter's secretary. Talbot also, most probably, gave instruction to young Wat. Lawrence Keymis, detained as a prisoner until New Year's Day 1604 and thereafter a most regular visitor, along with Thomas Hariot, provided

Walter with intellectual companionship. Ralegh's waterman, Owen, brought him beer and ale, since the drinking water in the Tower, like all London's water, was a risky beverage. Shelbury, a steward from Sherborne, came to take his master's instructions for the running of the estate, still effectively in Ralegh hands thanks to the legal stratagem that had transferred the property in trust for his son, while, most important of all, Walter was allowed to have Bess and Wat, now a lad of ten and getting ready for university, living with him.

So although Sir Walter Ralegh could not actually leave the confines of the Tower, his life was not otherwise a restricted one. He became one of the little village which still leads its own community life in the heart of twentieth-century London, and he quickly got on friendly terms with the garrison, dining frequently with the lieutenant, Sir George Harvey, and taking his exercise around the inner walls. He recaptured in the grounds the spirit of his botanic gardens at Sherborne, cultivating his own plot of land and planting it with the foreign shrubs and herbs that he loved, and he took over, too, a little shed in the lieutenant's garden where Bishop Latimer had been imprisoned before Queen Mary had had him burnt, and which had served more recently as a residence for chickens. In this hen house Walter installed copper tubing and retorts with which he could experiment with the essences of his exotic plants and produce cordials whose healing qualities now won him yet another type of renown: to Sir Walter Ralegh the courtier, poet, explorer, pirate, soldier, scientist and writer we must add Sir Walter Ralegh, doctor.

Ralegh's medical notes lie in the British Museum, to this day unexplored by a scientist able to expound the technicalities that defeat a non-expert examiner, but Walter won fame in his lifetime as a healer, and those parts of his notes that are susceptible to secular analysis endorse that reputation. To judge from the evidence, Sir Walter Ralegh never employed his own doctor but himself undertook responsibility for his own health and that of those around him: Dean the serving man, Talbot the teacher and secretary, Owen the waterman; there is no mention in Walter's Tower entourage, nor indeed in his household in more prosperous days, of a retained physician – and it is probably to Walter that the credit should go for bringing a hundred men out of the debilitating humidity of the Orinoco basin with not a life lost from sickness.

Some of his remedies smack of quackery. To recommend a particular stone to be clenched in the hand 'to cause to pisse bloode',[1] sounds neither plausible nor advisable, and to promote tobacco as a cure for headaches was just propaganda. But even in our own century rheumatism and the common cold remain the province of folk remedies, and Walter Ralegh's prescriptions seemed to work for many of his patients. His Guiana Balsam 'more mild and temperate than the black sweet Indian balsam' proved most efficacious, his cordial of strawberry water particularly soothed the symptoms of ailing ladies, while his 'Great Cordial' won renown that was to last for over a century. At one of the earliest meetings of the Royal Society in the 1660s, Charles II was to ask his French physician Lefebvre to recreate some of Ralegh's famous elixir, and the ingredients that the doctor ground up were formidable: some forty vegetable substances pounded in spirits of wine and distilled, then mixed with powders of pearl, red coral, deer's horn, ambergris, white sugar, musk and antimony – to which gruel was added, at the suggestion of Sir Kenelm Digby, the heart, liver and flesh of a viper. The resulting potion was palatable enough for the great chemist Robert Boyle to partake of it, but it seems unlikely that Ralegh would have assembled precisely this list of ingredients. It is rather more probable, in view of the malarial nature of so many English fevers of the period, that the principal constituent of his fabled medicines was some form of quinine from Guiana.

At all events, when Walter was working one day on his small plot of land in the governor's garden in the Tower of London, the wife of the French ambassador passed by on her way to see the Tower lions, and caught sight of him. In the course of their conversation she asked about his Guiana Balsam, and he promised to boil some up and send it to her – which he did.

Other foreign visitors whose company Walter enjoyed were the Indians he had brought back from Guiana and who had managed to survive the English climate for nearly a decade. Baptised Christians, these South Americans had lodgings near the Tower and came regularly to visit Walter for instruction in the English language and other subjects.

It was not, all in all, an unpleasant existence for a man condemned for treason, but the reports that reached the court did not please King James who was busy establishing another of his incongruous royal distinctions – as England's only pamphleteering king. In 1604 appeared his *Counterblast Against Tobacco*, a tract that took on in places the character of a personal attack on Sir Walter Ralegh, 'a father generally hated', who, James alleged, picked up the habit of smoking from his friends the 'beastly Indians, slaves to the Spaniards, refuse to the world, and as yet aliens from the holy covenant of God. . . .'

James was wrong, of course, in suggesting either that Ralegh had been to Virginia or that the 'beastly Indians' whom he had met in Guiana had introduced him to smoking. Yet the king scored some good points:

It [tobacco] makes a kitchen of the inward parts of men, soiling and infecting them with an unctuous and oily kind of soot. . . . Is it not a great vanity, that a man cannot heartily welcome his friend now, but straight they must be in hand with tobacco? . . . that the sweetness of man's breath, being a good gift of God, should be wilfully corrupted by this stinking smoke?

James, in fact, visited the Tower of London soon after Walter first arrived there, for the Easter festivities of 1604, but Walter was not a spectator at the ceremonies. When King James rode through the gates of the Tower 'under a rich canopy borne by six members of the Privy Council' – cabinet ministers had to work hard for their living in the seventeenth century – the great fortress had been entirely cleared of prisoners, all pardoned and released as an act of Easter mercy with the exception of three – Ralegh, Cobham and Grey. This trio, kept well apart lest they might discover what each was alleged to have said about the other during the trials of the previous November, were taken away to be lodged in the Fleet and then returned to discover that the royal party, and the populace who had come to cheer, had left behind them the plague.

It was a fortnight before the pestilence was notified, and in that time poor little Wat had been playing and sleeping near 'a woman with a running plague sore' and whose own child had died of the plague. Wat might have died. Walter wrote indignantly to Robert Cecil asking to be moved from the Tower. 'I cannot think myself to have been either such a viper but that this great downfall of mine, this shame, loss and sorrow, may seem to your lordship's heart and soul a sufficient punishment.' But his request was not granted, nor were other hopeful suggestions that he might be released and confined within the area of Sherborne. Bess had to move out of the Tower into the nearby lodgings where Carew was born.

Yet Robert Cecil was not Ralegh's worst friend in these years, for now straddled firmly in charge of James's government, he felt secure enough to extend a helping hand to the man whose ruin he knew he might have prevented. Cold fish though he was, Burghley's son had inherited his father's moral sense and, like his father, he was not averse to exercising it if it cost him nothing. So it was thanks to Cecil that as early as December 1603 Lady Ralegh was told she could keep her personal possessions free of distraint and that Walter's brother Carew continued to administer the wardenship of the Royal Forest of Gillingham and the lieutenancy of Portland Castle. The patent of wines could not be kept in the family, but Cecil was able to be of some help, for the new holder of the monopoly, Charles Howard, Earl of Nottingham, the Armada veteran, had lost no time in pestering the Raleghs for payment of certain arrears that Walter had not been able to collect, and he had forced the sale of the rich hangings of Durham House for only £500. Cecil put a stop to that and he was also of assistance so far as Sherborne was concerned. The tenants were refusing to pay their rents, creditors were cutting down the woods and selling off the cattle, and the whole estate was going to rack and ruin. Once again Cecil intervened and by letters patent dated 30 July 1604, the crown confirmed Lady Ralegh's and Wat's right to the lands subject to the control of trustees. Walter wrote thankfully to Cecil, 'I shall never forget your true honour and remorse of me.'[2]

Yet the Raleghs' position at Sherborne was a complicated one. In 1599 Walter had succeeded in exchanging his lease for a grant in perpetuity which he presumed his legal manœuvre of 1602 had transferred intact to young Wat. But when his son's legal title came to be checked, it was discovered that there was a fatal flaw in the 1601 deed of transfer. The clerk copying it out must have dozed off, and the point at which his mind wandered was the most crucial one of all, for omitted from the document were the words 'shall and will from henceforth stand and be thereof seised'. So young Wat had not actually been seised (put in possession) of Sherborne, which meant that the estate had, in fact, still been Sir Walter's personal property when he was found guilty of treason. It was therefore forfeited to the crown.

Back in October 1603, before Walter had even stood trial, Cecil had told a Scot anxious to have Sherborne for himself that a dozen other applicants had preceded him, and the Letters Patent of July 1604 had appeared to keep off all predators, for the moment at least. But now the clerk's conveyancing flaw threw all in doubt, and the strain of this blow proved too much for Bess. The troubles of the 1590s had been as much her fault as Walter's, but in this ridiculous business of Cobham she had been guiltless and yet had still had to bear alone the brunt of all the difficulties that flowed from it – for the worst inconveniences are always the practical ones. While Walter had fought grandly for his life in the public arena, Bess had had to scrabble less glamorously to keep a roof over her head, pawn the family plate and her own jewels, fend off creditors, comfort her confused son and keep up a steady stream of humiliating petitions to Cecil and the king. It had been at her entreaty that Cecil had called Lord Admiral Howard off his attempts to enforce arrears on the wine patents, and it had been Bess who had sought the interview that resulted in the Letters Patent apparently securing Sherborne in July 1604. In these times of trouble we see her spirit, why Walter loved her and how much he relied on her. Cobham and Grey of Wilton lost everything with their condemnation. It was largely thanks to Bess Ralegh's relentless efforts, which neither hard work nor pain nor humiliation could deter, that Walter found himself in less unhappy circumstances. She had fought like a tigress, but now the senseless, fatal errors in the Sherborne conveyance invalidated all her efforts.

Her total impotence in the face of this catastrophe was the last straw, and we discover why it was that Walter always stood somewhat in awe of his lady wife. For Bess dragged her son and newborn babe-in-arms to the Tower and there staged a magnificent scene, upbraiding her husband who lived such a carefree life among his plants and tubes and retorts, while she had to cope with all the miserable banalities of everyday survival. She told Walter to pull himself together. He must stir himself and get the Sherborne blunder put right if it was the last thing that he did, and in desperation Walter wrote urgently to Cecil, 'I shall be made more than weary of my life by her crying and bewailing who will return in post, and nothing done. ... These torments, added to my desolate life, ... are sufficient either utterly to distract me or to make me curse the time that ever I was born into the world.' Walter asked Lord Chief Justice Popham and Edward Coke, fierce adversaries but shrewd lawyers, to examine the legal position on his behalf.

But Robert Cecil evidently thought that he had done more than enough for the Raleghs, while Popham and Coke could come to no other conclusion but that the omission in the conveyance invalidated the transfer. Young Wat's title deed would not stand up in a court of law. So Lady Ralegh pocketed her pride to petition Robert Cecil yet again, and, when that proved to no avail, she pestered King James to such effect that he actually ordered Cecil to have a deed drawn up guaranteeing Sherborne to Lady Ralegh and her children – and there, for the moment, the matter rested, with Bess's obduracy having once again staved off total ruin.

James's solicitude was in 1605 one small reassurance to set against several other discouragements. In August of that year the amiable Sir George Harvey was abruptly removed from the lieutenancy of the Tower and in his place came the noxious Sir William Waad who had been Walter's jailor at the time of the trial in Winchester. There would be no more cosy dinners now for Walter in the lieutenant's apartments, for Waad took a poor view of all the comforts that Harvey had permitted his prisoners, and Ralegh in particular. Within a week of his arrival Waad was writing to Cecil complaining of the hen-house that Walter had converted 'into a still, where he doth spend his time all the day in his distillations'. It spoilt Waad's enjoyment of his garden, and so to guarantee his privacy against his prisoner's chemical concoctions, he got constructed a broad brick wall. Yet his prisoner promptly took to extending his exercise along the top of this same wall, which was visible outside the Tower, and the spectacle of the great Sir Walter taking the air in this fashion became one of the sights of London. What with Bess sweeping boldly into the Tower courtyard in her coach, it was as though the Raleghs considered the place their own home. Waad determined to set matters on a footing more befitting the premier prison of the realm, but in November 1605 more urgent concerns cropped up to occupy his particular talents.

In the cellars of Westminster had been discovered one Guido Fawkes with enough gunpowder to blow the king and members of parliament sky-high in the cause of Catholic emancipation. The indications were that the plot was wide-ranging and the Raleghs themselves were compromised, for, feeling somewhat more confident of her title to Sherborne, Bess had gone down to springclean the castle and had had all the rusty armour scoured. That, thought the Government's representatives in Dorset, was suspicious in the light of Catholic plans for a nation-wide rising, while when Walter had sent to the French ambassador's wife the Guiana Balsam that she had asked for on her visit to the Tower, he had chosen as a messenger from her entourage Captain Whitelocke, a dependant of the Earl of Northumberland who was an old friend of Walter's and was also implicated in the conspiracy. So on these grounds Walter had once again to appear before the Privy Council to answer their suspicions of treason. Yet this was an old game by now and Ralegh acquitted himself well.

The Earl of Northumberland, however, fared less successfully. His kinsman Thomas Percy was one of the principal gunpowder conspirators and, as the earl's steward, had laid plans to devote some £4,000 of the earl's money to a Catholic rising. Northumberland, vague and tied up in his scientific pursuits, knew nothing of all this, but the Privy Council, and Robert Cecil, in particular, chose to put the worst reflection on his negligence. The earl was fined the enormous sum of £30,000 – which he could, in fact, afford – and sent to the Tower. It cannot have helped Northumberland that he was such a good friend of Walter's, that he had been libelled with his friend by Henry Howard as one of the witches' coven at Durham House, and that he was said to have complained most bitterly at the treatment meted out to Ralegh in 1603. Still, his misfortune did mean that Walter was unexpectedly blessed with the companionship of the one man he would probably have chosen from all his friends to share his captivity.

Thomas Hariot had also suffered from the Gunpowder Conspiracy, being detained on account of his close links with both Ralegh and Northumberland – how the Privy Council must have delighted in the prospect of humbling the notorious 'conjuror'! But the charges against him would not stick, for he was no more than he set himself up to be, a mathematician interested in science for its own sake. He was set at liberty again, and so in the winter of 1605–6 he voluntarily took up residence inside the Tower with his two great patrons.

The Earl of Northumberland appears, Sir William Waad notwithstanding, to have been even more successful than Sir Walter Ralegh at providing himself with creature comforts in captivity. He kept a fine entourage of attendants, turned the warders into his servants by tipping them lavishly, paid Sir William no less than £100 per year for the privilege of enjoying his own food, built himself a bowling alley with a canvas roof, put fresh gravel down on the paths he used, had new windows pierced to bring more light into his rooms and, like Walter, set up a little laboratory for his scientific experiments.[3] As well as Hariot he enjoyed the scientific company of the medical enthusiast Walter Warner, and what with Walter Ralegh's pharmaceutical investigations there sprang up in the Tower a little colony of energetic, if somewhat unsystematic scientific researchers the like of which was not to be seen for more than sixty years in London – nor for several centuries in the classically constipated ancient universities of Oxford and Cambridge. The Durham House set lived on.

Precisely what Walter, Warner, Hariot and Northumberland discovered with their bubbling retorts we do not know. Northumberland's interest seems to have been directed towards distilling stale alcoholic beverages into exotic types of whisky, but Hariot's work was of greater moment. He was investigating the refraction of light through liquids, striking up a correspondence with the great Kepler and suggesting a rational explanation for the 'miracle' of rainbows with which we would not disagree. Walter, meanwhile, swung away from drugs and medicines to tackle a practical maritime problem – how to keep drinking water fresh during a long oceanic voyage. He devised a machine for distilling sea water so that it became palatable, but we have no evidence that the device was ever actually used at sea. It probably involved delicate glass apparatus ill-suited to nautical travel.

Then, in the spring of 1606, Ralegh fell ill. An official doctor suggested that he should be moved out of his dampish apartment into the snug 'little room which he hath built in the garden adjoining his still house', yet from the description of the symptoms it sounds as if the patient was suffering from something rather more serious than a simple chill. Walter seems to have suffered a stroke. He lost all feeling in his left side, which became cold and numb, the fingers of his left hand were paralysed and his speech was badly affected. With only partial control over his tongue, he slurred words painfully. For a man now in his mid fifties it was an unpleasant reminder of creeping age.

The paralysis disappeared, but life in the Tower became more tedious.

In July 1607 William Waad finally asserted his authority in a list of regulations he must have relished enforcing. Every afternoon at five a bell would ring at which signal all guests were to leave, while all prisoners were to retire with their servants to their own quarters. Prisoners were not to fraternize in the evenings and must dine alone while – most cherished prohibition of all – coaches were to stop outside the Tower's gates and not to enter the courtyard. Lady Ralegh would have to come and go with somewhat less of a flourish.

Still, all these complications were pinpricks and would have been quite tolerable for Walter and his wife had it not been for one sinister development. A young Scot named Robert Carr had broken his leg while jousting in front of King James early in 1607, and James, shambling over to study this beautifully shaped specimen wounded in the cause of his entertainment, found himself strangely moved. The youth's legs were particularly delectable, his face irresistible, and it was not long before the king found that he was head over heels in love. Carr was knighted, and when it came to arranging an estate to lend substance to his new title, Robert Cecil proved most helpful. Despite James's instructions to him, he had not, in fact, taken steps to secure the Ralegh lands to Bess and young Wat, so Sherborne was still as free as ever it was when Walter was condemned for treason.

Late in 1607 the court of exchequer began proceedings requesting Sir Walter Ralegh to show proper title whereby Sherborne should revert to his heirs, and Walter could only, of course, produce the fatally flawed conveyance. Lady Ralegh, however, was not going to let the matter go without a fight. She requested an audience with James and when she was ignored, stationed herself in a strategic position at Hampton Court and, as he passed, fell on her knees begging him to show mercy.

Greatly embarrassed James waddled on his way mumbling in broad Scots 'I mun have the land, I mun have it for Carr', while Bess let fly curses at all who had brought her family to this pass.

Poor James, caught between a young man's beauty and the fury of a tigress! He undertook to pay Lady Ralegh compensation that, given the forcible confiscation, was reasonably generous – £8,000 plus an annuity of £400 for the lifetime of herself and her son. But Sherborne was gone. Now indeed Walter Ralegh could say with Job, 'Naked came I into the world and naked will I go out.'

Sir Walter Ralegh, fortune's tennis ball, had been struck out of court in a decisive fashion. But, even in the Tower of London, there were several more games to play before the match was finally lost or won.

41

'The Story of All Ages
Past...'

It was always Walter Ralegh's great ambition to be the counsellor to a prince and it was, ironically, right in the middle of his detention in the Tower of London that he finally achieved his goal. Elizabeth had never taken him seriously as a political adviser, and James had mistrusted him before ever he met him, but in 1608 Walter Ralegh struck up a friendship with James's eldest son, Prince Henry, born in Scotland in 1594 and now Prince of Wales and heir to the throne. It was no relationship of passing curiosity, this companionship between the old Elizabethan and the bright fourteen-year-old lad who would be the next king of England and Scotland. Sharing common interests, similar temperaments and an attitude towards King James founded on separate but bitter personal experience, Walter and Henry became close and true friends.

The origins of their friendship went back to Walter's chance meeting in his Tower herb plot with the French ambassador's wife, for shortly after this lady had tasted Ralegh's Balsam of Guiana, Queen Anne sent to the Tower for her own sample of the cordial concocted by her husband's prisoner, and she also came in person to visit Walter. We know she was impressed for when, in 1606, her brother the king of Denmark came to London for a state visit he found time between the froth-blowing bouts in which he drank the entire Stuart court under the table to petition James to release Ralegh and allow him to become admiral of the Danish fleet. James refused, yet when his wife started taking with her on her visits their eldest son Henry, and when the youth started falling under the spell of old Ralegh's magic, James might well have wished that he had despatched Walter safely out of the kingdom. Even before he came under the influence of Ralegh, Henry had started to exhibit signs of a clear rejection of his father. Ostentatiously disdainful of the sickly revels of the Jacobean court, he made it a point never to swear, and cultivated sports involving self-discipline and fitness: riding, swimming and tennis. He was fascinated by the sea and ships and also by transatlantic colonization. He took a personal interest in the expedition which sailed for Virginia in 1607 to found Jamestown, and also in the voyage which Thomas Roe was to make in 1610 to Guiana, appreciating, obviously, the crucial part that Ralegh had played in the reign of Queen Elizabeth in first inspiring these ventures.

Henry exhibited too an earnest concern for the matters that were one day to be his daily responsibility, politics and the relations between nations, and this was the subject of the first treatise that Walter Ralegh composed for him, in the spring of 1608, a discourse on 'The Present State of Things, as they now stand between the three great Kingdoms, France, England and Spain'. This short essay[1] was an exposition of Ralegh's traditional Elizabethan world outlook, and in it one can see Walter grooming himself for the position of royal councillor for which he had waited so long.

Sir William Waad had, in some respects, proved a blessing in disguise, for with his officious bell ringing out at five and the Tower being cleared of all visitors, Walter now had long evenings to himself in which he could work hard at his papers for the prince. Taking up a particular interest of Henry's he set about compiling 'Observations and Notes concerning the Royal Navy and Sea Service', collaborating in the preparation of this treatise with Sir Arthur Gorges, who seems, like Ralegh, to have won the special affection of Henry. The prince wanted to build a new warship, the *Prince Royal*, and Walter placed all the expertise that had gone into the *Ark Ralegh* at his disposal. Some were advising the prince to construct the ship on a grandiose scale, but Walter sent him a paper arguing that exaggerated proportions would make for poor sea-worthiness.

In the event, the measurements Ralegh suggested were close to those of the finished vessel, and the launching of the *Prince Royal* in 1610, destined for a future as heroic as the famous *Ark Royal* – rebuilt at this period and renamed in honour of the queen the *Anne Royal* – was an implicit rebuke to King James, who had sorely neglected the great maritime fighting machine that had grown up in the previous century.

When James, in 1611 and 1612, proposed to marry his daughter Elizabeth and son Henry to a prince and princess of Savoy, Walter felt secure enough under Henry's protection openly to criticize an alliance with such a remote, weak and Catholic state. In two treatises on the proposed Savoy marriages and a discourse against Jesuits and recusants, Sir Walter Ralegh set out some forthright rebukes to the pro-Catholic policies pursued by James. As Henry Howard complained bitterly, Sir Walter Ralegh's decade of captivity seemed not to have subdued his 'boldness, pride and passion', but, on the contrary, to have 'cockered and fostered' his arrogance.

Prince Henry's friendship injected new life into Walter's dragging captivity, and a token of what Ralegh could hope for came when Henry spoke strongly to his father over the matter of the Sherborne estates to prevent him from assigning them to the beloved Carr – who was compensated with £20,000. Instead Henry held Sherborne himself against the day of Ralegh's release, a day when the restoration of his lands would be but one of many compensations for Walter's years of misery. A further obstacle to a pardon was removed when in May 1612 Robert Cecil died in Marlborough on his way back from taking the waters in Bath. A politician to the last, the little man had been hurrying up to London to forestall some Council intrigues against him, and with his death vanished the one man who, despite his small kindnesses to Walter and Bess, had always represented the strongest barrier to Ralegh's release. For whereas James, for all his spite, could be haphazard and was not immune to a certain tenderness, Robert Cecil, first Earl of Salisbury, did not forget. As far as he was concerned, Walter Ralegh had always been safest behind bars.

Prince Henry's famous remark, 'No king but my father would keep such a bird in a cage',[2] seemed about to take effect, but then, only a few weeks later, in the autumn of 1612, tragedy struck. Indulging in his favourite pastime of swimming – in the garbage-infested River Thames – Prince Henry was stricken down with a fever. The royal doctors tried their every trick, but still he sickened. The one beacon of hope in Jacobean England – not merely for Ralegh but for all who hoped for better times – flickered towards extinction. Quite beside herself, Queen Anne insisted that the young prince be given some of Walter Ralegh's famous cordial, but the Privy Council demurred. To invite a convicted traitor to administer drugs to the heir to the throne was unheard of madness. Lord Chief Justice Popham had asked for some of Ralegh's pills on his death bed in 1607 and had expired within the hour – a sequence of events into which it was not difficult to read a sinister significance.

Queen Anne, however, continued to insist, and it soon became obvious that the royal physicians had exhausted their quackery. The prince was dying and there was nothing to lose. So from the Tower was brought a phial of Walter's elixir – together with a gloomy warning from its distiller. The Balsam would cure any fever, said Ralegh, provided that poison had not previously been administered. As the cordial was poured between the lips of the comatose body, life was seen to revive. The prince opened his eyes. His complexion brightened. He sat up and he actually spoke. A miracle, it seemed, had occurred – and that would, of course, have been the absolute guarantee of Walter's salvation, for King James was quite prostrated with grief and the entire court with him.

But Prince Henry's revival was but a last rally before death, and with him on 6 November 1612, died all Walter's dearest hopes. There could now be no question of any immediate release for Ralegh, particularly in view of his gratuitous insinuation about poison. The manor and estates of Sherborne went to Robert Carr after all, and Walter Ralegh remained securely locked up with his books and the bittersweet memories of the greatest of all his many 'might have beens'.

Yet not quite all was lost, for from his four years of friendship with Prince Henry between 1608 and 1612 emerged the greatest of all Ralegh's writings, the creation of his which most deserves the title of masterpiece, *The History of the World*. Taking upon himself the mantle of tutor to the heir to the throne of England, Walter produced a history lesson that instructed not only the prince but whole generations of Englishmen, a stunning piece of work, astonishing both in its ambition and in its success. In the seventeenth century, *The History of the World* – a vast tome which might have been more accurately entitled the pre-Christian history of the world since it did not get beyond the year 168 BC – went through at least ten editions in England after the death of Ralegh, twice as many as either the works of Shakespeare or Spenser's *Faerie Queene*, and the influence it had was revolutionary. Oliver Cromwell recommended it to his son, John Locke thought it the ideal reading for 'gentlemen desirous of improving their education', John Milton's debt to it was incalculable, Marvell, Prynne and Lilburne praised it, the historian Digory Wheare said it placed Ralegh in the same class as Herodotus, and these were only the most eminent of a whole class of English society which, through one of the most formative periods in our history, had their thinking decisively shaped by what Walter Ralegh wrote. *The History of the World* came to be the backbone of anti-authoritarian thought through the years leading up to and following the Civil War, for it provided the average member of the English gentry with the context in which his revolt against the king could be justified, and it held the positive proof that the Protestant God was on his side.

If not quite *The Communist Manifesto* – the Puritan Bible was that – *The History of the World* could be called the *Das Kapital* of the seventeenth century for just as Marx analysed history in order to justify his thesis for proletarian revolution, so Walter Ralegh examined the past to illustrate the workings of God in political events – particularly in the punishment of unjust rulers.

It is this that gives *The History of the World* a significance that none other of Walter Ralegh's works possesses, and this too that contradicts the patronizing dismissal of the *History* which started in the mid-eighteenth century with the criticisms of Dr Johnson and David Hume. Johnson rejected Ralegh's work as a 'dissertation', Hume scoffed at 'the Jewish and rabbinical learning which compose the half of the volume', while, of course, any critic invited today to assess *The History* by modern historical standards would have to condemn it for its unscientific use of evidence and its subordination of objectivity to moralizing and propaganda. A modern historian might examine the 'cruelty [that] the kings and princes of the world have . . . committed to make themselves masters of the world', but he would not rely as Walter did on second-hand evidence, setting down myths and legends as established fact. Nor would his style or purpose be to turn his account into an enormous sermon: 'And yet hath Babylon, Persia, Egypt, Syria, Macedonia, Carthage, Rome and the rest no fruit, flower, grass nor leaf springing upon the face of the earth of those seeds. No! Their very roots and ruins do hardly remain!'

Yet it is precisely in these faults that the significance of the book lies. Walter's first concern was chronology, dedicating himself to proving that Prometheus and Atlas lived at the same time as Moses, or that Jason and the Argonauts, sailing off in search of the Golden Fleece, might well have bumped into Gideon who was alive at the same time.

If we hold up the world to be studied, he explained, it is through history that 'We behold how it was governed. How it was covered with waters and again repeopled. How kings and kingdoms have flourished and fallen, and for what virtue and piety God made prosperous, and for what vice and deformity he made wretched both the one and the other.'[3]

In this last sentence lay the sting, for Ralegh's concern with chronology was only the first stage of his argument. By establishing that there was no contradiction between history as set out by the classical authors and history as set out in the Bible, he was proving God's dominance over human affairs at all times in the past. Having proved that, he could then proceed to the essence of his argument, that the events of history, the rise and fall of kingdoms, the success and failure of kings, all directly illustrated the judgement of God. The example that he and all his readers had in mind – the reason why James banned *The History* and why parliamentarians like Prynne, Lilburne and Cromwell endorsed it – was, of course, the example of Queen Elizabeth's government in comparison to the régime of the early Stuart kings, how God had favoured one and not the other – and why.

This was the kernel of the book, and this was why, though it condemned republicanism as fiercely as it condemned absolute tyranny, *The History of the World* became a mainspring of revolutionary thought. For the sermons about God's judgements that it preached were read by seventeenth-century men in the context of the breakdown of relations between the early Stuarts and their parliaments. It was published in 1614, the very year in which relations between James and his new kingdom reached a new low. Under the influence of Carr, James tried to gerry-mander the elections, succeeding only in incensing both Commons and Lords to such an extent that the 'Addled Parliament' sat for two months refusing to pass a single act or to vote any supplies before it was dissolved, James then resolving that he would never call another parliament and would rule as an unfettered absolute monarch.

Against this background, Walter's thesis that God intervenes in human affairs to punish monarchs who have abused their power was positively explosive. And he also composed a Preface which set out his basic argu-ment in compact form, using examples drawn from history that were closer to his readers – the fortunes and misfortunes of English monarchs up to and including the Tudors. Walter's message could not have been clearer as he pointed out the catastrophes that had overtaken kings who had ruled tyrannically, from Henry I who was punished for his unjust treatment of his brother by the storm which wrecked the White Ship containing his son and his most 'dearly beloved' nobles, to Henry VIII whose treatment of his wives and closest advisers was rewarded by the extinction of the Tudor dynasty through the failure of his children Edward, Mary and Elizabeth to produce any children. Ralegh's list of royal sinners advances relentlessly, cataloguing the misdeeds and conse-quent divine punishment of Edward III, Richard II, Henry IV, Henry VI, Edward IV, Richard III and Henry VII and then – following Henry VIII and omitting Elizabeth who, of course, in Walter's eyes could do little wrong – it stops very obviously short at James I.

Of whom I may say it truly, that if all the malice of the world were infused into one eye, yet it could not discern in his life, even to this day, any one of those foul spots by which the consciences of all the forenamed princes (in effect) have been defiled; nor any drop of that innocent blood on the sword of justice with which the most that fore-went him have stained both their hands and fame.[4]

Ralegh's irony was palpable, especially as his readers knew well that the author who was praising James so extravagantly was a man himself cut down by the sword of justice which was supposed to be unstained by a single drop of innocent blood. It is impossible to believe that Walter intended his gross flattery of King James to be taken seriously, particu-larly as the entire *History* was intended as an instruction manual for the young prince who was to turn England away from the path into which his father was leading her.

The essential thing, Ralegh told Henry, was to rule only with the love of his people. Roboam oppressed his country with taxes and suffered for it, for 'what is the strength of a king left by his people?'[5] Artaxerxes II was handicapped by a similar delusion 'that his own will was the supreme law of his subject, and the rule by which all things were to be measured and adjusted to be good and evil'.[6] Such monarchs directly flouted the words of Elizabeth's fabled Golden Speech. 'And though God hath raised me high, yet this I count the Glory of my Crown, that I have reigned with your loves. . . . Above all earthly treasure I esteem my people's love, more than which I desire not to merit.'

In this speech lay the very distinction which Walter Ralegh made in his *History* between good kings and tyrants – the good prince cares for his people's affection, the tyrant is indifferent to it. And another section of Elizabeth's famous speech to her last parliament paraphrased precisely the doctrine that *The History* set up against James's theories of divine right: 'I know the title of a king is a glorious title; but assure yourself that the shining glory of princely authority hath not so dazzled the eyes of our understanding but that we will know and remember that we also are to yield an account of our actions before the great Judge.'

James's belief, in contradiction to this, was that the king, as God's representative on earth, could *not* be judged since he could not possibly do wrong. He was not accountable for his actions to anybody.

'I protest before the majesty of God', declared Walter in his *Preface*, 'that I malice no man under the sun.' But his audience knew why he took every opportunity he could in his book to pour scorn on famous sodomites, and James took the point. He banned *The History of the World* after its publication in 1614, because, said John Chamberlain, Walter Ralegh had been 'too saucy in censoring princes'.

It was more than a matter of isolated jibes, and it was far more than a matter of attacks on James's pet theories. *The History of the World* was a massively documented statement of political theory, a document as central to the English Revolution as Hobbes's *Leviathan* – which came, in any case, after the event. It articulated coherently a concept of divinely supervised government in which monarchs had obligations to their subjects that they ignored at their peril, and this was the more significant for being presented in the framework of a book of compulsive narrative style. Many a seventeenth-century gentleman must have swallowed his medicine without noticing it – and subsequent readers have done the same, notably in the final peroration that rounds off the argument:

O eloquent, just and mighty Death! Whom none could advise, thou hast persuaded. What none hath dared, thou hast done. And whom all the world hath flattered, thou only hast cast out of the world and despised. Thou hast drawn together all the far stretched greatness, all the pride, cruelty and ambitions of man and covered it all over with these two narrow words *Hic Jacet* [Here lies]. . . .

These are the words of a man a few years away from his own death, cast out of the world and despised, yet in reading them solely as Ralegh's statement of his own personal emotions, injustice has been done both to the ambition of his *History* and to the particular political argument which is its theme. For Walter Ralegh introduces death to his final paragraphs not as a vague moral sentiment but as a specific reference to 'the kings and princes of the world who . . . neglect the advice of God while they enjoy life or hope it' and who only come to their senses when they are confronted with the punishment for their sins – which is death.

Death thus becomes Ralegh's ultimate sanction, the only way of punishing a prince who refuses all advice, whom none dare offend, whom all flatter and in whom is epitomized 'all the pride, cruelty and ambition of man'. Ralegh saw death as a sanction to be applied to princes by God, but Cromwell, Lilburne, Milton, and other regicides who had read *The History of the World* were, of course, to take matters into their own hands.

The History of the World constitutes Walter Ralegh's most substantial claim to historical significance. He has always been acknowledged the great symbol of the reign of Queen Elizabeth, the epitome of an age, but in the last analysis, a reflection of it rather than a formative influence in his own right. In *The History of the World*, however, Walter Ralegh took the virtues of the age that he had outlived and created from them a framework of philosophy which affected deeply the way in which subsequent ages thought and acted.

He did this practically single-handed. We know that Prince Henry encouraged him in the early stages and made constructive comments as the work progressed. Thomas Hariot must have helped with the complicated chronology, and John Talbot appears to have taken down every word of the book in longhand as Walter dictated it to him. But the essence of *The History* was Walter himself.

Ben Jonson, whom Ralegh hired to act as young Wat's tutor for a period in 1612 and who took the lad to Paris, claimed in later years that he had written an essay on the Punic Wars which Walter had incorporated almost word for word into *The History*, and in the nineteenth century Benjamin Disraeli's father was to leap on this complaint and erect around it a thesis to the effect that Walter Ralegh was a plagiarist, stealing the work of others and presenting their ideas as his own. In fact, Jonson's remark apart, there is no evidence to justify any such allegation. Walter cultivated intellectual friends and would certainly have picked the brains of Hariot, Warner and Northumberland – as they picked his. When it came to straightforward narrative Ralegh had inevitably to rely on the specialist researches of others – he borrowed a veritable library of history books from Sir Robert Cotton at the start of the project – just as Ben Jonson got his material from some secondary source. But the important thing about *The History* was the philosophy animating it – which was Walter's – and the scope of it, which no Englishman had ever previously attempted.

The First Part of *The History* told the story of mankind from the creation to the emergence of Rome in the second century BC. The Second Part was to take up the story through the Christian era to the emergence of Britain, and the Third Part was to narrow the focus to Britain itself, telling its history up to the present day.

In fact, Prince Henry's death cut short the venture before Ralegh could start on the Second or Third Parts, and in that sense the work is incomplete. But the five books which make up the First Part have a completeness that is not impaired by the fact that they end in 168 BC. Walter sweeps majestically through the empires of the Babylonians, the Persians and the Greeks – 'the world' to Renaissance man meant the civilized world centred on the Mediterranean – to finish with the emergence of the fourth great empire, that of the Romans. Where the ground covered would be familiar to his readers – and this embraced most of the Old Testament – Walter forsook the narrative for the analytical approach, discussing, for example, the exact location, flora and fauna of the Garden of Eden or the dimensions and structure of Noah's Ark. This vessel would not need to be quite as large as some people imagined, he explained, since there are fewer truly separate species of animal in the world than people realize. The north Virginian thrush, for example, which has black and carnation feathers, is essentially the same as the English thrush and 'the dogfish of England is the shark of the south ocean'.

Simply as a compilation of knowledge *The History* was a monumental edifice, and Walter enlivened it at every stage with his own observations. Many of the things we know about his own life come from his accounts of the pre-Christian civilizations when he breaks off from his narrative to draw parallels, say, with his own experiences in the French Wars of Religion, or to describe the fig trees he had seen in South America. Some readers claimed to see King James satirized in the portrait of King Ninias who was 'esteemed no man of war at all, but altogether feminine and subjected to ease and delicacy', especially as Ralegh warmly praised Ninias's female predecessor as a just and wise queen. But when Walter stated that the 'end and scope of all history' is 'to teach by example of times past such wisdom as may guide desires and actions' in the present he was not thinking in terms of isolated examples, but of the broad sweep of the past under the eye of God's Providence.

Thanks to Prince Henry's influence, the book had been entered as early as April 1611 in the Stationer's Register – before it was completed – and typesetting appears to have started almost at once, so that the first part appeared in March 1614, only a few weeks after Walter had completed the fifth book. Since censorship usually occurred at the registration stage the book circulated freely for several months, selling well, and it was not until December 1614 that the agents of the archbishop of Canterbury set about seizing copies – by which time the damage had been done. The royal prohibition stayed in force for two years and then, in 1617, a new edition of *The History* appeared containing a portrait of Walter himself. James lacked the will, and Jacobean administration lacked the way to enforce the prohibition for long, particularly as times had changed since the days when *The History* was started. By 1617 new men had the ear of the king, new evidence had been discovered relating to the charges on which Walter had been sent to the Tower and, strangest of all, it seemed as if there was a particular task that the old prisoner and no one else could accomplish for James. So, despite having written in the summer of 1615 a sharp little treatise on *The Prerogative of Parliaments in England* which reflected on James no more credit than had *The History of the World*, Sir Walter Ralegh was, on 19 March 1616, released from the Tower of London. In his sixty-third year he was about to embark on a venture more dangerous, taxing and daring than any he had previously risked.

✿ 42 ✿

Freedom

The reasons for Sir Walter Ralegh's release from the Tower of London in the spring of 1616 had had an ironic connection with the castle and lands of Sherborne, for St Osmund's curse had operated for once in Sir Walter Ralegh's favour, and Sherborne's new owner, Robert Carr, not only lost the estate but had to move into Walter's own apartments in the Tower only a week after Walter had vacated them.

The affair stemmed from Carr's passion for Frances Howard, the niece of Lord Henry Howard, a lady more beautiful, but even more vicious than her uncle. For Frances had been married as a child bride in 1606 to Robert Devereux, himself only fourteen, the son of the great Earl of Essex, and in the four years the children had had to wait before they could live together as man and wife, Frances had met and fallen in love with Robert Carr, by 1610 riding the very crest of royal favour. Determined to give her all to Carr and that her young husband should never enjoy her, Frances went to an astrological quack who provided her with drugs to keep Robert Devereux impotent, and then, for good measure, this apothecary got one of his partners, a witch, to make assurance doubly sure. A wax effigy of Frances' husband was constructed with an anatomical precision that allowed a large pin to be run through Robert's testicles.

Under this combined assault, coupled with the fierce determination of his wife to resist his every advance, the young Earl of Essex struggled fruitlessly for three years to consummate his marriage until eventually the matter became the subject of divorce proceedings. Henry Howard used all his Privy Council influence on his niece's behalf, for he was anxious that Frances should marry Carr and reinforce his own position with James, but the young Earl of Essex proved recalcitrant. He was more than happy to get shot of his wife, but he was, quite naturally, unwilling to be publicly branded as impotent. So in May 1613 the matter was investigated by a commission on which were three bishops, among them George Abbott, the Archbishop of Canterbury himself.

To these reverend gentlemen Frances Howard offered uninhibited evidence as to the nature of her sex life – or the lack of it, servants who had examined the bed clothes of the couple solemnly giving their evidence at length. But the Archbishop of Canterbury was unconvinced, and Frances Howard, furthermore, had the reputation of a worn glove. So an additional commission 'of grave matrons, fearing God and mothers of children' was summoned together to examine the essence of the matter – Frances herself – and duly pronounced her to be *virgo intacta* – though her upper parts were so veiled that some suggested that Frances had substituted another woman. Archbishop Abbot remained suspicious, but after King James had added extra bishops to the commission who could overcome the archbishop's objections to the divorce with votes if not with arguments, Frances was freed to marry Carr at Christmas 1613.

But this was only the beginning of the tale, for Carr had a mentor, Sir Thomas Overbury, an *eminence grise* who had coached the young man in the best fashion to exploit the political power his physical beauty had won. Overbury resented the Howards so easily capturing his protégé and made no secret of his displeasure. So once again Frances and Henry Howard got to work on James and prevailed on him to send Overbury abroad as an ambassador. Overbury, however, would not be disposed of so easily, and, refusing James's offer, was sent to the Tower in 1613 where he was lodged near Sir Walter Ralegh's apartments.

We do not know if Overbury met Ralegh in 1613 – he had been present at his trial ten years earlier and had taken copious notes of the proceedings – but if he did, he had little time to get to know his fellow prisoner, for Frances Howard, consumed with the same style of hatred that could inspire her uncle, was now determined to compass his destruction. Her uncle, indeed, was himself an accomplice in her plot, for soon after Overbury arrived in the Tower, the officious but essentially honest William Waad was replaced by an obsequious creature of Howard's, Sir Gervase Elwys, who presided knowingly over the final act of the melodrama. Frances Howard herself lovingly cooked tarts, made jellies and mixed wines all heavily laced with poison which were carried to the Tower and administered to Overbury with the connivance of Elwys – with the inevitably fatal consequence to his prisoner. The corpse, reported Elwys, 'stank intolerably'.

For a year the secret was kept after a fashion, but then under the strain of increasing rumours the miserable Elwys lost his nerve. The whole story came out and, with the sniff of witchcraft in his nostrils, James became impassioned. He appointed Coke to investigate the depths of the affair, which the lawyer did with the greatest relish in a succession of spectacular trials that captured public attention for months. The role of Henry Howard, who had providentially died but a few months before, was revealed, together with the fact that he had for years been in receipt of a Spanish pension along with other eminent English politicians, including Robert Cecil. With his customary flair for unsubstantiated allegation Coke even contrived to suggest that Prince Henry himself had been cut down by poison.

This last innuendo, of course, echoed Walter Ralegh's dark warnings when he had offered his elixir to cure the young prince in 1612, but the implications of the Overbury affair for him extended beyond this. The disclosure about the bribes paid by Spain to Howard and Cecil threw an entirely new light on the campaign that those two men had sustained against Ralegh at the beginning of James's reign, and the literally venomous fashion in which Henry Howard had pursued the vendetta against Overbury put the scandalous letters which he had written to James about Ralegh in a new perspective.

Most important of all, the Overbury scandal confirmed the worst suspicions harboured about a court now revealed as rotten to the core. Carr was James's favourite and it had been the royal influence capriciously lent to corrupt practices that had made it possible for the Howards to have their murderous way. The Jacobean court and its king had been hopelessly compromised, and in a desperate attempt to salvage something of his reputation James moved towards new advisers.

Sir Ralph Winwood, the upright anti-Spanish Puritan who had become first secretary in 1614 now became more powerful, and George Abbott, the Archbishop of Canterbury who had from the first been suspicious of the Frances Howard divorce, was also able to swing James away from his pro-Spanish courses, for the moment at least. The primary instrument of their ascendancy was a young Buckinghamshire gentleman, George Villiers, whose beauty had dazzled James when he first appeared at court and whom Abbott pushed forward strongly as a replacement for Carr. Walter Ralegh also made the new favourite an instrument to his own ends, bribing Villiers' half-brother Edward with £750 and paying Sir William St John, one of Villiers's men, the same sum to have the arguments for his release presented forcefully to the king.

Winwood argued in the same direction, and there was no doubt that public opinion, scandalized by the Overbury case, would now respond favourably to the release from the Tower of the man it had once hissed and jeered. But the arguments that persuaded James seldom took account of public opinion. In 1615 the king's great preoccupation was the debt of £700,000 with which his own improvidence, the liabilities left by his predecessor, and his inability to get along with parliament had saddled him. It was not that the disgrace of insolvency worried James but the fact that, in the long term, the only way out of his dilemma was to throw himself on the mercy of parliament – and this his pride and political theory would not allow him to do. For two months in 1614 he had refused to contemplate the demands for reform with which the addled parliament had confronted him, and that parliament had refused equally steadfastly to vote any taxes that might ease his financial embarrassment. So determining that he would rule England without parliament, James was after 1614 looking desperately for a coup that would reduce his debts. For a time he had had high hopes of selling off his son Charles as a husband to the Infanta of Spain, but Spain's conditions for such a marriage included a system of education for any children of the marriage that would have produced a Popish heir to the throne of England. James at least had the nous to realize what sort of reception that sort of arrangement would get from his Protestant subjects, and so, desperate for money and ready to snatch at any straw, he lent a rather more sympathetic ear than he would otherwise have done to the plan Walter Ralegh offered him through Winwood and Villiers in 1615 to bring back treasure from Guiana.

It was not the first time that Walter had suggested to the Government that he should be set free in order to loot the gold that he said lay in South America. It had been the constant theme of his many petitions for release. In 1607 he had had some Guiana ore re-assayed and told Cecil that, on the strength of the results, he was sure he would be able to find shiploads more 'at the root of the grass in a broad and flat state'. Then in 1609, having found Cecil less than enthusiastic, Walter tempted the cupidity of one of James's Scottish friends, Lord Haddington – with equally little effect. Most powerfully of all, at the height of his friendship with Prince Henry in 1610 and 1611, Walter had bombarded Queen Anne, James himself, Cecil again and the entire Privy Council with proposals that did actually produce some response. Walter was told he could despatch Lawrence Keymis to Guiana to bring back solid substantiation of his claims – but that he could not go himself. There was obviously the suspicion that, confined within the Tower and desperate to be released, Walter was loading Guiana with a potential that the facts could not justify.

Keymis did not, in fact, sail as the Privy Council suggested, for freedom, not the suspense of waiting on another's explorations, had been the object of Walter's campaign, while there was already more than enough third party evidence on which the strength of Ralegh's propaganda could be assessed. *The Discoverie of the large, Rich and Beautiful Empyre of*

Guiana had had an inspiring effect on English explorers, and that area of South America had since 1595 been the object of more private attempts at trade and colonization than Virginia. If Walter was spellbound by the myth of the king who bathed in gold dust, he had also succeeded in spreading the enchantment widely.

In 1602 Captain Charles Leigh, a merchant who had examined all sorts of commercial possibilities on the eastern American seaboard, explored the Orinoco and discovered a site by the Wiapoco River he considered suitable for colonization, while in the same year Francis Sparrow, one of the men Ralegh had left living among the Indians, arrived back in England after being captured by the Spaniards, to write an account of his experiences. Englishmen could obviously survive both the climate and the natives of Guiana, and in 1604 a small group of adventurers set out with Captain Leigh and his brother Sir John, who knew Ralegh, to set up a trading post on the Wiapoco. While looking for gold they planted and raised crops of flax, cotton, sugar cane and tobacco with some success, but, not discovering the treasure they had hoped for, they were happy to come home on the Dutch and French ships that traded and raided in the area.

The same sort of fate befell an even more ambitious attempt at commercial exploitation undertaken in 1609 by Robert Harcourt, a Catholic who secured permission for his project through Prince Henry and who must, therefore, have had some contact with Ralegh. Harcourt tried deliberately to emulate Ralegh's policy of courting native friendship and met not only whole tribes who venerated the memory of 'Ralee' but one of Walter's own native protégés who had been to England and now, under his Christian baptismal name of Leonard, had become a much respected chief. Harcourt, who went through the formality of claiming Guiana for King James, had some success in setting up a main trading factory on the Wiapoco together with five small trading posts where English goods were exchanged for sugar cane, flax, tobacco, hardwood and dyestuffs. This little commercial network kept itself going for three years, but gold was the spur, and in its absence, despite vigorous explorations, the project petered out.

Sir Thomas Roe, later to win fame as the first English ambassador to India, was another explorer fired by Walter Ralegh's trail blazing, and Ralegh actually invested £600, which he – and Bess – could ill afford, in the expedition that Roe led to South America in 1610. Roe was an honest fellow who, as one of Queen Elizabeth's attendants, had moved in the same circles as Ralegh to win the trust not only of Walter but of the less impressionable Cecil, and Cecil went to not a little trouble to help Roe's party which left England secretly in February 1610. Cecil seems to have felt that if any man could get to the truth about Walter Ralegh's Guianan claims it was Roe, and Sir Thomas worked hard for over a year, sailing down the Amazon to approach the alleged site of Manoa from the rear.

Roe returned to England in 1611, and after his remarkably systematic and persistent investigations it was difficult to retain much faith in the accessibility or indeed in the existence of the city or empire of El Dorado. But although that myth now had to be acknowledged, even by Walter Ralegh, for the delusion it had always been, there was still the mine – or mines – which Walter's own explorations with Keymis had discovered, and no English explorer had brought back any evidence to contradict Ralegh's claims for these. Thomas Roe, indeed, had discovered in Trinidad that the Spaniards were maintaining San Thomé at the junction of the Orinoco and Caroni Rivers as a permanent military base, which indicated that they attached significance to the very area in which Ralegh insisted that gold lay, while Roe had spoken to renegade Spaniards who stated that rich mines *did* exist there.

So Roe's researches, while demolishing one of Ralegh's claims, appeared to strengthen another, and henceforward Walter's petitions from the Tower became more specific. He made no further mention of the golden city but concentrated instead on the mineral resources he claimed that he and Keymis could locate, citing the fort that the Spanish had constructed at San Thomé as substantiation of his claims. Gold, insisted Sir Walter Ralegh, lay beside the Orinoco for the digging, and with the ascendancy of Winwood's anti-Spanish policy, the diplomatic complications of trespassing on Spain's territory overseas were not allowed to loom large. James was, besides, cruelly tempted by the prospect of shiploads of South American bullion sailing into London and doing for his own regal power what Spain's treasure had, apparently, done for the absolute authority of King Philip and his successors.

So political circumstances flowed kindly at last for Sir Walter Ralegh and he was, in March 1616, finally released from the Tower of London to make preparations for the voyage he had begged so long to undertake. Another stage of Walter's long life was behind him, and though it had been the longest and hardest, it had also been the noblest and most creative. Walter had been cast down with a speed and injustice that would have destroyed many a character who was apparently more steadfast, and had started over a dozen years of imprisonment at an age when most of his contemporaries were already dead or resigning themselves to the decline of old age. But he had remained alive and more than alive. He had worked and hoped and struggled. With dignity he had come to terms with his confinement, and with bitter resolution he had fought to overcome it. *The History of the World* had overflowed with all the power

337

of a whole lifetime's work begun in the enthusiasm of youth, but Walter Ralegh had accomplished it almost as an afterthought behind bars at the end of his fifties.

It was a new man, not the broken shadow of an old one, that emerged from the Tower of London in the spring of 1616. The essential Walter was still there, boasting, posturing and, on occasions, deceiving, but his contemporaries, and posterity, had been shown beyond contradiction that there was more to the great Ralegh than just that.

Part 7

1616-18 Final Release

Oh what a noble mind is here o'erthrown!
The courtier's, soldier's, scholar's eye, tongue, sword,
The expectancy and rose of the fair state,
The glass of fashion and the mould of form,
The observ'd of all observers, quite, quite down!

Shakespeare, Hamlet. III, 2.

❧ 43 ❧

Admiral at Last

Walter Ralegh emerged from the Tower of London to prepare his voyage to Guiana – to find the face of his world
transformed. He strode round the streets of London looking at all the sights that had changed the capital since last
he had seen it over a dozen years previously. He had said farewell to a
Tudor city, the half-timbered world of King Henry VIII and his daughter
Elizabeth. He came out of captivity to discover a Palladian metropolis of
stone and mortar. Inigo Jones had started injecting into the winding,
haphazard streets of London the classical formality which still characterizes much of the city. The old royal banqueting hall where Walter had
dined so often with the queen had been torn down in 1606 to be replaced
with the be-pillared building that now graces Whitehall. In the Strand the
frontage of Durham House had been changed by Robert Cecil who had
erected the New Exchange, the two-storeyed arcade of shops that Pepys
was to enjoy half a century later, while dominating Charing Cross was
Northumberland House, the ostentatious memorial to the wealth that
Lord Henry Howard had succeeded in garnering with his own special
abilities.

The capital was larger than it had been in Walter's heyday. In Long
Acre, the narrow seven-acre field north of the Convent Garden, there was
a housing estate connected to the Strand by Drury Lane that had been
newly cobbled, and there was new building in the country around St
James's Park. It was a different city, a different generation to the one
Ralegh had known – as the new carved canopy in Westminster Abbey
emphasized. There lay the two redoubtable daughters of Henry VIII,
peacefully side by side in death as they had never been in life, Mary dour
and cold, Elizabeth, Ralegh's great mistress, sharp-featured, alert and
wide-eyed as ever.

Walter Ralegh himself, released to organize the voyage which, successful or otherwise, must surely be his last, was something of a sight to be gawked at in 1616. Tall, spare and upright, he was an authentic Elizabethan, the archetypal courtier of the great queen, preserved by her successor's vicious aspic to stride the streets of London as a grizzled *revenant*, the only survivor of that group of men who had thrashed the Armada. We have a dapper picture of Walter at this time proudly clasping his commander's baton for the Guiana voyage, his beard grey, his high brow wrinkled, but his eyes, like those of his dead queen, as piercing as ever.

Yet, though he put a brave face on it, Walter Ralegh was in 1616 weaker than he would allow himself to admit. He was over sixty and had had another stroke before he left the Tower. He had also become, with all his elixirs, something of a hypochondriac. So much depended on finding that mine in Guiana, and it was a strain keeping up the pretence that he and Lawrence Keymis really possessed definite information as to its whereabouts. The final act in Ralegh's life was to be flawed fatally by this basic fraud, a falsehood that was part wishful thinking and part deliberate deception in which Lawrence Keymis connived – for there was no mine, simply a belief in its existence.

Walter was still, furthermore, under sentence of death, going everywhere with a keeper as he had back in 1592 when sorting out the spoils of the *Madre de Dios*, forbidden 'to resort either to His Majesty's court, the queen's or the prince's, nor to go into any public assemblies whatsoever'. His job was simply to organize his intended voyage and so, eight days after his release, Walter was commissioning Phineas Pett in Deptford, the shipbuilder who had made such a good job of the *Prince Royal*, to build him a new warship in the *Revenge* class, slim, swift and heavily armed, to be known as the *Destiny*.[1] This was to be the flagship for Walter's last voyage.

A gambler all his life, Walter now staked everything on this final desperate fling – though most of what he had to risk was Bess's. Did *she* believe his traveller's tales? She had known Walter long enough to realize how easily he could outwit himself, but it was the only chance, so she worked hard to scrounge from her relatives the money that her husband needed. She called in £3,000 of the Sherborne compensation she had lent out to the Countess of Bedford to gather interest and sold the Mitcham estate that was her own property for £2,500, while her relatives the Earls of Huntingdon, Pembroke and Arundel chipped in with no less than £15,000 as sureties. Walter sold everything he possessed and, cajoling up to £50 out of each gentleman volunteer that he could rally to his flag, he managed to round off the capital invested in the expedition at some £30,000. This was sufficient to raise a fleet of over a dozen vessels, several of them very heavily armed.

But if the quality of the ships which it took Walter twelve months to gather was excellent, the thousand or so seamen he recruited for the expedition proved less satisfactory – 'the very scum of the world' he was to call them.[2] There were to be riots at Gravesend between the sailors and townspeople, and many of the 'gentlemen volunteers' also turned out to be riff-raff. Captain John Ferne was a privateer with an unsavoury reputation, while Captain Bailey was another pirate who was to prove a veritable Judas. There were all too few of the valued old Ralegh connections, Sir Warham St Leger, with whose father Walter had shared his first Irish command, George Ralegh his nephew, William Herbert, one of Bess's connections with the Pembrokes, Edward Hastings, the Earl of Huntingdon's brother, the faithful Keymis and Walter's own son, young Wat, now in his early twenties and named as captain of the *Destiny*.

Walter's first prose work written in the Tower in 1607 had been a set of *Instructions to his Son*, composed for young Wat's benefit before the boy went off to Oxford, an austere set of principles regimented into a morality that Walter had never observed himself and which young Wat wasted little time keeping. When his father had packed him off to Paris in 1612 under the care of Ben Jonson Wat had shocked the most libertine of Parisians by 'setting the favours [or love tokens] of damsels on a codpiece' and he had also got his tutor dead drunk – not a difficult task – and then wheeled him spread-eagled through the streets on a barrow crying out for every Catholic to hear that this was the best crucifix they could find in Paris.

Jonson told that story against himself, obviously delighted with his charge's blasphemous behaviour, while John Aubrey, always good for a story to capture the spirit if not the literal truth about a character, had an anecdote to match it. Walter and his son were invited to a dinner party together. Young Wat was,

> . . . very demure at least half dinner time. Then said he:
> 'I, this morning, not having the fear of God before my eyes, but by the instigation of the devil, went to a whore. I was very eager of her, kissed and embraced her, and went to enjoy her, but she thrust me from her and vowed I should not "For your father lay with me but an hour ago".'
> Sir Walter, being so strangely surprised and put out of his countenance at so great a table, gives his son a damned blow over the face. His son, as rude as he was, would not strike his father, but strikes over the face of the gentleman that sat next to him and said:
> 'Box about. 'Twill come to my father anon.'[3]

In April 1615, a year before Wat began helping his father organize the Guiana expedition, he had had to flee from England for a time after he had wounded an opponent in a duel. He was a full-blooded young man who obviously earned the deep love of both his parents and friends, but he was hot-headed and undiplomatic – and this recklessness held the gravest implications for the success of Walter Ralegh's venture. For though the Guiana fleet as it assembled around its flagship the *Destiny* took on the character of a powerful fighting force aimed at Spanish power in the Orinoco Basin, the strongest limitation imposed upon Sir Walter Ralegh by the king was a prohibition against fighting any Spaniards he might encounter. In the orders James gave Ralegh he pointedly erased the usual words 'trusty and well-beloved', emphasized that Walter was being despatched unpardoned 'under peril of the law' and franked his commission not with the Great Seal but with the less exalted Privy Seal. So Walter Ralegh was gambling his all, while King James was hedging his bets.

The reason for King James's ambiguous endorsement of Ralegh's incursion into the heart of the Spanish Empire was, as so often in that king's affairs, the consequence of a personal relationship which quite unbalanced him: Henry Howard, Robert Carr, George Villiers, all had had their impact on the king, and Walter Ralegh, a helpless third party, was rocked by the wash they left as they swept through the royal emotions. Now Walter was again threatened in this arbitrary fashion and this time by a character cast even more than Henry Howard in the mould of the pantomime villain, a dark and stumpy Spaniard, Don Diego Sarmiento de Acuna, ambassador to the English court since 1613 and better known to posterity by the title he was subsequently to receive, Count Gondomar. Gondomar was a relative of the Spaniard Pedro Sarmiento de Gamboa whom Ralegh had captured in 1586 and who first fired – or poisoned – Walter's imagination with tales of El Dorado. Now, thirty years later, Gondomar was to avenge his kinsman's capture.

It is difficult to see from his portrait what it was about Gondomar that captivated the king of England. Some said that he could rage in a fashion that terrified James – but he could also behave with a strange clownishness that tickled James's sense of humour. He flattered James with precision, allowing the wisest fool in Christendom to correct his Latin pronunciation with the apology that while he, a poor ambassador, could only speak Latin 'like a king', James could speak it 'like a Master of Arts'. He professed a love of things English – collecting twenty chests of tapestries and forty chests of books to take with him back to Spain – and he was a formidable conversationalist, talking his way into the royal confidence to such an extent that he was able subsequently to thank the king for making him an adviser not only to the Privy Council but also to James's own inner ring of confidants. He knew when to bribe James – offering him 2,000 ounces of solid plate – and he knew how to reveal his Castilian firmness, which he did in 1616 and 1617 as Walter Ralegh assembled the most powerful fighting force then ready for active service in European waters.

James was embarrassed. He was unwilling to forgo the possibility of solving all his financial problems with shiploads of gold from the Orinoco. But he was not prepared either to offend his Spanish friend, particularly as Gondomar represented the best channel for securing a Spanish dowry on reasonable terms for young Prince Charles. So James tried to have the best of both worlds, allowing Ralegh to sail, but forbidding him to get involved in hostilities with Spain; handing Ralegh a commission by which he, the king, would receive all taxes and duties on whatever Walter brought back plus one fifth of all bullion, but handing over to Gondomar a precise inventory of Ralegh's ships, armaments, ports of call and estimated dates of arrival. This was the cruellest deception of all – a kiss of Judas, for when Walter's men reached Guiana they were to find among the Spanish documents they captured there all these details of their strategy and plans passed on by Gondomar to Madrid and thence, in advance, across the Atlantic. As Walter was to remark with some justice 'All hands were loose, but mine bound'.

But it simply was not in the nature of the man to play safe. The very fact that his hands were bound while all others were free lent sport to the game, zest to the challenge, and Walter was, besides, not known as 'the fox' for nothing. He was not unaware of the game that the king was playing, for James's friendship with Gondomar was one of the scandals of London, while the purpose for which the *Destiny* was being built down in Deptford was no secret either. It was only sensible for Walter to assume that Gondomar, even without the special help that James extended him, could guess much of what Ralegh's plans were, and to anticipate that the ambassador would relay his suspicions on to his masters in Madrid – as George Carew wrote to Thomas Roe, now at the court of the Great Mongul:[4] 'The alarm of his [Ralegh's] journey is flown into Spain, and, as he tells me, sea forces are prepared to lie for him. But he is nothing appalled by the report, for he will be a good fleet and well manned.'

Walter knew that if he arrived home with enough gold dug from a mine or stolen from the Spanish treasure fleet then he would have achieved a triumph which – given the condition of the royal finances – Gondomar's special relationship with James could not cancel out. But if he came home empty handed, or worse, having fought the Spaniards to no avail, he would need some special relationships of his own – and this was the reason for some private negotiations that he conducted before he set sail for Guiana.

Ralegh had always enjoyed a special relationship with the French. The fact that he had fought in the armies of Henri of Navarre, the man who had emerged victorious from the Religious Wars, gave him strong political links with France's new Bourbon dynasty, and it was to the French that Walter turned now. He needed a safety net, an asylum against the possibility of his voyage to South America proving unsuccessful, and so he spoke to the French ambassador in London, Des Marets, who offered him a French privateering commission. If Walter captured any foreign ships or treasure in Guiana or on the way to or from Guiana, he could, if he wished, bring them safely into a French port.

Ralegh, after some consideration, accepted the commission, for it would mean that if anything went wrong in Guiana he could return across the Atlantic to a foreign, but not too distant port of refuge from which he could discover what James's reactions were. The French ambassador came away from his interview with Ralegh with the impression that the old pirate could even be recruited into the king of France's service, and he put forward a suggested method of collaboration that Walter actually passed on to the Privy Council – the possibility that the French might join up with Walter's invasion of Guiana and engage in diversionary hostilities with the Spaniards while the English got on quietly with digging up their gold. James appears to have considered this scheme along with other alternatives to a head-on confrontation with Spain – the great fleet marshalling in England was the talk of Europe and both Savoy and Venice put in bids for the services of *Sir Vate Rolo*[4] – but in the end James considered that he had least to lose from allowing Ralegh to set off in the fashion which he had already betrayed to Gondomar.

Only later was it to become apparent how fatally compromised the Guiana expedition had been before ever it set sail from Plymouth on 12 June 1617. But even in ignorance of James's treachery many doubted whether it was worth Sir Walter Ralegh's while to come back. With nothing to his name in England but a death penalty hanging over his head, he would do better, people thought, to turn pirate with his fleet and live off the high seas for the rest of his days.

44

The Voyage

The West Country gave Walter Ralegh a send-off in the old style. The mayor of Plymouth was voted 'by a general consent' a generous entertainment allowance to fête the man who had once ruled Devon and Cornwall as his own little kingdom and who was still well beloved among his own. The worthies of the Guildhall that was graced with the portrait of Drake and the arms of Hawkins gave the sole survivor of that heroic generation a grand reception, and then had a drummer beat a tattoo right to the gangplank of the *Destiny* as Sir Walter went aboard. It was over a decade since the privateers had been able proudly to sail in and out of the West Country ports, and Walter Ralegh provided a nostalgic reminder not only of past glory but of profits past as well.

The final preparations of the voyage had certainly recaptured the last minute panic that characterized many an Elizabethan privateering venture run short of funds. Captain Pennington of *The Star* had had to leave his ship at the Isle of Wight to beg cash from Bess Ralegh to pay for his bread, Captain Bailey had also found difficulty paying his grocery bills and Walter had had to sell what was left of the family plate to get Captain Whitney and the *Encounter* out of the hands of creditors. The ships' chandlers of the West Country had heard the rumours that Walter Ralegh might turn stateless pirate and were anxious to get their accounts settled while they could still be sure of their money.

Walter's orders to his fleet, however, were not those of a man about to turn renegade. They were godly in the extreme, establishing a regular routine of devotion twice a day with a psalm being sung to God whenever the watch was set. There were all sorts of commandments to safeguard sailors who had not been in the tropics before. Walter did not want to see another of his men devoured by alligators before his eyes, so sailors should only bathe where the Indians considered it safe to do so. There

347

was to be no sleeping on the ground, no sampling of unknown fruit – and no carnal enjoyment of 'any woman, be she Christian or heathen, upon pain of death'.[1]

The weather in 1617 was unkind to Walter. Scarcely had his ships left Plymouth on 12 June than they were blown back fiercely into the harbour, and though they made a little more progress on their second attempt, a storm then drove them into Falmouth. Taking advantage of this un-expected landfall to discharge sailors who, just in this short trip down the coast, had displayed both incompetence and insubordination, Walter set off for a third time, only to be struck by a tremendous gale off the Scilly Isles and be driven north to take refuge at the beginning of August 1617 in the harbour of Cork. It was a sour start to the enterprise, particularly as Walter had to impose on the hospitality of Robert Boyle, the man who now ruled from Lismore, the castle that Walter had had refurbished but had never enjoyed, estates even larger than the Munster fiefdom that had once been part of the Ralegh empire.

Yet Boyle, now Lord Boyle, proved a generous host. He had secured Walter's Irish lands back in 1602 for just £1,500 and had, after the pacifi-cation of Ireland, made them into a flourishing concern, so it was the least he could do in 1617 to lend his unexpected guest £350 cash. He also took Ralegh out for a day or so's falconry around Lismore, and provided his fleet with a hundred oxen, many other stores, fresh beer and a fine 32-gallon cask of whisky. He discussed the running of his estates with Walter and enlisted his support against that ever-troublesome entrepreneur Henry Pyne who had maintained a complicated dispute deriving from the Arcadian days when Walter lived at Youghal and went up the Blackwater to swap sonnets with Edmund Spenser. Pyne had brought little profit to Walter and now he plagued his successor. The old themes, and especially the less cheering ones, kept recurring in the twilight of Sir Walter Ralegh's life.

By 19 August, when his fleet was finally out at sea again and heading south in good order, Walter must have hoped that his course was now set fair as far as Guiana at least. After his long years in the Tower, the months of preparations and now these last weeks of delays, he was finally a free agent on the open ocean. He could rejoice in his liberty at last.

But in 1617 Walter Ralegh could never again be totally free, for even sailing on the wide Atlantic his fleet was reeling out an invisible thread that tied it back to London, James 1 and Gondomar, and every so often that thread twitched viciously to remind Walter that he was still in its power. When Bailey, one of his more dubious captains, caught up with four French ships carrying rich cargoes of fish oil he tried to seize the vessels as prizes, claiming that the oil had been stolen. But Ralegh, mindful of his sovereign's orders, could condone no privateering and insisted on paying the French in full for the oil and small pinnace that was taken. This infuriated Bailey and a further incident increased his anger. Seeking fresh water and provisions at Lancerota in the Canary Islands, three sailors from the English fleet were killed by the Spanish, and Walter forbade any violence: quite apart from James's instructions, there was in the harbour of Lancerota a defenceless English merchantman who would have suffered and Ralegh retaliated against the Spaniards.

But Captain Bailey had now had enough of his admiral's restraint. He took his ship back to England and, since he could hardly admit that it was he who had tried to turn pirate, he implied that Walter was guilty of that crime. 'He doth not charge him with any fact committed', wrote George Carew to Thomas Roe. But as a result of what Bailey had said, 'there is a doubtful opinion held of Sir Walter and those that malice him boldly affirm him to be a pirate, which for my part I will never believe'.[2]

Honest George and anti-Spanish Winwood would always think the best of Ralegh. But not all on the Privy Council were of their opinion. Sir John Digby, who had been James's ambassador to Spain and who was now the latest possessor of Sherborne, assumed the worst, and so did Sir John Lake, another privy councillor, who actually visited Gondomar to apologize for 'so atrocious a wickedness as this' and who also passed on to the Spaniard a remarkable message from the king: 'His Majesty is very disposed and determined against Ralegh, and will join the king of Spain in ruining him, but he wishes this resolution to be kept secret for the moment at least.'[3]

Gondomar crowed over this in a letter to Madrid, but he was to laugh on the other side of his face when Captain Reeks, the commander of the defenceless merchantman which had been inside Lancerota harbour as Ralegh restrained his aggressive captains, got back to England and told his tale. If it had not been for Walter curbing Bailey's bellicosity there would have been a fight – and Reeks's ship would have been the loser. Righteously indignant, the Privy Council flung Captain Bailey into jail for his perjury, though councillors Lake and Digby at least must have been moved more by embarrassment than by zeal for Walter Ralegh's good name.

Meanwhile, back in the Canaries, Walter had found hospitality on the island of Gomera at the hands of the Spanish governor's wife, a lady who turned out to be half English (her mother had been a Stafford). Hearing that the English fleet had fallen prey to illness she sent baskets of oranges, lemons, grapes, pomegranates and figs – exactly the food sick sailors needed. Ralegh responded with gifts of ambergris, rosewater, a fine ruff and 'a very excellent picture of Mary Magdalen' – not the only example of his taste for Catholic piety – and the lady's reply to this was more fruit, a basket full of fresh white bread, two dozen plump hens, unlimited supplies of fresh drinking water and, kindest token of all – a letter from the Spanish governor to Count Gondomar 'witnessing how nobly we behaved ourselves and how justly we had dealt with the inhabitants of the island'.[4]

These civilized courtesies are the kindest episode related in all Walter Ralegh's long journal of his voyage to Guiana, twenty-three wide parchment sheets closely scrawled in his own crabbed hand and vividly re-creating the texture of his last expedition. After Gomera the going got tough, and notwithstanding the presents of fresh fruit which Ralegh preserved in boxes of sand, sickness began to rage through the fleet. Ralegh had kept his first expedition to Guiana in the pink of health. Now his touch, and his luck, deserted him. By nightfall on the very day his ships left the Canaries fifty men were out of action on the *Destiny* alone, and forty-two were actually to die before land was sighted again. Captain Pigott, the chief assayer brought along to test ore samples, died, so did Bess's relative Edward Hastings and, saddest loss of all, John Talbot, the schoolmaster who had stayed in the Tower beside Walter throughout all his years of captivity and who had slaved over *The History of the World* so lovingly, also succumbed. Ready to follow his master to the ends of the earth, he died before ever sighting the promised land of which Walter had talked and written so much.

Every ship in the fleet had its fatalities, and their effect was disastrous. Caught in the storms of the mid-Atlantic the scarce-manned vessels received a severe buffeting, wallowing for days without the hands to shift their sails. One went down, and Walter Ralegh himself was pole-axed by a fever which prostrated him for four weeks. He was unable to take any solid food, so had it not been for the fruit of Gomera 'I could not have lived'.[5]

With favourable winds the run from the Canaries to Guiana could have been accomplished in as little as two weeks. But, with the storms that the weakened crews had to struggle through, it took nearer six. Not until 11 November 1617 was the mainland of South America finally reached, and when the battered English fleet dropped anchor three days later it presented a sorry sight. Walter was still on his sick-bed and so feeble he could scarcely hold his pen to write to Bess:

Sweetheart, I can yet write unto you but with a weak hand, for I have suffered the most violent calenture [fever] for fifteen days that ever man did and lived. But God that gave me a strong heart in all my adversities hath also now strengthened it in the hell-fire of heat.[6]

Walter sent Bess the good news that young Wat was well, and with the messenger that he despatched home with his letters and the worst of the invalids went a report entitled 'News of Sir Walter Ralegh from the River of Caliana'. It was an optimistic little treatise intended to put the best light possible on the promising features of Guiana. But the captain charged to carry it, Peter Alley, was a poor envoy, for when he got back to Portsmouth in February 1618 he quite overshadowed the written report with tales of the terrible pestilence and hurricanes that had nearly destroyed their expedition. Gondomar and his cronies were naturally cock-a-hoop, while even Ralegh's friends found it difficult to credit Walter with much chance of survival, let alone success in his hunt for the gold that had to save his life. As Sir Edward Conway told John Carleton, all Ralegh's letters from Guiana 'come charged with misfortunes and tears'.

❧ 45 ❧

Debacle

'To tell you that I might be here king of the Indians were a vanity', wrote Walter to his wife as he arrived in South America. 'But my name hath still lived among them.'[1] As the old campaigner was carried ashore to be fed on fresh pineapples and a little game thoroughly cooked, the Guianans who cherished his memory arrived to pay homage. Though Leonard, further down the coast could not be found, Harry, who had known Walter for two years in the Tower and was now also a chief, came bearing roasted mullet, plantains, pistachios and other tributes. Harry had almost forgotten his English, but he had not forgotten his master.

After the desperate voyage it was a reassuring welcome. Lying beneath the Caribbean palms, enjoying the fresh sea breezes instead of the foul odours wafting up from the bowels of the *Destiny*, Walter slowly recovered his strength. At sea he had been so debilitated he had been unable to eat anything except 'now and then a stewed prune'. But by the beginning of December 1617 he was organizing the expedition that would sail up the Orinoco – 150 sailors and 250 soldiers in five shallow draught vessels, though there could be no question now of Walter leading the party in person. His age had caught up with him cruelly and he was needing to lie down too often to contemplate the rigours of a jungle voyage. He would have to stay with the main body of the fleet patrolling to make sure that no Spanish ships arrived to bottle up the river party in the Orinoco.

The problem was who should lead the river party. Sir Warham St Leger, the obvious choice, was far sicker than Ralegh and would, like his commander, have to stay in his litter with the fleet. Young Wat, though fighting fit, was too imprudent to be given such weighty responsibility, for it was certain that there were Spaniards at San Thomé, and Wat was not the type, when tempted by the prospect of a scrap, to lend much heed to King James's wish to avoid violence. George Ralegh, Walter's cousin, was another possible leader, but he was also too red-blooded for the mission, and so it was to the Oxford don, Lawrence Keymis, that was entrusted command over the 400 Englishmen in their five little ships.

The academic was, in the circumstances, the best man for the job. He had proved his loyalty to Walter by staying close to him in both triumph and adversity for a quarter of a century; he was not a man dedicated to war for its own sake; and no one on the expedition, Walter included, had had more opportunity to discover the whereabouts of the crucial gold mine – or mines – that were the object of the entire venture. Keymis had travelled with Walter in 1595 and had in 1596 been in command of the small follow-up expedition sent to explore the Orinoco more fully.

On 10 December 1617, Walter Ralegh's 400 Englishmen set off with Keymis into the maze of the Orinoco Delta under detailed instructions which stood by both the letter and the spirit of King James's wishes. Reminding Keymis that George Ralegh, who was given military command of the soldiers and sailors, was inexperienced, Walter emphasized how much depended on Keymis's own good judgement as overall commander. He was not to approach or pass close by the Spanish town of San Thomé but to avoid it completely, to locate his mine and to use his soldiers only as a block between the site of his excavations and the Spaniards. If the situation proved too difficult for sustained excavations, Keymis should withdraw, bringing with him just one or two baskets of ore as an indication of the treasure available. To tangle with the Spaniards would be dangerous, 'for I know (a few gentlemen excepted) what a scum of men you have'. In the meantime Walter would stay to guard the rear of the party's advance to keep any hostile forces from following Keymis up the Orinoco, the conclusion to his orders forsaking politic caution to ring with Elizabethan bravado in the old style. Keymis, Ralegh said, could be certain that on his return he would find him, 'dead or alive, and if you find not the ships there, yet shall you find their ashes, for I will fire with the galleons if it come to extremity, but run away I never will.'[2]

Having set everything down on paper and wished his men God speed, Walter could do no more than wait – and carry out his own part of the plan. He took his fleet to Puncto Gallo (now Point Hicacos), the south-west tip of Trinidad, cruising up and down at action stations ready to engage the enemy fleet. He landed on Trinidad itself to explore again the great pitch lake and, after an attempt to·trade with the Spaniards there ended with cross-fire that cost the life of a sailor and a boy, he confined himself to searching for the medicinal plants and herbs he loved, while look-outs kept watch for Spanish attackers both by land and by sea.

Yet, Walter Ralegh had in truth little to fear from the Spaniards, for though Gondomar had faithfully passed on to Madrid all the relevant information about Walter's expedition, a combination of inefficiency and disbelief meant that his warnings were scarcely acted on. Guiana had never been the centre of Spanish concern in the New World, and though old Berreo's son was now governor-general of New Granada, he did not share his father's obsession with El Dorado, allowing Dutch and French traders to range Guiana in comparative freedom. It was difficult for him or for any of the Spanish authorities to believe that the incredibly detailed facts that Gondomar had passed on to them were not part of some English plot. Why should King James sanction such an assembly of military might and then betray to the Spanish ambassador exactly where and when this expedition was planning to invade the Spanish Empire unless he was attempting some decoy from Ralegh's real objective – possibly Virginia again, somewhere in the Jamestown area?

So Walter Ralegh waited off Trinidad through December 1617 and January 1618 with little to occupy him except his medicinal plants and worries as to how Lawrence Keymis was fulfilling the responsibility entrusted to him. Every day patrols went out to cross-question local tribesmen and, after a month, jungle rumours filtered back that the English had occupied San Thomé and that two English captains had fallen. That did not sound promising. Keymis was not supposed to approach the Spanish fort. But then, a full two months after Keymis and his men had set off up the mysterious river – on 14 February 1618 – came the definite news that Walter Ralegh knew was his death warrant. The English and the Spanish had indeed clashed, the Spaniards had been expelled from San Thomé, the fort had been occupied and, on top of all that, young Wat Ralegh had been killed.

It was a terrible blow, both politically and personally, for Sir Walter Ralegh. This flagrant contradiction of the expedition's pacific instructions – with no gold to show for it – meant the block or, at the very best, life imprisonment for him. While young Wat's death totally undermined the personal reserves with which Walter could have steeled himself against the inevitable. With the loss of his elder son the spirit which neither Elizabeth nor James at their most vicious had been able to conquer finally snapped. Walter Ralegh was a broken man and was to remain so until his death. Wat had been born at almost the same time as his father's involvement in Guiana, the two passions had grown together and helped sustain Walter through his years in the Tower – and now both, together, were cut down at the very moment that should have been the triumphant climax of a lifetime. There was nothing more left to live for. Walter Ralegh set down the pen with which he had been scribbling so industriously to chronicle the realization of his supreme ambition. His diary stopped with the arrival of Keymis's fateful letter.

What had gone wrong up the Orinoco River? Had Keymis had a brainstorm? Had his men got out of hand? Or had both Keymis and the 400 soldiers and sailors sent off in his care been despatched on a hopeless mission in the first place? Had their errand been a fool's errand, and the gold they were looking for fool's gold?

The answer is simple – and sad. Despite all the failings of Keymis, and despite all the failings of his men – notably young Wat – the essential blame must rest on the shoulders of Sir Walter Ralegh himself, for Walter had gambled against odds so overwhelming that men less courageous would never have ventured in the first place, while men more humane would have spared their families, friends, and followers the misery and death that the catastrophe involved.

The gamble went back to the ore samples that Walter had brought back from the Orinoco in 1595. The assayers had pronounced then that they were gold-bearing, but in the absence of any other first hand evidence of successful mining activity in the area, three important additional questions should have been asked. Were the gold traces they contained flukes, totally unrepresentative of the mineral resources of the locality? Were they perhaps representative but uneconomic, so that tons of ore would have to be processed in order to produce negligible amounts of gold? Most important, were the assayers' reports in themselves honest? Were they not, perhaps, only telling Walter Ralegh what they knew he wanted to hear?

If any single one of these objections were sustained, the entire Guiana expedition became a waste of energy, time, life and money, yet Walter Ralegh simply ignored them. On at least one occasion he offered the assayers he commissioned a special bonus if they *could* find ore in his samples – an active inducement to falsifying the facts; he had *no* evidence that his samples were representative of the area in which they were found, and he undertook *no* tests to discover whether they would be too expensive to process. The acid test of his confidence in his own claims was the eight years between 1595 and 1603 when he did not, as he had done in Virginia, send out a succession of regular expeditions to Guiana, but instead despatched Keymis – once – to prospect further. Not until Walter Ralegh was locked up in the Tower did Guiana suddenly become such an important goal for him, and then, of course, it possessed an attraction which outweighed all other practical considerations – it was a road to liberty. 'What will not one in captivity promise to regain his freedom?' asked James Howell in June 1618, 'Who would not promise not only mines but mountains of gold for liberty?'

That was the crucial fallacy of Walter Ralegh's last voyage. He simply did not possess the evidence that he claimed to have gathered, and it is not surprising that by the end of the 1617–18 expedition some of his closest associates had come to the conclusion that he was a confidence trickster or at best, a deluded old man.

According to Walter there was supposed to be a specific spot from which he and Keymis had in 1595 picked up the samples that were pronounced gold-bearing. But nowhere did he specify exactly where that spot was and when Keymis, the man who was supposed to be in on the secret, sailed up the Orinoco in December 1617 and January 1618 he patently did not know what he was looking for. He blundered, furthermore, into the Spanish fort at San Thomé, thus casting still further doubt on Ralegh's story, for again according to Walter – and this was a most important claim in the light of King James's anxieties – his gold mine could be reached without coming into contact with the Spaniards.

There have been several attempts to explain Ralegh's Guiana fiasco of 1617–18 – forgetfulness on Keymis's part, a belief in the existence of two mines or even three mines – but all must return to basic dishonesty on the part of Walter Ralegh himself. Whatever he claimed to put a good complexion on his first expedition in 1595, he had never discovered a specific gold mine. He had found samples which he took to indicate that gold could be found in a certain area near the Orinoco River, and the purpose of Keymis's expedition the following year was to locate a more precise position for this. Had Keymis made any specific discoveries in 1596 Ralegh would certainly have announced them triumphantly then, or else set about exploiting his secret knowledge as rapidly as possible before the Spaniards in the area forestalled him. But Keymis could produce no treasure chart, as his inept jungle wanderings of 1617–18 proved, and so the object of Ralegh's last voyage was born of his fertile imagination and frustrated ambition confined within the Tower of London between 1603 and 1616. Walter was compelled by Thomas Roe's explorations to stop talking of El Dorado, while fruitless explorations of the Orinoco region by other adventurers made it impossible to claim assistance for yet another vague prospecting expedition. Nothing short of a specific mine could possibly induce investors to back Walter or persuade the government to release him from the Tower, and so it was a specific mine that Walter offered. At his most convincing when lying, Walter Ralegh reached the very summit of his propagandizing powers preaching on behalf of Guiana.

Once released from the Tower Walter had been caught up by the momentum of his own deceit – hence his willingness to consider alternative objectives on behalf of Savoy or Venice and his interest in a privateering commission from France – and hence, too, his particular distress at being laid low with fever when he arrived in the Caribbean. It meant that Lawrence Keymis would have to search alone for the ore vein, and this was the reason for the gamble that Keymis took on 2 January 1618, when he gave orders for his party to land on the banks of the Orinoco only a few miles away from San Thomé. There was a better chance of picking up clues to the whereabouts of any mines or ore veins from the Spaniards, some of whom were said to be disaffected, than from wandering around the empty jungle. Camping well away from the town appeared to make the risk of a confrontation less likely.

But Keymis reckoned without the Spaniards, understandably alarmed at the large size of the English force, and without the impetuosity of young Wat Ralegh, burning to win his spurs. A dozen Spanish regulars made a midnight attack on a corner of the English bivouac, and Wat responded to their cries of *Perros Ingleses*! (English dogs) by rallying a company of pikemen to fight them off. Not content, however, with repulsing the enemy, Wat then pursued the Spaniards back to the very gates of St Thomé with the English all following him, and, when he saw his comrades hesitate at the sight of the citadel, leapt forward crying, 'Come on, my hearts! This is the mine you must expect! They that look for any other are fools!'[3] Thrusting his sword into the air the boy charged, to be felled almost immediately by a Spanish musket ball. But enthused by his heroism, the English continued the assault, broke into St Thomé and chased out the garrison. The citadel was theirs and its governor, with four other Spanish officers, lay dead.

Young Wat was buried with full honours as the hero of the hour – though he, more than anyone, had been responsible for the attack that was his father's death warrant, and it was nearly a week before poor Keymis could steel himself to write to Sir Walter with the news of the fatal night. In some attempt to excuse himself he wrote that the Spaniards had moved the site of San Thomé 20 miles downstream – but that was just a feeble lie, and then he betrayed his master's own far greater lie by failing totally to locate the much-promised gold mine, or even to make a plausible attempt at doing so. With George Ralegh and a special party of pioneers he embarked on a fruitless sally up the Orinoco, going further and further upstream in a desperate attempt to discover some indication that the whole venture had not been a fraud.

But he failed. He returned to Walter Ralegh with just two gold ingots looted from the Spaniards, three Negroes, two Indians and several tons of stolen tobacco – and left behind him 250 men dead and the Spanish settlement of San Thomé in ashes. For his master when he met him he had only excuses and apologies – and Walter dismissed them all with cold scorn. When Keymis tried to set down his justifications in a letter to be sent back to England Walter angrily declined to endorse his report. 'You have undone me by your obstinacy,' said Ralegh, 'and I will not favour or colour in any way your former folly.'[4]

It was a heartless way to treat an old retainer and friend, especially one who had devoted his life to giving some plausibility to Walter's falsehood, and Keymis took his master's rebukes very hard. He retired to his cabin humiliated, and shortly afterwards a shot rang out. Walter sent a servant to find out who had fired and Keymis, through his door, replied that he had been cleaning his weapons and had discharged a pistol that had been too long charged. But half an hour later Keymis's serving boy went into his master's cabin to find blood on the floor. Keymis had shot himself but the ball had bounced off his rib, so the former scholar of Balliol had taken a knife, inserted it precisely through his rib cage and stabbed himself to death through the heart.

It was the final rejection, the depth of degradation for Walter Ralegh. To have the blood of his son on his head was tragic enough. But it was even worse to know that he had brought about Keymis's death not so much from his fit of displeasure but from a deliberate piece of deception contrived over many years. The reckoning was bitter. The expedition broke up before Walter's very eyes, Captain Whitney, for whose sake the Ralegh plate had been sold, deserting to turn pirate, Captain Woollaston joining him, and the crew of the *Destiny*, who mutinied when the ship was left alone in the Atlantic, forcing Walter to set them ashore at Kinsale in Ireland. Since Keymis's one positive discovery had been Spanish documents in San Thomé that copied word for word the information that Ralegh had given King James before he sailed, Walter could have no illusions as to the fate awaiting him when he sailed into Plymouth harbour.

But as before, from the ashes of his destruction rose Walter's phoenix of life, for while no one would have blamed him now for deserting his responsibilities to turn pirate or beachcomber in the Caribbean, or to end his career in France as he had begun it, he did not flinch from what he saw as his duty. He had given his word to return home and friends had pledged large sums to the king as a guarantee of his good behaviour. Walter would not let them down. He had sunk low, but now his courage returned – and so did his creativity. In the depths of his misery he wrote to his wife a letter whose beauty soared above his despair, breaking to her as gently as was possible the death of their son – and preparing her for his own death that he now knew was to come:

I was loth to write, because I knew not how to comfort you: and, God knows, I never knew what sorrow meant till now. All that I can say to you is that you must obey the will and providence of God: and remember that the queen's majesty bare the loss of Prince Henry with a magnanimous heart. . . . Comfort your heart (dearest Bess) I shall sorrow for us both. I shall sorrow the less, because I have not long to sorrow, because not long to live. . . .[5]

❧ 46 ❧

Royal Welcome

When Count Gondomar heard from Madrid of the burning of San Thomé King James was occupied with other matters. The royal guards had orders to admit no one. But the Spanish ambassador was not used to the king of England keeping him waiting, and he had, besides only one word to say – which he burst in on James to repeat three times, '*Piratas! Piratas! Piratas!*'

Then on 23 May 1618, one of the English captains reached home with his own version of events, and it reflected little more creditably on Sir Walter Ralegh. His account made clear the deliberate deceit of which both Ralegh and Keymis had been guilty, and more seriously from Walter Ralegh's point of view, he bore back to England letters to Ralph Winwood setting out Walter's own justification of his actions, only to discover that Winwood was dead. The Puritan first secretary, the solid foe of Spain and friend to Walter, had succumbed to a fever the previous October. So Ralegh's only ally left on the Privy Council was George Carew – and he had to combat not only James's now notorious affection for Gondomar but Spanish pensioners like Sir John Digby, and, worst of all, George Villiers, who had been ennobled with the title of Buckingham and had become the leading advocate of a Spanish marriage for his young friend Prince Charles – since Prince Henry's death the heir to the throne of England.

On 11 June 1618, ten days before Walter Ralegh sailed into Plymouth, a royal proclamation appeared denouncing the 'hostile invasion of the town of San Thomé' which had 'maliciously broken and infringed the Peace and Amity' between England and 'our dear brother the King of Spain'. The lord admiral issued orders for Walter's arrest.

But when the *Destiny* tied up in Plymouth harbour on 21 June 1618, and Walter Ralegh stepped ashore to render safe the £15,000 worth of sureties pledged by the Earls of Arundel and Pembroke against his good behaviour, he was not taken into custody. He was allowed to range freely around the port, to write and despatch letters to London and to be reunited with Bess without Sir Lewis Stukeley, the vice-admiral of Devon arresting him. Stukeley, who was a kinsman of Walter's had definitely received the lord admiral's instructions, but for nearly a month Walter remained a free man – or rather a man in limbo, for he knew, as did everyone else, of James's and Gondomar's fury and of the fatal sentence suspended more menacingly than ever over his head.

The problem was that whatever James's anger – which stemmed as much from embarrassment as from any genuine outrage – it was not easy to wreak the vengeance that the royal displeasure demanded. Largely thanks to James himself, Walter Ralegh was no longer the vilified bogey-man that the crowds of London had jeered in 1603 – the reverse, in fact. Even the most abject Spanish pensioners like Digby appreciated the popular discontent that would be stirred up by arresting the great Sir Walter, let alone executing him or packing him off to Spain to be punished there as James had promised Gondomar. Feelings were running high against the Spaniard in London, as was demonstrated when one of his coachmen carelessly ran down a child in Chancery Lane: a furious mob several thousand strong attacked the Spanish Embassy and would have ransacked it had not the lord chief justice, the lord mayor and the aldermen of London all intervened to calm passions down.

Gondomar was due to go back to Spain in July 1618 at the end of his tour of duty, and once he was on his way to Madrid the problems raised by Walter's awkwardly honest return could be more easily dealt with. Evidence could be collected to build up a solid case against Ralegh, while any punishment would look less obviously Spanish-inspired. There was always the possibility, too, that Ralegh might, in the meantime, escape abroad. That would conveniently confirm his guilt whilst removing from the government the obligation to do anything too unpopular about it.

Escape abroad was certainly a possibility that Walter Ralegh considered seriously after his return to England. Poor Bess had spent most of her married life living with the consequences of royal displeasure, and un-willing now to suffer the ultimate sanction, she urged her husband to stop playing the hero and to flee the country. She recruited to her purposes one of Walter's old privateering captains, Captain Samuel King, a West-countryman who could make arrangements for a French vessel to slip the Raleghs across the Channel.

But Walter was not the man to fly – not yet, at least. He was brazen to the depths of his soul, in triumph and in adversity. So long as he was left at liberty he would fight, and he wrote to George Carew advancing a new argument in his defence. The Orinoco, he said, ran through British territory: 'That Guiana be Spanish territory can never be acknowledged, for I myself took possession of it for the queen of England, by virtue of a cession of all the native chiefs of the country. His Majesty knows this to be true.[1]

As with his mythical gold mine, Walter Ralegh's sudden claim that Guiana was part of the British Empire has received some sort of endorsement from events several centuries later, for the Blue Books published in 1896 and 1899 by the Foreign Office in pursuit of Britain's claim to land disputed between Venezuela and British Guiana were to maintain successfully that Walter Ralegh's visit to claim Guiana on behalf of Queen Elizabeth in 1595 was valid.

But this was by the way, for Sir Walter Ralegh had in 1617 accepted a commission from James that made no mention of Guiana being British, assuming he was entering the Spanish sphere of influence. And though James's endorsement of the expedition may have implied a belief in English claims to Guiana, James had been careful never to state that and had, on the contrary, been most anxious that Spanish claims should be respected. Walter had put his head into the noose knowingly, and now it had tightened he had to face the consequences.

Manfully he set off with Bess from Plymouth towards London in the second week of July 1618. He was still weak from his voyage home when he had been stricken down again with fever and had had to sit up all night in his cabin ready to deal with the *Destiny*'s mutinous crew. He had no idea of what his ultimate fate would be. But he had only gone 20 miles beyond Plymouth when any hopes of freedom that he may have entertained were dashed by a little posse riding up along the lanes behind him. It was Sir Lewis Stukeley who had finally received from London some sort of order to act. He was to escort Sir Walter back to Plymouth and, while awaiting further instructions, was also to sell off the looted tobacco that the *Destiny* had brought back.

Bess, still suffering under the shock of Wat's death, now intensified her efforts to persuade her husband to flee out of the country while there was still some chance of escape, for Stukeley, though he had brought the Raleghs back to Plymouth, left them at comparative liberty. Captain Samuel King used his contacts to persuade a French captain to take Walter to France, and late one night in July 1618, the Frenchman brought his vessel close to the shore so that Captain King could row Sir Walter Ralegh out through the darkness. But only a few yards from the vessel, Walter changed his mind. He asked to be rowed back to the shore.

Now close to seventy, Walter Ralegh was not the firm man of decision he once had been. He said himself after the death of his son that 'my brains are broken' and through these last weeks of his life he was to fall prey to dithering. Having changed his mind once, he then had second thoughts and allowed himself to be persuaded again to take flight. Once more he was rowed out over the dark night waters towards freedom. But once more, as the point of no return approached, his will wavered and he had himself rowed back into Plymouth. Sir Walter Ralegh was, in truth, an old man too weak to start a new life.

Meanwhile up in London another weaker but younger man was also in the throes of indecision. King James was torn between Count Gondomar and his own Council. To guarantee that Walter Ralegh was treated as his behaviour deserved, the ambassador had decided to postpone his departure for Madrid and to make sure that James stuck by the assurance which Digby and Villiers were sent to give him that 'Ralegh's friends and all England shall not save him from the gallows'. There was, furthermore, James's personal promise that he would hand Ralegh over for the Spaniards themselves to punish wherever and however they saw fit.

Gondomar demanded that a special meeting of the Privy Council be convened to hear his own thoughts on the matter. But when the councillors were casually informed by Gondomar of James's promise that Ralegh could be taken to Spain to be hanged in Madrid as if England were some colonial dependency, the hackles of the most abject rose. James had been too scared to tell his Council of this most slavish promise of all, and he was, consequently, given a rough time at a special meeting called two days later to discuss the problem further.

George Carew took Ralegh's side fiercely, and even the expedient Bacon felt constrained to protest at the power granted by James, without consultation with his Council, to the representative of a foreign country. Yet James was adamant, and Buckingham backed up his master. The Spanish faction possessed a clear majority when it came to a vote, and after the head count had been taken, James muttered darkly that he would consider the decision against Ralegh to be absolutely unanimous and treat all who spoke against it subsequently, in public or in private, as traitors. Sir Lewis Stukeley was ordered to bring his captive up to London, and James, before Gondomar left for Madrid, actually committed to paper his undertaking that not only Ralegh, but his leading captains, would be despatched to Spain in the *Destiny* to be dealt with if King Philip III so desired. Digby and Villiers were the witnesses of his promise handed by Villiers to Gondomar on the eve of his departure, the most staggering coup an ambassador could hope to bear home.

On 25 July 1618, Sir Walter Ralegh said goodbye to Plymouth for the last time and set off, also for the last time, along the route he had traced so often from the West Country to London, passing, sadly, by Sherborne, now the seat of the Spanish pensioner Digby whose family have enjoyed the estate to this day. 'All this was mine and it was taken from me unjustly', he was reported to have said as he rode down for a final sight of the shallow Yeo valley with its green meadows and rolling woods.[2]

There is no reason to doubt that Walter did give voice to this resentful sentiment, but the man who recorded it was a dubious character, a French physician by the name of Manourie. Stukeley had coopted the quack as one of his escort party because Ralegh was still far from well and also in the hope that Manourie, with his knowledge of exotic chemicals, might be able to worm his way into Walter's confidence by chatting as one medical man to another as they jogged the long miles up through Devon and Dorset.

Walter had never been a shrewd judge of character and now, feeling particularly in need of a friend, he took this unconvincing French physician into his confidence – though Manourie did, in fact, exhibit a readiness to help that extended beyond words to deeds. As Sir Lewis Stukeley's party dismounted from their horses to walk down one of the hills leading into Salisbury, Walter quietly asked the doctor if he could make him up some powerful purgatives and emetics. 'Give me a vomit,' he asked. 'It is good for me to evacuate many bad humours, and by this means I shall gain time to work my friends, give order of my affairs and, it maybe, pacify His Majesty.'

Walter was worried that he would be taken to London and executed rapidly without having had a chance to present a case in his own defence. He knew that King James was on progress near Salisbury, and he had in his head one last great pamphlet whose object was more urgent and desperate than *The Discoverie of Guiana* or *The Last Fight of the Revenge*. Walter wanted time to write down an *Apology* explaining what had gone wrong in Guiana and exonerating himself from blame. If Dr Manourie could give him some suitably noxious potions that would confine him to bed, he could plead illness as a pretext for delaying the journey and commit what he wanted to say to paper.

The Frenchman proved a willing accomplice to the stratagem, which he did not reveal until after Walter had had a chance to write his *Apology* and get it circulated. As the party arrived in Salisbury Walter counterfeited dizziness, and as Stukeley helped him up to bed he contrived to fall and strike his head sharply on a pillar, wounding himself genuinely. Walter was a consummate actor, and next day, after Lady Ralegh, Captain King and his own personal attendants had gone on their way to London, he threw himself stark naked onto the rushes in his room, rolled around like a senile lunatic, frothed alarmingly at the mouth and started gibbering

364

frantically. Manourie was sent for and he administered the drugs to complete the deception. Ralegh began vomiting and also to come out in a lurid rash of blotches, for Manourie had smeared irritants all over his skin. Not surprisingly the physicians of the Bishop of Winchester sent to diagnose this strange complaint had to confess themselves baffled, but they had no hesitation in signing for Stukeley a statement that the patient should not be moved.

It was a melodramatic device – the archetypal example of the histrionic tendencies that made up one side of Walter Ralegh – but it worked, for the moment at least. Manourie smuggled into the invalid's chamber 'a leg of mutton and three loaves' from the White Hart Inn, and Walter got to work, scribbling out furiously all his memories, hopes and justifications for the voyage to Guiana. He wrote all day and all night, his prose still burning today with the heat of his passion. He started straight in:

If the ill success of this enterprise of mine had been without example, I should have needed a large discourse and many arguments for my justification. But if the vain attempts of the greatest Princes of Europe ... have miscarried, then it is not so strange that myself, being but a private man, and drawing after me the chains and fetters wherewith I had been thirteen years tied in the Tower, being unpardoned and in disgrace with my Sovereign King, have by other men's errors failed in the attempt I undertook.[3]

He went on in *History of the World* style to list great kings and commanders who, with greater resources at their disposal, had failed at easier tasks than the exploitation of Guiana and then he went into all his arguments about England's right to the area. 'It seemeth to me that this empire is reserved for His Majesty,' he declaimed, and then pointed out what hypocrisy King James was guilty of: 'I have said it already and I will say it again, that if Guiana be not our sovereign's, the working of a mine there and the taking of a town there had been equally perilous to me.' If it was wrong for Walter's men to have captured San Thomé, in other words, it was equally wrong for the king to have sent someone to exploit a mine only a few miles away from that settlement.

But that was not the sort of logic to win the approval of James, and when the king arrived in Salisbury he angrily ordered Stukeley to convey his prisoner, spots or no spots, to London without further delay. Walter's days were numbered. He attempted, without success, to bribe Stukeley and Manourie to connive at his escape and then when, at Brentford, he met an agent from the French embassy, he seized the opportunity to arrange a meeting with Le Clerc, the new French ambassador, once he had arrived in London.

Walter was no longer the stoic hero. Now he was ready to resort to any intrigue to gain his ends. He was desperate to save his skin. Down in Devon it had seemed possible that he could stave off execution and so he had, after some indecision, rejected the chances of escape offered him. Now the omens were less favourable, and to stand on dignity or reputation when at the mercy of a king who acknowledged neither of those qualities was just foolhardy. So Ralegh began manœuvering actively to secure himself an escape route.

But, not for the first time, Walter was shown up as more flat-footed than he realized. James's government had anticipated his strategy at the Winchester trial in 1603, and now they caught him out again, for they had got wind of his escape plans and the role played in them by Bess and Captain Samuel King, and they deliberately allowed Walter to incriminate himself further. The government evidence against him was thin, and it would be strengthened considerably if he could be tempted to make a run for it.

Captain King had gone ahead from Salisbury with Bess to make the fresh preparations to get his master to France after Walter's fainting fit. But he chose the wrong accomplices for his scheme – a former boatswain of his called Hart who owned a Thames ketch and a one time servant of Walter's called Cottrell. Even while Walter was on the road towards the capital these men passed on the details of King's plans to one of Stukeley's relatives, William Herbert. He passed it on to Sir William St John – Buckingham's half brother who had, back in 1616, accepted Walter's money for helping to secure his release from the Tower. Now St John helped put Ralegh back inside again. He rode down to Bagshot to warn Stukeley of the escape plot.

The trap was sprung. Instead of being locked in the Tower when he got to London, Walter was allowed the comparative liberty of his wife's lodgings at Broad Street in the City while spies kept him under constant surveillance. He was being paid out all the rope he needed to hang himself.

When on 9 August 1618, Le Clerc, the French ambassador, visited him in Broad Street to invite him to take refuge in France, Walter was able to thank him for his invitation but to say that he preferred to travel in an English boat, and that very night he donned a false beard and stole under cover of darkness to the Tower dock where Captain King had two wherries waiting.

But Walter's comical disguise was not the only farcical element in this, his final night of freedom, for just as he had betrayed himself to Manourie, so now he told all his secrets to Stukeley, and when his jailer, instead of waxing indignant, calmly offered to come down the Thames to see him safely off, Walter actually agreed. Stukeley had carried out his responsibilities with comparative kindness so far as Walter was concerned, yet it was glaringly obvious that, unless he chose to go into exile along with Ralegh, he had absolutely no interest in allowing his prestigious prisoner to escape. Walter Ralegh's brains were indeed broken. When, as they got into the wherries, Stukeley had the nerve to enquire 'whether thus far he [Stukeley] had not distinguished himself as an honest man', Captain King was suspicious enough to say pointedly that he 'hoped he would continue so'. But Walter remained unsuspecting, even when a large and powerfully manned vessel loomed up behind the wherries and started to shadow them downriver.

Stukeley told the oarsmen to keep rowing, but when Ralegh began to inquire what they would do if ordered to stop in the king's name, and started elaborating a far-fetched story of a quarrel with the Spanish ambassador which was compelling him to leave the country, they started to be alarmed. They laid down their oars and refused to row any more, at which Stukeley harangued them for their obstinacy – while the shadowing craft waited all the time nearby in the darkness.

By the time the watermen had started rowing again the tide had been lost and it was impossible to get downriver to Gravesend, so Walter ordered the boats back to Greenwich. But as they turned, the strange boat that had been following them broke silence and hailed them in the name of the king. Ralegh now knew definitely that he had been betrayed – yet he still did not have the nous to tell his friends from his enemies. He turned to Stukeley, whispered to him and handed over some personal valuables to his kinsman. Stukeley embraced him – lovingly.

But when the boats touched shore at Greenwich the true nature of that embrace revealed itself and, ever after his arrest of Ralegh, Stukeley was to be dubbed 'Sir Judas'. Walter was so astonished he could only exclaim reproachfully, 'Sir Lewis these actions will not turn out to your credit', and, as dawn broke on the morning of 10 August 1618, the gates of the Tower of London opened on Sir Walter Ralegh for the third and final time. The Government could finally complete its dossier on its most embarrassing prisoner, and the personal possessions Walter had put together for his trip into exile were dourly chronicled by his jailers: £50 in gold; a native Guianan idol of gold and copper; a jacinth seal, set in gold with a Neptune cut in it and Guiana ore attached to it; a lodestone in a scarlet purse; an ancient silver seal bearing the proud Ralegh roebucks; a Symson stone set in gold; a wedge of 22 carat gold and a 'stobb' of coarser gold; a chain of gold with diamond sparks; a diamond ring of nine sparks; a naval officer's gold whistle set with small diamonds; sixty-three gold buttons with diamond sparks; an ounce of ambergris; a diamond ring given to Walter by the dead queen; a sprig jewel, embellished with soft stones and a ruby; a gold-cased miniature, the frame of which was set with diamonds: charts and a description of the Orinoco; a sample of Guiana ore and five silver-mine samples.[4]

These precious ornaments provided the most practical and portable form of wealth for a travelling man – but beneath their crustings of jewels Ralegh's knick-knacks made up essentially the pocketful of an overgrown schoolboy.

❧ 47 ❧

Final Judgement

Given the inflation between AD 33 and 1618, Sir 'Judas' Stukeley was paid generously for his betrayal of Walter Ralegh – nearly £1,000 – and his subsequent history also paralleled the fate of history's most famous traitor. For after both he and Dr Manourie had been caught, only a few weeks later, clipping gold coins and had been spared the death sentence which that offence carried, Sir Lewis was driven to live like a hermit on the lonely Bristol Channel island of Lundy, and on that cheerless rock he died a madman only two years after he had embraced Sir Walter Ralegh and handed him over to be arrested. He had tried to get James to deal with the men and women who made the last two years of his life such purgatory, but the king had been contemptuous. 'On my soul,' he exclaimed, 'if I should hang all that speak ill of thee, all the trees in my kingdom would not suffice.'

But that was not only Stukeley's problem. It was James's as well. For though Sir Walter Ralegh had by his attempted escape on the night of 9 August 1618, provided enough justification for being locked in the Tower, public opinion was not in a mood to tolerate his execution, let alone to see him handed over to the Spanish authorities. Many were speaking out openly on Ralegh's behalf, most notably Queen Anne, who begged the Duke of Buckingham to speak to the king: 'If I have any power or credit with you, I pray you let me have a trial of it at this time in dealing sincerely and earnestly with the king that Sir Walter Ralegh's life may not be called in question. . . .'[1]

Yet the days were gone when Buckingham, then Villiers, had relied on Queen Anne for his access to the royal presence, and her letter was just ignored. James, who scarcely ever saw his wife, was too occupied searching for the pretext he needed to destroy Ralegh. The stratagems that had worked so well in the weeks since Walter had been taken into custody were resorted to again, and Sir Robert Naunton, Winwood's successor as secretary, sent to the Tower as Ralegh's special keeper Sir Thomas Wilson, giving him orders to repeat the tactics that Dr Manourie and Stukeley had employed with such success. But by now even Walter was aware of the game that his succession of friendly jailers were playing, and Wilson had been one of Robert Cecil's most notorious spies. Though the fellow did everything he could to ingratiate himself with Ralegh, he was fobbed off with bland replies, so that he had to resort in his reports to the Government to insinuations of his own in an attempt to lend some colour to his exertions. Ralegh, he reported, had been moved to a higher lodging 'which though it seems nearer Heaven, yet is there no means of escape from thence for him to any place but Hell'. His prisoner seemed, he wrote, to be primarily interested in chemical spirits of which he had such an enormous collection that 'there is none wanting that ever I heard of, unless it be the spirit of God. . . .'[2]

It was poor stuff, sprinkled as it was with vague denunciations of 'this arch-hypocrite', and the government knew it. An attempt to coerce Lady Ralegh by locking her up also proved fruitless. The affection between Walter and Bess was an unbreakable bond, and they kept in touch with each other with little notes smuggled in and out of the Tower by the under-keeper, Edward Wilson.

I am sick and weak. This honest gentleman, Mr Edward Wilson, is my keeper and takes much pain with me. My swollen side keeps me in perpetual pain and unrest. God comfort us!

Yours, W.R.

I am sorry to hear amongst many discomforts that your health is so ill. 'Tis merely sorrow and grief that with wind hath gathered into your side. I hope your health and comforts will mend and mend us for God. I am glad to hear you have the company and comfort of so good a keeper. I was something dismayed, at the first, that you had no servant of your own left you, but I hear this knight's [Sir Alan Apsley, lieutenant of the Tower] servants are very necessary. God requite his courtesies and God, in mercy, look on us.

Yours, E.Ralegh.[3]

Through August and September 1618 a special commission of privy councillors worked on the problem of building a substantial case against Sir Walter Ralegh. Bacon and Coke were particularly skilled at that sort of task, but they found the going difficult. Piracy on the Atlantic, trespass in Guiana, and Walter's intrigues with the French in London were their main lines of attack, but none possessed much bite: Ralegh's conduct on the journey out to Guiana had been the very reverse of piratical; so far as trespass was concerned, it would be necessary to launch a prosecution against all the survivors of the attack on San Thomé, and as for the French involvement in the whole affair, it was difficult to see what treasonable motive could have been involved. The French offers of help to Walter had been simply that of assistance to an old friend, and Le Clerc, the French ambassador who was asked by the Privy Council what Sir Walter would have done if he had escaped to France replied quite simply: '*Il mangera il boyera il fera bien*'. [He would have eaten, drunk and had a good time.] There was nothing more sinister than that. Bacon advised King James to drop the French charges.

After over a month of fruitless investigations the commissioners had to confess themselves baffled, and on 24 September 1618, Walter sent to the king a fierce statement of his defence, pointing out that he had refrained from avenging his men killed in the Azores, had left Spanish shipping untouched and had ignored all the Spanish Caribbean towns that he might have sacked. The sacking of San Thomé was a mistake at which he had not been present, and paled into insignificance beside the way in which the Spaniards, peace treaty or no, had on other occasions massacred English merchants whom they encountered peacefully trading. Other Englishmen had raided the Spanish Main since peace was signed with Spain and been allowed home without being troubled, and, Walter argued, the fact that he had returned home voluntarily demonstrated that he was no trickster.

Like his *Apology* Walter's letter was a powerful piece of advocacy. But it avoided the crucial issue that clouded his handling of the entire Guiana venture, whether or not the oft-promised gold mine actually existed. Walter rightly concentrated on the good faith he had shown in coming home of his own free will. He had only tried to escape once *after* he had been arrested. 'My mutineers told me that if I returned to England I should be undone. But I believed more in Your Majesty's goodness than in their arguments.'

Yet it was the goodness of the king of Spain that mattered more than whatever mercy the king of England might feel moved by. On 15 October 1618, the orders from Madrid duly arrived. King Philip III was pleased graciously to spare Sir Walter Ralegh and King James the problems of an execution in Madrid. The penalty should be exacted in London instead, and, given the delicate nature of the negotiations surrounding Prince Charles's marriage into the Spanish royal family, the execution should take place immediately. Sir Walter Ralegh was not to live out the month.

Three days later, on 18 October 1618, Sir Edward Coke presented to King James the recommendations that his own special commissioners had drawn up. They had been unable to discover any substantial grounds for executing Ralegh on new charges, but there was still the old death sentence dating back fifteen years hanging over his head, and this could now be implemented in one of two fashions. Either the old warrant for execution could be supplemented by a printed declaration of his 'late crimes and offences', a narrative which would hold no legal status but would be a political instrument to combat public indignation arising from the fact that James had given Ralegh 'employment by Your Majesty's commission'; the declaration could explain how this commission in no way constituted a pardon. Or the alternative course was some sort of informal Privy Council hearing (not a trial) before a small hand-picked audience of nobles and gentry. Ralegh would be denounced, have a chance to reply and then be executed.

James did not like the sound of the second suggestion. He could remember Winchester, 'where by his wit he turned the hatred of men into compassion for him'. He did not want any audiences, no matter how small and hand-picked, getting the benefit of Ralegh's oratory. On the other hand he realized that he could not execute Ralegh without some form of ceremony. So the mechanism he suggested was a further and final hearing in front of the commissioners who had been examining Ralegh, followed by a rapid execution, and then the publication of a *Declaration* to justify the deed. To emphasize that the hearing was a mere formality, he ordered the execution warrant to be sent to him to sign in advance.

Four days later, on 22 October 1618, Sir Walter Ralegh was brought from the Tower to face his accusers. The attorney general, Sir Henry Yelverton, recited the catalogue of his offences dividing them into 'faults before his going on this last voyage', 'faults committed in his voyage', and 'faults committed since'. There was nothing new brought up against Walter, and the solicitor general, Sir Thomas Coventry, who developed the tale, could produce little of capital seriousness either.

It was Walter Ralegh's speech in his defence which brought the proceedings to life. James had been right to insist on proceedings in camera. With nothing to lose Walter claimed boldly that King James had never believed him truly guilty of treason back in 1603, citing James's remark about the dangers of being tried by a Middlesex jury and also the subsequent deathbed repentance of one of his judges, Justice Gawdy, who had stated that in his opinion 'the justice of England was never so depraved and injured' than by Ralegh's condemnation.[4]

Turning to the accusations made against his conduct of the Guiana voyage he crisply rejected them all, and then pointed out that he had only attempted to flee abroad after he had been arrested, trusting totally in truth and the king until then. In defence of his Salisbury charade with the help of Dr Manourie's potions he cited a Biblical precedent: 'David, a man after God's own heart, yet, for safety of his life, feigned himself mad and let the spittle fall down upon his beard, and I find not that recorded as a fault in David, and I hope God will never lay it to my charge as a sin.'[5] Curious though Ralegh's behaviour had been, it was hardly the stuff of which treason charges could be made.

The only new and remotely substantial evidence against Walter produced by the commissioners was the testimony of two of his Guiana captains who asserted that Ralegh had proposed to attack the Spanish treasure fleet if the attempt on the mine failed. But this was so much hearsay. Walter had *not* attacked the Spanish treasure fleet, and was able plausibly to state that he had voiced his proposal solely as a means of keeping together his mutinous and piratical fleet.

After Walter had spoken, Lord Chancellor Bacon, fresh in the enjoyment of this great legal office, had a hard job lending conviction to the death sentence with which he closed the proceedings, and when, next day, the law officers met to discuss the proper form of execution, they had to conclude that a simple warrant issued solely on the judgement of 1603 was not, after all, enough. Ralegh would, for the sake of legal form, have to appear before the King's Bench for the sentence of death to be pronounced with more validity.

So the stage was set for the final legal act. Five days later on 28 October 1618, Sir Walter Ralegh appeared before his judges for the very last time. Demoralized by his weeks of questioning and only too aware of the futility of the agonizingly long rigmarole that could now only end one way, he was taken by his captors past the London landmarks he knew he would never see again, and crowds gathered quietly and respectfully to do homage to the passing of the last Elizabethan. All the way from the Tower to the Palace of Westminster he went, past St Paul's Cathedral and Ludgate Hill where Essex's revolt had foundered, past the great palaces on the Strand that had once housed the giants who had attended on Gloriana, and most poignant of all, past the towers of Durham House with his little study in the turret looking out over the Thames where he had worked and talked with Gorges, Hariot, Keymis and Northumberland, the earl who was still in the Tower but who had, at least, been able to keep his life. It was a humbling final journey, and Walter, still shaking with the fevers he had contracted on his voyage to Guiana, looked a broken man. He had not bothered to comb his curling white hair that straggled down matted and unkempt, and one of his former servants who was standing in the silent crowds called out in dismay at his master's tousled locks.

'Let them kem [comb] it that are to have it,' smiled Walter quietly in reply. 'Peter, dost thou know of any plaster to set a man's head on again when it is off?'

The spirit still flickered, but the body was defeated. As the most famous of the Elizabethans slouched wrinkled and untidy in front of him, Attorney-General Yelverton could not help but be touched. 'Sir Walter Ralegh hath been a statesman,' he declared, 'and a man who in regard of his parts and quality is to be pitied. He hath been a star at which the world hath gazed. But stars may fall, nay, they must fall when they trouble the sphere wherein they abide.'[6]

Was it the star's fault that the sky in which it glittered was troubled by its brilliance? When asked to give cause why he should not forfeit his life, old Walter had to apologize for his voice which, never strong, had now been weakened sorely by his jail fever. He began to point out how his former conviction could not be resurrected against him since the king had, in the meantime, entrusted him with a royal commission that gave him the power of life and death over others. This was an argument Francis Bacon had suggested to him back in 1616 when Walter was wondering whether to pay out still more money to Villiers and his cronies to buy a full pardon. It was not worth the expense, Bacon had then advised, because the royal commission implied pardon.

But now, on 28 October 1618, Lord Chief Justice Montague told Walter that to pursue that argument was to rest on a broken reed, for treason must be specifically pardoned, 'by words of a special nature and not by implication'. In law the lord chief justice was absolutely right. Walter Ralegh had, in law, been a dead man for fifteen years 'and might at any minute have been cut off'. Now the only sentence that could be passed was of death – though Montague, who had studied the 1603 case carefully, made a deliberate correction to the vicious slander pronounced by Lord Chief Justice Popham.

'Your faith hath heretofore been questioned,' he said, 'but I am satisfied you are a good Christian, for your book, which is an admirable work, doth testify as much.'[7]

If the high judiciary of England were noting and approving the philosophy of *The History of the World*, it boded ill for any king who attempted to meddle with them – as events were shortly to prove. The revolt of the judges against both James and Charles I was only one example of the way in which 'the ghost of Ralegh pursued the House of Stuart to the scaffold',[8] and King James was to be plagued for the rest of his life by books, satires, songs and demonstrations in which the spirit of Walter Ralegh returned to mock him – not least when England was lit with bonfires from end to end to celebrate the final breakdown of negotiations for the Spanish marriage which the death of Walter Ralegh was intended to purchase.

Yet on 28 October 1618, that final triumph lay far in the future, for it was decided that Walter Ralegh was to be executed on the very morning following this, his final condemnation. It was not even worth sending him back to the Tower again. He would be lodged overnight in the Abbey Gatehouse near Westminster Hall while a scaffold was hastily prepared outside. His judges went their separate ways, the news went to King James that the royal will could finally be put into effect, and to the Abbey Gatehouse came Walter Ralegh's friends flocking to pay their final respects. Among them was his kinsman Thynne, one of the Longleat Thynnes whose faith had been called in question at the Cerne Abbas enquiry back in 1595. Poor Thynne was worried that the fortitude with which Walter was now facing death might be misinterpreted by his audience.

'Do not carry it with too much bravery,' he counselled. 'Your enemies will take exception if you do.'

'It is my last mirth in this world,' Walter Ralegh replied wryly. 'Do not grudge it to me. When I come to the sad parting you shall see me grave enough.'[9]

❧ 48 ❧
Execution

The last months of Walter Ralegh's life had been tortured not simply by all that was inflicted on him, but more profoundly by the disturbances within his own spirit. His rejection of Keymis, his vacillating attempts at escape from England, his undignified feigned illness at Salisbury, all these were symptoms of a mind that was sick, and Walter's final unkempt appearance before his judges on the eve of his death had shown plainly to all the world that stress had torn apart his pride. The Ralegh on whom the sentence of death was finally pronounced in 1618 was the feverish Ralegh in disintegration who had, back in 1592, stabbed Arthur Gorges for a sight of Queen Elizabeth, who had attempted suicide in 1603 and who had cast dignity to the winds in his cringing efforts to avoid execution after his condemnation at Winchester in that same year.

But with the final confirmation of the inevitable, and now knowing definitely that he had not twenty-four hours to live, the other Ralegh, the noble Ralegh, rallied. Sick in body he might be, but on the eve of his execution his mind and soul moved back into harmony and he faced his death with sharpness and with courage. Death, indeed, became his supreme triumph, the victory which did not simply round off his life but which gave his entire career its meaning, for had King James let Walter Ralegh die quietly in his bed of old age, posterity would merely have acknowledged the passing of an ambitious, gifted and flawed personality. As it was, Walter Ralegh died an ambitious, gifted and flawed martyr, the symbol of an age superseded, an eternal parable of passing time, an immortal.

Walter's hardest task as he prepared himself for death was to say goodbye to Bess. It was when he had met her that his glittering career had started to go wrong, and yet she had compensated him for all his misfortunes with love and loyalty and energy that had added a new and human dimension to his life. She had made him a rounded human being. Her pride had matched his and strengthened him through the most testing times, and now they had to say their final farewell. The Council had promised her that her husband's body would not be exhibited to the common rabble and that she could have it to bury herself, but that was gruesome consolation for her in her final hours with her man – as Walter himself said: 'It is well, dear Bess, that thou mayst dispose of that dead which thou hadst not always the disposing of when alive.' The clock struck midnight even as they spoke and Bess clung to the great brigand who had plundered life and counted her his greatest spoil. She left in tears to be taken home by the Carews, good faithful friends who were waiting outside, and when she got home and could not sleep she sat down to write to Sir Nicholas Carew at Beddington a letter whose spelling betrayed, as always, the turbulence of her feelings:

I desiar, good brother, that you will be pleased to let me berri the worthi boddi of my nobell hosban, Sur Walter Ralegh, in your chorche at Beddington, wher I desiar to be berred. The Lordes have geven me his ded boddi, though they denied me his life.[1]

Back in the Abbey Gatehouse Walter was writing too. He had business affairs he wanted to make tidy before he went, and he ordered them with all his old precision. Remembering his conversation with Lord Boyle in Munster on his last journey to Guiana he now said that he withdrew the support he had given Boyle in his dispute with Henry Pyne and that he wished to be considered neutral in the argument. He asked his wife to make provision for the widows of two men who had served him faithfully, and he remembered too the tobacco that he had brought back from Guiana, his only spoil from his final quest for El Dorado. Sir Lewis Stukeley had sold the tobacco in the hold of the *Destiny* and had pocketed the proceeds. He should be brought to account.

Then he set out in another note nine neat headings to answer the various accusations made in connection with his Guiana voyage and return. He summarized his old arguments and marshalled his facts for the speech he was planning to deliver next morning from the scaffold. He had always tried to live as a lion and he intended to die one:

Cowards may die. But courage stout,
Rather than live in snuff, will be put out.[2]

His last mortal words committed to paper had to include some verse. He wrote that little distich, and then his mind went back to the loveliest of the love poems that he had written in the green springtime of his love for Bess – 'Nature that washt her hands in milk':

Her eyes he would should be of light,
A violet breath and lips of jelly,
Her hair not black, nor over bright,
And of the softest down her belly. . . .

They were his most life-filled lines, and he wrote down again in the flyleaf of his Bible the last brooding stanza of the poem, changing just the opening invocation and adding to the end two lines to make an epitaph fit to match his mood in these last hours of his life:

Even such is Time which takes in trust
Our youth, our joys and all we have,
And pays us but with age and dust,
Who in the dark and silent grave
When we have wandered all our ways
Shuts up the story of our days.
    And from which earth and grave and dust
    The Lord shall raise me up I trust.[3]

Walter had come face to face with his old enemy, Time, and drawn on his Christian faith to triumph in the encounter. His scepticism was quietened, his searching mind sought only for spiritual composure, and his old arrogance was refined into quiet dignity. He was ready to meet his maker, and was so composed, indeed, that the official priest sent to minister to him in his final hours was rather annoyed to find that his consolation was so obviously redundant. Dr Robert Tounson, Dean of Westminster and later Bishop of Salisbury, was a po-faced fellow and, disconcerted by Walter's tranquillity, he reproved the condemned man, as Francis Thynne had done, for taking death so calmly. But Walter simply replied that to end with the axe was less painful than to die of a slow wasting fever, and that he met his fate with cheerfulness and courage knowing that 'he were assured of the love and favour of God unto him'.

When at dawn the reverend doctor gave communion to his charge, Ralegh rose from the sacrament 'very cheerful and merry', and talked of persuading the spectators to his death that he died an innocent man. This gave Tounson the opportunity he wanted to moralize, pointing out that Walter's 'pleading innocency was an oblique taxing of the justice of the realm upon him', and that, whatever the legal rights or wrongs of the case, the catastrophe about to descend stemmed from some other action, perhaps hidden, that had incurred divine displeasure and was being punished in this fashion. Had Walter, the cleric ventured to inquire, anything for which he should reproach himself so far as the destruction of the Earl of Essex was concerned?

But if Walter felt moved to anger, he did not show it. Nothing disturbed the serenity of his final hours, and Tounson's presumption reminded him that he could take advantage of his scaffold speech to answer the old smear that he had been responsible for Essex's destruction. He would have a lot to say – and in preparation for that he ate a hearty breakfast.

Walter Ralegh, the old trouper, was positively relishing his final hours on the stage. When he had finished eating his breakfast he sat back and enjoyed a good pipe of tobacco. It was the least that the most famous victim of James I could do, to bow out puffing on the noxious weed, and he dressed immaculately for his curtain call: a satin doublet, a black wrought velvet waistcoat, ash-coloured silk stockings, black taffeta breeches, a ruff band and a black wrought velvet cloak over all. There was no more question of letting his hair go uncombed. Sir Walter Ralegh would face his last audience trim and immaculate from top to toe.

King James, of course, had done his best to ensure that the applause he won would be thin. The morning chosen for Sir Walter Ralegh's execution was Lord Mayor's Day, when, as John Aubrey said, 'the pageants and fine shows might draw away the people from beholding the tragedy of one of the gallantest worthies that ever England bred.' But the stratagem failed, for early that morning in late October 1618 a huge crowd was waiting for Walter Ralegh as he strode proudly out of the Gatehouse. He was offered a cup of sack wine which he drank, and when asked if it pleased him he replied, 'I will answer you as did the fellow who drank of St Giles's bowl as he went to Tyburn: "It is a good drink, if a man might but tarry by it".'

It was a day for epigrams, an unforgettable moment in the lives of all who were present, and many were to record for posterity what they saw and felt.

The most significant of the chroniclers present was Sir John Eliot, the follower of the Duke of Buckingham who was to be given the vice-admiralship of Devon vacated by Sir Lewis Stukeley, and whose entire life was to be changed by witnessing the death of Sir Walter Ralegh. The execution turned him from being a supporter into the most scornful opponent of the Stuart monarchy, and he, like Ralegh, was to pay for his scorn with his life – at the hands of Charles I. His description of Ralegh mounting the scaffold can stand for the impression that Walter made on all who saw him:

All preparations that are terrible were presented to his eye. Guards and officers were about him, the scaffold and the executioner, the axe and the more cruel expectation of his enemies. And what did all this work on the resolution of our Ralegh? Made it an impression of weak fear to distract his reason?

Nothing so little did that great soul suffer. His mind became the clearer, as if already it had been freed from the cloud and oppression of the body. Such was his unmoved courage and placid temper that, while it changed the affection of the enemies who had come to witness it, and turned their joy to sorrow, it filled all men else with emotion and admiration, leaving them only with this doubt – whether death were more acceptable to him or he more welcome unto death.[4]

It was Winchester all over again. Men who had come to gloat at the humiliation of a proud spirit brought low were lost in admiration at a great soul.

In the cold morning air many shivered, and the sheriff lit a fire for the condemned man to warm himself. But Ralegh declined. It might start him shivering himself once he stood high on the scaffold. He had been taken from his sick bed quaking with fever only the previous morning and he did not want any waverings put down to fear. 'I thank God of His infinite goodness,' he cried, 'that He hath sent me to die in the sight of so honourable an assembly and not in darkness.'

But his words were not reaching the nobles up in the windows looking down on him and so Lord Arundel cried 'We will come down to you' – at which all the lords threaded their way through the crowd to come up onto the scaffold and shake hands with Walter one by one. Some men at least were not afraid to stand up and be counted – and as Walter launched into his long speech it became more and more obvious what a potent demonstration of rejection the whole gathering was to the character, policy and reputation of King James I.

Walter did not deign to waste words on the ostensible reason for his execution – his 1603 conviction. That was a legal convenience and everybody knew it. He concentrated rather on the way in which he was being sacrificed to satisfy Spanish bloodlust, and, as the oldest and most notorious enemy of Spain, he revelled in his declamation.

For a man to call God to witness to a falsehood at any time is a grievous sin, and what shall he hope for at the Tribunal Day of Judgement? But to call God to witness to a falsehood at the time of death is far more grievous and impious, and there is no hope for such a one. And what should I expect that am now going to render an account of my faith? I do therefore call the Lord to witness, as I hope to be saved, and as I hope to see Him in His Kingdom, which I hope will be within this quarter of an hour.[5]

Within a quarter of an hour. . . . That was how literal the faith of Walter Ralegh could be, and he had a lot to say in the fifteen minutes before he met his Maker. He denied suggestions that he had acted improperly towards France. 'If I speak not true, O Lord, let me never come into thy Kingdom.' He denied the various allegations that the hirelings Manourie and Stukeley had made against him, and he invited God's mercy on Stukeley's particular treachery 'as I hope to be forgiven'.

Looking down at his notes – he had been thorough to the end – he surveyed the other points he wished to make. 'Now a little more, and I will have done by and by.' He wanted to deal with all the charges of disloyalty made in connection with the Guiana voyage and then, turning to Arundel standing on the scaffold with the other lords beside him, he asked if it were not true that he had given his word to return home no matter what happened on the voyage.

'So you did,' Arundel spoke out boldly for all the crowd to hear. 'It is true.'

Walter nodded politely at the sheriff.

'I will speak but a word or two more,' he said, 'because I will not trouble Mr Sheriff too long.'

He wanted to answer the slanders about his malice towards the Earl of Essex and he went to some lengths to explain how on the day of Essex's execution, he had tried to get a word with the earl.

'I confess,' said Walter, 'I was of a contrary faction. But I knew that my Lord of Essex was a noble gentleman and that it would be worse with me when he was gone. For those that set me up against him did afterwards set themselves against me, and were my greatest enemies.'

That was true enough, and since the revelations about Robert Cecil's Spanish pension, all Ralegh's hearers had good reason to believe what he said.

Now came the final peroration. 'I have long been a seafaring man, a soldier and a courtier,' he confessed, 'and in the temptations of the least of these there is enough to overthrow a good mind and a good man.' But he was happy to tell Tounson that he died 'in the faith professed by the Church of England. I hope to be saved, and to have my sins washed away by the precious blood and merits of our Saviour Christ. . . . So I take my leave of you all, making my peace with God. I have a long journey to take and must bid the company farewell.'

When the sheriff had cleared the scaffold of the nobles, Walter took off his gown and doublet and asked to see the axe. The executioner hesitated.

'I prithee let me see it,' said Ralegh. 'Dost thou think I am afraid of it?'

He felt the blade and it was well honed.

'This is a sharp medicine,' he smiled, 'but it is a sure cure for all diseases.'

Sir Dudley Carleton wrote that Ralegh's 'happiest hours were those of his arraignment and execution',⁶ and another observer noticed how the victim 'seemed as free from all manner of apprehension as if he had been come thither rather to be a spectator than a sufferer'.⁷

The executioner flung down his own cloak for Walter to kneel on and knelt down himself to beg his victim's forgiveness. Ralegh placed both hands on the prostrate man's shoulders.

'When I stretch forth my hands,' he said, 'despatch me.'

As Walter got down himself someone asked if he would not rather lie towards the east looking towards the promised land. Such symbolism was important to a Renaissance Christian. But Walter, that modern man, demurred.

'So the heart be right,' he said 'it is no matter which way the head lieth.'

He also refused a blindfold.

'Think you I fear the shadow of the axe when I fear not the axe itself?'

His faith was with him to the last. He prayed for a minute and then stretched out his hands. But the axeman could not move. So Walter stretched his hands out again, and again there was the long agonizing hesitation.

'What dost thou fear?' Walter cried. 'Strike, man, strike!'

The axe fell. The body did not move – and nor did the head. Again the axe fell, and this time the head did fall – to be picked up and brandished by its bloodied silver hair to the crowd.

But the axeman did not pronounce the time-honoured words 'Behold the head of a traitor', and it was a voice from the crowd that supplied a better epitaph.

'We have not another such head to be cut off!'

References

Bibliographical Note.
Professor Pierre Lefranc's *Sir Walter Ralegh, Ecrivain, l'œuvre et les idées*, Librairie Armand Colin, Les Presses de l'Université Laval, 1968, lists the definitive canon of Ralegh's prose and verse works. It also contains an 18-page bibliography that sets out and evaluates all source and secondary material in detail. The only significant addition to be made to that exhaustive survey since 1968 is the 1597 will of Ralegh which is at Sherborne Castle, Dorset, and can be examined on application to the archivist there.

Chapter 1
1 John Aubrey, *Brief Lives*, ed. A. Clark, II, p. 179
2 *Otterton MS.*, Bicton House, and *Ralegh, Letters*, E. Edwards, London 1868, II, X, p. 26.
3 Sir Robert Naunton, *Fragmenta Regalia*, Arbers' English Reprints, p. 48.
4 T.N.Brushfield, *Trans. Devon Assoc.*, 1883, p. 163.
5 Parish Records, East Budleigh, Devon.
6 M.J.G.Stanford, *A History of the Ralegh Family of Fardel and Budleigh in the early Tudor Period*, London University MA Thesis, 1955.
7 Holinshed, *Chronicle of England*, cited in Edwards, I, p. 17.
8 Stanford, op. cit.
9 John Foxe, Acts and Monuments, ed. Townsend, vol. 8, p. 500.

Chapter 2
1 Cal. Hatfield MSS., IV, p. 438.
2 Humphrey Gilbert, *A Discourse of Discoverie for a New Passage to Cataia*.
3 Lefranc, op. cit., p. 26.

4 'Pour avoir venus contra la volunté de la Royne d'Angleterre au service des Huguenots.'
5 Ralegh, *History of the World*, V, chapter 2. All references to Ralegh's prose writing are taken from the 1829 collected edition except where otherwise specified: *The Works of Sir Walter Ralegh, Kt, now first collected* (Oxford, 1829, reprinted New York 1965).
6 ibid.
7 ibid.

Chapter 3
1 Lefranc, p. 26.
2 Francis Bacon, *Apopthegms*, London 1625, p. 292.
3 Aubrey, II, p. 179.
4 Middlesex County Records, London 1886, I, p. 110.
5 Sir William Sanderson, *Aulicus Coquinario*, from *The Secret History of King James VI*, ed. W. Scott, 1811, p. 175.
6 Macgeach and Sturgess: *Register of Admissions to the Honorable Society of the Middle Temple*, London 1949, I, p. 38.
7 Aubrey, II, p. 179.
8 Agnes M. Latham *The Poems of Sir Walter Ralegh*, Routledge 1951, I. All references to Ralegh's poems are taken from this definitive collection except where otherwise specified. References are to the poem numbers.
9 Naunton, op. cit., p. 48.
10 Lloyd Williams, *Ralegh*, 1967, p. 14.
11 W. Monson, *Naval Tracts*, p. 547.
12 Richard Hakluyt, *The Principal Navigations*, III, p. 174.
13 Edwards, II, p. 12.

Chapter 4
1 *Register of the Privy Council, Eliz*, IV, p. 726.
2 Latham, op. cit.
3 B.M.Ward, *The Seventeenth Earl of Oxford*, 1550–1604, London 1928, pp. 207–24.
4 Lefranc, p. 341.

Chapter 5
1 Ralegh, *History*, op. cit.
2 Edwards, II, p. 17.
3 ibid, II, p. 11.

Chapter 6

1 Aubrey, op. cit.
2 Sherborne Castle MSS.
3 J.L.Vivian, Visitations of Devon 1895, p. 638.
4 E.McLysaght, *More Irish Families*, Dublin 1960, p. 125.
5 R.R.Lemprière, *Bulletin Annuel de la Société Jersiaise*, St Helier 1919, IX, pp. 96–106, cited in Latham, *Review of English Studies*, XXII, no. 86, May 1971, p. 133.
6 Thomas Fuller, *Worthies*, 1663, p. 262.
7 ibid.
8 Naunton, op. cit.
9 ibid.
10 Latham, XLIX.
11 Edwards, I, p. 61.
12 M.A.S.Hume, *Ralegh*, 1847, p. 36.
13 Cal. State Papers, Ireland, 1574–85, p. 406.
14 Edwards, II, p. 22.
15 ibid.

Chapter 7

1 W.B.Rye, *England as Seen by Foreigners*, 1865, p. 113.
2 Edwards, I, p. 63.
3 T.N.Brushfield, *Trans. Devon Assoc.*, 1903, p. 546.
4 Neville Williams, *Elizabeth I*, p. 86.
5 Naunton, op. cit.
6 Rye, op. cit., p. 134.

Chapter 8

1 Hakluyt, op. cit., III, pp. 297–301.
2 ibid., Epistle Dedicatory to Sir Francis Walsingham.
3 ibid., III, p. 301 ff.
4 A.L.Rowse, *The Expansion of Elizabethan England*, p. 161.
5 Samuel Eliot Morison, *The European Discovery of America*, 1971, p. 601.
6 Cotton Roll, XIII, p. 48.
7 Trattner, *Dr John Dee*, p. 24.
8 D.B.Quinn, *Ralegh and the British Empire*, 1947, p. 52.
9 Rye, op. cit., p. 323.

Chapter 9

1 The description of the Virginia colonization in this and subsequent chapters is based on accounts in Morison op. cit. and in David B. Quinn, *The Roanoke Voyages, 1585–1590*, Hakluyt Society, 1955.
2 Cal. State Papers, Spanish, 1580–1586, p. 532.

REFERENCES

Chapter 10
1 HMC App. Fourth Report, p. 338.
2 Edwards, II, p. 26.
3 Brushfield, *Trans. Devon Assoc.*, 1896, p. 272.
4 Cited in Rowse, *Tudor Cornwall*, p. 62, on which the preceding and following paragraphs relating to tin mining are based.
5 Cal. State Papers, Dom. Addenda, 1580–1625, p. 182.
6 K. Andrews, *Elizabethan Privateering*, 1964, provides the documentation for this and other data relating to privateering cited in this chapter.
7 Quinn, *Ralegh*, p. 99.

Chapter 11
1 Quinn, *Ralegh*, p. 106.
2 ibid., p. 213.
3 Morison, op. cit., p. 667.
4 J. Howell, *Epistolae*, p. 552.

Chapter 12
1 Rye, op. cit.
2 Latham, IX.
3 ibid., III.
4 ibid., XV.
5 ibid., V.

Chapter 13
1 Cal. State Papers, Spanish, 1587–1603, p. 23.
2 ibid., p. 56.
3 Edwards, II, p. 33.
4 Hatfield, III, p. 96.
5 Warrant Book, Add. MSS., British Museum, V, p. 750.
6 Aubrey, op. cit.
7 Tanner MSS., Bodleian, 76, fol. 84b–85a.

Chapter 14
1 Quinn, *Ralegh*, p. 138.
2 ibid., p. 136.
3 Namely, the very best lands on either side of the Blackwater River, the town of Tallow, the castles of Shean, Lisfinny, Kilnacowiga, Strancally, Ballynatray and Templemichael in Waterford, areas running up into the Knockmealdown Mountains, together with the castle of Mocollop, and in County Cork the whole of the barony of Inchiquin, the castle of Mogeely and White's Island.

4 Quinn, *Ralegh*, p. 138.
5 White corresponded in 1593 with Richard Hakluyt from Newtown in Kylmore.
6 Quinn, *Ralegh*, p. 143.
7 ibid., p. 141.
8 ibid., p. 142.

Chapter 15
1 Lefranc, p. 347.
2 ibid.
3 *An Advertisement Written to a Secretary*, 1592, p. 18.
4 See E.A.Strathman, *Sir Walter Ralegh, a Study in Elizabethan Scepticism*, 1951, chapter 3, for this and other examples of Elizabethan use and abuse of the word 'atheism'.
5 MS. Stonyhurst, Anglia VI, p. 117, cited by Philip Caraman in *The Other Face*, 1960.
6 Lefranc, p. 351.
7 Latham, XLVIII.
8 ibid., p. 15.
9 ibid., XVI.
10 Morison, p. 657.

Chapter 16
1 See Quinn, *The Roanoke Voyages*, op. cit.

Chapter 17
1 E.Thompson, *Ralegh*, 1935, p. 37.
2 Rowse, *Tudor Cornwall*, p. 396.
3 Quinn, *Roanoke Voyages*, II, p. 559.
4 Hakluyt, VII, p. 39.

Chapter 18
1 Latham, XVIII.
2 Edwards, II, p. 41.
3 ibid.
4 Latham, XI.
5 ibid., XII.
6 ibid., Critical Comments, lxii.
7 ibid.
8 ibid., XLVI
9 ibid., XLVII.
10 ibid., X.
11 Lefranc, pp. 112, 113.

Chapter 19
1 Latham, XX.
2 ibid., XIX.
3 Cited in Rowse, *Ralegh and the Throckmortons*, 1962, p. 102.
4 ibid., p. 104.
5 ibid., p. 57.
6 ibid.
7 Latham, XVII.
8 Rowse, *Ralegh etc.*, p. 160.
9 Lefranc, *La Date du Mariage de Sir Walter Ralegh*, Études Anglaises, IX, 1956, pp. 193–211.
10 Latham, XX.

Chapter 20
1 W.Wallace, *Sir Walter Ralegh*, 1959, p. 56.
2 Quinn, *Ralegh*, p. 121.
3 ibid.
4 Morison, p. 675.
5 Bacon, *Essays*, Everyman edition, p. 104.
6 Wallace, p. 57, and Morison, p. 677.

Chapter 21
1 Ralegh had tried to secure Sherborne for himself in 1589.
2 Harington, *Nugae Antiquae*, 1779, I, p. 105.

Chapter 22
1 Rowse, *Ralegh*, p. 160.
2 Edwards, I, p. 147.
3 ibid., II, p. 46.
4 Rowse, *Ralegh*, p. 160.
5 ibid.
6 Lefranc, p. 138, note 10.
7 Edwards, II, p. 50.
8 MS. Ashmol., 1729, fol. 177.
9 Thompson, op. cit., p. 83.
10 Edwards, II, p. 51.
11 Latham, XXIII.

Chapter 23
1 MS. Lansdowne, LXX, fol. 88.

2 Andrews, p. 115.
3 ibid.
4 Dom. Corr. Eliz., Sept. 1592.
5 Edwards, II, p. 72.
6 ibid., II, p. 76.
7 ibid., II, p. 70.
8 ibid., II, p. 76.

Chapter 24
1 Bacon, *Essays*, p. 137.
2 Acta Cancellariae, London 1847, ed. Monroe, p. 177.
3 Cal. MSS. Sal. (Hatfield), HMC, London, XII, p. 206.
4 Latham, XLIV.
5 ibid., XLIII.
6 ibid., XXIV, II, p. 120.
7 ibid.
8 ibid.
9 ibid., XXV.
10 ibid., XXI.

Chapter 25
1 Sir Simonds D'Ewes, *Journal*, 1693, p. 517.
2 ibid.
3 ibid.
4 ibid.

Chapter 26
1 Nashe, *Works*, II, p. 116, cited by Strathman, p. 86, on which much of this chapter is based.
2 Cal. S.P.Dom., 1581–1590, p. 107.
3 Strathman, p. 210.
4 Lefranc, p. 390.
5 ibid., p. 387.
6 Cited by Strathman, p. 48.
7 Latham, XXVI.
8 Rawlinson Poetry, p. 212, cited in Lefranc, p. 91, together with a detailed discussion of the authorship of 'The Lie'.
9 Latham, p. 132.
10 Cited in Lefranc, p. 93.
11 *Records of the English Province of the Society of Jesus*, 1878, III, p. 462.

Chapter 27
1 Hakluyt, op. cit.

Chapter 28

1 Ralegh, *Discoverie of Guiana*, 1596 edition, on which this chapter is based.

Chapter 29

1 ibid.
2 Latham, *Selected Writings of Sir Walter Ralegh*, 1951.
3 ibid.
4 ibid.

Chapter 30

This account of the assault on Cadiz is based on Hakluyt, *The Principal Navigations*; Harrison, *An Historical Description of the Ilande of Britain*, 1577, and Monson's *Naval Tracts*.

1 Ralegh, *Works*, VIII, p. 677.
2 Edwards, II, p. 131.
3 Rowse, *Ralegh*, p. 199.
4 W.B.Devereux, *Lives and Letters of the Devereux*, 1835, I, p. 493.
5 Edwards, II, p. 151.
6 ibid., p. 152.
7 ibid., p. 154.
8 J.S.Corbett, *The Successors of Drake*. 1919, p. 86.
9 Edwards, II, p. 137.

Chapter 31

1 Wallace, op. cit., p. 140.
2 Lefranc, p. 347.
3 Lloyd Williams, *Ralegh*, p. 217.

Chapter 32

1 The will can be examined at Sherborne Castle. Agnes Latham set out its main points in *Sir Walter Ralegh's Will*, Review of English Studies, XXII, p. 86, May 1971, p. 129.

Chapter 33

1 The narrative here of the Islands Voyage is based on the accounts in Hakluyt, Harrison and Monson.

Chapter 34

1 Devereux, op. cit., I, p. 497.
2 Lloyd Williams, op. cit., p. 191.

3 ibid., p. 192.
4 Edwards, II, p. 161.
5 Edwards, I, p. 259.
6 ibid., II, p. 198.
7 ibid.
8 Devereux, op. cit., I, p. 493.
9 Lloyd Williams, p. 201.
10 ibid.
11 HMCS, VIII, p. 358.

Chapter 35
1 Ralegh, *Works*, VIII, p. 521.
2 G.B.Harrison, *Elizabethan Journal*, 1938, III, p. 174.
3 ibid.
4 D'Ewes, op. cit., p. 659.
5 *Secret Correspondence of Sir Robert Cecil with King James the Sixth*, edited by Lord Hailes, p. 68.
6 ibid.
7 Cecil Papers, XCIX, p. 54.
8 ibid., p. 76.
9 John was the son of Walter's half-brother Humphrey. He had been knighted at Cadiz.
10 Edwards, II, p. 194.
11 Sully, *Mémoires*, 1814, III, p. 29.
12 Edwards, II, pp. 226–7.

Chapter 36
1 Aubrey, II, p. 186.
2 ibid.
3 ibid.

Chapter 37
1 Aubrey, op. cit., II, p. 187.
2 Cecil Papers, CII, p. 77.
3 Edwards, II, p. 383.
4 ibid., II, p. 485.
5 HMC Sal., XV, p. 284.

Chapter 38
1 CSP, Dom (James I), IV, p. 76.
2 Carew Ralegh, *Observations*, p. 8.
3 Jardine, *Criminal Trials*, I, p. 451.

4 Bruce Williamson, *Sir Walter Ralegh and his trial*, a reading delivered to the Honourable Society of the Middle Temple, 13 November 1935.

5 Strathman, op. cit., p. 57.

6 This account of Ralegh's trial has been based on Howell, *State Trials*, II, 1–31, and Jardine, Criminal Trials, I, pp. 384–452, the latter of which is drawn principally from Harleian MSS. vol. 39 and the eye-witness report of Sir Thomas Overbury.

Chapter 39

1 Latham, XXX.

2 C. Williams, *Court and Times of James I*, I, p. 20.

3 Edwards, II, p. 279.

4 ibid., II, p. 280.

5 ibid., II, p. 284.

6 Williams, op. cit., I, p. 31.

7 Edwards, II, p. 282.

Chapter 40

1 Lefranc, p. 681.

2 Edwards, II, p. 319.

3 MSS. at Syon House, HMSC, 6th Report, 1877, App.

Chapter 41

1 Printed in Lefranc, Appendix C.

2 Osborne, II, p. 141.

3 Ralegh, *History*, Preface.

4 ibid.

5 Ralegh, *History*, II, XIX, I, p. 505.

6 ibid., III, XII, IV, p. 148.

Chapter 43

1 G.J.Marcus, *Naval History of England*, 1961, p. 180.

2 Edwards, II, p. 347.

3 Aubrey, op. cit.

4 V.T.Harlow, *Ralegh's Last Voyage*, p. 39.

Chapter 44

1 From V.T.Harlow, op. cit., on which this, and much of the succeeding chapters, is based.

2 Carew, p. 129.

3 Spanish letter from Gondomar to Madrid, translated in Harlow, op. cit., p. 159.

4 Edwards, II, p. 347.
5 ibid.
6 ibid.

Chapter 45
1 Edwards, II, p. 349.
2 Ralegh, *Works*, VIII, p. 490.
3 Harlow, p. 344.
4 ibid.
5 Edwards, II, p. 359.

Chapter 46
1 Edwards, II, p. 375.
2 From King James's Declaration published to justify the execution of Ralegh, cited in Harlow.
3 Ralegh, *Apology*.
4 Edwards, II, p. 496.

Chapter 47
1 Edwards, II, p. 487.
2 Acts of the Privy Council, James I, VIII, p. 509.
3 Edwards, II, p. 370.
4 Bruce Williamson, op. cit.
5 Edwards, I, p. 677.
6 Thompson, p. 339.
7 ibid., p. 340.
8 G.M. Trevelyan, *History of England*.
9 Edwards, I, p. 690.

Chapter 48
1 Edwards, II, p. 413.
2 Latham, XLI.
3 ibid., XL.
4 Monarchy of Man, Harleian MSS., 2228.
5 The transcript of Ralegh's scaffold speech in Archbishop Sancroft's handwriting is in the Tanner MSS., Bodleian Library, Oxford.
6 Edwards, I.
7 Thompson, p. 342.

Index